ORGANIZING
DEVIANCE

ORGANIZING DEVIANCE

Joel Best

California State University, Fresno

David F. Luckenbill

University of Illinois, Chicago Circle

PRENTICE-HALL INC., ENGLEWOOD CLIFFS, N.J. 07632

Library of Congress Cataloging in Publication Data

BEST, JOEL.
    Organizing deviance.

    Bibliography: p.
    Includes index.
    1. Deviant behavior. 2. Crime and criminals.
3. Social structure. I. Luckenbill, David. II. Title.
HM291.B398   302.5   81-13850
ISBN 0-13-641605-5   AACR2

©1982 by Prentice-Hall, Inc., Englewood Cliffs, N.J. 07632

Printed in the United States of America

10 9 8 7 6 5 4 3

ISBN 0-13-641605-5

Prentice-Hall International, Inc., *London*
Prentice-Hall of Australia Pty. Limited, *Sydney*
Prentice-Hall of Canada, Ltd., *Toronto*
Prentice-Hall of India Private Limited, *New Delhi*
Prentice-Hall of Japan, Inc., *Tokyo*
Prentice-Hall of Southeast Asia Pte. Ltd., *Singapore*
Whitehall Books Limited, *Wellington, New Zealand*

For Joan and Diane

CONTENTS

PREFACE

Sociological research on deviance expanded dramatically during the past twenty-five years. Dozens of reports described deviants of all sorts: murderers, rapists, thieves, juvenile delinquents, heroin addicts, schizophrenics, marijuana smokers, prostitutes, and so on. Another large group of studies dealt with those charged with controlling deviants, including police officers, psychiatrists, and school psychologists. For many readers, this research seems exotic; it describes scenes outside the experience of most students and instructors, making the study of deviance especially interesting. Unfortunately, courses about deviance often lean too heavily on this interest in the exotic; they tend to treat the topic as a kind of carnival sideshow. Just as a sideshow features separate exhibits, this one with a two-headed calf and that one with a bearded woman, courses about deviance tend to display a series of exotic "freaks"—criminals this week and prostitutes next week. These courses fail to develop an analytic framework, a systematic perspective from which to view the topic. They make little or no connection between different types of deviance. One critic charges that the sociology of deviance often becomes the study of "nuts, sluts, and preverts [sic]"—sideshow exhibits, not analysis (Liazos, 1972).

This book attempts to move beyond the carnival atmosphere to a more analytic treatment of deviance. Our title, *Organizing Deviance,* contains a double meaning. First, we want to organize much of the knowledge that sociologists have about deviance. Rather than examining different types of deviance one by one, in isolation from one another, we classify all deviance within an overall, theoretical framework. This framework lets us compare and contrast different types of deviance. In doing so, we develop the framework as a way of understanding deviance as a whole, and we also learn to recognize some of the key features of each type of deviance. The theoretical framework organizes our knowledge about deviance. Second, we use social organization as the foundation for our theoretical framework. While there are many competing theories of deviance, this book does not try to give them all equal attention. (In our minds, books which present one theory after another simply offer a different kind of sideshow—one with theories, rather than deviants, as the exhibits.) Instead, we try to understand deviance in terms of social organization. Social organization is not the only framework for looking at deviance; it cannot answer every question we might ask. However, it is a useful, though neglected, way of thinking about deviance. There are important differences in the ways deviants organize themselves and in the ways deviant activities are organized; these differences have important consequences. Thus, our title's two meanings become clear; we want to organize our thoughts about deviance around a particular theoretical framework; and we want to use social organization as the basis of that framework.

This book represents the culmination of several years of thinking about deviance and social organization. At various times, we benefited from the comments of friends, colleagues, and students, as well as several anonymous reviewers. We want to thank all of these people, with special thanks to Donald R. Cressey, Patrick G. Jackson, Weldon T. Johnson, and Earl Rubington. Some of the following chapters contain material which first appeared in a different form in *Social Problems, Urban Life,* and *Deviant Behavior.*

ORGANIZING DEVIANCE

CHAPTER ONE
INTRODUCTION:
Deviants, Deviance, and Social Organization

Reflecting on his career as a criminal, John Allen recalled the following incident:

> . . . during this time, around the spring of '70, I was sticking up legal joints as well as drug dealers. Most of the time I had my regular mob with me. I remember this little bar where a lot of sissies used to go—a lot of homosexuals. Sophisticated sissies I call them. . . . Only reason a young dude would be in there is for the purpose of somebody picking him up and giving him fifty dollars.
>
> The guy that owned the joint was a pretty die-hard dude. A week or two previous to our going in there, he had actually shot two people that tried to rob him. So I'm telling Cub, "Man, when we get in this joint, you and I going to have to get him." My brother Nut's job was to get the cash; and Leo, Cub's brother, was to stand in the middle of the place with a shotgun and make all the sissies get on the floor and put all their hides, all their wallets, in one pile.
>
> When we went in, we got a booth and sat down to look the joint over. There was a dude at the bar drinking a beer, and I immediately saw that he had a shoulder holster. I looked at him close, especially at his shoes, and I said, "This a roller." Evidently the guy that owned the place had hired a special police that didn't wear a uniform to keep an eye on the joint.

So we order some beer, 'cause we gotta rearrange our plans. . . .

So we just sitting there, and finally we come up with the idea that the dude that owned the place a pretty tough dude, so I got to get him. Okay. Cub got to get the police. Nut's job is still to get the cash, and Leo's job the same—get all the hides piled up, pick them up, stand around with that shotgun, and watch everything. The signal was, I get up and go play a number on the jukebox. So I go over and drop a quarter in, punch the number three times so it play over and over. I turn around, and the owner of the joint is sitting at a little special table with a broad. She can see me, but his back is to me.

I turn away from the jukebox, pop my fingers a couple of minutes, then move closer to him. I come out with my gun, and the broad panic. She say, "Don't play with that thing around here." The owner went to turn, but when he did, I put that gun against the back of his head and said, "I know you got a gun. Put it on the table."

"Punk. You better get the motherfuck out of my place."

"Yeah?" I stepped on back and shot him in the leg. He fall on the floor. I say, "You want some more?"

"No, no! You got it! You got it!"

After I shoot him, the [waitress] . . . just about turned blue. She looking all funny, just wanting to please everybody now. She scared to death; and Leo . . . standing there with that big shotgun. Now, Cub immediately stepped up to the police, politely put his pistol right up on his neck, took his gun, and told him to be cool. The man just kept on drinking his beer. Another dude was on the telephone. I made him get off. . . .

We got everybody laying on the floor. Nut goes to the cash registers and takes out the cash. All the faggots were trying to sound like women, but they was piling their hides up on the floor, and we had them crawling around. . . .

So we get the wallets and things on the floor, and we take the keys to the joint and go on out to my old raggly car. The money man always leave first. If anybody gets busted, get away with the money. Just before Leo steps out, he takes the shotgun and smashes all the glasses and bowls on the table that we had been using, and turns the table over. Then he comes out, and I just pull the door, lock it, and go the car. (Allen, 1977:186-89)

This robbery is an example of deviance. One can ask several important questions about robbery. Why do people rob others? What kinds of people become robbers and what kinds of people get robbed? How often do robberies occur? How can robbery be controlled? Another important issue involves the social organization of robbery. Social organization refers to the patterns of relations among people—in this case, among those involved in the crime. Actually, two kinds of social organization appear in Allen's tale of robbery. First, the four criminals organized themselves to perform the robbery. They planned the crime, selecting their target and deciding which tasks each member would perform; they obtained weapons and a car for their getaway; and they cooperated during the crime itself. Second, the interaction between the robbers and their victims was organized. The robbers threatened the victims with death and took their money, while the victims evaluated the robbers' threats and decided to comply.

This book examines social organization and deviance. It focuses on both the ways in which deviants organize themselves and the ways in which deviant transactions are organized. Before exploring social organization in greater detail, the concept of deviance should be examined.

DEFINING DEVIANCE

Sociologists define deviance in different ways. Some define it as any violation of any social norm in any social system; the norm may be of major or minor significance, the violation may elicit a strong or mild reaction, and the social system may range from two people to a complex society (A. Cohen, 1966; Denzin, 1970). Other sociologists argue that deviance is a violation of a major social norm which brings a strong negative reaction, such as imprisonment (Black and Reiss, 1970; DeLamater, 1968; Gibbons and Jones, 1975; Lofland, 1969; Schur, 1971). Still others expand the term to include discreditable conditions, such as obesity, mental retardation, and blindness (Clinard and Meier, 1979; Sagarin, 1975). Rather than focusing on violations of norms, some sociologists define deviance in terms of people's reactions: deviance is whatever someone labels deviant (Becker, 1963; Kitsuse, 1962).

In this book, deviance will refer to any behavior that is likely to be defined as an unacceptable violation of a major social norm and elicit strong negative reactions by social control agents. In turn, deviants are persons who commit such acts. Several features of this definition require comment.

First, deviance refers to *behavior,* not merely to any condition that makes a person discreditable. While such conditions as obesity and mental retardation sometimes elicit harsh reactions, they reflect what people are, not what they do. This book focuses on the ways people organize themselves to carry out deviant activities and on the ways these activities are themselves organized.

Second, deviance is an *unacceptable* violation of a norm. Behavior that violates social norms varies in its social acceptability (cf. Wilkins, 1964). Risking one's life in battle to save one's comrades breaks the norm of self-preservation, yet it is considered praiseworthy. In contrast, deviant activities are unacceptable, seen as wicked or harmful.

Third, deviance violates *major social norms.* Norms vary in their importance for society's well-being. Some are of minor significance—their violation does not threaten the society's welfare, and offenses can elicit mild reactions, such as ridicule. Breaches of etiquette, such as failing to cover one's mouth when coughing, break minor norms. At the other extreme are norms of major significance—their violation is believed to threaten the society's well-being, and infractions can elicit strong sanctions, such as incarceration or execution. The criminal law contains many major social norms, such as those requiring citizens to maintain their loyalty to the state and refrain from stealing one another's property. Defining deviance as a violation of major social norms is problematic. In a large, heterogeneous society, people disagree about which norms are significant and which violations are threatening. One common way of resolving this dilemma is to define major social norms as those which are formalized in law (McCaghy, 1976:97-101).

Fourth, deviance makes the offender eligible for *negative reactions* from social control agents. Social control agents are designated officials who enforce major social norms. Such officials include agents of the criminal justice system, such as police, prosecutors, and judges, psychiatrists, and school psychologists. These officials work to detect, apprehend, and sanction deviants. Sanctioning may entail punishment, such as incarceration or fines, or treatment, such as hospitalization or education. In either case, sanctioning typically aims at the prevention of further deviant activity. Whether sanctioning involves punishment or treatment, the deviant is likely to dislike it; hospitalization may be as painful as imprisonment.

Fifth, deviance is *likely* to be defined as a major norm violation and attract the attention of social control agents. Not all activities which might be defined as deviant actually get labeled. Some are instances of secret deviance—they are never discovered or reported (Becker, 1963:20-21). Other activities are normalized, defined as instances of normal, rather than deviant, behavior (Rubington and Weinberg, 1981:29). Thus, a group of boys that forcibly takes a basketball from a youngster on the playground may be seen as "bullying," not "robbing," and a person who hears strange voices may be thought to suffer from a "loss of sleep" or "overwork," rather than from "mental illness." Further, there are many laws on the books which social control agents do not enforce because they are not deemed important for the society's welfare—laws that forbid jaywalking, premarital sexual relations, and smoking tobacco by teenagers are enforced infrequently. Only activities which are likely to be defined as violations of major norms and make the offenders liable to sanctioning should be considered deviant. This "likelihood" can be measured; an activity is deviant if it frequently leads to social control efforts. Of course, some acts which might elicit such sanctions are never noticed, get normalized, or, for some other reason, are not labeled deviant. The point is not that sanctions are inevitable, but that they are likely.

Thus, deviance is any unacceptable violation of a major social norm that makes the offender eligible for the sanctioning efforts of social control agents. Deviance covers a very broad swath of human conduct, and sociologists have asked a number of different questions in their efforts to understand deviance.

CENTRAL PROBLEMS IN THE
STUDY OF DEVIANCE

Social organization, the focus of this book, has not been a central concern in the study of deviance. Most sociological studies of deviance focus on four other problems: causes of deviance, consequences of deviance, creation of deviance, and control of deviance. This section briefly examines each of these topics before offering social organization as a fifth problem for investigation.

Causes of Deviance

The problem which receives the most attention from sociologists is the cause of deviance: why do people commit deviant acts? Efforts to answer this question typically involve identifying one or more conditions that distinguish offenders from nonoffenders and account for the offenders' deviance. Sociologists have divided the problem of causation into several specific questions. One question concerns individual behavior, attempting to explain why a particular individual performs a deviant act; for example, why did John steal the purse? Another focuses on systematic deviant behavior, trying to explain why some individuals engage in deviance regularly; for example, why does Carol engage in prostitution daily? A third question deals with the distribution of deviant behavior within society. Here the problem is to explain why deviant behavior varies in particular ways along such dimensions as age, sex, and social class; for example, why does the lower class have a significantly higher rate of violent crime than the middle class? To answer these causal questions, scientists develop theories of deviance causation and test them through research. To understand the diversity of these efforts, consider some of the prominent theoretical approaches to these causal questions.

Theories explaining an individual's deviant behavior draw from different disciplines, including biology, psychiatry, and social psychology. Biological theories generally argue that deviant behavior is due to some deficiency in the individual's biological constitution (cf. Vold, 1979:51-123). While respectable people are biologically normal, deviants are biologically inferior. In an early variant of this idea, Lombroso (1918) argued that deviants are atavists, biological throwbacks to earlier stages of evolution, and they are distinguished from normal, respectable persons by their physical characteristics, including protruding jaws, small craniums, and huge ears. Other early investigators attributed deviance to feeblemindedness, which they considered a product of biological degeneracy (H. Goddard, 1914). Unlike persons with normal or high intelligence, feebleminded persons were said to be predisposed toward deviance—they cannot manage everyday problems in a normal, socially acceptable way. Modern versions of the biological approach emphasize other factors (cf. Mednick and Christiansen, 1977). For example, some theories link deviance to defects in the nervous system, while others point to genetic defects, such as the possession of an extra Y chromosome.

Psychiatric theories are another prominent approach to explaining an individual's deviance. These theories emphasize the importance of the individual's personality; they link deviance to some personality disturbance (Abrahamsen, 1960; cf. Vold, 1979:124-158). One version, for instance, explains deviance in terms of a disturbance in personality controls, those internalized forces (such as the Superego and the Ego) that constrain one's inherent, animalistic impulses so that the individual can satisfy his or her needs in a socially acceptable way. When personality controls develop improperly, impulses are given free expression, often resulting in deviant behavior. Other psychiatrists argue that deviance solves problems caused by the deprivation of basic needs, such as the need for security. When needs are not satisfied during childhood, the individual experiences anxiety, which ultimately can lead to mental disequilibrium. Deviant behavior reduces anxiety and restores mental equilibrium by satisfying unmet needs.

Social-psychological theories, deriving from sociology and psychology, are a prominent modern approach to explaining the individual's deviant behavior. These theories view deviance as the product of social conditions. In general, they argue that the socialization or learning process accounts for deviance. Just as some people learn to engage in respectable activities in certain situations, others learn to commit deviant acts in those same situations. For example, differential association theory argues that individuals learn attitudes favorable to deviance through interaction with significant others, and they will engage in deviance when they acquire more attitudes favorable to deviance than attitudes unfavorable to deviance (Sutherland and Cressey, 1978:80-83). Thus, social psychological theories view deviance as the product of normal social processes operating on normal human beings, not of some biological or psychological deficiency.

The second causal question concerns systematic deviance. Most people commit occasional deviant acts, but they do not see themselves as deviant. Their deviance is episodic; they do not organize their lives around deviance. But others define themselves as deviant; they organize their lives around that identity, regularly engaging in deviance. Why do some people engage in systematic deviance? Labeling theory provides one explanation (Becker, 1963; Lemert, 1967:40-64; Lofland, 1969). According to labeling theory, a person's deviant career develops in a series of stages. When an actor violates a major social norm, respectable others identify the violation as an instance of deviance and label the actor a deviant. Labeling thrusts the actor into an inferior social status. Respectable others consider the actor as evil, morally inferior, untrustworthy, and so on. Also they increasingly treat the actor in a negative manner. This negative treatment ranges from distrusting the actor and refusing to interact with him or her to punishing the actor for his or her deviance. The actor responds to the stigma of the deviant label by increasingly turning to other deviants. Deviant others protect the actor from negative reactions. They give the actor an ideology justifying participation in deviance and praise the actor for engaging in deviance. The unfavorable reactions of respectable others and the positive reactions of deviant others lead to the actor's developing a deviant identity. The actor comes to view himself or herself as others do—as a deviant—and act in a manner consistent with that identity—regularly engaging in deviance.

A third causal question involves the distribution of deviance within society. Research demonstrates that deviance is unevenly distributed. For example, lower-class people commit more property crime than middle-class people, and teenagers commit more violent crime than older persons. Sociological theories explaining the distribution of deviance argue that social conditions shape the distribution patterns. Shaw and McKay (1942), for instance, developed a theory explaining why many juvenile delinquents live in lower-class, inner-city neighborhoods. They argued that the areas' poverty, physical deterioration, and conflict between residents lead to social disorganization—an absence of conventional norms owing to the breakdown of organizations that transmit those norms. In turn, social disorganization weakens control over youngsters; demoralized parents provide little direction for their children, and churches and schools are inadequate in socializing youth. Young people are free to join peer groups, such as play groups and gangs, which pass along attitudes and skills that encourage delinquency. To belong to these groups, youngsters must conform to their delinquent traditions. Another effort to explain why the lower-class has higher rates of deviance is anomie theory (Merton, 1957). Merton argues that American culture encourages everyone to aspire to financial success and to use certain legitimate means, such as hard work and thrift, to achieve this goal. However, people have different opportunities for achieving success through legitimate means. Because they face discrimination, limited economic resources, and the like, lower-class people have fewer opportunities to obtain wealth legitimately. Lower-class members adjust to this dilemma in different ways. Some simply conform to conventional norms, with little hope of achieving success. But others turn to some form of deviance: they may employ illegitimate means, such as theft, to achieve success; or they may retreat from the competitive struggle, becoming tramps, alcoholics, or drug addicts. Thus, differential opportunities help explain why many lower-class people engage in deviance.

The problem of deviance causation has been divided into three questions: why individuals commit deviant acts, why some people engage in systematic deviance, and why deviance is distributed unevenly through society. Each of these questions has attracted considerable attention. Many theories, drawing from different disciplines, attempt to explain deviance. Hundreds of studies test these theories, and heated debates over the logical and empirical bases of different theories are common. Despite this enormous effort, causation remains a central problem in the investigation of deviance.

Consequences of Deviance

Identifying the consequences of deviant behavior for society is a second problem studied by sociologists of deviance. Deviance has both negative and positive consequences. On the one hand, deviant behavior can be dysfunctional for a society, threatening its well-being in at least three ways (A. Cohen, 1966:4-6). First, deviance threatens society by interfering with important system activities. Just as a living organism requires its parts to perform certain tasks to maintain life, a social system's members must perform certain vital activities. Deviance can obstruct these activities. For instance, governmental corruption can impede the activities of the political subsystem, in turn affecting the smooth operation of the economic and military subsystems and thereby threatening the society's well-being. Second, deviance can destroy members' willingness to perform their prescribed roles and meet the system's requirements.

> It may do this by offending their sense of justice, of the proper ratio between effort and reward. "Idlers," "fakers," "chiselers," "sneaks," "deadbeats," and the like, even if their activities do not directly threaten the interests of the virtuous, offend the virtuous because they share the rewards, sometimes disproportionately, without undergoing the sacrifices and discipline of the virtuous. (A. Cohen, 1966:4)

Thus, by provoking resentment and undermining members' commitment to prescribed roles, deviance threatens society's well-being. Third, deviance disrupts a society by damaging members' trust in one another. The system's smooth operation depends on trust, on confidence that others will honor their obligations. Deviance violates these expectations and damages members' confidence in one another. For example, street crime leads to the distrust of strangers and the belief that some urban areas are unsafe, and many citizens avoid these areas for fear of being attacked. In turn, their withdrawal from participation makes these areas more dangerous and may damage the areas' economy.

When people consider the consequences of deviance, they usually think about its dysfunctions. This is not surprising; it seems reasonable that evil actions bring negative consequences. However, some sociologists argue that deviance also is functional for a society, helping to maintain its well-being. In a classic essay, Emile Durkheim (1938) claimed that crime is a normal feature of society; it is universal, found in every society at every point in history. According to Durkheim, crime's universality suggests that it must serve some social function; otherwise, crime would disappear over the course of societal evolution.

Sociologists identify several functions of deviance. First, deviance helps to define the society's moral boundaries. A social system requires norms which distinguish unacceptable from acceptable action. Because norms are abstract and changing, it can be difficult to clearly draw the boundaries of morality.

> ... seldom is the precise meaning of a rule obvious simply from a verbal statement of it. ... Just what is included within each term of the rule; the exact limits of its applicability; its qualifications and reservations; the intensity of feeling associated with it; whether it is a pious sentiment or an injunction to be taken seriously—all these can seldom be communicated in a few words, or even in a complicated formula. (A. Cohen, 1966:8)

People learn where the boundaries are by observing which actions are identified and sanctioned as deviant (cf. Erikson, 1966). For instance, individuals learn that selling marijuana is deviant by observing that those who sell marijuana are routinely labeled and sanctioned. Similarly, people learn that premarital sexual relations are not deviant by observing that those who engage in such activities are rarely labeled and sanctioned.

Second, deviance unites members of a society against a common enemy—the deviant. When an individual violates important norms, respectable members of society feel anger and hostility toward the deviant. Sanctioning the offender not only relieves these feelings but serves to integrate respectable people by reaffirming their collective support for the moral norm. Thus, deviance increases social solidarity: "Seemingly without the criminal the cohesiveness of society would disappear and the universal goods of the community would crumble into mutual repellant individual particles" (Mead, 1969:582). Third, deviance facilitates social change. Durkheim (1938) argued that deviance exposes defects in the social system:

> Where crime exists, collective sentiments are sufficiently flexible to take on a new form, and crime sometimes helps to determine the form they will take. How many times, indeed, it is only an anticipation of future morality—a step toward what will be! (Durkheim, 1938:71)

For example, while many Americans considered the civil rights protests in the late 1950s and early 1960s deviant, the demonstrations brought discrimination into plain view and led to changes in the treatment of blacks and other disadvantaged minorities.

Deviance has diverse consequences for society. Some sociologists speak of its dysfunctions, while others point to its functions. There are elements of truth in both positions. The important point is that sociologists focus on the problem of consequences because they are concerned with the effects of deviance on the social system. When they examine the creation of deviance, sociologists turn to the social system's effects on deviance.

Creating Deviance

Deviance is behavior which is defined as illicit by those who set social control policy. Deviance is not inherently evil; there is nothing about the behavior itself which makes it wrong. Rather, an activity is deviant because others define it as deviant (Becker, 1963:8-18). Thus, it is not the act but the definition which leads to social control efforts. For instance, before Congress passed the Harrison Narcotics Act in 1914, the use of narcotics was acceptable. Many patent medicines contained opiates and millions of people used these medicines for their soothing qualities. In 1914, Congress redefined the use of opiates as deviant, making users subject to strong sanctions. Using narcotics is not necessarily evil; Congress formally defined it as deviant.

Some sociologists study the creation of deviant labels. Specifically, they ask why certain classes of behavior are formally declared deviant. One answer is that behavior is labeled deviant if it threatens society's welfare. But why are some activities defined as threatening, and declared deviant, while others are not? Do deviant labels protect all of the society's members, or do they favor the interests of some groups over others? Because many of the norms whose violation is considered deviant are formalized in law, these questions link the sociology of deviance with the sociology of law.

Two rival models explain the creation of laws. The pluralist model holds that laws are an objective response to problems of social order in complex society (Pound, 1942). Complex society is heterogeneous, composed of many groups with different interests. While these groups may share some norms and values, they conflict over others. For example, in the United States, there is considerable disagreement over the moral status of smoking marijuana, purchasing pornography, and having an abortion. Lawmaking bodies, such as Congress, serve to resolve conflict and maintain order among diverse groups. When groups conflict, lawmakers consider the different sides of the controversy and support that side which benefits the interests of the larger number of the society's members. Thus, laws protect the majority's interests; behavior is labeled deviant when it threatens those interests. For instance, stealing is labeled deviant because theft threatens the widespread interest in preserving private property. The pluralist model views law as the outcome of a political process which reconciles conflicting interests and restores harmony.

The elitist model claims that law protects and perpetuates the interests of the society's elite, that group controlling significant economic and political resources. Law is a tool of the elite (Chambliss, 1976; Quinney, 1974). Like the pluralist model, the elitist model views complex society as heterogeneous; many groups compete to protect their interests. But the elitist model contends that these groups do not compete on an equal basis; they differ in their control of economic and political resources. The greater a group's resources, the greater its power. The elite uses its considerable power to shape the creation and administration of laws to favor its interests. When its interests are threatened, the elite has them protected by law, even at the expense of less powerful groups. When the interests of less powerful groups are threatened, they can do little to protect their interests under the law, unless they obtain the elite's support. According to the elitist model, activities are labeled deviant when they threaten the elite's interests.

Considering deviance as a label that makes a class of behavior illicit is a relatively recent development in the sociology of deviance. In studying the creation of deviance, sociologists usually try to understand and explain the history of deviant labels; such studies test the pluralist and elitist models of law. Perhaps more than any other topic in the sociology of deviance, the creation of deviance will capture increasing attention from sociologists.

Controlling Deviance

For many people, including laymen, policy makers, and sociologists, an important problem is to control deviance—to regulate, reduce, or completely suppress it. They want to control deviance because they believe it would enhance social welfare and reduce citizens' pain and suffering. Under the general topic of control, sociologists address many issues, including the techniques used to control deviance, the justifications for different techniques, the administration of control, and the effectiveness of different techniques. A brief examination of these issues shows the scope of sociological discussions of deviance control.

Every society has techniques for controlling deviance, and sociologists seek to understand and use them. The most prominent technique is punishment—pain intentionally inflicted on the deviant by agents of the state (Sutherland and Cressey, 1978:304-5). Punishment can range from death to incarceration, financial penalties to social degradation (Korn and McCorkle, 1959:373-414). Punishment has been justified on several grounds. One justification is retribution. From the retributive standpoint, good and evil are moral absolutes; deviance disturbs the moral order. Inflicting punishment on the deviant equal to the harm caused by the offense restores the moral order and reestablishes the balance between right and wrong. Thus, retribution requires that deviants get their "just desserts" (cf. Pincoffs, 1966). Another justification for punishment is its contribution to the society's solidarity. While deviance calls certain values or standards into question, punishing the offender reaffirms those values or standards, thereby integrating respectable citizens. Indeed, failure to punish the offender may produce ambiguity over what is right and wrong, which in turn might lead to the disintegration of society (cf. Coser, 1962). A third justification is that punishment prevents deviance—it serves a deterrent function. There are two principal types of deterrence. Specific deterrence affects the individual offender. Punishment teaches the offender not to commit the same act again; he or she wants to avoid the pain of future punishment. General deterrence affects the public. When an individual is punished, other citizens learn about the painful consequences of deviance and choose to refrain from deviance to avoid punishment (cf. Andenaes, 1974).

Treatment is an alternative to punishment. While punishment assumes that the offender intentionally committed the deviant act, treatment assumes that the offense is caused by conditions over which the offender has no control. Because they are not responsible for their actions, deviants should be helped rather than punished. Different disciplines offer strikingly different kinds of treatment techniques. For example, psychiatrists who locate the cause of deviance in the actor's disordered personality use clinical techniques, such as psychoanalysis, to treat the actor. Social psychologists who locate the cause in the actor's social relations use techniques to alter those relations so that the actor will learn attitudes promoting respectable behavior (cf. Cressey, 1955). While other techniques, such as the sheer incapacitation of offenders, may be used to control deviance, punishment and treatment are the two principal modes of control.

Sociologists also try to explain why specific control techniques exist in particular societies or historical periods. For instance, several theories account for the use of specific punitive techniques. According to the cultural consistency model, "societal reactions to lawbreaking and the methods used to implement or express those reactions show a general tendency to be consistent with other ways of behaving in the society" (Sutherland and Cressey, 1978:348). Thus, in a society where physical suffering is regarded as the natural lot of mankind, physical torture is common; a society where freedom and liberty are highly valued may use incarceration as its most severe punishment. In contrast, one psychoanalytic theory claims that the severity of punishment reflects the society's alternatives for satisfying aggressive drives (Menninger, 1968). The fewer the alternate routes which members can use to release aggression, the more severe the techniques used to punish deviants.

Sociologists investigate the administration of social control. There are hundreds of studies examining the ways in which police, courts, prisons, and other social control agencies perform their duties (cf. Daudistel et al.,

1979). For example, there is considerable research on the manner in which police officers maintain order and enforce the criminal law; studies focus on officers' acquisition of information about crime and criminals as well as their decisions to arrest or release suspects (Bittner, 1970). Similarly, researchers have considered the ways in which individuals suffering from mental illness are evaluated by psychiatrists, processed into mental institutions, and treated for their illnesses (Scheff, 1967). Recent years have witnessed the development of evaluation research. Here, investigators evaluate the efficiency of administrative operations and recommend ways for improving them.

Related to administration is a concern for assessing the effectiveness of control techniques. There has been a continuing effort to determine the effectiveness of punishment in deterring deviants and the general public. Much of this research centers on discovering the effectiveness of capital punishment in preventing murder (Gibbs, 1975; Zimring and Hawkins, 1973). There also has been a growing effort to determine the effectiveness of treatment in reforming deviants. For the most part, investigators find that traditional treatment methods do not significantly reduce recidivism (Robinson and Smith, 1971). In explaining this failure, some argue that the theoretical foundations of particular treatment practices are dubious; others point to obstacles that hinder the implementation of treatment, such as political opposition or the lack of necessary resources (cf. Sutherland and Cressey, 1978:366-83). Accompanying efforts to assess the effectiveness of punishment and treatment is controversy regarding the political, economic, and humanitarian implications of these techniques.

Controlling deviance is an important topic for sociologists of deviance. They address many different issues, ranging from theoretical problems, such as why societies use different techniques to control deviance, to policy questions, involving the choice and use of control techniques. Whatever the objective, the problem of control is central to the investigation of deviance.

SOCIAL ORGANIZATION AND DEVIANCE

Three Levels of Analysis

The four problems discussed in the preceding section account for most of the work in the sociology of deviance. Sociologists studying these problems usually adopt one of two levels of analysis: social-psychological or social-structural (A. Cohen, 1965; Gibbons and Jones, 1975:30-39). At the social-psychological level, the deviant individual is the center of attention. Social-psychological research focuses on the conditions which lead individuals to commit deviant acts, the stages in the deviant's career, the ways in which the deviant copes with social control efforts, and so forth. Whatever the issue, social-psychological attention focuses on the individual. At the social-structural level of analysis, the center of attention is the network of social institutions which makes up society. Social-structural research examines the distribution of deviance within society, the consequences of deviance for society, the role of political and economic institutions in the creation of deviant labels, and so forth. In each of these cases, all or part of society is the focus of attention. Between the social-psychological and social-structural levels is an intermediate level of analysis—social organizational. At this third level, the focus is the group, rather than the individual or the society. This book explores social organization.

The individual and society are bound together in a dialectical relation (Berger and Luckmann, 1966). On the one hand, the society shapes the individual, molding the biological creature into a competent societal member. On the other hand, the individual shapes the society, reaffirming some practices, calling for change in others, voting in elections, contributing to production, and so on. But the relation between the individual and society is not direct; it is mediated through organizations of various kinds. The society molds individuals into competent members through such organizations as the family, school, and church, and individuals shape the society through their participation in these and other organizations. Thus, social organization constitutes a third, intermediate level of analysis. Before examining social organization and deviance, a conceptual framework for understanding social organization is needed.

Generally, social organization refers to a network of social relations (Martindale, 1966:129-30; Mott, 1965:13-14). This broad definition includes two different kinds of networks. First, social organization can be viewed as an *association,* a network of relations between a number of individuals who form some sort of group. Organizations may be formal, with well-defined hierarchies, goals, rules for operation, and exact rosters of members (Caplow, 1964:1). Universities, corporations, and government agencies are formal organizations. Or organizations may be informal, involving personalized relations among a small number of persons, as exemplified by a family or a high school clique. Second, social organization can be seen as a *transaction,* a network of relations between two or more individuals involved in a common activity, whether or not they belong to the same association (Blumer, 1962). Transactions also may be formal, governed by impersonal rules and backed by authority. Political elections and church weddings are formal transactions. Or they may be informal, guided by norms which the participants develop and back with mutual consent. Examples include lovemaking, weekly poker games, and family picnics. Viewing social organization in terms of associations emphasizes the structure of groups; viewing social organization in terms of transactions emphasizes the structure of joint activities.

It is difficult to distinguish association from transaction. Associations are dynamic; their members act. And transactions involve associations of many kinds. Each form of organization shapes the other. The transactions pursued affect the structure of associations. For instance, if a hospital wants to provide psychiatric services to a community, it must add a special ward staffed with trained psychiatric specialists. Likewise, the type of association influences the structure of the transaction. Military battles, for example, are more complicated if the opponents are large, complex armies rather than small platoons. Although they are intertwined, association can be distinguished from transaction for purposes of analysis.

Whether attention centers on associations or transactions, the social organizational level of analysis uses two important concepts: position and role (cf. Blau and Scott, 1962; Caplow, 1964). A *position* refers to a category of membership whose incumbent is expected to act in a specific way (Caplow, 1964:64). President of a company, leader of a high school clique, and mother of a family are organizational positions. *Role* is the dynamic side of position. A role refers to the pattern of action expected of a person in a particular position (Shibutani, 1961:46). Thus, the role of company president may include meeting with the board of directors, setting company policies, directing executives to implement policies, and so forth. Position and role are inseparable—there are no roles without positions, and no positions without roles.

A role cannot be isolated; it is part of a larger social network. A role's meaning derives from its relationship to other roles. What a wife does, for example, depends on the expectations and activities of her husband. A role involves both obligations—activities that a person must perform because of the position he or she occupies—and claims—activities that a person expects others to perform because of his or her position. Students are obligated to perform course work—take notes during lectures, write term papers, and take examinations—but they also make claims on their instructors—to give lectures, make assignments, and give examinations. The relations between roles are supported by a system of norms and sanctions. Whether they are formal or informal, written or unwritten, stable or fleeting, norms specify roles' obligations and claims. Sanctions back norms by rewarding conformity and punishing violations. The relations between linked positions and roles constitute social organization.

Social organizations mediate between the individual and the society. On the one hand, they mediate the impact of the society on the individual. The individual is trained and directed by other members of organizations, such as family members, school teachers, and fellow workers. They teach the individual about his or her obligations and claims in particular settings; they supply the resources for meeting these obligations; and they reward the individual for satisfying obligations and punish for failures to do so. These obligations and the associated rewards and punishments are themselves shaped by the society. For instance, a man holds a full-time job in a factory because he learned from his parents and teachers that men should be gainfully employed, and his work is rewarded by payment. He uses his wages to pay the rent and buy food and clothing for his wife and children because he also learned that men should support their families. But these obligations which the family and school passed on to him are shaped by the larger society. Industrialization changed the basic activities pursued by the family. The family-based economy, where family members produced their own food, clothing, and shelter, gave way to an alternate system, where men left home, produced goods for others, and used their wages to purchase necessities. The society's industrial economy requires wage-earning laborers, as well as such organizations as the family and school to transmit this requirement to individuals. Thus, society shapes the individual through social organizations.

On the other hand, social organizations mediate the individual's impact on the society. In rare cases, an individual affects society directly. For instance, by assassinating a major political leader, an individual may alter the society's economic and political institutions. However, most individuals affect society through their participation in associations. By operating within a labor union or political interest group, for example, the individual may influence the society's economy or government.

The Social Organization of Deviants and Deviance

This book employs conceptions of social organization, both as association and transaction, to analyze deviance. First, deviants have relationships with one another; they form associations. The features of these deviant associations can be examined, including the ways members join and leave the association, how they act toward and feel about one another, how they acquire the knowledge and skills needed to participate as members, how they develop and work toward the association's goals, and how they distribute resources and benefits among themselves. These issues involve the social organization of deviants; they focus on relationships among deviant actors. Second, deviants undertake deviant transactions, and these transactions can be studied, including the specific acts which comprise the transaction, the ways these acts are coordinated, the resources needed to complete the transaction, and the actors' objectives in the transaction. These issues involve the social organization of deviance; deviant activities are the focus.

To illustrate the differences between the social-psychological, social-structural, and social-organizational levels of analysis, consider juvenile delinquency. At a social-psychological level, the sociologist might study the causes of an individual's delinquent act or the development of an individual's delinquent career. At a social-structural level, the sociologist might

look at rates of delinquency, the consequences of delinquency for the society, or the creation of the delinquent label. However, at the social-organizational level, the topics are the structure of relations between delinquents
(the social organization of deviants) and the structure of relations during
delinquent activities (the social organization of deviance). In the former
case, the sociologist might examine the ways juveniles organize themselves
into delinquent gangs. Focusing on one gang, the researcher might consider
the ways juveniles join and leave the gang, the gang's objectives, how members acquire the knowledge and skills needed to participate together, how
authority and tasks are divided within the gang, the gang's norms, and the
sanctions used against members who break those norms. When studying
the social organization of delinquency, the sociologist would focus on delinquent transactions. For any given transaction, the researcher might study
the actors' objectives, the roles of the delinquents and other participants,
the specific acts involved and the way they are coordinated, and the knowledge, skills, and resources necessary for the transaction. Both delinquent
associations and delinquent transactions can be studied at the organizational
level of analysis.

Deviant organizations, like respectable forms of organization, mediate
between the individual and the society. The delinquent gang illustrates the
relationship between the individual, the deviant social organization, and
the society. On the one hand, the gang mediates the society's impact on the
individual. For example, this explains why some middle-class adolescents
engage in delinquency. Middle-class adolescent peer groups shape delinquent behavior, and the society shapes the attitudes which these groups
transmit. Basic changes in America's labor market and educational system
facilitated the development of a youth culture favorable to middle-class
delinquency (A. Cohen, 1967). The occupational system changed in such
a way that adolescents have been removed from the labor force, while the
educational system extended its control over adolescents until they reach
adulthood. Released from adult responsibilities, middle-class adolescents
developed a youth culture which values pleasure-seeking and makes certain
delinquent activities, such as drinking, sexual promiscuity, and drug use,
acceptable. The middle-class adolescent's peer groups transmit attitudes
that encourage these forms of pleasure-seeking (cf. Myerhoff and Myerhoff, 1964). Thus, the peer group shapes the individual's delinquent behavior, while the society shapes the peer group's values and standards.

On the other hand, the gang mediates the individual's impact on the
society. Albert Cohen (1955) wrote *Delinquent Boys,* a classic study demonstrating this point. He asked why delinquent subcultures develop predom-
inately among lower-class males. He argued that lower-class youngsters
acquire middle-class success goals, especially those calling for the achievement of high social status. However, they lack the skills necessary to compete
with middle-class youngsters in achieving these goals. Their inability to

compete successfully leads to frustration and a sense of personal failure. Lower-class youngsters who share this experience come together, collectively examine ways of solving their frustration, and work out a mutually beneficial solution. One solution involves forming a gang and carrying out delinquent activities—activities which are nonutilitarian, malicious, and negativistic. These activities demonstrate their rejection of middle-class success goals and thereby resolve their problems in achieving status. According to Cohen, the gang mediates the frustration of the individual.

Studying Social Organization and Deviance

Sociologists of deviance have not ignored social organization. First, there are several studies about the social organization of specific types of deviance. Some studies examine the associations formed by certain kinds of deviants, such as racketeers, armed robbers, homosexuals, burglars, and marijuana users (Cressey, 1969; Einstadter, 1969; Mileski and Black, 1972; Shover, 1973; Zimmerman and Wieder, 1977). Other reports describe the organization of deviant transactions, such as extortion, impersonal homosexual intercourse, murder, and pickpocketing (Best, 1982; Humphreys, 1970; Luckenbill, 1977; Maurer, 1964; McIntosh, 1971). These studies provide valuable descriptions, but they do not develop a comprehensive theory of social organization and deviance.

Second, some typologies of deviance use social-organizational features to classify offenders or offenses. One example is Clinard and Quinney's (1973) typology of criminal behavior systems. They state that a criminal behavior system consists of four elements: the offender's criminal career, the group's support of criminal behavior, the correspondence between criminal and legitimate behavior patterns, and the societal reaction to the behavior. Some of the dimensions for distinguishing behavior systems include organizational features; the offender's criminal career, for instance, includes the social roles he or she performs, and group support of criminal behavior reflects the degree to which criminals share norms, encouraging crime. In another typology, Gibbons (1977) classifies criminals on the basis of variables which touch on the organization of crime and criminals, including the sophistication of the offense behavior and the structure of the offense setting. These typologies note the relevance of social organization, but they do not explore it systematically.

Finally, there are some attempts to consider deviance in terms of an organizational framework. For instance, Cressey (1972) critically examines the social organization of criminals. He argues that criminal associations vary along a dimension of rationality. The greater the division of labor, coordination by rules, and pursuit of announced goals, the greater the association's rationality. Cressey then arrays six basic forms of criminal association along this dimension, ranging from the most rational form, a confederation of mafia families, to the least rational form, a task force. Similarly, Gale Miller (1978) analyzes deviant occupations in terms of their organizational features, such as the occupation's work roles, its related and supportive roles, and its ideology justifying deviants' participation.

These treatments of social organization suffer from one or more flaws. First, they often are too narrow. Some focus on a single form of deviance, such as murder or armed robbery. Others focus more broadly on crime, constructing typologies of criminal offenses or offenders. But even this focus is narrow, for it ignores other kinds of deviance, such as mental illness and suicide. Further, these typologies generally are inadequate; a large proportion of deviance does not fit into any of their categories (Gibbons, 1979:85-92). Second, most studies of social organization limit themselves to description. They fail to either locate organizational forms along a dimension of social organization or examine the consequences of organizational variation for deviants and social control agents. Finally, these studies often confuse the two different bases for analyzing social organization. A comprehensive theory of social organization and deviance must distinguish between the social organization of deviants—the patterns of social relations among deviant actors—and the social organization of deviance—the patterns of social relations among the roles performed in the deviant transaction.

By adopting social organization as the level of analysis, sociologists can ask several important questions. Consider the social organization of deviants. First, in what basic ways do deviant actors organize themselves to pursue their deviant activities? How do these basic forms differ in organizational features, such as their division of labor, coordination among the deviant actors, and objectives? Second, what are the consequences of organizational variation for deviants and social control agents? How does social organization affect individuals' deviant careers, their rewards from deviance, and their management of social control efforts? How does deviant organization affect social control agents' attempts to locate, apprehend, and sanction deviants? Third, what conditions facilitate the development and transformation of organizational forms? What conditions shape the development of different forms of deviant organization? How do basic organizational forms change over time, and what conditions account for these changes? These questions address some of the same issues found in traditional research on deviance—the causes, consequences, and control of deviance. But they examine these issues at the social organizational level of analysis.

When considering the social organization of deviance, similar questions arise. First, in what basic ways are deviant transactions organized? How do these basic forms differ in their organizational features, such as their principal roles, the relations between those roles, and the transactions' outcomes? Second, what are the consequences of organizational variation for deviants and social control agents? How does variation influence deviants' strategies for conducting the operation? How does it affect social control agents' tactics for detecting and apprehending deviants? Third, what conditions facilitate the development and transformation of basic organizational forms? What conditions cause different forms of deviance? How do these forms change, and what conditions account for their change? Again, these questions examine traditional issues using the social-organizational level of analysis.

The social psychological and social structural levels of analysis have dominated deviance research. Social organization offers an intermediate level of analysis that has not received as much attention. Although some sociologists consider social organization when studying deviance, their writings do not produce a comprehensive understanding of deviance and social organization. This book to addresses this broader topic.

PLAN OF THE BOOK

This book does not examine deviance from the social-psychological or social-structural level of analysis. Rather, it concentrates on the middle level— deviance and social organization. Accordingly, the book has two principal objectives. First, it seeks to develop a comprehensive framework for understanding the social organization of deviants and deviance. This requires identifying and describing the basic organizational forms of deviant associations and deviant transactions. Second, the book develops propositions about the consequences of organizational variation, how variation in deviant associations and deviant transactions affects deviants and social control agents.

This book's approach is inductive. Many theories of deviance are deductive; they are derived from broader sociological theories and then evaluated in light of empirical evidence. Unfortunately, these deductive efforts sometimes lack a broad base of empirical support, or they fail to account for some empirical cases, a problem with many of the typologies discussed earlier. In contrast, the inductive framework is "grounded" (cf. Glaser and Strauss, 1967). Empirical research is used to identify the basic forms of deviant associations and deviant transactions and to develop propositions about the consequences of organizational variation. Instead of moving from theory to empirical tests, the inductive approach moves from empirical research to theory in the hope of developing a framework that has a broad base of support.

This book is divided into two major parts. Part I focuses on the social organization of deviants. Chapters 2 and 3 describe the basic ways deviants organize themselves to pursue deviant activities. Chapter 4 identifies some consequences of the social organization of deviants for deviant actors and social control agents. Part II focuses on the social organization of deviance. Chapters 5 through 8 describe the basic forms of deviant transactions. Chapter 9 examines some of the consequences of the social organization of deviance for deviants and social control agents. Finally, chapter 10 examines the interrelationship between the social organization of deviants and the social organization of deviance.

PART ONE
THE SOCIAL ORGANIZATION OF DEVIANTS

Every person has ties to other people. Even a hermit, living in isolation, interprets experiences using a language learned from others. Of course, few people are as isolated as hermits; most of us have many different, ongoing relationships with others. These relationships can be purely sociable, or they can be instrumental. People in a relationship may place few constraints on one another, or their actions may be tightly coordinated. At one extreme, an actor in a relationship may have power over another and, when the other person acknowledges that that power is legitimate, the relationship involves authority. In short, people's ties to one another can involve relationships of varying qualities.

Relationships between deviants take many forms. A physician who is addicted to drugs and tries to keep it secret from everyone else, a group of prostitutes talking as they wait for customers, a gang of delinquents riding in a stolen car, a team of robbers carrying out a carefully planned, tightly coordinated robbery, and a family of organized criminals operating a numbers racket are examples of deviants who are linked to one another in very different ways. The social organization of deviants refers to the patterns of relationships among deviant actors involved in the pursuit of deviance.

The social organization of deviants varies along a dimension of sophistication. Organizational sophistication involves the elements of complexity, coordination, and purposiveness (cf. Cressey, 1972:11-17). Organizations vary in the *complexity* of their division of labor, including the number of members, the degree of stratification, and the degree of specialization of organizational roles. Members can range in number from one to many; they may consider one another as equals or they may be arrayed in a clearly defined hierarchy; and members' contributions may be defined very roughly or their responsibilities may be specialized, with each individual performing a designated task. Organizations also vary in their *coordination* among organizational roles, including the degree to which rules, agreements, and codes regulating relationships are defined and enforced. Some organizations are essentially casual; others are governed by rigid rules. Finally, organizations vary in the *purposiveness* with which they specify, strive toward, and achieve their goals. Forms of organization which display high levels of complexity, coordination, and purposiveness are more sophisticated than those forms with lower levels.

Deviants' relations with one another can be arrayed along the dimension of organizational sophistication. Beginning with the least sophisticated form, chapters 2 and 3 discuss five forms of the social organization of deviants: loners, colleagues, peers, mobs, and formal organizations. These organizational forms are defined in terms of four variables: whether the deviants associate with one another; whether they participate in deviance together; whether their deviance requires an elaborate division of labor; and whether their organization's activities extend over time and space (see Table I-1).

Loners do not associate with other deviants, participate in shared deviance, have a division of labor, or maintain their deviance over extended time and space. Colleagues differ from loners because they associate with fellow deviants. Peers

Table I-1 CHARACTERISTICS OF DIFFERENT FORMS OF THE SOCIAL ORGANIZATION OF DEVIANTS

| | | CHARACTERISTIC | | |
FORM OF ORGANIZATION	MUTUAL ASSOCIATION	MUTUAL PARTICIPATION	ELABORATE DIVISION OF LABOR	EXTENDED ORGANIZATION
Loners	no	no	no	no
Colleagues	yes	no	no	no
Peers	yes	yes	no	no
Mobs	yes	yes	yes	no
Formal Organizations	yes	yes	yes	yes

not only associate with one another, but also participate in deviance together. In mobs, this shared participation requires an elaborate division of labor. Finally, formal organizations involve mutual association, mutual participation, an elaborate division of labor, and deviant activities extended over time and space.

Classifying deviants' relations in terms of organizational sophistication offers some important analytical advantages. Sociologists recognize the importance of other deviants in convincing newcomers to experiment with deviance, giving advice about deviant techniques, and supporting each other's deviant life style. Some theories of deviance, such as differential association theory (Sutherland and Cressey, 1978:79-83) and social learning theory (Akers, 1973:45-61), consider the ways deviants influence one another. However, these relations have not been analyzed thoroughly. Most sociological discussions generalize about deviant *subcultures* —an ambiguous term which encompasses a wide range of relationships and ignores important differences (cf. A. Cohen, 1955; Cloward and Ohlin, 1960; Rubington and Weinberg, 1981). A group of prostitutes, a gang of delinquents, a team of robbers, and an organized crime family all have subcultures, but they also differ in important ways. The scheme of classification developed here distinguishes among those forms and includes loners, individuals who have little or no contact with other deviants. In addition, the five organizational forms affect the lives of deviants as well as social control agents. Each form poses special problems for the deviants, placing limitations on their deviant actions. But each form also offers advantages, making it easier to carry out some kinds of deviance successfully. The social organization of deviants also affects social control agents; they must tailor their reactions to fit the deviant organization they want to control.

The description of these forms of organization and their consequences must be qualified in two ways. First, the forms appear as ideal-types. There is variation among the types of deviants within each form, as well as between one form and another. This book tries to sketch the typical features of each form, recognizing that specific deviants may not share all of the features of their form. Organizational sophistication can be viewed as a continuum, with deviants located between, as well as on, the five points noted here. Describing only five forms along this continuum inevitably understates the complexities of social life. Second, the descriptions of these forms draw largely from field studies of deviants in the contemporary United States. A particular type of deviant can organize in various ways in different societies or at different times. The references to specific field studies serve to place familiar pieces of research within this analytic framework; there is no claim that particular types of deviants invariably organize in a given way.

The three chapters which follow describe each of the five forms and then examine the consequences of organizational sophistication. Chapter 2 discusses loners, colleagues, and peers. Chapter 3 considers the more sophisticated forms, mobs and formal organizations. Finally, chapter 4 examines the consequences of the social organization of deviants for the deviants themselves and for social control agents.

CHAPTER TWO
LONERS, COLLEAGUES, AND PEERS

Deviants, like respectable individuals, face practical problems. Deviant acts require resources, such as special equipment or knowledge. Consider marijuana smoking, an apparently simple act (Becker, 1963:41-78). The novice smoker needs to get the necessary equipment. At a minimum, marijuana is required; other smoking paraphernalia, such as rolling papers and a roach clip, are helpful. In addition, the novice needs knowledge. To get high, the marijuana smoker must know how to smoke and how to recognize and interpret the drug's effects. Equally important, the novice needs an ideology, a rationale for trying marijuana. Most people's early socialization encourages respectable behavior. The decision to commit a deviant act goes against what the individual has learned. The act must be justified by an ideological account which explains why it is appropriate under these circumstances. For example, the novice marijuana smoker may argue that marijuana is harmless. Deviants face the practical problem of avoiding sanctions. By definition, deviants are subject to discovery, apprehension, and sanctioning by social control agents; they must devise ways of avoiding officials. For marijuana smokers, this may involve smoking in a private place and concealing one's deviance from outsiders who might report it.

Deviants' practical problems center on the acquisition of resources, the management of the deviant act, and protection from social control agents. The deviant must acquire the resources necessary to commit the deviant act. Resources include techniques for carrying out the act, an ideology to justify it, whatever equipment is necessary, and, if they are required, other people to serve as partners or victims. Deviant acts often involve several stages which must be managed. Each stage poses its own problems and the deviant must attend to the act's progress, coordinating the different elements to bring it to a successful conclusion. Finally, deviants must protect themselves from social control agents. There are many protective tactics, ranging from keeping one's deviance secret to bribing the authorities, but some form of protection is needed to avoid sanctioning.

The solutions to these practical problems depend upon the social organization of deviants. The more sophisticated the form of organization, the more likely the deviants can help one another with their problems. Deviants help one another in many ways: by teaching each other deviant skills and a deviant ideology; by working together to carry out complicated tasks; by giving each other sociable contacts and moral support; by supplying one another with deviant equipment; by protecting each other from the authorities; and so forth. Just as respectable persons rely on one another in the course of everyday life, deviants find it easier to cope with practical problems when they have the help of deviant associates.

This chapter considers three relatively unsophisticated forms of deviant organization. It begins with loners, individuals who lack contacts with other deviants, in order to examine how deviants deal with practical problems when they are on their own. Then it considers colleagues, who associate with other deviants but commit their deviant acts by themselves, and finally peers, who cooperate with each other in committing deviant acts. Deviants in each of these organizational forms must cope with the practical problems of resource acquisition, task management, and protection from social control.

LONERS

Loners do not associate with other deviants. They are on their own in coping with the practical problems posed by deviance. Examples of loners include most murderers (Luckenbill, 1977), rapists (Amir, 1971), physician narcotic addicts (Winick, 1961), check forgers (Klein and Montague, 1977; Lemert, 1967:99-134), heterosexual transvestites (Buckner, 1970), embezzlers (Cressey, 1953), compulsive criminals (Cressey, 1962), amateur shoplifters (Cameron, 1964), women seeking illicit abortions (N. Davis,1974; N. Lee, 1969), gamblers (Lesieur, 1977), the mentally ill (Scheff, 1966), and computer criminals (Parker, 1976). In each of these cases, the deviant often works alone, without the benefits of associating with fellow deviants.

At first glance, it may seem appropriate to interpret the loner's experience in psychological, rather than sociological, terms. After all, the loner appears to lack any social support. But loners are affected by their relations with others. Every loner has been socialized—taught a language, social skills, and the norms which govern life in his or her group. Socialization also teaches the individual how to interpret personal experiences so that when faced with a problem, the person can recognize it as a problem, interpret his or her reactions, consider a range of possible responses, select the one which seems most appropriate, and carry out that response. Even when cut off from all contact with other people, an individual's choice of action and the reasoning behind it derive from his or her social experiences. This is true for deviants as well as respectable persons. What makes loners particularly interesting is that, having been socialized by respectable persons who presumably encouraged respectable behavior, they should choose respectable, rather than deviant, courses of action. Loners choose deviance because they face situations where respectable courses of action are unattractive, not because they want to contradict their socialization. For example, a loner may decide to commit a deviant act because the costs of breaking a norm seem less than the costs of respectable conduct. A pregnant woman living in a society which prohibits abortion may decide that completing her pregnancy would cause more problems than having the abortion. Moreover, the costs of deviance may be minimized by concealing the deviant act from others, particularly social control agents.

Most individuals have more difficulty deciding to commit their first deviant act than with decisions about subsequent deviant actions. Once the deviant develops a personally acceptable justification for deviance and acquires some experience in carrying out deviant acts, successive violations can be committed with greater confidence. Following Lemert's (1967:99-134) discussion of check forgers, a distinction can be drawn between naive and systematic loners. In the initial decision to commit a deviant act, the loner is naive, confronting the practical problems posed by deviance for the first time. Every loner is naive at first. However, some loners go on to engage in systematic deviance, regularly performing the deviant act. While one person may decide to solve pressing financial problems by writing a bad check (naive forgery), another may forge checks regularly (systematic forgery). While systematic loners have the advantage of experience, they run greater risks.

This section focuses on two types of loners. Embezzlers serve as an example of naive loners. The decision to embezzle reveals some of the problems involved in entering deviance alone. Physician narcotic addicts illustrate systematic loners. The physician addict engages in regular deviance at considerable risk.

Embezzlers

Not everyone has an opportunity for embezzlement (Cressey, 1953:19-32). The embezzler must occupy a position of financial trust; he or she must be entrusted with other people's money, as when a company treasurer controls the firm's funds. Embezzlement involves the intentional violation of that trust, taking other people's money for the embezzler's personal use. The position of financial trust gives the embezzler an opportunity to steal, but he or she must overcome two additional obstacles in order to commit embezzlement. First, the embezzler must avoid discovery. Persons in positions of financial trust usually are among the first suspects when an embezzlement is discovered. While some embezzlers simply abscond, taking the money and fleeing, many try to retain their positions of trust after the theft occurs. To do so, they must find a way to cover up the theft, such as manipulative bookkeeping, where funds are moved from one account to another ahead of the inspectors so that each examination of an individual account reveals the correct sum in place. The second obstacle is psychological. Persons are not given positions of financial trust unless they have a record of honesty. Such people usually see themselves as honest. Before they steal, embezzlers must justify their dishonest action to themselves. In addition to devising techniques for taking money and hiding the loss, they must be able to account for their entry into deviance.

Opportunities for embezzlement vary with the technology for keeping track of entrusted funds. Traditionally, positions of financial trust involved handling cash or keeping written records of financial transactions; bookkeepers, bank tellers, and accountants occupied the positions of trust from which embezzlement could be staged. As the economy shifts to electronic records of financial transactions, programmers and others with access to computer systems have opportunities for embezzlement. In either case, those who entrust their money to others try to protect themselves against embezzlement. A first line of defense involves carefully selecting those who occupy the entrusted positions, trying to insure that they are honest. Auditing systems which keep track of funds and make it difficult to conceal a theft form a second line of defense. A third line of defense involves procedures which require that two or more people cooperate in all financial transactions. Such procedures assume that the risk of embezzlement is highest when an individual can commit the offense alone. It is more difficult for two or more people to conspire to embezzle funds, if only because each will be reluctant to reveal a willingness to steal to the other, who might notify the authorities. Thus, among the experts' recommendations for protecting computerized records from abuse are:

> Separation of responsibility of people in sensitive jobs, dual control over sensitive functions where separation is not practical, . . . prohibiting computer programmers from entering the computer room except for emergencies, formal software developmental methods including independent quality assurance testing of all software. . . . (Parker, 1976:281)

Most systems do not require cooperative financial transactions. As a result, the typical embezzler is a loner. Without assistance from others, the deviant devises techniques for stealing money and concealing the loss, as well as a justification for doing so.

Why does a previously honest employee turn to theft? Cressey (1953) answered this question in a classic study. He argued that the criminal violator of financial trust goes through three stages in committing the crime. The first stage involves identifying a nonshareable problem involving a need for money (Cressey, 1953:33-76). The nature of this problem varies; the person may suffer a business loss, have an extravagant life style which leaves him or her in debt, or simply want more status. The specifics of the problem are less important than the individual's definition of it as nonshareable. The individual believes that he or she cannot afford to tell others about the problem—sharing the problem would risk losing the others' esteem and receiving sanctions. This may not be an accurate assessment; if told about the problem, other people might be more supportive than the individual believes. What is critical is that the individual holds these beliefs and decides not to share the problem. While the problem cannot be shared, it can be solved, or at least reduced, with money. For example, a person with heavy gambling debts may be unwilling to reveal this fact to employers, family members, and so on. At the same time, the individual believes that additional money would make it possible to pay off the debts and eliminate the problem.

The second stage is the person's perception that the entrusted funds can be used to solve the problem (Cressey, 1953:77-91). Embezzling rarely presents a technical problem—the person holding a position of financial trust already knows how to violate that trust. One embezzler explained:

> . . . I would have to say that I learned all of it in school and in my ordinary accounting experience. In school they teach you in your advanced years how to detect embezzlements, and you sort of absorb it. . . . In my case I did not use any techniques which any ordinary accountant in my position could not have used; they are known by all accountants, just like the abortion technique is known by all doctors. (Cressey, 1953:82)

The key in this second stage is the recognition that embezzlement offers a means of solving the nonshareable problem. Individuals who fail to make this connection do not go on to embezzle.

Finally, the individual must devise a rationalization for carrying out the theft, an account which explains to the individual why violating the trust is an appropriate, acceptable action (Cressey, 1953:93-138). For first-time embezzlers, the most common rationale is that they are "borrowing" the money and intend to repay it in the future. This rationale draws from the larger culture—borrowing is a reasonable, respectable method of taking something belonging to another. So long as the borrowed article is returned, the borrower harms no one. By defining their actions as borrowing, rather than as theft, embezzlers can retain their definition of themselves as respectable, trustworthy people, even while knowing that others would see their actions as deviant. The borrowing rationale may become less effective if the person repeats the theft. A person with gambling debts may embezzle, reasoning that he or she will return the money, but then decide that, rather than simply paying off the debts with the stolen money, it makes more sense to gamble with the money, trying to win enough to *both* pay off the debts and return the stolen sum. Of course, if the stolen money is lost, the nonshareable problem grows and additional funds may be embezzled. Repeated embezzlements eventually are defined by the offender as criminal acts, rather than instances of borrowing.

Nettler (1974) challenged Cressey's account of entry into embezzlement. In an examination of six major Canadian embezzlements, he found only one that fit Cressey's model. Nettler argues that two traditional models of embezzlement better fit the facts of his cases. The "detective's theory" recommends looking for the "Three B's—babes, booze, and bets." That is, embezzlers begin to steal after they become involved with sex, alcohol, or gambling. The "auditor's hypothesis" says that embezzlement results from a combination of desire and opportunity—the individual wants the money and sees a means of taking it. In short, Nettler argues that some cases start with simple greed or involvement in vice, rather than a nonshareable problem. But even if Cressey cannot account for every instance of embezzlement, his analysis retains considerable usefulness. Many embezzlements involve persons with no deviant past who make the transition into deviance. For these naive individuals, the sequence of defining a problem as nonshareable, perceiving embezzlement as a solution, and devising a rationale may be a particularly common pathway into deviance.

The first act of embezzlement typically involves a naive loner, a respectable person with no deviant experience. According to Cressey, the process of becoming an embezzler is a lonely one. Defining a problem as nonshareable isolates the individual from others. The individual perceives an opportunity for deviance; because he or she already has whatever skills and knowledge the theft requires, there is no need for instruction from an experienced deviant. The rationale justifying the deviance often is a familiar one, such as "borrowing," derived from the larger culture to fit the requirements of the situation. While subsequent thefts may require less thought, the naive embezzler is likely to view the first theft as a major step.

Physician Narcotic Addicts

By definition, narcotic addiction is a form of systematic deviance—an addict requires regular doses of narcotics. Acquiring and using drugs becomes a regular, systematic activity in the addict's life, around which other concerns are scheduled. The stereotype of the "street addict" is familiar: he or she is young, poor, addicted to heroin, involved in crime to support the habit, and associated with other addicts who help the individual find and use drugs. Physician addicts violate every aspect of this stereotype.

Addiction is a major problem in the medical professions. Estimates of the proportion of physicians who are addicted to narcotics range from 1 percent to 2.5 percent—numbers far greater than the rates of addiction in the general population (Hessler, 1974). Addiction also is relatively common among nurses and other health professionals. Physician addicts have little in common with the street addict. They are typically middle-aged, rather than young, and prosperous, rather than poor; they are addicted to meperidine (Demerol), rather than heroin; they take their drugs from medical supplies, rather than stealing to support their habits; and they operate as loners, rather than as part of a group of addicts (Winick, 1961).

The physician's entry into deviance bears several similarities to the embezzler's initial experiences. Many physicians' deviant careers begin with a problem, such as overwork, chronic pain, or marital difficulties (Winick, 1961). As doctors, they already know about the effects of various drugs, appropriate dosages, and methods of administering drugs, and they have access to drugs, typically in clinic or hospital supplies. They begin "treating" their own symptoms by using drugs taken illicitly from medical supplies. While this action is deviant, they justify it to themselves as a medical decision. Thus, like the embezzler, the physician addict enters deviance in response to personal problems, adapts professional knowledge for deviant purposes, and devises an account which draws on respectable explanations.

The key difference between the two forms of deviance is in their schedules. Embezzlement is an episodic action undertaken once or at irregular, relatively infrequent intervals. Initially, the physician who uses narcotics also may have an infrequent, irregular schedule for drug use (Winick, 1961). However, some doctors begin to use the drugs with greater frequency, and they become addicted. Recognizing his or her addiction forces the physician addict to confront two problems beyond those faced by naive loners. First, physician addicts must reinterpret the meaning of their activities in terms of their knowledge that they are addicted. Like street addicts, many physicians begin using narcotics believing that they can control their usage and avoid addiction. In fact, physicians often view themselves as professionals and scientists who are particularly qualified to judge and understand the risks of addiction and thereby avoid becoming dependent on drugs. Recognition of addiction contradicts these beliefs and physician addicts must redefine their actions in terms of their new identity as an addict. Second, as the incidence of drug taking increases—particularly after they recognize their addiction—physician addicts must devise methods of regularly acquiring drugs. A doctor can take an occasional dosage from medical supplies without drawing attention, but the amount of drugs required by an addict cannot simply disappear without being noticed. Government agencies regularly audit narcotic supplies held by legitimate medical professionals, and those professionals are required to keep complete records of the disposition of their narcotics. The physician addict must devise some way of taking drugs from medical supplies while simultaneously altering the records to avoid detection. For example, a physician may fake records to show that the missing narcotics were prescribed for a patient. Since the same patient cannot receive narcotics for an indefinite period, the records must be altered frequently, making it appear that different patients received narcotics. Through such manipulations, the physician addict can solve the problem of supplying a drug habit.

With rare exceptions, physician addicts are isolated from other addicts (Winick, 1961). Street addicts view long-term addiction in terms of several practical problems—locating sources for illicit drugs, acquiring enough money to pay for the drugs, avoiding the attention of officials, and so on —which throw them into contact with one another; but physician addicts are loners, able to solve these problems on their own. They do not associate with other addicts, use drugs in one another's presence, or introduce others to narcotics use. The physician addicts' drugs come from a medical setting, such as hospital supplies; even if they pay for the drugs, pharmaceutical drugs are relatively inexpensive. Because they have no need to contact drug dealers or steal to support their habits, physician addicts rarely become known to the police. Rather than adopting the street addict's slang, physician addicts continue to define their addiction in medical terms, using medical language to describe the drugs and dosages. Often, the doctor's addiction becomes known to another person; a trusted nurse may help maintain the physician's secret and falsify the drug records. This knowledgeable other is not addicted; the physician addict remains a loner.

The principal risk for physician addicts is discovery through the periodic checks of drug supplies conducted by government agents (Winick, 1961). When drug records reveal a substantial increase in the level of narcotics prescribed by a physician, agents may investigate and detect inconsistencies in the physician addict's records. In most cases, the newly discovered addict is not turned over to the criminal justice system; instead, the medical profession levies its own sanctions. The local medical society usually revokes the addict's license to practice and orders the doctor to enter a drug treatment program. If treatment progresses satisfactorily, the physician's license may be reinstated, although his or her drug records continue to receive special scrutiny from the authorities. Although returned to practice, former addicts often do poorly; they frequently move their practices or quit their profession (Putnam and Ellinwood, 1966).

Physician addicts are sociologically interesting for two reasons. First, their experiences differ from those of street addicts, even though both are biologically dependent on narcotics. These differences point to ways in which the addict is affected by social, rather than simply biological, circumstances. Second, a physician's problems with maintaining a drug habit illustrate the difficulties faced by loners who engage in systematic deviance.

In systematic deviance, this isolation means they must devise their own routines for managing deviance as an everyday activity over prolonged periods.

Isolation and Instability

Loners' involvement in deviance often is defensive; they commit their initial deviant act in order to ward off some perceived threat. According to Lofland (1969:39-103), the pathway into a defensive deviant act involves three stages: perception of some threat to the individual's physical or social well-being; encapsulation, during which the individual considers various methods of managing the threat and comes to focus on an immediate, short-term solution; and closure, the selection of a deviant act as the response to the threat. An accountant who embezzles to solve a nonshareable problem and a physician who turns to narcotics to cope with pain or pressure are both trying to preserve some valued element in their lives. Not every loner's deviance is defensive, but the pattern fits a large proportion of the cases, particularly those involving people with no previous deviant experience. Loners are more likely to be female, middle-class, or middle-aged than deviants organized in more sophisticated forms. These people choose deviance because they want to protect their status and they perceive that their respectable options are less likely to offer protection. Lacking deviant contacts, they act as loners, developing their own deviant methods.

Loners draw upon their respectable training and experiences for the resources their deviance requires. Without instruction or support from other deviants, loners must develop their own deviant techniques and their own rationales for deviance. The knowledge and skill required to perform respectable roles provide vital resources for would-be loners; in an accountant's case, knowledge of bookkeeping and a position of trust can be converted into embezzlement, while a physician's knowledge of drug dosages and effects and access to drug supplies provide the opportunity for addiction. Narcotic addiction is not a severe problem among accountants, who have no access to drug supplies, and most physicians lack the knowledge of bookkeeping techniques required to embezzle funds. Similarly, loners usually borrow or adapt respectable rationales for their deviance, rather than create new ones. To account for their deviance, loners draw upon explanations they use in conventional life, modifying these accounts to fit the circumstances of their deviance. Embezzlers justify their theft by using the respectable account that they are merely "borrowing" the money; physician addicts justify their narcotics use in terms of their professional judgment that it is an appropriate "treatment" for their condition. Because loners do not receive instruction in a deviant ideology from experienced deviants, modifications of conventional rationales are the simplest means of accounting for their deviance. These respectably derived accounts may become weaker if the deviant act is repeated and the individual settles into systematic deviance. Systematic loners may be forced to acknowledge that their behavior is deviant, rather than a special case of ordinarily accountable action.

Systematic deviance creates other forms of stress for loners. Some loners who engage in repeated acts of deviance come to question the meaning of their actions. Lemert (1967:109-34) studied the behavior of systematic check forgers who made a living by traveling from town to town and forging checks. These forgers had to maintain a respectable appearance in order to convince storekeepers and others to accept their checks with insufficient identification; they could not afford to be seen in the company of other thieves. Their expenses from living on the road were high and, since they encountered less resistance to cashing smaller checks, they sometimes had to forge several checks a day. To protect themselves from discovery, the forgers gave false names and told phony stories about why they needed to cash the checks. Many forgers reported that they eventually became confused; it became hard to keep their stories straight and the rationale for their deviance was lost as their travels continued. Contact with other criminals might have reassured the forgers about the reasonableness of their actions, but the loners in Lemert's study became disoriented and suffered personal crises. Some reported making obvious mistakes, such as remaining in a town long enough for the authorities to find them. Other forgers began to drink heavily or run added risks by signing checks with give-away names, such as "U. R. Stuck." Not surprisingly, such behavior led to arrest. This example suggests that systematic loners are involved in a particularly unstable pattern of deviance; without the support of fellow deviants, it is difficult to sustain deviance over prolonged periods. Deviants, like respectable persons, depend on contact with others who share their perspective and reaffirm the meaning of their actions.

COLLEAGUES

Aside from loners, all forms of deviant organization feature social contacts between fellow deviants. Even minimal contacts are important. A basic sociological observation is that individuals are affected by their ties to others. Contacts with fellow deviants can have various effects—deviants may learn how to behave from one another; they may learn a deviant ideology, a systematic perspective toward their world; and they may receive social support for who they are and what they do. Deviants are outside respectable society, subject to the sanctions of social control agents, and fellow deviants can offer help and support in an otherwise hostile world.

The relationship between deviant colleagues involves limited contact. Like loners, colleagues perform their deviant acts alone. But unlike loners, colleagues associate with one another when they are not engaged in deviance. The collegial relationship is found in many respectable occupations, as well as among deviants. Teachers, for example, usually organize as colleagues: each teacher works alone with his or her students in a separate classroom; but after class, teachers interact with one another in the teachers' lounge. In effect, there is a division between two settings: onstage, where each individual performs alone; and backstage, where colleagues meet (Goffman, 1959:106-40, 159-66). In their backstage meetings, colleagues discuss matters of common interest, including techniques for performing effectively, common problems and how to deal with them, and ways of coping with the outside world. In most occupations, members recognize insiders, who have personal experience in the role and "know what's going on," and outsiders, who lack this experience and "can never really understand what it's like." Just as teachers may feel frustrated with outsiders who have never taught and cannot understand what teaching involves, deviants find themselves isolated; they turn to their colleagues for understanding.

While loners construct their own deviant techniques and justifications, deviant colleagues build a body of shared knowledge through their contacts. This knowledge is called a *subculture* because it exists as specialized knowledge within the larger culture. The colleagues' subculture contains several items. Deviants may share a special vocabulary, called an argot, composed of special words or special meanings given to ordinary words. Argot terms identify important persons, objects, or events in the deviants' world. Colleagues are also likely to develop a cognitive perspective, a framework for interpreting their deviant activities. This perspective has its own values, specifying what is desirable, and these values are translated into behavioral expectations or norms. Using these values and norms, colleagues justify their deviant actions. Colleagues distinguish appropriate from inappropriate behavior by whether an act supports or violates their norms, and they evaluate one another's performances in terms of these norms. On the basis of these evaluations, colleagues are ranked within a system of stratification; each individual's status depends, in part, on the degree to which his or her behavior approaches the subcultural ideal described in the values and norms. Whereas the loner borrows heavily from the larger culture in constructing and interpreting his or her situation, colleagues often develop a rich subculture for guiding their actions and evaluating their experiences.

This section describes two examples of deviant colleagues. Pool hustlers have collegial relationships because they work in a limited number of poolrooms where they routinely come into contact. Prostitutes are colleagues who meet in a variety of ways. Both groups develop rich subcultures, although they emphasize different features.

Pool Hustlers

Pool hustling is probably the most familiar type of sports hustling (Polsky, 1967:41-116). Hustling always involves a game of skill which features "action" or players betting on the outcome of the game, wagering that they can beat their opponent. The size of the bet is unimportant—players can hustle for a few cents or for thousands of dollars. Hustling involves misrepresenting one's skill so that the opposing player (called the "sucker" in pool hustling) overestimates his or her own chances of winning. Even when the sucker knows that the hustler is the more skillful of the two, hustling remains possible. The sucker can receive a "handicap" which appears to make the game even but actually fails to compensate for the full amount of the hustler's advantage. Once the bet is made, the hustler plays to win, but by the smallest margin possible. The hustler cannot afford to play his or her best game because the sucker would then know the real difference in their skills. Pool hustlers have a saying: "Never show your true speed." A sucker who loses by a narrow margin may be willing to play again—with a slightly better handicap. So long as the hustler does not show his or her "true speed," this handicap can be kept low enough to insure the hustler another victory. Hustling should be distinguished from simple cheating, where players arrange the outcome of the match in advance. Hustlers usually play within the game's formal rules; they only violate the norm that players should not deceive one another.

Hustling is found in any "action" sport where players bet with each other. The most familiar games are pool, tennis, and golf, but hustlers also play table tennis, bowling, chess, and any other game where they can match their considerable skill against an opponent who has an exaggerated estimate of his or her own ability and is willing to bet. Many hustlers are amateurs, playing in "friendly" games, but some are professionals who make a living at hustling. Most types of hustling have not received systematic study and it is difficult to determine their form of organization. Many amateur hustlers probably operate as loners. Professional pool hustlers, however, organize as colleagues.

Pool is well suited for hustling (Polsky, 1967:44-49). The poolroom is a classic action scene; players frequently bet on the outcome of their games. Pool is a game of precise skill; players can conceal their ability through fine manipulations. Because it is difficult to tell when a player deliberately misses a shot, pool is particularly conducive to hustling. The basis for the association between pool hustlers is ecological; they meet in the action poolrooms, establishments where players customarily bet against each other. Pool hustlers, searching for suckers, come together in a relatively small number of locations. Because they frequent the same poolrooms, spending much of their time there, hustlers have extensive contacts with one another. In their games against suckers, each hustler works alone; but in their moments away from hustling, hustlers see a good deal of their deviant colleagues.

As colleagues, pool hustlers share a distinctive subculture (Polsky, 1967: 68-76, 106-16). There is a sense of we-ness—hustlers distinguish between themselves and outsiders. The hustlers' ranks are stratified; individuals earn prestige according to three criteria. First, players are ranked by their skill at playing pool: the greater one's skill, the higher one's prestige. Second, hustlers are judged by their ability to "make a game." Making a game involves setting the odds for a particular match—the more the odds favor the hustler, the more certain the hustler's success. One hustler criticized another's ability to make games: ". . . he'll never be a good hustler, 'cause he's always giving away too many points. He's part sucker, that's what he is" (Polsky, 1967:71). Finally, hustlers are ranked by their "heart." Heart refers to courage, to playing well under pressure, as the following hustlers' comments suggest:

> You can't bet on A because you don't know how he's going to stand up for more than $20. No heart.
>
> I tell you one thing about Boston Shorty, the real great thing, is that the guy kisses icewater. He don't frighten out. One time I seen a game where somebody runs over 100 balls on him, and Shorty comes right back with 89 and out. It takes plenty heart to do that. (Polsky, 1967:72)[1]

Among hustlers, individuals develop reputations for playing well, making games well, and working effectively under pressure. Because they spend so much time with one another, hustlers also share a rich argot, a specialized vocabulary for describing their world. Every social group modifies the basic language to fit its own circumstances, creating new words or using ordinary words in special ways. For example, hustlers use the word "fish" to describe a sucker who, after losing to a hustler, leaves the poolroom to get more money for another game. Hustlers also use monikers, or nicknames (such as Boston Shorty). Mutual use of this language reinforces the hustlers' sense of we-ness, reaffirms their ties as colleagues, and, by implication, defines the boundaries between hustlers and outsiders. Hustlers also share a rich oral tradition; in their conversations, hustlers pass along lore about famous pool hustlers and their games.

The hustlers' subculture defines the set of expectations hustlers have for one another. Although hustlers ordinarily work alone, these norms demand that they cooperate in some specific ways.

> Often a hustler will tell a colleague about a fault he has noticed in the latter's game, although there appears to be no clearly defined collegial obligation to do this. . . . A clearly defined obligation, the strongest in the hustlers' colleague code, has to do with regulating the competition for opponents: when a hustler has started to make a game (be it with a sucker or another hustler), any hustler who is a third party is not supposed to cut in with a better offer or otherwise queer the pitch. . . . When a hustler from out of town is cleaned out by some local hustler, the latter is obligated to give the former, on request, "get-out-of-town-money." And whatever the winner's personal feelings about the loser, he doesn't fail to honor the request, so severe would be the castigation from his colleagues otherwise. . . . When a hustler is preparing for a road trip

> to towns he doesn't know, or hasn't visited in a long time, colleagues who have recently been to those places provide him with information on where the action is, who the best players are, what kind of cons they go for, and what their skill levels are. (Polsky, 1967:73)

Without interfering with the individual's freedom, these cooperative acts reaffirm the collegial ties among hustlers.

The practice of dumping is another way in which hustlers cooperate (Polsky, 1967:59-60). Dumping violates the overall pattern of colleagues' relationships in that two hustlers work together to carry out a deviant act. Dumping is a method of cheating the spectators who bet on games where two hustlers play against each other. In these games, the two players pretend to bet with each other on the outcome, while secretly agreeing to dupe the poolroom spectators. The spectators, assuming that each hustler is playing to win, watch the game and bet among themselves on the outcome. The players offer to make side-bets on the match with the spectators. If the match is an interesting one, the amount wagered in side-bets with spectators probably will be greater than the amount at stake between the two hustlers. As the game proceeds, the player with the smallest side-bets loses the match, using the deceptive maneuvers normally used to conceal one's true speed from suckers. When the match is over, all bets are paid off and the two players later split the profits from the winner's side-bets. Dumping is a secretive activity; the hustlers cannot afford to let the spectators learn that they were duped. Dumping is uncommon, an exception to the rule that colleagues do not commit deviant acts together; most of the time, hustlers work alone.

Pool hustling is an unstable occupation in the midst of a long-term decline (Polsky, 1967:13-40; 76-95). At the turn of the century, pool halls flourished throughout the United States; today, there are fewer players in fewer rooms. These dwindling numbers mean that there is less action and fewer opportunities to hustle pool. Hustlers find it harder to make ends meet. Indeed, many quit hustling when they find it too difficult to make a living or when they get married and find the all-hours poolroom routine difficult to maintain. Among those hustlers who remain, many moonlight, working at second jobs to earn enough to support themselves during periods when hustling profits are low. Although hustling attracts many people, few make it their life's work.

Pool hustlers offer one another limited support. Hustlers can draw on their subculture to make sense of their activities; they can describe their actions using its argot and evaluate what they do using its norms. Hustlers know that their colleagues will see fooling a sucker as a reasonable, admirable act. Colleagues support each other through minor favors, such as giving advice about the hustling scene in other cities. At the same time, this support has limits. Each hustler works alone. Success is up to the individual; colleagues cannot protect one another from individual failure or the broader conditions forcing pool hustling into decline.

Prostitutes

Prostitutes sell sexual services (Goldstein, 1979:23-39). Prostitutes vary in their commitment to deviance and in their style of work. Some prostitutes are amateurs who occasionally "turn a trick" without being committed to prostitution, while others are professionals who earn their living selling sexual services. Female prostitutes can work as streetwalkers (who patrol public places in hopes of attracting customers from the passers-by) (B. Cohen, 1980), brothel prostitutes (who work in a house under the management of a madam and whose customers visit the brothel) (Heyl, 1979), call girls (who entertain customers by appointment) (Bryan, 1965; Greenwald, 1970), and massage parlor prostitutes (who typically masturbate the establishment's customers) (Rasmussen and Kuhn, 1976). Not all prostitutes are women. Some males act as homosexual prostitutes, selling sexual services to other men (Ginsburg, 1967; Harris, 1974; Lloyd, 1976). Other males serve as heterosexual prostitutes, sometimes working in special brothels which cater to women (Pittman, 1971). Thus, the label of "prostitute" applies to a wide variety of people who sell sexual services under very different circumstances. This section focuses on female prostitutes—and call girls in particular—because they are the subject of several detailed sociological studies.

At first glance, it seems difficult to generalize about the social organization of prostitutes. Some prostitutes—especially amateurs who occasionally commit acts of prostitution—work as loners. At the other extreme, a city's brothels may be controlled by a deviant formal organization employing hundreds of prostitutes. But most prostitutes organize as colleagues. Their deviant acts typically occur outside one another's presence; each prostitute entertains her customers in private. The women also have contacts with one another. Even those who enter prostitution as loners are likely to acquire colleagues. Streetwalkers frequent the same neighborhoods, even the same corners; brothel and massage parlor prostitutes see each other in their establishments. Even call girls, who usually live separately, are likely to meet their colleagues in all-night beauty parlors, restaurants, and after-hours bars (Greenwald, 1970:10-30; Roebuck and Frese, 1976). In part, prostitutes' contacts with one another reflect their shared schedules—they tend to work in the afternoons and evenings and have their leisure time late at night or during the day. Since they are free when most people are asleep or at work, prostitutes are more likely to meet and associate with one another.

Prostitutes use the argot expression "in the life" to distinguish between themselves and nonprostitutes (Greenwald, 1970:23-34). Women in the life share a set of experiences and a subculture including a system of stratification and an ideology. Prostitutes rank one another according to their method of doing business and their fees (Greenwald, 1970:24-27). All prostitutes, from the most accessible streetwalker to the most exclusive call girl, provide essentially the same sexual services for their customers. Customers patronize more expensive prostitutes for several reasons. They may believe that expensive prostitutes are less likely to be diseased, find them more attractive or more cultivated companions, or prefer to visit the women in nicely furnished settings. A prostitute's income, and her status among those in the life, depends upon her ability to attract and satisfy high-paying customers. In this system of stratification, the streetwalker has little status, the call girl considerably more. A streetwalker may see several customers a night, earning a small fee from each and completing each contact in a matter of minutes. At the other extreme, an exclusive call girl may limit herself to one customer per night. Her fees are far higher and the couple may spend the evening together, perhaps dining out. Within a type of prostitution, prostitutes are ranked according to their prices—a call girl who charges $200 per customer outranks a colleague who charges only $100. Prostitutes understand that their method of business and their fees can vary enormously, and their rankings of one another depend upon these factors. A call girl's "status is based on her attractiveness, financial standing, political connections, dress, apartment, manners, and the state in which she keeps her 'old man' or pimp" (Greenwald, 1970:24-25). Each of these items reflects the woman's ability to charge high prices or limit herself to an exclusive style of doing business.

Prostitutes also share an ideology, a system of ideas about their world (Bryan, 1966). Several themes run through their ideology. First, prostitutes believe they serve an important social function—offering an outlet for their customers' sexual impulses. If prostitutes were not available, they argue, rape would be more common. Second, males in general and customers in particular are seen as exploitative. They take advantage of the prostitute and deserve to be exploited in return. Prostitutes recognize that their success depends upon effectively controlling their contacts with their customers. One reported, "99% of this business is in the living room, not the bedroom" (Samovar and Sanders, 1978:32). Prostitutes use the word "trick" in several revealing ways: the customer is called a trick, the sex act is "turning a trick," and so on. "Trick" implies deceit; when a prostitute fakes an interest in her customer or pretends to feel passion, she is tricking him. He takes advantage of her, but she exploits him in return; without his knowledge, she controls the encounter (Johnson, 1973). Third, the ideology defines others in the life as more trustworthy than outsiders. Fourth, all relationships between the sexes are equivalent to acts of prostitution. In this view, all women exchange sexual services for material goods. Some marry for security, others work as prostitutes. Taken together, these themes form the prostitutes' ideology; "the professional perspective argues that customers can and should be exploited, that the role of the prostitute is no more immoral than the role of the 'square,' and that colleagues are more honest and helpful than women outside the profession." (Bryan, 1966:444).

Prostitutes acquire their ideology when they enter deviance. Most prostitutes serve a period of apprenticeship under an experienced deviant, such as another prostitute, a madam, or a pimp (Bryan, 1965; Heyl, 1979; Milner and Milner, 1972). This apprenticeship involves instruction in the skills prostitution requires: collecting money, interacting with customers, sexual techniques, coping with violent or difficult customers, and so forth. Having these skills gives the prostitute more control over her customers. In addition to learning specific skills, prostitutes learn the professional ideology for interpreting their experiences. The ideology helps the newcomer differentiate between her conventional past and the deviant life she is beginning. However, once the prostitute gains experience, the ideology becomes less important. Bryan (1966) found that call girls were familiar with the ideology and often reported that these attitudes were held by "professionals," yet their own experiences taught them a different set of attitudes. They learned that all clients were not equally exploitative and that some colleagues could not be trusted not to take advantage of them. While they were familiar with the ideology, these prostitutes were not bound by it. They modified the ideology in line with their own experiences.

There are some occasions when the collegial relationship among prostitutes leads to an exchange of favors (Greenwald, 1970:14-24). Prostitutes are sometimes hired to "put on a show" in which two prostitutes simulate lesbian intercourse before one or more customers, usually before having sex with the customers. The prostitute who is hired to put on a show contacts a colleague and asks her to help. This favor obligates the second prostitute to invite the first woman along the next time she learns of a similar opportunity. Call girls, who keep lists of their customers, also may exchange clients' names. Some customers want a variety of sexual partners, and, by trading names, call girls can bring colleagues and customers together. Of course, prostitutes only trade names with others who charge the same prices and who reciprocate with the names of some of their customers.

The collegial relationship between prostitutes is not especially strong. According to their ideology, prostitutes should trust one another, but their work is not structured to encourage trust (Bryan, 1966). Prostitutes are in competition and, except for occasional favors, such as invitations to put on shows, colleagues are rarely in a position to reward one another for cooperative behavior. As a consequence, most prostitutes keep some distance between themselves and their colleagues. One survey of twenty-nine prostitutes found only one who reported being "close" to other prostitutes, while twenty said their relationships with colleagues were "very distant" (Decker, 1979:477). The prostitutes' argot reflects these limited ties. Maurer (1939) argues that prostitutes have a less elaborate argot than many other career deviants; their limited contacts with one another, as well as their relatively limited specialization of skills, give them less reason to develop a specialized vocabulary. Moreover, in contrast to pool hustling, where a few deviants make the occupation a lifelong pursuit, prostitutes have shorter careers. Prostitutes' customers place a premium on physical attractiveness; each year makes the women less competitive in their marketplace. While some move up to become madams of brothels (Goldstein, 1979; Heyl, 1979), many simply drift back into respectability, finding legitimate work or marrying. The population of prostitutes is constantly shifting, making stability among colleagues even less likely.

Contact and Commitment

Colleagues retain the independence of operation which characterizes loners. But unlike loners, colleagues benefit from regular contact with one another. Usually, this contact is based on the urban ecology. Deviants involved in similar activities find themselves frequenting the same places: pool hustlers must play in action poolrooms, streetwalkers are most likely to find customers if they work in "red-light districts," and so on. In addition, deviant colleagues often see one another during their leisure hours. Prostitutes and pimps frequent the same bars and clubs, attracted in part by the opportunity to be with others who share a common subculture (Milner and Milner, 1972; Roebuck and Frese, 1976).

The existence of a subculture sets colleagues apart from loners. The subculture gives colleagues a framework for interpreting their experiences. The argot supplies terms which can be used to precisely describe events; the values and norms provide the context for assessing those events. Subcultural knowledge makes it possible to predict others' behavior with some accuracy. This helps the individual choose appropriate responses in different situations. The subculture is transmitted through the colleagues' contacts. During an individual's entry into deviance, an experienced colleague may act as a coach, providing guidance and instruction in the subculture (Strauss, 1959:109-18). Later, the acquired subcultural knowledge is reaffirmed during the deviant's regular contacts with other colleagues.

While their contacts with one another make colleagues' lives easier, their careers are relatively unstable. Some individuals enter deviance and spend decades with their colleagues, but the typical career is much shorter, lasting only a few years. Individuals enter deviance and learn the subculture, only to find that a deviant career offers limited opportunities. A pool hustler may discover that his or her personal skill is insufficient to win regularly or that other occupations are more profitable; a prostitute may tire of the life or recognize that her increasing age makes her less attractive to customers. Although a few people make a great deal of money as pool hustlers or prostitutes, most find their earnings erratic. Contacts among colleagues do not provide much support for individuals under these pressures. Each individual acts alone and is responsible for the success of his or her deviant operations. Colleagues are expected to pay each other a few modest favors, but they are not obliged to support fellow deviants whose careers are near collapse. In fact, colleagues often must compete with one another. There are only so many suckers in pool halls and so many customers looking for prostitutes. If one colleague ends his or her career, the prospects for those remaining are improved. Therefore, colleagues find it in their interest to let others drift out of deviance, rather than to help them adjust to its pressures. To remain a deviant colleague, an individual must carry out successful operations alone and be committed to the career itself, because the ties between colleagues are relatively weak.

PEERS

Deviant peers are distinguished from colleagues by their shared participation in deviance. While colleagues carry out their deviant operations alone, peers commit deviant acts in one another's presence. Peers cooperate in carrying out deviant operations, but they have a minimal division of labor, with each individual making roughly comparable contributions. Peer relationships also tend to be egalitarian and informal; some peers may be acknowledged leaders or admired for their skills, but there is no set division of authority. Like colleagues, peers share subcultural knowledge, but peer groups typically provide their members with more support. In addition to cooperating in deviant operations, peers may recruit and socialize newcomers and supply one another with deviant equipment and social support. Thus, the bonds between peers are stronger than those linking colleagues.

Peer groups can emerge under various conditions. In contemporary society, illicit marketplaces and youth roles have features which encourage deviants to organize as peers. Whenever a good or service is forbidden but the demand for it continues, an illicit marketplace can emerge. Peer groups organized around illicit marketplaces include: sadists and masochists (T. Weinberg and Falk, 1980), swingers (Bartell, 1971), skid row tramps (Spradley, 1970; Wiseman, 1970), illicit drug users (Blumer, 1967; Carey, 1968; Feldman, 1968; Stoddart, 1974), and group-oriented gamblers (Lesieur, 1977). An illicit marketplace is composed of people who seek the deviant good or service and those willing to supply it. (The exchanges between these customers and suppliers are discussed in Chapter 6.) For example, in spite of the laws against heroin, addicts continue to want the drug and, so long as this demand exists, drug dealers will find it profitable to sell heroin. Not all markets involve monetary purchases. For instance, there are illicit markets where people exchange sexual services; a sadist and a masochist may give each other sexual satisfaction without any money exchanging hands. There are several reasons why illicit markets encourage deviants to organize as peers. First, relationships with other deviants make it easier to obtain information about supply within the marketplace. Because an illicit market operates underground, deviant customers need such contacts to keep in touch with suppliers. For example, heroin addicts must make regular drug purchases but they do not always know who has heroin for sale. Through their contacts with deviant peers, addicts can learn who is selling heroin. If the dealer is a stranger, peers also can vouch for one another, assuring the dealer that they can be trusted. Second, in some illicit marketplaces, deviant peers exchange sexual services with one another. In a sexual marketplace based on monetary payments, the participants are not peers. There are sharp distinctions between prostitutes and their customers, for example. But where the sexual marketplace does not involve payment, participants typically organize as peers. Sadists and masochists, homosexuals, and swingers need partners for mutual participation in deviant acts; intercourse is impossible without the cooperation of a peer. These relationships are egalitarian; each person gives and receives sexual satisfaction. Third, in many deviant marketplaces, participants define their deviant activities as sociable. People engaged in illicit drinking, drug use, and gambling view their deviance as recreation which is more enjoyable in the company of others. A person with a reliable drug connection may not need the peers' "grapevine" about current supplies, yet may prefer to use drugs in the company of other users. By their mutual participation in these deviant activities, such individuals become deviant peers.

Like illicit marketplaces, the roles assigned adolescents in complex modern societies encourage associations of deviant peers. Adolescence is defined as an intermediate stage between childhood and adulthood. As adolescents become physically mature, they want the independence and rights of adults. However, many adult privileges, such as smoking and drinking, are forbidden to adolescents. Extended education and limited opportunities for employment prolong adolescence into early adulthood. At the same time, many adolescents have considerable free time as well as extensive contacts with others their own age. These conditions facilitate the emergence of deviant peer groups among young people. Examples include delinquent gangs (Cloward and Ohlin, 1960; Matza, 1964; Rosenberg and Silverstein, 1969), illicit drinkers and drug users (Blumer, 1967; Carey, 1968; Feldman, 1968; Schwartz et al., 1973), and motorcycle gangs (S. Cohen, 1972; H. Thompson, 1966).

Relationships among peers vary—some are long-lived, others are fleeting. When peer groups consist of members with a common background who see one another regularly, the groups can exist for years. For example, a group of boys from the same neighborhood may organize a gang when they enter adolescence. So long as the gang members live near one another and have enough free time, they can stick together. Only the assumption of adult roles, such as full-time work or marriage, breaks up the gang. At the other extreme, peers can have fleeting relationships which last only a few hours or minutes, as when two individuals meet and quickly decide to take advantage of an opportunity to engage in an illicit sexual encounter. At the end of the transaction, they may separate and never see one another again. Some peer groups contain both kinds of relationships; while a core group exists over relatively long periods, other deviants form temporary relationships with one or more of the core members (Yablonsky, 1959). The strength of peers' ties to one another depends, in part, on the length of their association. The longer their associations, the more peers invest in their relationships with each other. The peer group's subculture becomes more important to long-term members than to those deviants with little involvement in the scene.

This section examines two cases of deviants organized as peers. Recreational drug users organize around a deviant marketplace. Relationships between drug users range from fleeting to long-term, but a substantial proportion are short-lived. In contrast, delinquent gangs are composed of adolescent peers. Some delinquents have fleeting relationships, but gang members often maintain their ties over relatively long periods. Thus, the two examples span some important dimensions along which deviant peers vary.

Recreational Drug Users

Most illicit drug use is recreational—users take the drugs for pleasure. Many drugs have been considered illicit at one time or another. During Prohibition, alcohol was an illicit drug. Other societies have prohibited the recreational use of tobacco, ether, and coffee (Best, 1979; Connell, 1968: 87-110; Ellis, 1956). Currently in the United States, social control agents try to enforce prohibitions against the recreational use of heroin, cocaine, marijuana, LSD, PCP, amphetamines, barbiturates, and even glue and paint (Brecher, 1972). Whatever the prohibited substances in a given society, drug users face the problem of supply. Most drug users cannot grow or manufacture their own drugs; they must get their drugs from a dealer in the illicit marketplace. Once they enter the illicit marketplace, drug users are likely to organize as peers. In the illicit marketplace, drug users must cluster around the limited number of drug dealers. This clustering has the effect of bringing users into contact with one another. These contacts serve a valuable function by spreading information—users can tell each other which suppliers have drugs on hand and warn one another about contaminated drugs or dishonest dealers. The peers' network helps them cope with the practical problems posed by recreational drug use. Further, recreational drug use often is defined as a sociable occasion, where the drug's effects are enhanced by the companionship of other users. Drug users want to share the deviant experience.

Illicit drug users who organize as peers can acquire a substantial body of subcultural knowledge, including techniques of drug use, a practical pharmacology of drug effects, norms for conduct during drug use, methods of acquiring drugs and the money needed to pay for them, and justifications for drug use. Peers frequently teach newcomers the correct techniques for using drugs. For example, the beginning marijuana user must learn the technique of smoking—how to inhale deeply and hold the smoke in the lungs, maximizing the drug's effects (Becker, 1963:41-58). Similarly, heroin addicts learn how to prepare the drug and inject it (Agar, 1973). In contrast to the physician addict, who learns about administering drugs in medical school, most recreational drug users learn about dosages and techniques of administration from their peers. Peers also help the novice interpret the drug experience. The beginner must learn to recognize the physical effects of drugs and interpret them as pleasurable (Becker, 1963:41-58). When a drug is taken without the guidance of experienced users, the novice may become frightened and have an adverse reaction to the drug experience (Becker, 1967). For example, individuals who unwittingly take LSD may become confused and disturbed by the hallucinatory perceptions caused by the drug, while persons taking the same drug under the guidance of experienced users learn to appreciate these effects as part of the "trip."

As users gain experience with drugs, they acquire and pass along practical pharmacological knowledge about drugs and their effects. For example, LSD users exchange a great deal of information about the drug experience, the range of possible outcomes when taking LSD, and methods of controlling these outcomes (Stoddart, 1974). LSD users divide the drug experience into several phases: the rush (the initial impact of the drug); getting off (the beginning of psychedelic effects); the peak (the high point of those effects); and coming down (when the effects begin to wear off). This scheme for classifying the drug experience is not founded on clinical research; rather, it is constructed on the basis of the peers' experiences and provides a useful framework for interpreting their own and others' reactions to the drug. LSD users distinguish between pleasant drug experiences ("good trips") and unpleasant experiences ("bummers" or "freakouts"). Subcultural knowledge offers users practical rules of thumb for controlling a trip's outcome. For instance, users tell one another that outcomes are affected by one's state of mind before and during the trip, the setting in which the drug is taken, the user's experience with LSD, the specific chemical composition of the LSD being taken, and the interaction between LSD and any other drugs taken during the trip. Armed with this knowledge, an LSD user can control a trip's outcome to some degree, making good trips more common and bad trips less frequent. For example, users who become unsettled while coming down are advised to drink, for alcohol is thought to calm users. This pharmacological knowledge need not be accurate. It offers rules of thumb which may ease the tension simply by giving the user a sense that the trip is controllable, just as superstitious habits give gamblers confidence that they can control chance (Henslin, 1967). This pharmacological knowledge passed along to peers probably includes both accurate and inaccurate information, but any information helps prepare users for the drug experience.

The subculture of drug users also includes norms for conduct. When peers use drugs in one another's company, they observe an etiquette for proper behavior in that setting (Agar, 1973; Cavan, 1972:112-39; Zimmerman and Wieder, 1977). For example, a study of marijuana users in a university community identified several norms for smoking in the presence of peers:

1. Persons possessing marijuana are expected to share it.
2. Given that marijuana is to be smoked on some occasion, the joint or pipe is passed around to everybody present.
3. Smoking marijuana with others entails a commitment to the ongoing social occasion. [That is, smokers should be sociable.]
4. Within the limits of the marijuana available, persons may smoke as much as they desire: persons are free to get as stoned as they wish. (Zimmerman and Wieder, 1977:201)

Among these users, any individual had the right to initiate marijuana smoking during virtually any informal gathering. As a consequence, users argued that smoking was a spontaneous, unplanned activity. Under these norms, smoking was an easily initiated, easily joined ceremony and peers therefore could be fairly confident that "spontaneous" drug use would occur in their gatherings. In consequence, one smoker noted, "you can't help but get stoned."

The subculture offers guidelines for activities outside the situation of drug use. For example, heroin addicts require regular supplies of a drug which is almost always expensive and hard to locate (Agar, 1973; Waldorf and Reinarman, 1975). Since failure to take sufficient drugs to maintain one's habit will lead to physical distress, heroin addicts confront two problems nearly every day: they must locate a dealer and get enough money to pay for the drugs. Addicts usually buy their drugs from a regular dealer. However, if social control agents restrict the drug supply, by either capturing drug shipments or arresting drug dealers, the addict's regular dealer may be unable to supply his or her customers' demand for heroin. In such cases, addicts may help one another find an alternate "connection." Similarly, the addict subculture contains knowledge about methods of "hustling." Here, hustling refers to ways of getting the money to buy drugs. Many female addicts work as prostitutes, while males often steal the money they need. Frequently, a hustling technique which works one day will not bring in enough money the next. Addicts must improvise—if prostitution does not produce enough money, women may try shoplifting. In search of a steady income, many addicts turn to drug dealing. They buy a supply of drugs, sell part of them at a profit sufficient to replenish their supply, and keep the remainder for themselves.

Finally, the subculture of drug users typically includes an ideology justifying drug use. This ideology may justify the initial decision to try an illicit drug. For example, Feldman (1968) argues that lower class youths are especially likely to experiment with drugs in order to establish their credentials as "stand-up cats." Lower-class culture puts a premium on bravery and a willingness to take risks; individuals, particularly males, who fall short of this standard are denigrated as "punks." Trying a new drug is one way to demonstrate courage. In fact, the more dangerous a drug's reputation, the more effectively drug use proves one's bravery. In addition to justifying the initial experiment with drugs, drug subcultures explain continued drug use (Cavan, 1972:55-76). For example, marijuana users argue that they are "mellow," while nonusers are "up-tight." The subculture's ideology minimizes the dangers of drug use, praises the drug for providing enlightenment, relaxation, or other valued sensations or experiences, and describes those who refuse to use drugs in invidious terms.

Recreational drugs are not all alike; there are important differences in their effects, legal status, and users' commitment to drug use. Heroin addicts, LSD users, and marijuana smokers differ in many ways. But in each case, drug use often is a shared experience among peers whose relationships are cemented by a subculture which supplies both technical information and an ideology justifying drug use.

Delinquent Gangs

Delinquency refers to violations of juvenile law by juveniles. Delinquent offenses range from serious violations, such as murder and robbery, to minor offenses, such as drinking and truancy. Delinquents organize in various ways, ranging from loners to formal organizations, but many organize as peers. Most delinquent acts involve two or more youths (Erickson, 1971). Sometimes delinquents form a social club or gang and adopt a name for themselves. But delinquent gangs do not account for all delinquency; many delinquents are not gang members. Moreover, delinquency accounts for only a portion of the gangs' activities. Much of the time, gang members simply "hang out" with one another or engage in other legitimate pursuits. By focusing on delinquent gangs as an example of deviant peers, this section considers only one of delinquency's many facets.

Ties of friendship link gang members to one another (Suttles, 1968:157-73). Friendship usually precedes organization; gangs form around existing relationships. Neighborhood children grow up playing and going to school together. When they enter adolescence, they may decide to give themselves a name and become a club or gang. This is particularly likely if older youths in the neighborhood belong to gangs. Admiring these older youths, the younger adolescents imitate them by creating their own gangs; sometimes they become an affiliate of the older group, taking its name. For example, a gang called the Earls may spawn an affiliate called the Junior Earls. The new gang may invite others to join. Because the gang is founded on friendships, its members tend to be alike. Even in heterogeneous urban neighborhoods, gangs tend to be homogeneous. Members are almost always of the same sex (usually males) and they tend to be within a year or two of the same age and from the same ethnic group. Most urban gang members also live near one another.

Gang members are peers bound by informal ties (Suttles, 1968:175-220). In addition to adopting a name for themselves, gang members may wear a distinctive jacket, sponsor dances and other social functions, or formally designate leadership positions and even elect officers to fill them. In spite of these sometimes elaborate trappings, gangs are fundamentally informal organizations. Gang leaders tend to be those members who already have the others' confidence; their election to office merely confirms their existing leadership. In the rare cases when a gang prepares a written set of rules, that document carries little weight in the members' everyday activities. Interaction within a gang reflects the pattern of personal relationships that developed among gang members over what may have been years of contact. In fact, most gang activities involve only some of the gang's members, rather than the whole gang. On important occasions, such as a gang-sponsored dance or a fight with another gang, it may be possible to mobilize all of the gang's members, but day-to-day activities typically involve "traveling groups," cliques of friends within the gang who spend most of their free time together. Names, jackets, and other trappings say something about the members' commitment to the gang and its importance in their lives, but very little about the formality of their association.

At various times, gang members may become involved in several different types of deviance, including fighting, stealing, and drug use. One famous sociological interpretation argues that gangs specialize in deviance, adopting either conflict (fighting), criminal (stealing), or retreatist (drugs) values (Cloward and Ohlin, 1960; cf. Spergel, 1964). Yet many gangs have members who occasionally engage in all of these deviant activities. The gang's operations involve little specialization or division of labor; its members cooperate as peers. Shared activities are the gang's lifeblood, the reason for its existence; when members stop doing things together, the gang dies. A study of one gang over a three year period found that whenever its members began to spend less time with the gang, the active members would start operations, often delinquent activities such as a fight with another gang, which served to attract and reinvolve their absent peers, thereby increasing the gang's solidarity (Jansyn, 1966). Considerable variation over time in the type and level of gang activities demonstrates the informal nature of gang relationships. Gangs provide a focal point for youths with similar interests. They know their fellow gang members are available as companions for almost any undertaking, deviant or respectable. Gangs do not organize for the sole purpose of carrying out deviant operations; rather, deviance is one kind of activity gang members occasionally carry out as peers.

As a consequence, the gang members share a subculture which includes, but is not limited to, knowledge about deviance. Delinquents are by definition juveniles, and many gangs form around the time their members enter adolescence. Gang members acquire much of their subcultural knowledge from older people, especially members of older gangs. What one gang member learns from an older delinquent can be passed along to the rest of the gang through interaction. Most adolescents gain some knowledge of delinquent argot as they get older, but gang members learn more argot terms than nonmembers (Lerman, 1967). In addition to learning from older gang members, the gang's subculture borrows from the surrounding adult culture. For example, lower-class gangs' values are consistent with central concerns of the larger lower-class culture, such as toughness, smartness (the ability to recognize and take advantage of opportunities), and excitement (W. Miller, 1958). These concerns are translated into norms for members' behavior. For example, most lower-class gang members command limited resources. Because toughness is a valued trait, their peers expect gang members to defend the resources they do have. Members are obliged to fight to preserve their personal honor (Horowitz and Schwartz, 1974) and their control over their neighborhood "turf" (Werthman and Piliavin, 1967). Affronts to honor or invasions of territory often lead to fights between members of rival gangs (Short and Strodtbeck, 1965; Suttles, 1968:195-202). In addition to an argot, values, and norms, the gang subculture includes justifications for delinquent acts. Sykes and Matza (1957) identify five accounts delinquents use to justify their deviance: (1) denial of responsibility ("It's not my fault; I had a deprived background"); (2) denial of injury ("We didn't hurt anyone"); (3) denial of the victim ("It's alright to beat up homosexuals"); (4) condemnation of the condemners ("Police are corrupt"); and (5) appeal to higher loyalties ("My friends were counting on me, so I had to go along"). While less integrated than some other deviant ideologies, these accounts help gang members justify their actions.

Gang membership is an option for adolescents. Most gang members have a limited commitment to deviant behavior. Although gang members sometimes commit delinquent acts, deviance is not the sole, or even the central, focus for most gangs. Rather, gang members "drift" into delinquency on those occasions when it seems appropriate (Matza, 1964). Because most delinquent activities require few resources, such as special skills or equipment, many occasions can be transformed into situations for delinquency. For example, delinquent vandals rarely plan their operations; rather, vandalism develops as a spontaneous activity in which delinquents make use of whatever materials happen to be at hand (Wade, 1967). Because delinquency is a common part of the adolescent experience and most gang members have a limited commitment to their deviant identities, members eventually leave the gang, usually for marriage or respectable work. Although they can span several years, the delinquents' peer relationships are relatively weak.

Shared Participation in Deviance

The defining feature of peers is that they share participation in deviant activities. Loners and colleagues commit their deviant acts apart from other deviants, while peers act in one another's presence. Shared participation can offer several advantages. By cooperating, deviants find it easier to carry out more complex operations quickly and efficiently, thereby reducing the risks posed by social control agents. Shared participation also offers sociability; deviants can enjoy the companionship and support of their peers.

The subcultures developed by peers tend to be more elaborate than those of colleagues. Colleagues and peers have subcultures with similar elements, including an argot, values, norms, criteria for stratification, and ideological justifications for deviance. However, colleagues do not normally perform under each other's scrutiny. Peers watch each other performing deviant acts; they share the experience of deviance and their subculture reflects this more intense contact. Peers develop rules of etiquette to govern their interactions during deviance; drug users, for instance, have norms about sharing drugs. Peers also are more likely to make gestures of commitment and solidarity toward one another and to expect similar gestures in return; for example, gang members must wear the club jacket. Finally, peers are obliged to offer moral support, helping each other cope with the problems they face. Because peers see each other in action, they can judge individuals against the subculture's standards. Among their peers, individuals acquire reputations based on their deviant performances (cf. E. Anderson, 1978).

Peer relationships have the potential for relative stability. To be sure, some peers are involved in fleeting relationships—chance acquaintances who share a brief deviant encounter. In these circumstances, the participants have limited expectations of one another, a minimal subculture, and no plans for a lasting relationship. At the other extreme, peers can remain companions for years. While peer relationships can prove stable, they are vulnerable. Peers usually control few resources which they can draw upon in case of trouble. A delinquent gang's members may pledge to help one another, but they are unlikely to have the money needed to hire a lawyer to defend an arrested member. These limited resources for defense against outside pressure account for the eventual failure of most peer groups. For instance, a delinquent gang cannot hold its members once they reach adulthood because the rewards the gang can offer are far less than those from respectability. Similarly, social control agents may disrupt peer relationships. When arrested drug users cannot afford the services of a lawyer, they may betray their peers in order to save themselves. Thus, limited resources make it unlikely that peer relationships will endure. Even when a person remains deviant, his or her peer network is likely to change as members surrender to outside pressures.

SUMMARY

Deviants operate outside the boundaries of respectable conduct. As outsiders, they encounter some obvious disadvantages. Deviants face the threat of social control agents' sanctions if they are discovered. They also may be blocked from drawing upon the resources of respectable society—known deviants cannot expect to qualify for bank loans or assistance from social service agencies. As a consequence, when they confront practical problems, deviants must devise their own solutions, alone or with the help of fellow deviants.

Obviously, the form of deviant organization affects the kinds of solutions deviants can devise. The three organizational forms examined in this chapter—loners, colleagues, and peers—are less sophisticated than the forms discussed in chapter 3. By definition, loners are on their own—each individual must cope with whatever problems arise. Those who fail get caught or abandon deviance. Colleagues and peers do assist one another, but the ties that bind them are weak. Arrangements among colleagues and peers tend to be informal; there are few rigid rules of conduct and it is hard to enforce those that do exist. Moreover, many colleagues and peers command little in the way of resources, so that members cannot depend upon one another for a great deal of aid. While less isolated than loners, colleagues and peers cannot be sure that their associates will behave as expected or that they will have the resources required to overcome a particular problem. As a consequence, individuals in these less sophisticated forms of deviant organization often fail to solve practical problems and choose to leave deviance.

Before examining these and other consequences of organizational sophistication in detail, it is necessary to explore the rest of the dimension of sophistication. Chapter 3 continues the analysis, describing mobs and formal organizations—two forms of deviant organization of greater sophistication.

NOTES

[1]Excerpts from Ned Polsky, *Hustlers, Beats, and Others,* reprinted with permission of Aldine Publishing Company, New York.

CHAPTER THREE
MOBS AND FORMAL ORGANIZATIONS

Loners, colleagues, and peers share an important characteristic—within a type of deviance, each deviant performs roughly the same set of actions. More sophisticated forms of deviant organization have a more elaborate division of labor; deviants work in teams, performing specialized, coordinated roles. Specialization means that members of the team perform different roles that often demand particular qualifications, such as special knowledge and skill. In addition to specialization, teamwork requires coordination. Coordination means that each member's actions bear the proper relationship to the others' actions; every member of the team must be in the right place, doing the right thing at the right time for the operation to succeed. Coordination demands discipline. During the operation, members must put aside their own interests and pay attention to their responsibilities to the team. Further, teamwork usually requires a division of authority. One member may act as the leader, making plans and giving instructions to the team, while others carry out the operation's necessary tasks.

Two distinctive forms of deviant organization involve teamwork: mobs and formal organizations. In this book, "mob" does not refer to a disorganized crowd, such as a lynch mob. Rather, the term is borrowed from early twentieth century thieves' argot; it refers to a small team of deviants who regularly engage in a particular type of deviance, usually a form of theft, and who perform specialized roles in coordination. An elaborate division of labor is the distinctive characteristic of mobs. Deviant formal organizations also have a division of labor, but they can be distinguished from mobs. Formal organizations are deliberately constructed to perform complex operations with considerable efficiency. They are usually much larger than other forms of deviant organization; their operations extend over time and space. The members form a team, but it is a team on a very large scale.

Mobs and formal organizations share a purpose—they are designed to amass money or, more rarely, power. While deviants organized in less sophisticated ways sometimes seek to make a profit or gain power, this is always true for mobs and formal organizations. Moreover, their deviant operations are systematic, carried out regularly.

In meeting their objectives, mobs and formal organizations confront several problems. First, they must find ways of maximizing their profits, of making their operations as efficient and effective as possible. This requires specialized skills and careful coordination of action. Second, they must develop the means for acquiring those skills and maintaining the discipline needed for coordination. Members must think beyond the current deviant operation, to the team's continued, systematic working. Third, if the team is to operate over an extended period, it must have ways of maintaining morale and curbing dissension. Teams must be concerned with their members' relationships with each other, in addition to their conduct during deviant operations. Finally, teams must devise means of neutralizing the efforts of social control agents. If teams are to operate on a regular basis, they must be able to cope with their opposition. These problems and their solutions become focal issues for mobs and formal organizations.

MOBS

In 1937, Edwin Sutherland published a classic study in criminology, *The Professional Thief,* based on his conversations with "Chic Conwell," a confidence man who operated from roughly 1905 to 1925. The book distinguished professional theft from other types of crime, arguing that professional thieves were a criminal elite, highly skilled and committed to their work and to one another. Sutherland used "professional" in two senses: professional thieves earned their living from stealing; and more importantly, they shared many of the characteristics of legitimate professions (such as law or medicine), including "technical skill, an exclusive group, immunity from punishment which almost amounts to a license from the state to steal, a degree of monopoly growing out of their exclusive group relationship and of their recognition by the agents of the state"

(Sutherland, 1937:216). In later studies, sociologists examined armed robbers, safecrackers, and other full-time thieves, comparing them to Sutherland's model of the professional thief (Einstadter, 1969; B. Jackson, 1972; Lemert, 1967:109-34; Letkemann, 1973). These studies argued that many full-time thieves were not professionals; they displayed less cohesion than the thieves described by Sutherland. The terms "career thief" or "career criminal" refer to full-time thieves who are not professionals.

Both professional and career thieves can organize in forms of varying sophistication. Chapter 2 discussed systematic check forgers and pool hustlers—two types of deviants who engage in theft as a full-time occupation. Both types of deviance are precarious. In their isolation, systematic check forgers often find it difficult to maintain the life of deception and mobility their work requires; the limited earnings from pool hustling force many hustlers to moonlight in other jobs. Forgers and hustlers also are constrained by their limited support from fellow deviants. Most professional or career theft involves a more sophisticated form of organization—the mob. A mob is a small group of thieves which engages in repeated acts of theft, using a relatively elaborate division of labor. (The term "mob" is dated; modern criminals are more likely to speak of a "crew.") Mobs often specialize in particular forms of theft; for example, Sutherland (1937) spoke of cannon mobs (pickpocketing), boosting mobs (shoplifting), and confidence mobs (confidence games).

Mobs develop because an elaborate division of labor allows thieves to operate more effectively and in greater safety. Some types of theft require substantial skill. Pickpocketing, for example, is a specialized crime; only an accomplished thief can pick pockets undetected (Maurer, 1964). Thieves need one another for socialization into theft; it is almost impossible to teach oneself the techniques of pickpocketing. Even more importantly, mobs provide the support needed to carry out theft safely. Division of labor increases efficiency and safety. A lone individual can rob a bank by walking up to the teller and presenting a note demanding money, but a mob can make more money with less risk. A three-person mob of bank robbers can have one member "cover" the people in the bank, while a second vaults over the counter and takes the money held by each teller and a third member waits outside in a running car, prepared to get the mob away from the bank before the police arrive (Einstadter, 1969; Letkemann, 1973:90-116). Using a mob increases the amount which can be stolen (taking cash from all the bank's tellers) and makes the task safer (by covering guards, other employees, and customers, and by arranging a quick getaway). A relatively elaborate subculture, including a technical argot and a code of conduct for members, and a network of contacts with other criminals facilitates the mob's coordination of these complex operations.

This section will examine one type of mob in detail. Robert Prus, a sociologist, and "C. R. D. Sharper," a former professional gambler, have described mobs of road hustlers—professional card and dice cheats (Prus and Sharper, 1977). Road hustlers remain active in contemporary society, whereas other types of mobs, such as those specializing in confidence games and pickpocketing, are less common than they were fifty years ago. After examining road hustlers' mobs, this section compares them with other mobs.

Road Hustlers

Road hustlers are professional gamblers who cheat at cards or dice. A road hustlers' mob, called a "crew," travels from town to town, cheating "suckers"—people who gamble with members of the crew. Typically, a crew attends conventions, parties, lodge picnics, and other celebrations where some participants gamble as part of the festivities. The hustlers join these games and use various methods to cheat the suckers and take their money. (The term "hustler" is used here in a different sense than in the discussion of pool hustlers [Chapter 2]. In pool hustling, the mark is tricked into underestimating the hustler's skill and thereby betting in situations where it will be very difficult to win. The pool hustler does not cheat; dishonesty takes the form of deception about the hustler's skill. In contrast, road hustlers, although they are typically highly skilled gamblers, do not rely on their skills; they cheat.)

There are two basic methods of cheating: using illicit equipment and manipulating the gambling equipment (Prus and Sharper, 1977:11-20). In the former, the hustler introduces special playing equipment which puts the other players at a disadvantage. Marked cards (which have slight variations in the pattern on the backs, indicating the cards' values) can be purchased, or a hustler can mark a new deck using ink, pin holes, or "daub" (a wax). Similarly, one can buy "bogus" dice: "percentage dice" are unevenly weighted, making some outcomes more likely; "tops" are dice which have some numbers missing (for example, a player throwing two tops which have only odd numbers [1-3-5] cannot throw a seven); and other bogus dice can be controlled with magnets. Obviously, hustlers using illicit equipment have a considerable advantage over their naive opponents. Manipulations are manual techniques for cheating. In card games, the dealer may stack the deck (arrange the cards in a particular order), deal seconds (or otherwise give certain cards to other players), or peek at the cards as they are being shuffled or dealt. Manipulations sometimes involve illicit equipment; in dice games, the most common manipulation involves switching one set of dice for another.

The division of labor among road hustlers during a game involves three roles: mechanic, shoot-up man, and muscle (Prus and Sharper, 1977:31-46). The mechanic is the player who introduces the illicit equipment into the game and carries out the manipulations. In a dice game, the mechanic stands where the dice fall and picks them up, switching the dice for the next shooter. In card games, the mechanic manipulates the deck during the deal. The shoot-up man is responsible for manipulating the social occasion, keeping the suckers involved in the game while calming their suspicions. The shoot-up man must be personable because, through the mechanic's efforts, the shoot-up man will emerge the game's winner and suckers are less likely to object to losing when the winner is friendly and well liked. In card games, the shoot-up man sits at the table. In dice games, while the shoot-up man may throw the dice occasionally, most of the money is made on side bets (where the suckers are less likely to notice that the hustlers are winning substantial sums). The muscle functions as the protector, someone who can defend the mob from angry suckers who suspect they have been cheated. Obviously, the more proficient the crew's deceptions, the less it needs to use the muscle. In actual play, a crew of three or four hustlers may use more than one mechanic or shoot-up man, with members doubling in two roles or switching roles as circumstances dictate.

Road hustling also involves roles outside the game itself (Prus and Sharper, 1977:35-36; 64-66). The contacts man is responsible for scheduling the crew's travels and planning its route. To maximize profits, a crew should work nearly every night, preferably in high-stakes games. This requires considerable advance planning, phoning ahead to learn the dates and locations of annual conventions, parties, and so on. The boss of the crew serves as its manager, setting policy and disciplining members. Often the boss is also the contacts man. In addition to the members of the crew, road hustlers use noncrew members as bird-dogs and sponsors. A bird-dog tips the crew about a game and receives a small fee for this information. A sponsor "fronts" for the crew, taking the members to the event and vouching for them, thereby reducing the suckers' suspicions about the hustlers (who are, after all, outsiders). Sponsors also play in the games, giving the crew added legitimacy. In return, the sponsor receives the same share of the profits as each of the crew members.

Road hustlers distinguish their work from the "rough hustle"—cheating by amateurs (Prus and Sharper, 1977:21-31). Many players, even in "friendly" games, try to cheat. Road hustlers have four characteristics which set them apart from amateur cheats. First, road hustlers view card and dice hustling as a full-time job. Second, they have a high level of skill. In part, their skills are technical—the ability to read marked cards or manipulate a deck comes only with long practice. Moreover, these technical skills must be used in stressful situations—if the suckers discover they are being cheated, the inept hustler will face their anger. But hustlers' skills are also social; they must be able to get the suckers to play—preferably for high stakes—win without making the suckers resentful, and manage accusations of cheating and other problems. Third, road hustlers must be flexible. It is impossible to predict all of the ways a game can develop as the evening goes on. Suckers may have more or less money than expected, they may want to quit early or continue playing, or they may become drunk, argumentative, or suspicious. In each case, professional hustlers must be able to adjust. In hustling, as in other situations where people must perform under pressure, coolness is a prized virtue (cf. Lyman and Scott, 1970:145-57). Finally, professional hustlers are mobile; they travel with a crew and have connections with other hustlers and career criminals.

Most professional hustlers begin as amateur cheats (Prus and Sharper, 1977:47-59). While a few individuals with no hustling background are recruited by crews, most professionals are spotted by crews while they are amateurs with limited hustling skills. The transition to professional status requires additional socialization:

> But you really never stop learning and even when you think you're on top of it, you still have to practice and watch your moves. Like sometimes your partners might tell you to slow down on your deal. Sure enough, I would be concentrating on the game and just whip those cards out on the table. "Just deal like a sucker," they might say, so you slow down and make sure you are holding the deck sort of sloppy like. You try to reduce suspicion throughout the game, you try to keep the suckers happy. (Prus and Sharper, 1977:55)

Other lessons are less technical ones. The newcomer must acquire "larceny sense," becoming sensitive to opportunities to steal. Amateur hustlers might not cheat handicapped players or other suckers who gain their sympathy; a professional learns to overcome these feelings. Newcomers also must learn their place in the crew; until they can carry a full share of the load, they must acknowledge the more experienced members' right to more privileges. Crews "shortcake" newcomers, paying them less than a full share of the winnings. Newcomers cannot protest this inequity until they become accomplished hustlers, able to contribute fully toward the crew's success. Finally, newcomers must learn how to "make the nut," to limit expenditures while on the road. Hustlers routinely cheat hotels and restaurants out of their bills and otherwise minimize expenses. Learning these lessons marks the transition from rough hustling to professionalism.

Professional hustlers tend to have stable careers. Prus and Sharper (1977:43-46) examined forty professionals who had been involved in hustling between five and forty years. All were males of respectable appearance. Most could play more than one role for their crews—a hustler might be an accomplished mechanic, but also have the strength to act as the muscle or the social skills needed to perform as the shoot-up man. Because hustling's physical skills require dexterity rather than strength, hustlers can remain active as they grow older. In contrast, deviant activities which demand considerable agility or strength tend to be limited to younger people; most burglars and robbers are under thirty. For the road hustler, middle age adds respectability to one's appearance, making it easier to fit in at con-ventions and lodge picnics, and reducing the likelihood that suckers will become suspicious of cheating. Relatively few people have the skills hustling requires. As a consequence, a crew with compatible members is likely to work together for years without any turnover in its membership. Moreover:

> It's tough to get out of the business. First, where else can a guy like this make this kind of money, say without getting into other kinds of crime. A man with a good crew will make $20,000 a year plus. If you're with a top-level crew, maybe $30,000 or more. And that's after deducting your expenses. (Prus and Sharper, 1977:131)

Crews usually limit recruiting to those occasions when they have an opening. Since these are rare, the rate at which newcomers enter professional ranks stays low.

Road hustlers run some risks, but they are limited (Prus and Sharper, 1977: 107-23). Even professionals make mistakes during an operation, and they must be prepared to cover them.

> We had a spread going, and on a switch he threw out three dice. His reply to this was, "Fifteen the hard way," like three fives. A couple of the guys chuckled, and one guy said "Shoot, shoot!", but that was all. (Prus and Sharper, 1977:112)

This incident could have caused trouble—seeing three dice in a game where only two are needed should have made the suckers suspicious, but the hustler managed to convince them that it was a prank. Not all problems can be handled this easily. If the hustlers believe the other players are becoming suspicious, they will try to allay their doubts. In dice games, the mechanic may casually show the suckers empty hands or display a seven on the dice to reassure them that the game is legitimate. If suckers become convinced that cheating is taking place and threaten to make a scene, the hustlers may take them aside and try to buy their silence, returning the money they have lost plus a bonus. On rare occasions, a suspicious player's drink may be drugged. "Hey Rubes"—incidents which lead to violence—are extremely rare, but they represent the most serious threat to professionals.

Although hustlers steal considerable sums of money, they face minimal legal sanctions. If caught, they may bribe the authorities, who often view hustling as a relatively minor offense. Hustlers who do get arrested usually face misdemeanor charges, such as "conspiring to cheat," which are rarely punished by a sentence more severe than a small fine. Road hustling is a comparatively safe form of deviance; the hustlers run minimal risks of serious injury or severe punishment. Of course, their safety contributes to their long, stable careers.

Other Mobs

Road hustlers resemble other mobs in that they share the same basic structure. All mobs have an elaborate division of labor with members performing specialized roles. Among road hustlers, the key roles are mechanic, shoot-up man, and muscle. Mobs of pickpockets (discussed in chapter 7) use a tool (who actually picks the pocket), aided by one or more stalls (who maneuver the victim into a position from which the wallet can be taken) (Maurer, 1964). In confidence games (treated in chapter 8), the mob's basic roles are the roper (who locates a potential victim) and the insideman (who convinces the victim to part with some money) (Maurer, 1974). Mobs committing armed robberies assign a member to cover the robbery scene, another to actually take the money, and a third to drive the getaway car (Einstadter, 1969; Letkemann, 1973:90-116). A "troupe" of shoplifters usually includes a stall (who attracts the attention of the salespeople), a clout (who steals the articles), "and perhaps a cover to take the goods from the clout or to conceal the clout's exit" (Cameron, 1964:45). In each of these cases, the roles assigned to the mob's members make it possible to steal efficiently with maximum safety.

Road hustlers are atypical of mobs in other ways. Cheating at cards or dice is not viewed as a serious crime (in spite of the fact that road hustlers steal enough to live comfortably), and there is little risk of sanctioning from social control agents. In contrast, pickpocketing, confidence games, armed robbery, and professional shoplifting are relatively serious offenses, carrying more severe penalties. Unlike road hustlers, other mobs must find ways of dealing with these greater risks. Their traditional solutions involve codes of conduct and corruption.

Sutherland's professional thief described, at great length, a code of conduct governing the relationships between mob members. In summary:

> The normative imperatives of the professional underworld, in their purest form, may be stated as follows: (1) do not hold out money or property from fellow criminals; (2) pay debts to other criminals as rapidly as possible; (3) members of a mob must deal honestly with one another; (4) mob members must not cut in on one another's operational roles; (5) mob members must endeavor to fix cases involving other members; and, most important, (6) thieves must never inform the police as to the crimes of fellow thieves. (Inciardi, 1975:69)

These rules are considerably more elaborate than those found in less sophisticated forms of deviant organization. Mobs are organized to pursue profit, and their code specifies the way money should be handled within the mob. In addition, mobs face potentially severe sanctions from social control agents, and their code of conduct emphasizes members' responsibilities to thwart social control efforts. The existence of these rules does not mean that members inevitably follow them. As noted above, road hustlers shortcake newcomers—directly violating the first rule. Just as in respectable groups, mob members sometimes violate their own rules, but those rules still reflect the group's values. In general, mobs subscribe to a code of conduct which specifies the members' responsibilities to one another.

While codes of conduct reduce the likelihood that one mob member will betray the others, social control efforts remain a risk. Many mobs try to neutralize social control agents through corruption. Because mob operations are usually systematic, it is difficult to remain undetected by social control agents once the agents begin receiving complaints from victims. Therefore, mobs turn to corruption to gain the agents' cooperation. This can take several forms, grouped under the traditional term "the fix" (Maurer, 1974:181-208; Sutherland, 1937:82-139). Police officers may be paid in advance to allow mobs to work in their precincts. Officers agree to ignore the thieves at work and, if citizens point out the thieves, the police will not arrest them. Other mobs try to bribe officers after their crimes come to police attention. Where police cannot be corrupted, thieves may subvert the courts. Some mobs retain a lawyer who has the contacts to fix cases. If a judge or prosecutor is known to accept bribes and if the mob's attorney can contact that official, court cases may result in dismissal or minimum penalties. For example, a professional shoplifter who has a number of prior arrests may be brought before a court where cooperative officials treat the thief as a first offender whose penalty is a small fine (Cameron, 1964:48). If the officials cannot be corrupted, the mob may subvert the trial by bribing witnesses. Mob members may offer full restitution to the victim of a theft in return for dropping the charges. The fix flourished in the early twentieth century, when urban governments were notoriously corrupt. Modern social control agencies are less corruptible than their earlier counterparts and the fix is no longer routine, although thieves sometimes locate cooperative social control agents (Gardiner, 1970; Sherman, 1974).

Greater difficulty in arranging a fix suggests the changes affecting mob operations. McIntosh (1971) described a broad change in the organization of mobs—from craft crime to project crime. Craft crime involves a perfected technique, a routine which a mob repeats against individual victims. For example, pickpockets use the same techniques to steal from one person after another. In contrast, corporate bodies, such as banks, are the targets of project crime. Each project theft requires special planning. Although a group of thieves may work together on several projects, their division of labor varies from one project to the next, with particular individuals performing different roles in different thefts. The one-of-a-kind, large-scale thefts which achieve notoriety, such as the Brink's robbery, exemplify project crime (Behn, 1977; cf. Feiden, 1980). As the economy changes from cash to credit as its principal method of exchange, traditional forms of mob theft become less profitable, and some criminal crafts, such as pickpocketing, begin to disappear (Inciardi, 1977). Thieves must direct their attention toward profitable targets; increasingly, these are corporate bodies which must be attacked through specially planned project thefts.

Although these external conditions transform the mob's work, mob structure and subculture remain relatively unaffected. The mob offers an efficient form of organization for routinizing theft; members band together because they need one another to insure their operations' success and their own safety. In addition, few individuals can invent the technical and social skills needed for complex operations. Mobs provide a forum for socializing newcomers. (Exceptions do exist. A person can enter the rough hustle or even start picking pockets without instruction from an experienced thief, but prolonged, successful operations by such loners are uncommon [Maurer, 1964: 166-68; Prus and Sharper, 1977:22].) Because their members depend on one another, mobs often develop a rich subculture. In part, this reflects the technical nature of their work. Maurer (1964) identified hundreds of words in the argot of pickpockets, including special terms for various pockets and the items found within them. Codes of conduct are another aspect of mob subculture. The subculture flourishes because mobs travel; on the road, members not only work together but also spend their free time socializing with one another. In many cities, a bar becomes known among thieves as the place where they can meet other professional and career thieves. Meetings between mobs are occasions for describing recent experiences, passing along information about new techniques or about opportunities and dangers in particular cities, assessing the characters of those present and gossiping about thieves who are not, and so forth. Such conversations enrich the thieves' oral tradition and help bind them into a loose social network so that established thieves can locate new partners if their old mob breaks up. As a result of their contacts in this network, mob members are more likely to maintain long, stable careers.

Coordinating Small Teams

On the surface, mobs resemble colleagues and peers. Each form of deviant organization involves a small group with considerable face-to-face contact among the members. Some sociologists lump these forms together as "deviant subcultures." Yet there are important differences among the three forms. Colleagues' contacts are largely sociable, with each individual operating alone, except under special circumstances. Peers and mobs are differentiated by the former's lack of a specialized division of labor. This difference reflects the mob's purpose—to make deviance safe and profitable. Mob members usually steal for a living, using routine procedures which feature a specialized division of labor. The mob's organization is purposeful—a mob should be no larger than necessary, since each additional member means that profits must be split into smaller shares. At the same time, a mob must be large enough so that the operation's required tasks can be performed efficiently (so that the theft has the maximum chance of being successfully completed) and safely (so that chances of being apprehended by social control agents are minimized). With its concern for profit, the mob's organization takes on a rationality which is usually absent in less sophisticated forms of deviant organization.

FORMAL ORGANIZATIONS

Formal organizations are the most sophisticated form of deviant organization. Deviant formal organizations have not received a great deal of scholarly attention, but the study of respectable formal organizations is a recognized specialty within sociology. Scholars working in this specialty define formal organizations in terms of their intentionally designed character. Etzioni states: "Organizations are social units (or human groupings) deliberately constructed and reconstructed to seek specific goals" (Etzioni, 1964:3; cf. Blau and Scott, 1962:5). Another leading authority notes: "The defining criterion of a formal organization . . . is the existence of procedures for mobilizing and coordinating the efforts of various, usually specialized, subgroups in the pursuit of joint objectives" (Blau, 1974:29). In short, formal organizations, such as industrial and governmental bureaucracies, have characteristic features: a clear division of labor; a hierarchical structure of authority; a set of written rules; a specialized administrative staff; an impersonal orientation toward the organization's clients; and members' commitment to extended careers within the organization (Blau, 1974:30; Weber, 1946:196-204). While these characteristics may describe General Motors or the Internal Revenue Service, they do not all fit deviant formal organizations. Deviant formal organizations are less elaborately organized than their respectable counterparts. However, they share the quality of being intentionally designed.

Deviant formal organizations involve relatively large numbers of deviants, cooperating over extended time and space to accomplish the organization's deviant goals. Like mobs, deviant formal organizations exist to amass money or power. But mobs rarely have more than a handful of members, while formal organizations have dozens, even hundreds. In order to coordinate its members' actions, a deviant formal organization needs a deliberately designed structure within which members are assigned positions. These positions are differentiated along both a vertical hierarchy of authority and a horizontal division of responsibility, and there are channels for efficient communication within this structure. A deviant formal organization may have special departments for planning, processing goods, public relations, and rule enforcement, with positions for strategists, coordinators, accountants, lawyers, enforcers, and dealers in illicit goods. Once this structure exists, members' actions can be coordinated even when their operations are physically separated. Moreover, the structure lends itself to systematic operations and steady productivity over time; deviant formal organizations can survive for decades. Maintaining the structure demands that members be replaced when they leave their positions and that the organization be able to recruit new members to fill vacant positions or expand its membership. Deviant formal organizations usually have binding, albeit unwritten, rules for guiding members in organizational action, and these rules are actively enforced.

Before considering some specific examples, deviant formal organizations should be distinguished from two related organizational forms. First, there are *extended mobs*—small teams of deviants whose operations extend over time or space. Extended mobs have a degree of organizational sophistication somewhere between mobs and formal organizations. Like mobs, their membership is small; like formal organizations, their operations involve either members located at considerable distances from one another or continuous, stable operation over a prolonged period. For example, smuggling can involve a small but highly specialized group with members located in different countries. In this small group, one member purchases the goods; another arranges the transportation across international borders; and a third sells the smuggled goods (T. Green, 1969). While smugglers operate at considerable distances from one another, other extended mobs carry out prolonged operations on a fixed site. Brothels, for instance, may operate for years under the management of the same madam, while dozens of prostitutes pass through the house, each working for a short period (Heyl, 1979). Smuggling rings and brothels resemble formal organizations in their rational methods of making a profit. At the same time, the small size of these groups makes an elaborate formal structure unnecessary; the madam of a brothel is clearly in charge, but she can deal directly with each of her prostitutes. Their small size and informal procedures set extended mobs apart from deviant formal organizations.

Deviant formal organizations must also be distinguished from *organizational deviance*, where members of a respectable formal organization use deviant means to achieve their organization's goals. Schrager and Short (1978:411-12) offer a definition: "Organizational crimes are illegal acts of omission or commission of an individual or a group of individuals in a legitimate formal organization in accordance with the operative goals of the organization, which have a serious physical or economic impact on employees, consumers or the general public." For example, price fixing involves representatives of different firms in an industry who meet to decide how much they will charge their customers. Price fixing can involve huge sums; for example, the conspiracies to fix prices in the forest products industry, exposed in a series of federal cases between 1972 and 1978, led to fines and damage payments of over $535 million (Briggs, 1979). Organizational deviance also includes illicit activities by government agencies, such as the illegal covert intelligence campaigns waged by the FBI, the CIA, and the White House Plumbers during the Nixon Administration. Organizational deviance need not involve all, or even most of the organization's members—a handful of members or even a single person can carry out the deviant operations. In a price-fixing scheme, for example, knowledge of the illegal plan typically is limited to a small group of executives (cf. Geis, 1967). This fact separates organizational deviance from deviant formal organizations. In organizational deviance, the deviants are members of a formal organization, but they are not formally organized as deviants. Organizational deviance may be committed by single individuals (loners) or small groups (peers or mobs) within the larger, legitimate formal organization. Further, organizational deviance is unlike deviant formal organizations because the formal organization itself is legitimate, designed to achieve respectable, not deviant, goals.

This section focuses on deviant formal organizations, considering two examples in some detail. First, the Vice Lords, a large Chicago street gang, provides an example of a relatively unsophisticated deviant formal organization. Second, organized crime families, formal organizations of greater sophistication, will be examined.

The Vice Lords: A Large Street Gang

In 1958, the Vice Lords began as a typical delinquent gang. The members were about a dozen adolescent males, living in the same neighborhood in Chicago's West Side black ghetto and linked by friendship ties (Dawley, 1973:28-49; Keiser, 1969:1-11). They started the Vice Lords while inmates of an Illinois reformatory. Upon their release, they decided to continue operating as a social club, sponsoring parties. At that time, the West Side had several rival fighting gangs and the Vice Lords were drawn into combat. In order to protect themselves from the established gangs, the Vice Lords sought to increase their own numbers. They grew by fighting other gangs and absorbing their defeated opponents:

> The first target for takeover was the Barons, another little club. There were about twenty-four of them. . . . "It took us about a week to dust 'em and make 'em join the Vice Lords. We got 'em jammed up tight and told 'em instead of goin' ahead, why don't they come on and join us since we're the strongest. Ain't no sense in them tryin' to make it on their own, because they can't make it." (Dawley, 1973:33)

As their membership grew, it became easier for the Vice Lords to overcome opposition; they were able to absorb increasingly larger rival gangs. On Chicago's South Side, the same process of conflict and absorption produced another very large gang—the Blackstone Rangers (McPherson, 1969; Sale, 1971).

By the mid 1960s, the Vice Lords, renamed the Vice Lord Nation, was the largest gang on the West Side. The size of the gang at its height is a matter of debate. Keiser (1969:12, 20) believed that there were six to nine branches, totaling between six hundred and three thousand members. Dawley (1973:65) claimed: "There were at least twenty-six branches and eight to ten thousand Lords." Regardless of which estimate is correct, the gang grew far beyond the point where its members could conduct their affairs as a peer group. The Vice Lords needed a structure for coordinating activity—they had to become a formal organization.

By 1966, the gang had an elaborate structure (shown in Figure 3-1).

FIGURE 3-1
Organization of the Vice Lords in 1966*

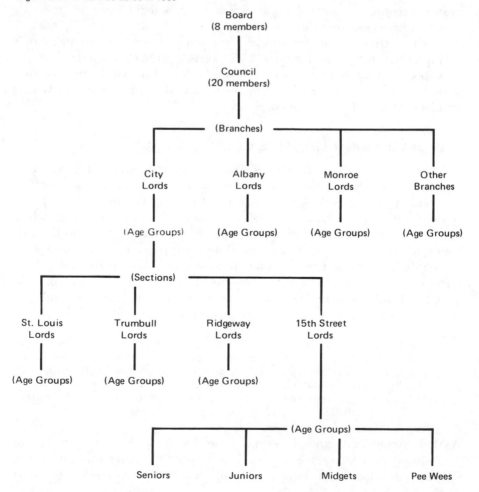

*Based on Keiser (1969).

Control over the Vice Lord Nation was then vested in an eight-member board, which was supported by a council of twenty other members (Keiser, 1969:12-19). Board and council members represented the gang's major branches and sections. The Vice Lord Nation was divided into several branches, named for neighborhoods within the Vice Lords' territory. The largest branch, the City Lords, was subdivided into geographically-based sections. Each section, like each of the other branches, had three or four age groups. The criterion for belonging to an age group varied; most City Lords' Seniors were 18 or over, the Juniors were 16 or 17, and the Midgets 15 or under. Each branch of the Vice Lord Nation had formal offices which varied from one unit to the next. Keiser found seven named offices: president, vice-president, secretary-treasurer, supreme war counselor, war counselor, gunkeeper, and sergeant-at-arms.

This description probably exaggerates the Vice Lords' formal structure. Because the gang grew too large to settle its affairs informally, some structure was necessary to coordinate its operations. The designation of formal leadership positions also functioned to assure stability in the face of inevitable personnel changes. The Vice Lords attracted the attention of the police, and members frequently were arrested and imprisoned. The establishment of a board and council not only gave the gang a central decision-making body, it also provided a means for replacing lost leaders. When a member of the board was arrested, a replacement was selected from the council. Similarly, the arrest of the president of a branch, section, or age group elevated the vice-president to the unit's presidency (Keiser, 1969:17-19). Yet, for the average member, the formal workings of the gang remained unimportant. Most members spent their time in small cliques— equivalent to a typical delinquent gang. In day-to-day activities, the informal life of the clique outweighed the formal structure of the larger gang (Keiser, 1969:18-19).

While informal clique relationships governed most routine activities, the gang's formal organization became important in some situations. The Vice Lords remained rivals with fighting gangs from surrounding neighborhoods. When intergang hostility erupted, the Vice Lords' formal structure provided the means for efficiently mobilizing members (Keiser, 1969:31-33). When members of a rival gang attacked a Vice Lord, units within the Vice Lord Nation could be mobilized:

> The status of the Vice Lord beaten up by an enemy club is also the crucial factor in determining which subgroup will be mobilized for retaliation. If the person jumped on is an influential leader in a section or strongly allied with an important section leader, but is not allied with any of the important branch or Nation leaders, then the group that may be mobilized for retaliation would be the section; if he has high status in a branch, but not the Nation, then the branch may be mobilized; and finally, if he is considered one of the "top Lords" in the Nation, then the entire Vice Lord Nation may be mobilized for the purpose of retaliation. (Keiser, 1969:33)

Similarly, when any rival gangs were expected to invade the Vice Lords' territory, whole branches or sections were mobilized for defense. By providing lines of communication and allocating responsibility, the gang's formal structure maximized the effect of one of the Vice Lords' most important resources—the gang's size. Leaders could send part or all of the gang to meet outside threats.

In addition to fighting, the Vice Lords engaged in other deviant activities. The gang experimented with a variety of rackets:

> There were a million different ways to get money. Nothing was safe on the streets. We would get money from liquor stores, liquor salesmen, clothing stores, dudes off the street, dope peddlers, reefer peddlers, pill pushers, barbecue places, stickups, boosters—any way we could get it. Boosting was when the girls would go in stores and steal clothes and we would sell them on the streets for discount prices. . . .

> You needed cats that wouldn't fight but would be car thieves, hubcap thieves, battery thieves. . . . Money came from small rackets like hubcaps, snatching pocketbooks or knocking a dude in the head. Protection required too much bookwork. (Dawley, 1973:59-60, 89)

None of these rackets became a systematic source of income for the Vice Lords; the organization was not as effective in coordinating these deviant activities as it was in mobilizing members to fight. The early attempt to organize a protection racket—a systematic source of income for many deviant formal organizations—failed. But more recently, some other large street gangs, such as El Rukn (formerly the Blackstone Rangers), have successfully gained control of narcotics distribution and other profitable rackets in Chicago (Petacque, 1980).

The Vice Lords were successful in providing some services for their members. One gang leader became a powerful figure within a prison. He recalled:

> Eventually we took care of any Lord that came in. They ate the best, they wore the best, and they slept in the best places. Any dude on the street that was a Lord knew when he was busted that he would be well taken care of when he went in the place, so being locked up was no threat for the Lords. . . . As dudes came in, they saw it was profitable to be a Vice Lord. (Dawley, 1973:56)

In spite of their limited successes with any profitable rackets, the Vice Lords' fighting strength and ability to provide services enabled them to recruit new members.

The Vice Lord Nation is an interesting example of a deviant formal organization, precisely because of its limited scope. The Vice Lords needed a formal structure in order to manage their large membership. However, beyond efficiently mobilizing members for fights with other gangs, there is little evidence of either formal control over the members' activities or the disciplined coordination which characterize more sophisticated deviant formal organizations.

Organized Crime Families

The Vice Lords had a large membership, organized to achieve dominance among the Chicago West Side's gangs. Other deviant formal organizations have fewer members, but they operate more profitable illicit enterprises, such as bookmaking (taking bets on sporting events), numbers running (illegal lotteries), loan sharking (lending money at exorbitant interest), and drug smuggling. There is disagreement about the best term to describe such formal organizations; "organized crime" is popular, but experts also speak of syndicate crime (Albini, 1971), racketeering (McIntosh, 1973), and mafias (Hobsbawm, 1959). Critics of the term "organized crime" argue that it is misleading because criminal activities can be organized in many different ways. Of course, this is a major theme in this book. Within the context of this book's larger discussion about the social organization of deviants, this analysis will speak of organized crime in a narrow sense, referring to activities by members of deviant formal organizations in pursuit of the organizations' goals.

The debate about organized crime is not merely over terminology. Sociologists also disagree about the history and operation of organized crime in different societies, and specifically about the role of organized crime families in modern America (D. Smith, 1975). Some recent accounts describe individual families (cf. Ianni, 1972; Talese, 1971), but observers cannot agree about the organization of these groups or their relationships to one another and to the larger society. One position argues that the families form a conspiracy, "a nationwide illicit cartel and a nationwide confederation" which threatens "basic economic and political traditions and institutions" (Cressey, 1969:1); another counters that this conspiracy is imaginary, a "most seductive and persistent" myth, but "extraordinarily fanciful" (Morris and Hawkins, 1970: 203, 234). This section does not resolve all of the issues about organized crime families; rather, it focuses on social organization, using the families as examples of deviant formal organizations. This discussion explores three topics: the reasons why some deviant activities become controlled by organized crime; the ways one organized crime family manages its deviant operations; and the nature of the relationships among family members.

Two general types of deviance form the foundation for organized crime (Block, 1980; McIntosh, 1973; Schelling, 1971). First, organized crime supplies illicit goods and services. Wherever there is a demand for prohibited goods or services, such as prostitution, drugs, pornography, gambling, or smuggled goods, there is an opportunity for organized crime to become the major supplier for an illicit marketplace. The American experience with Prohibition is an obvious example. Although the law prohibited alcohol, people wanted to drink and organized crime supplied the liquor to meet this demand. Second, organized crime engages in systematic extortion, collecting payments from people through the use of threats. For example, organized criminals may insist that restaurants subscribe to their linen service; those which refuse may be attacked. McIntosh (1973:38) explains why the provision of illicit goods and services and systematic extortion are the basic operations of organized crime:

> ... the two have the same organizational potentiality, a potentiality that is rooted in their common characteristic, that the so-called 'victims' know what is going on and for some reason accept it, for a time at least. The reason may be different in each case. It may be that they see the extortionist as having more power in their particular parish than the agents of the state, or that they desire the goods and services supplied by the racketeer. Either way, they see it as in their interest to acquiesce or positively to encourage the criminals. In the short run, at least, they are not willing to co-operate in the prevention of the crime.

These two types of crime share another characteristic: they offer regular sources of income. Most illicit markets involve a fairly steady demand, and extortionists can arrange to collect their payments at regular intervals. The criminals' organization must be sophisticated enough to manage regular supply or collection activities but, in return, they can count on a steady flow of income and, because they set prices, a profitable operation. These profits help to insure the organization's safety; a portion of the money goes to corrupt social control agents, who may, in turn, receive regular payments (Cressey, 1969:248-89; Gardiner, 1970; Sherman, 1974). Large-scale illicit operations are difficult to conceal, especially when they continue over time. Corruption insures the cooperation of the authorities and protects the organization's operations.

Most studies of organized crime face serious problems of evidence (Morris and Hawkins, 1970:203-35). Their authors have little or no direct experience with organized crime, and they focus on events visible to outsiders, such as the murders of reputed Mafia leaders, or on material made available by social control agents, such as transcripts of wiretapped conversations between organized criminals. The evidence often is ambiguous, subject to different interpretations. Contradictory conclusions are not uncommon, partly because some writers seem to interpret the evidence in terms of their preconceived notions about organized crime. To minimize this problem, this section draws heavily on one study based on firsthand observation and interviews with members of an organized crime family. *A Family Business,* by Francis Ianni (1972), focuses on the Lupollos—an Italian-American organized crime family.

At the time of Ianni's study, the Brooklyn-based Lupollos controlled an empire of legitimate and illegitimate enterprises (Ianni, 1972:89-99). Fifteen men, related to one another through blood or marriage, ran the family businesses, under the leadership of Joe Lupollo. Other family members were employed at intermediate levels in family enterprises. The Lupollos owned eleven legitimate firms, including real estate, food processing, trucking, and public relations businesses, with assets totaling over $30 million. In addition, the family had an interest in at least ten other legitimate

FIGURE 3-2
Organization of the Lupollo Numbers Enterprise*

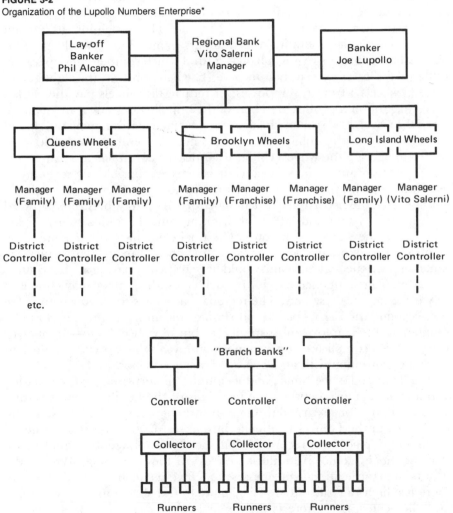

*From *A Family Business* by Francis A. J. Ianni, p. 95, © Russell Sage Foundation, Basic Books, Inc., Publishers, New York, 1972.

businesses. Ianni limits his discussion of the Lupollos' illicit activities to two enterprises—numbers running and loan sharking. It is not clear whether the family was involved in other kinds of deviance.

The organization of the Lupollo numbers racket, outlined in Figure 3-2, suggests the scope of one of the family's illicit activities (Ianni, 1972:91-96). In the numbers game, individuals make small bets (often one dollar) on a lottery. Each bettor selects a three digit number (such as 4-8-6), betting that number will be the day's winner. The winning number is determined through a random process, such as using the last three digits in the total amount of money wagered that day at a particular race track. The odds against winning, of course, are a thousand to one, but the winner's payoff is much smaller—usually six hundred to one. The remaining 40 percent goes to the people operating the numbers game. The Lupollo game is backed by the family's regional bank—a fund which compensates operators if their day's losses exceed their income. The bank protects the eight games (called "wheels") from severe losses; in return, the wheels pay the bank a percentage of their profits. Members of the Lupollo family own and manage six of the wheels. Two other wheels are run by Puerto Ricans who purchased a franchise from the family. Each wheel's manager employs a district controller to operate the wheel. Under each district controller are controllers who operate branch banks. Each controller is responsible for several collectors who pick up the day's bets from runners. At the bottom level, the runners take the bets from the actual bettors. Each day, bets filter upward through this system and, after the winning number is determined, payments to winners filter back down. The final element in the scheme is the layoff bank, operated by another family member. If many bettors pick the same number, the regional bank would have difficulty paying all the winners if that number happened to win. In such cases, the banker may choose to "lay off" some of these bets. The regional bank pays the layoff bank a fee for accepting the risk of paying off should this number win. The Lupollo numbers game employs an unspecified—but obviously large—number of people. It is a complicated operation which reveals the capacity of a deviant formal organization with an elaborate division of labor.

The Lupollos' legitimate and illegitimate enterprises are not separate entities; funds move between the two sides of the family business (Ianni, 1972:99-103). Money earned through the numbers game and loan sharking is invested in the family's legitimate businesses. In this way, the money is "laundered," placed on record so that social control agents cannot prove that the money comes from illicit sources. At the same time, some of the profits from the legitimate businesses are reinvested in loan sharking, where there is a high rate of return. This ability to transfer money between licit and illicit enterprises protects the family against social control efforts and maximizes profits.

Are organized crime families formal organizations? Experts disagree on the issue. The 1967 federal Task Force on Organized Crime described organized crime families in terms usually reserved for legitimate formal organizations: "Family organization is rationally designed with an integrated set of positions geared to maximize profits" (President's Commission, 1967a:7). It supported this claim with a chart depicting a typical family as a hierarchy with five levels: a boss, an underboss, lieutenants, soldiers, and nonmembers (President's Commission, 1967a: 9). In short, the Task Force saw the family's structure as that of a formal organization. Ianni (1972:153) challenges this view:

> Secret societies such as the *Mafia* . . . are not rationally designed and consciously constructed; they are responsive to culture and are patterned by tradition. They are not hierarchies of organizational positions which can be diagrammed and then changed by recasting the organization chart; they are patterns of relationship among individuals which have the force of kinship, and so they can only be changed by drastic, often fatal, action. Secret criminal groups such as the *Mafia* and the *Camorra* are not formal organizations; they are traditional social systems.[1]

The Lupollos' bonds are familial, not formal. In Ianni's view, the family members' behavior is understandable only within the context of the traditional Italian culture. Authority in the Lupollo family depends less on one's position in the organizational hierarchy than upon one's generation (the older the member's generation, the greater the authority), lineage (Lupollos have more authority than members related through marriage), and specialization (a member with special knowledge, such as an accountant, or special contacts, such as acquaintances in the government, has more authority) (Ianni, 1972:107-31). Allocating authority on the basis of one's generation and lineage is consistent with traditional Italian values. Similarly, power within the Lupollo family depends upon informal alliances. While Joe Lupollo, the family head, theoretically controls the family, small groups of family members, linked by informal arrangements, maneuver to gain power and influence. Ianni emphasizes informal, rather than formal, relationships among the Lupollos.

Ianni's claim that the Lupollos do not constitute a formal organization joins the larger sociological debate about the relationships among organized criminals. Two competing perspectives exist (Albini, 1971:155-214). The evolutional-centralization perspective argues that Italian-American organized crime families, such as the Lupollos, evolved from the Sicilian mafia into a centralized criminal conspiracy (R. Anderson, 1965; Cressey, 1969; President's Commission, 1967a). This view emphasizes the formal hierarchy of authority within each family and charges that the families are united in a conspiracy which is controlled by a national commission of powerful family heads that sets policy and settles disputes between families. The evolutional-centralization perspective treats organized crime families and the nationwide conspiracy as formal organizations. In contrast, the developmental-associational perspective views Italian-American organized crime families as informal associations which developed in response to oppressive conditions which confronted Italian immigrants in urban America (Albini, 1971; D. Bell, 1960; Ianni, 1972). The experiences of Italians paralleled those of immigrants from other countries who entered American society at the bottom (D. Bell, 1960:115-36). Italian and Sicilian immigrants arrived in the United States in the late nineteenth and early twentieth centuries. For the most part, they were poor people from rural villages. Immigrating to large cities in a foreign country, they faced discrimination against their poverty and ethnicity. Discrimination blocked them from conventional routes for upward mobility through education or business, so some chose other, less conventional routes to success, including organized crime. The ethnicity of American organized criminals changed as new ethnic groups entered the country and faced discrimination. Many nineteenth century criminals were Irish; Jews became prominent around the turn of the century; and Italians rose to power in the 1920s. Some observers believe that a similar shift is occurring in modern America, with Blacks, Chicanos, and Puerto Ricans developing new deviant formal organizations (Ianni, 1974; Lewis, 1980). In this view, Italian-American organized crime families did not simply evolve from the Sicilian mafia; rather, they developed in reaction to the discrimination against Italian immigrants. At the same time, the new criminal organizations reflected the immigrants' culture, valuing respect, age, lineage, and so on. Family members were tied together, not by a formal, bureaucratic structure, but by blood and friendship. Ianni's portrait of the Lupollos fits this developmental-associational perspective.

Resolving the debate between the evolutional-centralization and the developmental-associational perspectives would clarify the nature of the ties between organized crime family members. Both interpretations may be partially correct. Their disagreement reflects, in part, their different research subjects. The evolutional-centralization literature tends to look at the organized crime family as a web which links small-time street criminals—the drug dealer, the bookie, the numbers runner—to deviants at successive hierarchical levels, culminating in the family head or the national commission. In contrast, developmental-associational studies tend to focus on the group at the top—the family's leadership. Ianni (1972) limits his attention to fifteen men who run the Lupollo family; he does not consider other individuals who actually carry out the family's criminal operations. In this view, the Lupollo numbers racket involves only three of the fifteen family leaders; yet Figure 3-2 shows that dozens of other criminals work in the racket's lower levels, from manager to runner. To argue that relationships among the fifteen family leaders reflect informal ties of lineage and respect does not prove that these same ties bind all of the persons involved in the family's criminal activities. Throughout most of the organization, relationships, particularly between supervisors and subordinates, reflect formally defined rank and authority.

McIntosh (1973:43) charts a middle path between the two interpretations, arguing that mafia families "may be bureaucrat*ish*, but they are not bureaucratic" (emphasis in original). Respectable formal organizations operate in a legally defined arena—their actions are legally binding. Criminal formal organizations lack this advantage:

> For none of the contracts, which for most businesses are enforceable at law, that are made by racket bosses have any legal status. This is important at four junctures: in connection with the holding and accumulation of racket capital, and in connection with control over relations with subordinates, competitors, and customer-victims. (McIntosh, 1973:43; cf. Block, 1980)

Because criminals have no legal right to their profits, the members of organized crime families must transform their money into legitimate investments (as when the Lupollos shift funds into the family's respectable businesses). Nor can subordinates be held accountable with legally binding contracts. Consequently, families must devise other ways of binding members to the organization, including rituals of indoctrination, implicating members in the organization's activities (e.g., ordering a new member to commit a murder), or using enforcers to punish disloyal members. With competing criminal organizations:

> There can be no formal procedures for mergers, takeovers or price-fixing and any procedures for hiring, firing or promotion are purely local. So the boundaries of the organization may often be in flux. The same methods—i. violence, ii. control over law enforcement and effective and profitable organization of the racket, iii. loyalty to traditional and criminal norm [sic] and 'fear of being out in the cold'—are used to control relations both with rivals and with subordinates. (McIntosh, 1973:44-45)

Finally, the family leaders solve the problems of controlling customers and victims by using low-ranking members as a buffer. A bettor does not deal with the Lupollo family; he or she bets with a specific number runner who is responsible for dealing with that bettor. Family leaders do not consider number runners and other low-level deviants to be family members. In short, because organized crime families engage in deviant activities, they are unlike respectable formal organizations. Legitimate organizations can turn to the law to enforce their dealings; deviant formal organizations cannot. As a consequence, deviants depend upon informal ties, such as kinship, loyalty, respect, and fear, to bind their arrangements.

These informal bonds reinforce a relatively sophisticated structure. The Lupollo numbers game is complex, but it is just part of the family's elaborate division of labor. Other family operations serve other functions, such as warding off social control efforts. Like a mob, a deviant formal organization uses corruption to protect itself against social control agents. Members may bribe individual agents to overlook particular operations. But corruption also takes other, subtler forms, such as fostering links to legitimate political parties or official agencies. In the Lupollo family, members with connections to city, state, and federal officials have considerable influence (Ianni, 1972: 114). An organized crime family which helps a lawyer become a judge may be repaid when the judge's influence protects family members from severe sanctions. Just as a family must devise methods of corrupting officials, it must develop ways of carrying out other important tasks. Members may be assigned to gather intelligence, enforce the organization's rules by punishing violators, socialize promising newcomers, and so forth. These operations must be coordinated over space; family leaders set policy regarding finances, personnel, and relations with customers, social control agents, and other families. Long-term planning is necessary because an organization's operations may extend over years. This stability reflects the organization's sources of income; systematic extortion and supplying illicit goods and services return high profits at a steady rate so long as the organization's members coordinate the necessary parts of their operations.

Coordinating Large Teams

Members of the Vice Lords and the Lupollo family occupy positions in formal structures of deviants. Much of this section asked whether these structures should be considered "formal" organizations. The largest deviant formal organizations are relatively small, numbering a few hundred or, at most, a few thousand members, while respectable formal organizations, such as armies or corporations, may have hundreds of thousands of members. Deviant organizations do not have all of the trappings of large corporations or government agencies. They also lack the protection which the law provides legitimate formal organizations. At the same time, deviant and respectable formal organizations share some important characteristics: both are intentionally designed to solve the problems they face; both articulate their structure and their rules for operation; and both efficiently carry out complicated operations over extended time and space. Complicated mob operations, such as hustling a dice game, require skill and a specialized division of labor, but they are simple in comparison to some operations by deviant formal organizations. In a numbers racket, dozens, perhaps hundreds, of members take bets, send the appropriate sums of money up the organizational hierarchy, and, after the winning number is known, pay the appropriate winnings to the lucky bettors. These tasks must be done accurately and efficiently, there must be precautions against cheating and social control interference, and this complicated operation must be coordinated day after day. For such tasks, the informal ties which bind less sophisticated forms of deviant organization simply cannot provide adequate cohesion and coordination. Managing operations which extend over time and space requires a formal structure.

DEVIANT COMMUNITIES: AN ASIDE

This book has described a continuum of organizational sophistication for deviants, ranging from loners, through colleagues, peers, and mobs, to deviant formal organizations. In this scheme, formal organizations are the most sophisticated form of deviant organization. Their members associate with one another, commit deviant acts in each other's presence, have an elaborate division of labor, and extend their operations over time and space. Before considering some consequences of the social organization of deviants, two questions arise. Do deviants ever organize in forms more sophisticated than formal organizations? And if so, under what conditions do these highly sophisticated organizational forms emerge? Two additional organizational forms—worlds and communities—deserve consideration.

Individuals involved in different types of deviance often know and have sociable contacts with one another. They may even frequent the same places—an after-hours club may attract career thieves, prostitutes, and organized criminals as regular patrons (Roebuck and Frese, 1976). Deviants who share these contacts may view each other as belonging to the same "scene" or "world," sharing some of the same attitudes and problems (Irwin, 1977; Unruh, 1979). A deviant world has a large but imprecisely defined membership. Its members share a sense of their common deviant status and an argot composed of words common to different deviant groups, but they do not share a code of conduct or a sense of responsibility for one another. Relationships between members of a deviant world resemble the loose ties between deviant colleagues. Deviant worlds exist, but they are not a highly sophisticated form of organization.

On the other hand, communities are highly sophisticated, and deviants sometimes form communities. For example, sociologists often speak of contemporary American homosexual communities (Dank, 1971; Delph, 1978; Harry and DeVall, 1978; Hooker, 1967; J. Lee, 1979; Leznoff and Westley, 1956; Warren, 1974; Wolf, 1979). Before evaluating the claim that homosexuals form communities, the term "community" must be defined— a surprisingly difficult task.

Sociologists use the term "community" to refer to such different phenomena as a small village, an urban ethnic group, and a prison population. There are many competing definitions, but "most students would agree that the human community is a social group inhabiting a common territory and having one or more additional common ties" (Hillery, 1968:11). These ties can include a sense of shared identity, a common subculture, institutions which function to meet the members' needs, and so on. Communities differ in the number and strength of their ties; some are self-sufficient, while others depend on the larger society for many services. Self-sufficiency strengthens the ties between members; dependency on a larger society weakens them. A community which maintains its own institutions to serve its members' needs is institutionally complete:

> Ethnic communities can vary enormously in their social organization. At one extreme, there is the community which consists essentially in a network of interpersonal relations: members of a certain ethnic group seek each other's companionship; friendship groups and cliques are formed. But beyond this informal network, no formal organization may exist. . . . Institutional completeness would be at its extreme whenever the ethnic community could perform all the services required by its members. (Breton, 1964:194)

Communities, then, take different forms and this range must be kept in mind when applying the term to deviants. Using the term in a loose sense, to refer to "friendship groups and cliques," means that deviant worlds, peers, and even colleagues can be considered communities. This section adopts a narrower definition of community—groups which share a common territory and a higher degree of institutional completeness.

Homosexuals offer the most promising example of a contemporary deviant community. Politicians, the media, and homosexuals, as well as sociologists, speak of the "the gay community." Like heterosexuals, homosexuals form a market composed of people looking for sexual partners. In societies which consider homosexuals deviant, this market is illicit and the members must be discreet. As chapter 2 noted, illicit markets often form the focus for deviant peer groups whose members participate in deviant activities together. Peer groups usually involve small circles of acquaintances, but homosexual markets sometimes develop in gathering places which attract many individuals, most of whom do not know one another personally. There are many reasons for frequenting these places. Like heterosexuals, homosexuals want to find compatible partners, and success is more likely if they can choose from a large group of candidates; discrimination against homosexuals makes it especially hard to maintain long-term relationships, so that a relatively large proportion of homosexuals are likely to be seeking partners; some homosexuals pursue promiscuity as a goal; and social control agencies may try to limit the number of homosexual gathering places (J. Lee, 1979; Styles, 1979). Because a shared territory is one attribute of a community, these gathering places—particularly gay bars—deserve more attention.

The gay bar is the central institution for urban homosexuals. These establishments have a long history (Jonathan Katz, 1976:61-81; Trumbach, 1977). A bar typically is a city's first gathering place for homosexuals. Where homosexuality is deviant, the gay bar offers a solution to several problems. Since most heterosexuals do not know which bars are gay, homosexuals can go to a gay bar discreetly, without arousing suspicion. The bar provides an opportunity to meet strangers who are homosexual; it functions as a sexual marketplace (Achilles, 1967). Patrons "cruise" one another; each individual examines the others and indicates an interest in some, hoping that one of these overtures will be accepted so that they can leave the bar as a couple. In addition, the bar provides a place for sociable interaction. Individuals can relax and acknowledge their sexual preferences without worrying about exposure.

Gay bars mirror the gay population. They only operate where there are enough homosexuals to support them (Harry and DeVall, 1978:134-54). One homosexual guide book lists at least one gay bar in every American city with a population over 250,000, in 74 percent of cities with 100,000 to 250,000 citizens, but in only 39 percent of cities with 50,000 to 99,000 people, and in 7 percent of cities with 10,000 to 49,000 people. Moreover, the bars in smaller cities tend to cater to a mixed homosexual clientele, whereas gay bars in larger cities specialize—some offer dancing or entertainment, others attract clientele of a particular age, race, or sexual preference. The policies of local social control agencies also affect gay bars (Achilles, 1967; A. Bell and Weinberg, 1978:233-63). Some agencies ignore the bars; others set standards for patrons' conduct, such as forbidding slow dancing or any bodily contact, such as holding hands. Still others harass gay bars and their patrons—agents may try to entrap patrons or demand payoffs from the proprietors. These policies sometimes face resistance by the patrons. The 1969 Stonewall riot in New York, which marked the beginning of the gay liberation movement, began in response to a police raid on a gay bar (Humphreys, 1972; M. Weinberg and Williams, 1974: 33-46).

In many American cities, gay bars became less important as other gay institutions developed (A. Bell and Weinberg, 1978:233-63; Harry and DeVall, 1978; Humphreys, 1972; J. Lee, 1979). In the political arena, for example, gay interest groups take stands on public issues. The early homophile organizations, such as the Mattachine Society, lobbied against discriminatory laws. Their successors, gay liberation groups, demonstrate for a variety of gay rights. In some cities with large gay populations, homosexuals have organized as a political force, endorsing politicians who support gay rights or running their own candidates. Large cities also feature services for gays, such as gay magazines and newspapers and churches with gay congregations. Gay bookstores and coffeehouses may be designed as gathering places (Wolf, 1979:106-35). Gay businesses, often owned and operated by homosexuals, advertise in gay media in hopes of attracting gay customers. Of course, to the degree that a city's homosexuals trade with the same firms, those establishments become part of the network of locations frequented by gays, so that the central function of the gay bar as gathering place becomes less important as other gathering places emerge. Some urban neighborhoods become defined as gay, with homosexuals composing a large proportion of the residents and local bars, restaurants, and businesses catering to gay customers.

The territories controlled by a city's homosexuals can range from a single gay bar to institutionally complete neighborhoods:

> A gay citizen of Toronto can buy a home through a gay real estate agent familiar with the types of housing and neighborhoods most suitable to gay clients. He can close the deal through a gay lawyer, and insure with a gay insurance agent. If he is new to the community and cannot ask acquaintances for the names of these agents, he can consult the Gay Yellow Pages, a listing of businesses and services which is available in many larger cities. Or he can approach a typical source of connection with the gay community, such as a gay bookstore, or he can consult a local gay newspaper or periodical. . . . He can contribute money to tax-deductible gay foundations, participate in gay political groups, and enjoy gay-produced programs on cable television. To keep him up to date on everything happening in his gay community he can telephone the Gay Line, which is updated weekly. (J. Lee, 1979:179-80)

A critic might argue that the ties among the patrons of a city's only gay bar are not strong enough to form a community. But certainly homosexuals in cities such as Toronto, with their wide range of businesses, service organizations, media, and interest groups, constitute a community.

But is this gay community a *deviant* community? In recent years, public attitudes toward homosexuality have changed dramatically (Humphreys, 1972; Spector and Kitsuse, 1977:13-20). Twenty years ago, the American Psychiatric Association formally defined homosexuality as a type of mental illness and the vast majority of homosexuals remained "in the closet," afraid to acknowledge their sexual preferences. People who admitted their homosexuality could lose their jobs or even be committed to mental hospitals. Police harassment of gay bars was common. While homosexuals remain a minority, rejected by some heterosexuals, they are moving toward equal status under the law. In 1974, the American Psychiatric Association passed a resolution declaring that homosexuality was not a psychiatric disorder. Many states and municipalities passed legislation protecting homosexuals' rights. In several states, homosexual acts, when carried out by consenting adults in privacy, are no longer illegal. The gay liberation movement, advocating "gay pride," brought many gay people out of the closet to publicly acknowledge their homosexuality. Gay candidates run for and are elected to state and local offices.

In short, the emergence of the institutionally complete gay community paralleled homosexuality's vindication from deviance. Although sociologists traditionally included homosexuality in their discussions of deviance, this characterization has become increasingly questionable. To a substantial degree, homosexuality has been vindicated (Best, 1979). This is not to say that everyone accepts homosexuality as respectable behavior. At this writing,

the issue is hotly debated. But many behaviors which were once defined as deviant, such as cigarette smoking, are no longer sanctioned by social control agencies—and are therefore no longer deviant—even though some people retain moral objections to the behaviors. For homosexuals in large cities, the question is no longer whether there is a homosexual community, but whether that community should be considered deviant.

Contemporary homosexuals sometimes form communities but, with homosexuality's vindication, they are not communities of deviants. However, there are historical examples of deviant communities which existed in spite of social control efforts. In each case, the deviant community was isolated from the larger society. Isolation fosters a sense of community and makes it more difficult for social control agents to interfere (Breton, 1964). The basis of isolation varies. Seventeenth century pirate crews, for example, were physically isolated from conventional society; living on ships or in secret camps, they had to be self-sufficient (Rediker, 1981). In nineteenth century London, class formed the basis for isolation:

> The areas occupied by the lowest classes were called 'rookeries,' and until the latter part of the century, a rookery was a thieves' quarter. From the rookery criminals would move out to do their day's or their night's work; to the rookery they would retire if they were pursued or when they had made enough for their needs. Their meeting-places—usually called 'flash-houses' in the earlier part of the century—were usually in the rookery, and there too the receivers were mostly found. (Tobias, 1967:68)

Rookeries thrived because the police chose not to enter them. Early police concentrated on protecting respectable neighborhoods; they lacked the resources to control the rookeries. Similarly, deviant communities developed in late nineteenth century red-light districts (Rose, 1974). In addition to brothels, these districts supplied supporting services, such as musicians, bars, printers (of guide books, handbills, and so on), and laundries. The districts' isolation reflected social control policy; the authorities sought to restrict the spread of vice to respectable neighborhoods by ignoring it in the red-light districts.

These examples suggest two conditions under which deviant communities emerge. First, isolation from the larger society can serve as the basis for a community. While pirates, rookeries, and red-light districts offer examples of communities built on isolation, it is more difficult to identify contemporary examples. This reflects the relatively efficient operation of modern social control agencies, which attempt to extend enforcement into all corners of society. While the ability to enforce laws varies from place to place and group to group, agents usually can supply enough pressure to inhibit community formation. Second, the example of contemporary homosexual communities suggests that communities may form as social control efforts diminish during the process of vindication.

This section began by asking whether deviants organize in forms more sophisticated than formal organizations. Deviants do participate in deviant

worlds, but the bonds between a world's members are weak and a deviant world is not a highly sophisticated organizational form. In contrast, communities are highly sophisticated, but social control efforts in modern society usually are too extensive to permit community formation. For practical purposes, then, the dimension of sophistication outlined in this book, ranging from loners to formal organizations, encompasses virtually all deviants.

CONCLUSION

Much of the discussion about deviant formal organizations and deviant communities focused on the applicability of standard sociological definitions of these terms—definitions which describe respectable organizations—to deviant phenomena. Sociologists are comfortable applying some organizational terms, particularly subculture, to deviants, but they often argue that deviants cannot form "true" formal organizations or "true" communities. Yet the terms do seem appropriate. If formal organizations are characterized by their intentional design, then some deviant organizations fit this category. The differences between deviant and respectable formal organizations are largely a consequence of two factors. First, deviant formal organizations tend to be smaller than their respectable counterparts. Second, deviant formal organizations are deviant—an obvious but easily neglected fact. The activities of respectable formal organizations depend on the support of social control agencies; companies enter into contracts because they know the courts will insure that those agreements will be honored. In contrast, social control agents are likely to interfere with a deviant formal organization and the deviants cannot afford to place their activities on a permanent, accessible record.

The question of deviant communities is somewhat different. The stronger the ties among community members, the more institutionally complete and the more visible the community becomes. So long as social control agents try to eradicate a type of deviance, communities can emerge only where they are isolated from the agents' attacks. Or, when those policies are challenged and the deviance is vindicated, communities of former deviants can form. In modern America, the dimension of sophistication for forms of deviant organization does not extend beyond deviant formal organizations.

Chapters 2 and 3 described five principal forms of social organization: loners, colleagues, peers, mobs, and formal organizations. Some of the differences among these forms were considered in passing. Chapter 4 focuses on these differences and, in a more systematic fashion, explores the consequences of organizational sophistication for deviants and social control agents.

NOTES

[1]Excerpt from *A Family Business* by Francis A. J. Ianni, p. 153, © Russell Sage Foundation, Basic Books, Inc.,Publishers, New York, 1972.

CHAPTER FOUR
THE SIGNIFICANCE OF RELATIONS BETWEEN DEVIANTS

Forms of deviant organization can be arrayed along a dimension of organizational sophistication. Chapters 2 and 3 described five basic forms: loners, colleagues, peers, mobs, and formal organizations. Loners operate as individuals—they do not associate with one another. Although colleagues perform their deviant acts alone, they share a subculture and interact with one another outside the deviant transaction. Peers perform deviant acts together, at the same time and in the same place. They have a minimal division of labor, with members performing similar roles, and limited stratification, with members operating as equals. Mobs are small teams which conduct coordinated deviant operations requiring an elaborate division of labor, with specialized, often highly skilled roles. Deviant formal organizations extend over time and space. They usually have a large membership, an elaborate division of labor and authority, and a set of rules that is actively enforced. This chapter compares these different forms of deviant organization. It develops five propositions about the consequences of deviant organization for deviants and social control agents. These consequences reflect differences in the ways deviants in different organizational forms manage the problems posed by their deviance.

Deviants face several problems. First, they must acquire the resources needed for their deviant operations. Resources include knowledge and skill for undertaking deviant operations; to enjoy marijuana, for instance, the individual must know how to prepare the drug and smoke it. Resources also include any equipment needed for performing deviance. For example, safecracking may require explosives, a heavy-duty drill, or a hammer and chisel. Resources vary with the type of deviance. Some deviance requires few, if any, resources; a suicide can simply jump off a building. Other types of deviance, however, require special resources which may be hard to acquire. Most resources needed for respectable activities are widely available through conventional channels, such as schools, books, and businesses. In contrast, some deviant resources are restricted, available only through illicit channels. For instance, to learn how to crack a safe, an individual must be taught by an experienced safecracker; to obtain illicit drugs, one must locate a dealer.

Second, deviants encounter the problem of ideology—how to look at, make sense of, and refer to their particular world. People involved in respectable activities have less need to justify their activities, carefully consider how to relate to others, or use a special vocabulary to communicate with others. However, because deviance involves a violation of major social norms, deviants must justify their offenses, interpreting them as morally acceptable. Furthermore, because conventional guidelines do not cover deviant behavior, deviants also must learn to regulate their own activities and relations with others. For instance, prostitutes must learn how to attract customers and collect payments as well as how to relate to their colleagues. Finally, because deviants may need to talk about their activities with some precision, they need to acquire an argot, a special vocabulary for describing their world. A deviant ideology provides justifications for deviance, norms for regulating deviant action, and special terms for describing deviance.

Third, deviants face the problem of gaining satisfaction from deviance. The rewards individuals seek from deviance vary considerably, ranging from physical satisfaction to monetary profit. Deviants, like respectable people, seek sufficient rewards to make their participation worthwhile. However, their rewards are relatively problematic. Deviants must ask whether their deviant involvement is worth the risk of being sanctioned by social control agents. They also face the possibility of exploitation by other deviants who might attack, cheat, or betray them. While respectable people can report exploitation to the authorities, deviants cannot turn to social control agents if other deviants take advantage of them. Thus, deviants seek rewards which compensate for their time and effort as well as the additional risks of sanctions and exploitation.

Fourth, deviants confront the problem of security. While respectable people worry about security from exploitation by deviants, deviants must worry about social control agents' sanctions as well as exploitation by other deviants. Since they cannot get help from the authorities, deviants must devise their own ways to maintain security. These techniques include concealing their activities and identities, insuring that their associates and victims do not give damaging information to the authorities, and neutralizing social control efforts.

Social organization helps deviants solve these problems. Deviant associates can provide an individual with necessary resources, a deviant ideology, rewards, and security. However, the degree to which associates can help solve these problems varies with the sophistication of their organization. The more sophisticated the deviant organization, the greater its capacity to solve its members' problems. In turn, the greater the organization's sophistication, the more difficulty social control agents have in apprehending and sanctioning the deviants. This chapter's propositions develop these points.

Although the propositions were derived from reports of field research, including the studies summarized in chapters 2 and 3, they must be qualified in two ways. First, the propositions deliberately concentrate on organizational sophistication and ignore the impact of other factors, such as the deviant's background or the character of the deviant activity. These other factors may have different, even opposing, consequences for deviants and authorities. Further study of the propositions is needed to determine the circumstances under which they apply. Second, the field studies which provide the empirical foundation for the propositions generally describe deviants in the contemporary United States. Accordingly, the consequences of organizational sophistication outlined in the propositions may not apply to other societies or historical periods. Comparative research is needed to discover the impact of social organization on deviants and social control agents in different societies and at different times.

CONSEQUENCES OF ORGANIZATIONAL SOPHISTICATION

Proposition 1: The more sophisticated the form of deviant social organization, the greater its members' capability for complex deviant operations. Deviant activities, like respectable activities, vary in their complexity. Compared to simple activities, complex lines of action demand more careful preparation and execution, and they take longer to complete. The complexity of a deviant operation refers to the number of elements required to carry it through to completion; the more component parts to an activity, the greater its complexity.[1] The complexity of a deviant act depends on two identifiable types of elements. First, there are the *resources* needed for the operation's completion. Complex activities often require special knowledge, skill, or equipment. Simple acts, however, can be carried out without such resources. Second, there is the *organization* of the deviant transaction—the number and types of roles needed for the operation's completion (see Part II). Some deviant acts can be accomplished by a single actor. Other deviant acts require joint participation by two or more people; the actors in a transaction may perform a similar role, as when marijuana smokers share a joint, or they may perform different roles, such as attacker and victim or seller and buyer. Further, the coordination among these roles varies from minimal coordination, as in a group of juvenile vandals, to precise routines, as in a mob of road hustlers. The more people involved, the more roles they perform, and the more coordination among those roles, the more complex the deviant transaction's organization. The more resources and organization involved in a deviant operation, the greater the operation's complexity.

In general, deviants in more sophisticated forms of organization tend to engage in more complex activities. The deviant acts of loners often are simple, requiring little in the way of resources or organization. The person who commits suicide, for example, usually needs no assistance from others and only minimal knowledge and skill. Similarly, while a murderer needs a victim, the act is relatively simple. Most murderers do not have associates; they grab whatever weapon is handy and use everyday knowledge and skill in the attack. Although colleagues work apart from one another, their operations typically involve other people. Pool hustlers require suckers, and prostitutes need customers. Further, colleagues may require special resources to perform their deviant operations—pool hustlers must have money to bet, the skill to shoot a good game of pool, and the ability to dupe the sucker. Colleagues share other resources, such as geographic areas. The hustlers' pool hall and the prostitutes' red-light district contain the elements necessary for deviant operations, including suckers and customers. Peers may undertake operations in which they are the only ones present, performing complementary or comparable roles, as when two persons engage in illicit sexual intercourse or skid row tramps share a bottle of cheap wine. Other peer activities involve nonmembers, as when a delinquent gang robs a passer-by. In either case, while several people may be involved, peers' operations tend to be fairly simple, requiring few special resources. Mobs' deviant activities involve substantially more specialization and coordination among the members' roles, as well as special knowledge, skill, and equipment. A road hustlers' crew, for instance, includes a mechanic, a shoot-up man, and muscle with special skills and, in the mechanic's case, deviant equipment. Finally, the operations of deviant formal organizations tend to be particularly complex, requiring substantial resources and elaborate organization. Major off-track betting operations, with staff members at local, district, and regional offices who carry out a variety of clerical and supervisory tasks on a daily basis, are an exceedingly complex form of deviance.

The relationship between the sophistication of deviant organization and the complexity of deviant activities is not perfect. Deviants organized in less sophisticated forms sometimes perform relatively complex operations. Loners, for instance, can commit acts of considerable complexity.

The computer criminal who single-handedly devises a complicated scheme for breaking into and stealing from computerized records, the embezzler who carries out an elaborate series of illicit financial manipulations, and the physician who juggles drug records in order to maintain his or her addiction to narcotics are engaged in complex violations that call for substantial resources. However, these offenses cannot be committed by everyone. These loners draw upon resources which they command through their conventional positions, turning them to deviant uses. The computer criminal is usually an experienced programmer, the embezzler occupies a position of financial trust, and the physician has been trained in the use of drugs. Possessing these special resources makes the loner's complex operations possible. Most loners lack the resources necessary for more than one type of complex deviance. For example, physicians cannot commit computer thefts or embezzlements. In short, the more concentrated the resources necessary for a deviant operation, the less sophisticated the form of deviant organization required. If one person commands all the necessary resources, that person can operate as a loner. Conversely, where the necessary resources are dispersed, more sophisticated forms of deviant organization are needed to undertake complex deviant operations.

On the other hand, members of more sophisticated organizational forms sometimes commit relatively simple deviant acts. For instance, a deviant formal organization which operates an illicit gambling operation assigns members to perform such simple tasks as taking bets and paying off winners. However, these simple acts are components of larger, more complex endeavors. While taking a bet is a simple act, the mechanics of the gambling operation, managing thousands of bets over considerable time and space, are complex indeed. Similarly, a barroom dispute between two friends which ends in murder is very different from an execution which is ordered and carried out by members of a formal organization, even though the two acts may appear equally simple. In the latter case, the killing may be intended as a means of maintaining discipline by demonstrating the organization's capacity to punish wayward members. Thus, actions by members of sophisticated forms of deviant organization must be understood within the broad context of the organization's operations.

Sophisticated forms of deviant organization have advantages beyond the ability to undertake complex operations by coordinating the actions and pooling the resources of their individual members. Some deviant activities require a minimal level of organization. Illicit sexual intercourse demands the participation of two parties, and pickpocketing usually calls for the precise coordination of at least two partners. In many other cases, it may be possible to conduct a deviant operation using a relatively unsophisticated form of organization, but the operation is considerably easier if a more sophisticated form of deviant organization is used. This is because more sophisticated forms of organization enjoy several advantages. They can manage several types of deviant operations; a mob can shift from picking pockets to shoplifting in order to avoid the police, and an organized crime family can operate several different rackets simultaneously (Maurer, 1964:55; Ianni, 1972:87-106). These operations can occur with greater frequency and over a broader range of territory, and, as discussed below, the members of sophisticated organizational forms are better protected from the efforts of social control agents.

Proposition 2: The more sophisticated the form of deviant social organization, the more elaborate the socialization of its members. Beginning deviants need to acquire two types of knowledge. First, they must learn how to perform deviant acts, acquiring the appropriate *skills and techniques.* Second, they must learn a *cognitive perspective,* a distinctive scheme for understanding and making sense of their new, deviant world (cf. Shibutani, 1961:118-127). The perspective includes an ideology which accounts for deviance, the individual's involvement in it, and the organizational form to which the individual belongs, as well as a special vocabulary for speaking about these and related matters. In many cases, newcomers acquire both the skills and techniques and a cognitive perspective from experienced deviants through the process of socialization.

As forms of deviant organization increase in sophistication, the socialization of newcomers becomes more elaborate. Loners do not depend on other deviants for instruction in deviant skills or a cognitive perspective. Instead, they acquire the skills and ideology needed for deviance through their participation in conventional social scenes. For example, murderers learn in conventional life that situations of interpersonal conflict can be resolved with physical force, and they use culturally widespread justifications for killing people (cf. Bohannon, 1960; Wolfgang and Ferracuti, 1967). Embezzlers learn techniques for subverting a financial trust in the course of respectable vocational training, and they adapt justifications, such as "borrowing," from conventional business ideology. In contrast, colleagues teach one another a great deal. Although pool hustlers usually know how to shoot pool before they begin hustling, their colleagues provide a rich cognitive perspective, including a sense of "we-ness," norms for conduct, a system for stratifying the hustling world, and an extensive argot. Similarly, experienced deviants teach new prostitutes a variety of skills, including sexual techniques and methods for managing troublesome customers and collecting payment, as well as a cognitive perspective for interpreting the activities of colleagues, pimps, customers, and others.[2] Peers also may receive training from experienced deviants. In other cases, inexperienced peers teach one another through a process of emerging norms; members collectively decide to perform a particular deviant act, devise a rationale to justify it, and develop some norms to regulate their behavior in the course of the offense (cf. Turner, 1964). For instance, vandalism may emerge through a mutually constructed interpretation by juvenile peers that destructive activities are suitable to the particular situation (Wade, 1967). Sometimes the knowledge peers acquire serves largely symbolic functions, affirming the group's identity and solidarity, as when a club of motorcycle outlaws drafts a written constitution (Reynolds, 1967:134-136). In mobs and formal organizations, members receive extensive instruction in deviant skills and techniques. Often, this instruction involves an experienced deviant coaching an apprentice over an extended period of time. For instance, under an experienced safecracker's supervision, a novice learns about the different kinds of safes and the ways they can be opened, as well as the ways to obtain the equipment needed to open them (Chambliss, 1972). Members of these sophisticated organizational forms also acquire an extensive cognitive perspective that focuses on relatively practical matters. Their codes of conduct specify the responsibilities members have in their dealings with one another, social control agents, and others; these codes call for secrecy about members' activities and identities, honesty in dealings among members, and assistance for members in trouble with control agents.

Two circumstances affect socialization in different forms of deviant organization. First, organizational sophistication affects the scope and style of the training process. The amount of training tends to increase with the sophistication of the deviant organization. While the skills and techniques required to perform deviant roles vary, there is a tendency for more sophisticated forms of organization to incorporate one or more highly skilled roles which require lengthy training and practice to perfect. For instance, the road hustler who works with a mob acquires and uses substantially greater skill than the rough hustler who operates as a loner. Also, more sophisticated forms of organization often have broad perspectives; members must learn a large body of specialized knowledge. In general, loners do not have a distinctive perspective, while colleagues and peers may share a loose and relatively limited perspective and members of mobs and formal organizations have a strong and encompassing perspective. The method of socialization also tends to be organized differently according to the sophistication of the deviant organization. While loners operate as their own agents of socialization, colleagues and peers usually socialize one another. Mobs and formal organizations, in contrast, typically apprentice newcomers to experienced deviants.

Second, the newcomer's motivation for entering deviance affects his or her socialization experiences. Loners, of course, choose deviance on their own. In more sophisticated forms of organization, some newcomers may request admission, but many are recruited by experienced deviants. Peers often recruit widely, as when a delinquent gang tries to enlist all of the neighborhood boys of a given age and ethnicity. In contrast, mobs and formal organizations recruit selectively; they judge the character and commitment of prospective members, sometimes demanding evidence of their skill and prior experience. For loners, entry into deviance is often a defensive act, intended to ward off some immediate threat (Lofland, 1969:41-103). A person in a position of financial trust embezzles in order to resolve a nonshareable problem. Peers frequently commit deviant acts in search of stimulation. Swingers, recreational drug users, skid row winos, and motorcycle outlaws find their deviance physically or emotionally satisfying; their deviance has an adventurous quality (Lofland, 1969:104-117). Mobs and formal organizations adopt a more instrumental approach to deviance. For members of these organizational forms, deviance is a calculated means of gaining profit or power. Whether a newcomer chooses or is chosen by his or her fellow deviants shapes the relationships during socialization. Similarly, the motives behind entry into deviance affects the newcomer's commitment to and perception of socialization.

These differences in the scope of socialization, the way the process is organized, and the novice's motivation for entering deviance help demonstrate the relationship between organizational sophistication and the elaborateness of the socialization process. Yet this relationship is not perfect. Colleagues represent a partial exception to the pattern. They resemble members of mobs and formal organizations in that they adopt an instrumental perspective, view their deviance as a career, accept deviance as a central identity, and sometimes learn through apprenticeship to an experienced deviant. While peers have a more sophisticated form of organization, their participation in deviance typically rests on their shared involvement in an illicit marketplace or leisure-time activity. In contrast, most colleagues are committed to deviance as a way of earning a living. However, because colleagues share a relatively unsophisticated form of organization, they labor under restrictions that are greater than those faced by members of mobs and formal organizations. Their socialization is of limited scope. Pool hustlers, for example, learn about dealing with suckers and other hustlers, but they learn very little from their colleagues about playing pool. The code of conduct governing colleagues is less encompassing and less binding than the codes for more sophisticated forms, and the deviance of colleagues usually is less profitable. Thus, despite their similarities to members of mobs and formal organizations, the absence of advantages associated with organizational sophistication places colleagues in an unstable situation, where many individuals drift away from deviance after a short time. While colleagues are partial exceptions to the relationship, more sophisticated forms of deviant organization usually provide more elaborate socialization for their members.

Proposition 3: The more sophisticated the form of deviant social organization, the more elaborate the services provided its members. Whether deviant or respectable, every social role poses practical problems for its performers. Some can be solved by providing the actors with resources of various kinds. First, actors may require special *equipment* to perform a role. Just as a dentist needs special instruments to extract a tooth, a safecracker requires explosives, drills, and so on. Second, actors may require *information* about their situation in order to coordinate their behavior with the ongoing action and successfully perform their part in the operation. The dentist needs information about the patient's dental history as well as his or her current problem, and the safecracker needs to know about the type of safe, its location and contents, and the best time to open it without attracting attention. One function of deviant organization is to help solve members' practical problems by supplying them with the necessary equipment and information. In general, the more sophisticated forms of deviant organization provide more of these services.

Deviants differ in their requirements for equipment. Some need little equipment—a mugger can rob a passer-by with a piece of pipe. In such cases, supply poses little problem; deviants can make do with commonplace, conventional objects. Other deviants, however, need unconventional, specialized items which have few, if any, respectable uses, such as the booster boxes used in shoplifting. Some of this equipment may even be illicit; for instance, possessing heroin is a crime. Obtaining such equipment requires access to illicit sources, such as drug dealers. Deviants who require unconventional equipment must develop contacts with an illicit market.

The greater the sophistication of the deviant organization, the greater its members' needs for equipment and the greater its capacity to meet these needs. Loners usually require little equipment. When special needs exist, they are satisfied through conventional channels accessible to the deviants. Physician narcotic addicts obtain drugs from hospital or clinic supplies, and computer criminals gain access to computerized records through their positions as programmers. For the most part, colleagues also supply their own equipment; for example, pool hustlers own their cues. Yet, colleagues also may get assistance; hustlers sometimes turn to financial backers for funding. Peers use equipment in different ways. In some cases, their equipment is merely a symbol of their deviant status, as when the members of a delinquent gang or motorcycle club wear distinctive clothing designating their membership. In other cases, peer groups provide vital equipment to meet their members' needs, as when they organize for purposes of distributing and consuming illicit goods. Networks to supply illicit drugs are the most obvious example. Members of mobs need more equipment, and this equipment tends to be utilitarian. Professional or career theft often requires specialized, unconventional tools, such as explosives for safecracking and booster boxes for shoplifting. In addition to each member's personal equipment, the mob may need special materials for specific projects, such as a getaway car for a robbery. Often, the mob's norms specify the manner of financing such equipment purchases. In still other instances, individuals who own expensive pieces of equipment may cooperate with several different mobs who make use of them; several confidence mobs can use a centrally located "big store." Formal organizations also have extensive equipment needs. Because their operations extend over considerable time and space, formal organizations may invest in an elaborate array of fixed equipment. Off-track bookmaking, for instance, may involve the purchase or rental of offices, office supplies, calculators, computer lines, and automobiles. Special staff members may have the responsibility of maintaining this equipment for the organization (D. Bell, 1960:134). In addition, some formal organizations produce or distribute deviant equipment for other deviants; drug smuggling offers one example.

Deviants need information in order to plan their courses of action. In order to operate efficiently, they must know about opportunities for deviance. In order to operate safely, they also need information about social control agents' movements. The more sophisticated forms of deviant organization have advantages in acquiring and processing such information. Loners depend upon themselves for information. Their knowledge about opportunities and social control efforts comes from such conventional, readily accessible sources as newspapers, television, and radio, as well as their firsthand observations. Their plans cannot take into account opportunities and threats outside their personal notice. In contrast, colleagues and peers can learn considerably more by virtue of their contacts with the deviant "grapevine," a network for relaying information of special interest, such as knowledge about covert social control efforts. In addition, colleagues and peers may have norms that call for members to share relevant information; for example, prostitutes should warn one another about undercover police officers. Mobs cultivate information in more systematic ways. Mob members develop perceptual skills that enable them to "case" victims; in planning a robbery, thieves may observe a bank to learn about daily movements, schedules, protective devices, and so forth (Letkemann, 1973). Some mobs rely on outsiders for necessary information, paying spotters a commission for pointing out opportunities for theft. The deviant grapevine and members' contacts with corrupted officials also help mobs learn the current tactics of social control agents. Formal organizations acquire and process an even more extensive amount of information. Widely distributed members provide information about new opportunities and competition. Also, informants, including corrupted officials, supply information about social control tactics. Deviant formal organizations sometimes learn about the plans of social control agents before they can be implemented, allowing the deviants to adjust their operations to avoid disruption. For instance, a corrupted official notifies the organization about an impending police raid on its regional bookmaking office, and the office members destroy the evidence and vacate the office before the police arrive.

Therefore, more sophisticated forms of deviant organization not only feature more elaborate socialization of members, but they also have a greater capacity to provide members with the equipment and information needed to carry out deviant operations.

Proposition 4: The more sophisticated the form of deviant social organization, the greater its members' involvement in deviance. The first three propositions reflect the importance of interaction among deviants. Complex deviant activities require planning as well as coordination during the operation; socialization often involves interaction between newcomers and experienced deviants; and supplying equipment and information brings deviants into contact with one another. In addition, interaction with other deviants is an important source of social support. Because deviants face the hostility of respectable citizens, as well as the sanctions of social control agents, they turn to one another for support. Fellow deviants may denigrate respectable others, provide an ideology justifying deviance, praise deviant acts, and offer a setting in which offenders can relax without fear. Forms of deviant organization differ in their ability to provide social support for their members, and this difference has important social psychological consequences for deviants' careers and identities. More sophisticated forms of deviant organization are more likely to involve intense contacts between members which provide social support. In turn, the more contact and support the organization provides, the greater the members' involvement in deviance.

The length of deviant careers varies with the form of deviant organization. Longer deviant careers tend to occur in more sophisticated forms of organization. For naive loners, deviance may comprise a single episode, a defensive act to ward off an immediate threat. For systematic loners and many colleagues and peers, involvement in deviance is limited to one period in their lives. Check forgers eventually tire of the constant deceptions, prostitutes grow too old to compete in the sexual marketplace, delinquents move into respectable adult roles, and so on. Members of mobs and formal organizations are more likely to have extended careers, sometimes lasting decades. When their roles are not too physically demanding, deviance can continue until the individual is ready to retire from the work force (Inciardi, 1977).

Deviant careers also vary in their intensity, the amount of time they demand while an individual is active. Some deviant roles take up only a small portion of the person's hours, but others are equivalent to full-time, conventional jobs. In general, the more sophisticated the organizational form, the more time members devote to their deviant careers. Loners' deviance usually takes up only a small fraction of their time; the embezzler and the physician narcotic addict limit their deviance to a few minutes each day. In part, this reflects the relative simplicity of their deviant operations. But many loners have only a marginal commitment to deviance, so they continue to allocate most of their time to their respectable roles. While the deviance of colleagues and peers takes up a larger portion of their daily lives, it typically remains a part-time activity, if only because the profits from deviance are low. Pool hustlers often moonlight to make ends meet. For motorcycle outlaws and many other peers, deviance is a leisure-time activity, rather than a source of income. Mobs and formal organizations commit deviant acts to make a profit; members' deviant roles are full-time occupational roles. Thus, deviant careers tend to be longer and more intense as organizational sophistication increases.

Social organization also affects the relative prominence of the deviant identity in the individual's self. Individuals can view their deviance as tangential to the major themes in their lives, or they can see it as a central theme, an identity around which much of one's life is arranged. The latter pattern is more likely to develop among members of sophisticated forms of deviant organization because several factors associated with deviant organization facilitate the assumption of a deviant identity (Lofland, 1969). These include frequenting places that are populated by deviants, acquiring deviant equipment, and being taught deviant skills and a deviant ideology by experienced deviants. These factors also help maintain deviance as a central identity. Loners seem to be especially adept at isolating their deviance, considering it a minor exception to the generally conventional pattern of their lives (cf. Cressey, 1962). This is particularly true when their deviance was initially undertaken to defend that conventional life style from some threat. Even when individuals are relatively committed to deviance, respectable identities can serve as an important resource. In his discussion of the World War II underground, Aubert (1965) notes that respectable identities served to protect members from capture, functioning as fronts behind which members could engage in subversive operations. Similarly, an established normal status shields deviants from the suspicion of social control agents and, if the members refrain from revealing their respectable identities to one another, against betrayal by deviant associates. These considerations seem to be especially important in middle-class peer groups organized around leisure-time participation in a deviant marketplace. For example, swingers keep their contacts on a first-name basis and avoid giving away information which could be used to identify them (Bartell, 1971:92-95), and men who engage in impersonal sex in public restrooms are attracted by the setting's assurance of anonymity (Humphreys, 1970). Other deviants, particularly members of mobs and formal organizations, may associate with deviant associates away from deviant operations, so that both their work and their sociable interaction involve contact with deviants. This is also true for peer groups which expand into deviant communities, offering members an institutionally complete range of services. Active members of urban gay communities, for the most part, can restrict their contacts to other homosexuals (Harry and Devall, 1978; Wolf, 1979). In these cases, there is little need to perform respectable roles, aside from their value as a cover for deviance, and the deviant identity is likely to be central for the individual.

The degree to which an individual finds a deviant career and a deviant identity satisfying depends, in part, on the form of deviant organization to which he or she belongs. As in any activity, persons continue to engage in deviance only as long as the rewards it provides are greater than the rewards which could be gained through alternative activities. Of course, the relevant rewards vary from one person to the next and from one type of deviance to another; a partial list includes money, physical and emotional satisfaction, valued social connections, and prestige. Because the relative importance of these rewards varies with the individual, it is impossible to measure the differences in rewards between forms of deviant organization. However, there is some evidence that monetary profits are generally higher in more sophisticated forms of deviant organization (cf. Plate, 1975:87-108). While an occasional loner can steal a very large sum through an embezzlement or a computer theft, mobs can earn a relatively steady income and formal organizations consistently yield high profits. Perhaps a more revealing measure of satisfaction is career stability. As suggested earlier, members of more sophisticated forms of organization are more likely to remain in deviance. Loners' careers are short lived, even when they engage in systematic deviance. The failure of professional check forgers to remain at large suggests that the loner's lack of social support is critical (Lemert, 1967:119-134). As noted above, persons frequently drift out of their roles as colleagues and peers when other options become more attractive. The long-term careers of members of mobs and formal organizations suggest that these forms are more likely to satisfy their members.[3]

Thus, organizational sophistication affects individuals' involvement in deviance. The more sophisticated the form of deviant organization, the greater the length and intensity of members' deviant careers, the more prominent their deviant identities, and the more satisfying their involvement in deviance.

Proposition 5: The more sophisticated the form of deviant social organization, the more secure its members' deviant operations from social control efforts. The social organization of deviants affects the interaction between deviants and social control agents. This relationship is complicated, for increased sophistication has consequences which would seem to make social control efforts both easier and more difficult. On the one hand, the more sophisticated the deviant organization, the greater its public visibility and chances of becoming the object of social control efforts. Because more sophisticated forms of organization undertake more complex deviant operations, there are more people involved with the organization as members, victims, customers, and bystanders. Consequently, there are more people capable of supplying the authorities with information about the identities, activities, and locations of organizational members. This visibility makes the deviant operations of more sophisticated forms relatively vulnerable to social control efforts. On the other hand, more sophisticated forms of deviant organization are more likely to have codes of conduct requiring members to be loyal to the organization—to maintain its secrets and be discreet about the identities and activities of the other members. More sophisticated forms also command resources which can be used to protect the organization and its members by corrupting or subverting social control efforts. Therefore, while highly sophisticated organizations find it more difficult to conceal the fact that they are involved in deviance, they typically are more successful at shielding their members from severe sanctions. This complex relationship becomes apparent through a review of the problems which members of different organizational forms face in coping with social control.

Loners' operations are relatively insecure because loners must provide their own protection against social control efforts. To protect themselves, many loners depend upon concealing their deviance from others, as when a physician addict uses narcotics in private. Physical isolation facilitates secrecy and stability, but this isolation is easily shattered. Because loners use limited, conventional channels of information to learn about social control practices they can fall prey to surreptitious control techniques. For instance, spot checks of narcotics prescriptions can uncover the physician's addiction, and unexpected audits of computer transactions can reveal the computer criminal's theft. Even without surreptitious control practices, ignorance or mistakes can expose the loner's secretive operations. Others may observe signs of the loner's deviant involvement in his or her appearance, behavior, or life style. In some cases, loners commit deviant acts in the presence of respectable persons; others may witness the loner's hallucinatory behavior. Given their knowledge of the loner's deviance, these others can notify the authorities. Mobilization of social control agents brings a likelihood of apprehension and legal processing, for loners must rely on their personal, usually limited resources to combat control efforts. Some naive loners may have enough social margin—leeway for lapses from respectability—to call upon relatives or friends for support (Wiseman, 1970:223-226). But those with records of systematic deviance are especially vulnerable. They cannot combat the authorities on their own and they no longer have enough social margin to get support from relatives or friends.

Colleagues' and peers' deviant operations also are insecure. To be sure, the deviant grapevine gives colleagues and peers access to special information about social control practices, such as covert police operations, and they can adjust their operations to avoid detection and apprehension. Also, colleagues and peers share codes of conduct which call for secrecy about fellow deviants' identities, activities, and locations. Despite these advantages, these deviants confront several conditions which make their deviant operations insecure. First, colleagues and peers engage in activities which are generally more visible than those undertaken by loners. Sometimes, their deviance requires that they make themselves accessible to others; prostitutes must find customers and pool hustlers must locate suckers. In other cases, they enter public illicit marketplaces to contact and trade with other deviants, as when drug dealers and their customers do business on street

corners. In still other cases, their resources are so limited that they cannot command private places; skid row tramps drink in vacant lots and delinquent gangs gather on the streets. Second, while loners operate alone, colleagues and peers associate with other deviants. Hence, the number of people who know about the member's deviant involvement is considerably larger. Individuals often develop a local reputation, becoming known for their deviance. A reputation facilitates the attribution of deviance; known deviants are more likely to be apprehended and blamed for reported violations. Third, colleagues and peers have limited organizational resources with which to manage social control efforts. Even when members feel obliged to assist an arrested associate, they rarely can do more than arrange for bail or recommend an attorney.

Mobs' operations are more secure than those of loners, colleagues, or peers. Because most mobs engage in routine theft, more people are aware of the members' identities, activities, and locations, including victims, fences, tipsters, fixers, attorneys, and members of other mobs. To offset their heightened visibility, mobs have several features which facilitate security. First, mobs organize their operations so as to pose minimal danger to themselves. In some cases, mobs include roles designed to protect deviant operations from the interference of social control agents. For instance, burglars who post a lookout and armed robbers who have a driver waiting in a running car have anticipated some threatening contingencies. In other cases, the nature of the relationship between the mob and victim offers protection; because confidence games require dishonesty on the part of the mark, victims are reluctant to complain to the police and thereby reveal their involvement in an illicit scheme.

Second, mob members learn and use specialized skills to carry out their deviant operations safely. Members case targets in order to learn when they are most prosperous and vulnerable and plan attacks against them to minimize risk. Members use other specialized skills to complete their operations safely. A burglar needs considerable skill in detecting and offsetting burglar alarms to enter a locked building; a pickpocket requires a deft touch to take a man's wallet without his knowledge. By assessing the risks and devising methods of coping with them, mob members protect their operations.

Third, while they possess damaging information about one another, mob members share a code of conduct which offers them some protection. These codes warn against revealing the mob's secrets to outsiders. For example, a central rule embraced by career thieves prohibits informing: "Be a stand-up guy," "Keep your eyes and ears open and your mouth shut," and "Don't sell out" are variations of this rule (Sutherland and Cressey, 1978:278). In addition, these codes specify members' responsibilities toward associates who are captured by social control agents; those who remain at large must use the mob's resources to aid the captured deviants.

Fourth, mobs provide resources for managing social control efforts. Where possible, mobs try to ward off arrests by corrupting the authorities in advance. If a member is caught, the mob may pay a corrupted official to "fix" the case's outcome. Or it may compensate the victim in exchange for dropping the charges, try to influence the testimony of witnesses, or at least hire an experienced attorney to defend the deviant in court. Because mobs carefully assess the risks of deviant operations and adopt tactics to minimize the danger, and because they have the resources necessary to use these tactics, the operations of mobs are relatively secure.

Deviant formal organizations are relatively secure from social control efforts. Because these organizations touch the lives of so many people, including victims, customers, bystanders, lawyers, police, politicians, and members of the mass media, their existence is no secret. Indeed, popular novels and movies, social scientists' and journalists' accounts, and the reports of official investigations describe deviant formal organizations and their operations. Nonetheless, these organizations and their members enjoy considerable security, as suggested by their stability over time. It is possible to trace the histories of some specific formal organizations over several decades. For example, some American organized crime families developed before Prohibition and endured in spite of personnel turnover, succession of leadership, mergers with other organizations, and conflict with other deviant groups and social control agents (Nelli, 1976).

There are several reasons for the relative security of deviant formal organizations. First, a code of conduct enjoins members from revealing organizational secrets and violations of this rule may be punishable by violence. Some formal organizations have specialists ("enforcers") to punish betrayal (Cressey, 1969). Second, deviant formal organizations go to considerable lengths to protect their members against social control efforts. They may maintain a network of informants who can warn about covert social control investigations, impending raids, and so on. Organizations may employ their own attorneys to defend arrested members. As importantly, they insure against aggressive law enforcement by corrupting the authorities. Some organizations have positions for "corrupters" who pay control agents ("corruptees") to insure immunity for the organization and its members (Cressey, 1969). While mobs limit their corruption to lower echelon officials, such as patrol officers, formal organizations can corrupt officials at all levels of the social control hierarchy, from police officers to legislators. Third, even when arrests occur, formal organizations can avoid serious damage. Their hierarchical division of labor places the lowest ranking members in the positions that are most vulnerable to apprehension. Because organizational leaders rarely commit public violations, law enforcement agencies find it difficult to compile evidence against them. Moreover, the arrest and conviction of a ranking member is not enough to cripple the organization; another member can move into the captured deviant's

organizational position. When Mussolini tried to destroy the Sicilian mafia by assassinating its families' leaders, other organizational members immediately filled the vacated positions, and the families survived (Cressey, 1972:100). The failure of authorities to destroy several contemporary deviant formal organizations reflects some of the advantages of organizational sophistication.

Because organizational forms differ in their vulnerability to social control, officials must adapt their tactics to fit the form of organization if they hope to disrupt its operations and apprehend its members. In general, agents must invest greater resources in apprehending and sanctioning deviants as the sophistication of the deviant organization increases. Relatively unsophisticated forms of organization demand few social control resources. The legal processing of vagrants and tramps, for example, involves minimal time and energy (Foote, 1956; Wiseman, 1970). On the other hand, organizational sophistication carries advantages—greater loyalty among members, mechanisms for enforcing such loyalty, better information about control agents' plans and movements, operations designed to minimize risks, and so forth—which must be overcome before the deviants can be captured and sanctioned. Therefore, in dealing with deviant formal organizations, social control agents need extraordinary resources. For instance, in order to protect them from an organization's revenge, members who defect and inform on their associates may be placed in specially guarded settings or given new identities and set up in legitimate careers in new cities (cf. President's Commission, 1967a:19-20). Special strike forces of agents, such as the Organized Crime and Racketeering Section of the U.S. Department of Justice, may be established and permitted to operate independently of the police and other low level officials who are thought to be corruptible. These strike forces may use elaborate techniques for gathering evidence and present their cases to special grand juries organized for this investigation (cf. President's Commission, 1967a). Or, where deviants cannot be prosecuted for their "real" crimes, agents may attempt to compile evidence on ancillary violations, such as income tax evasion. Thus, conspiracy charges are brought against leaders of organized crime families, because a person can be found guilty of conspiracy even if it cannot be shown that he or she physically participated in an illicit transaction (Rich, 1975:198). Despite these control strategies, some deviant formal organizations have proven able to withstand officials' attacks for decades.

The more sophisticated the form of deviant organization, the greater its operations' security from social control efforts, in spite of their heightened visibility. The more sophisticated forms have codes of conduct emphasizing secrecy and loyalty and substantial resources with which to neutralize and fight social control efforts. Consequently, to capture and sanction the members of sophisticated organizations, the authorities must use extraordinary resources.

CONCLUSION

Deviants can be arrayed along a dimension of organizational sophistication. Chapters 2 and 3 described five basic forms of deviant organization: loners, colleagues, peers, mobs, and formal organizations. This chapter examined some of the consequences of organizational sophistication for deviants and social control agents (see Table 4-1). In general, the more sophisticated the deviant organization, the greater the deviants' capacity for complex deviant operations, the more elaborate their socialization, the greater the services provided to them, the greater their involvement in deviance, and the greater their operations' security from interference by social control agents.

These propositions reflect the relationship between the social organization of deviants and the individual's management of several problems in pursuing deviance: the more sophisticated the organization, the greater its capacity to help the deviant acquire the resources needed for deviance, an ideology for understanding and justifying deviance, greater satisfactions from deviance, and greater security. Thus, social organization affects the texture of the deviant's life.

While these propositions were derived from dozens of empirical studies of deviants, two qualifications should be repeated. First, while the propositions emphasize the impact of organizational sophistication, sophistication cannot explain all behavior by deviants and social control agents. Other factors also affect their lives. The preceding discussion identified some exceptions to the propositions—circumstances where other factors are particularly important. Second, the field studies which served as data for the propositions generally focus on contemporary America. Only additional, comparative research can determine whether societies in other places or at other times feature the same organizational forms and whether those forms have the consequences specified in the propositions.

Table 4-1   CONSEQUENCES OF THE SOCIAL ORGANIZATION OF DEVIANTS

AS DEVIANTS' ORGANIZATIONAL SOPHISTICATION DECREASES:	AS DEVIANTS' ORGANIZATIONAL SOPHISTICATION INCREASES:
1. Deviants have less capacity for complex operations.	1. Deviants have more capacity for complex operations.
2. Deviants receive less elaborate socialization.	2. Deviants receive more elaborate socialization.
3. Deviants receive less elaborate services from the organization.	3. Deviants receive more elaborate services from the organization.
4. Deviants are less involved in deviance.	4. Deviants are more involved in deviance.
5. Deviants' operations are less secure from social control efforts.	5. Deviants' operations are more secure from social control efforts.

The dimension of organizational sophistication also applies to respectable relationships. For reasons that follow, it is difficult to identify many respectable occupations filled by loners; an unpublished writer, laboring on a manuscript, is one example. In contrast, many respectable professionals, including physicians and attorneys, organize as colleagues. While professionals do much of their work alone, they associate with one another through shared communication channels, such as journals, professional meetings, and sociable interaction. Ignoring relationships with supervisors, interaction within work groups in factories and farm labor resembles the contacts between deviant peers; members work together with little division of labor or authority between them. Just as many deviant peer groups focus around leisure-time activities, peers also populate respectable leisure scenes, such as the tavern or bowling alley (LeMasters, 1975). The staff in a small business operates as a small team or mob; members perform specialized roles, sometimes calling for considerable skill and training, in tight coordination. And, of course, bureaucracies and other legitimate formal organizations are easily identified. An analysis analogous to the one developed in this chapter, comparing the complexity of operation, patterns of socialization, supply, and member involvement, and security from external threats among the different forms of respectable organization, could lead to a more general statement about the effects of organizational sophistication on members and relevant outsiders.

    While analogies can be drawn between deviant and respectable forms of organization, the two should be distinguished, for they occupy different positions in the larger social structure. Deviant activities are subject to sanctioning by social control agents. As a consequence, secrecy forms a central theme in deviants' lives. While conventional workers may conceal some details of their work from competitors who might steal their secrets or outsiders who might be shocked by backstage revelations, relatively few respectable occupations require individuals to completely conceal their career involvement. This explains the scarcity of respectable loners—virtually every worker has ties to a larger social network. Moreover, the links between people involved in respectable occupations are affirmed in written records, such as licenses, contracts, deeds of ownership, company rules, and the like. Deviants are much less likely to commit their activities to a written record; they attempt to operate outside the larger institutional network. Although this has the advantage of preserving their secrecy, it also carries several disadvantages. Written records increase efficiency, particularly in large organizations. Also, links to the institutional order provide respectable organizations with protections; social control agents enforce laws prohibiting unfair competition or contract violations, for example. In contrast, deviants cannot turn to the authorities for protection. Finally, respectable workers usually have relationships in which they produce, as well as consume. However, those deviants who exploit victims without providing a compensating good or service, such as robbers or rapists, consistently perform a consumer role. Workers who produce have stronger ties to the social network; a producer must be visible if someone is to purchase his or her wares. Thus, secrecy is both necessary for the deviant's protection and a consequence of his or her exploitative role. In spite of certain similarities, deviant and respectable forms of social organization can be distinguished by their need for secrecy, their use of written records, their involvement in the production of goods or services, and their reliance on the authorities.

NOTES

[1] The complexity of a deviant activity must be distinguished from two other uses of the term complexity. First, the definition of organizational sophistication, given in Part I, included complexity of the division of labor among the deviants in a given organizational form as one criterion of sophistication. However, the complexity of a deviant activity refers to the structure of the deviant transaction. Thus, a relatively unsophisticated organization without a complex division of labor can undertake a very complex transaction, as when a lone embezzler steals a large sum from the corporate treasury. Second, the complexity of a deviant activity should not be confused with the complexity of its explanation. Suicide, for instance, usually is not a complexly organized act, even though a complex social psychological analysis may be needed to explain it.

[2] Within a given form of organization, some perspectives may be more elaborate than others. Pool hustlers have a strong oral tradition, founded on the many hours they spend together in pool halls, while prostitutes have a relatively limited argot. Maurer (1939) argues that this is due, in part, to the restricted contact prostitutes have with one another during their work.

[3] During their careers, deviants may shift from one organizational form or one type of offense to another. For example, the habitual felons interviewed by Petersilia et al. (1977) reported that, while many of their offenses as juveniles involved more than one partner (presumably members of a peer group), they preferred to work alone or with a single partner on the crimes they committed as adults. The most common pattern was for juveniles who specialized in burglaries to turn to robbery when they became adults.

PART TWO
THE SOCIAL ORGANIZATION OF DEVIANCE

Chapters 2, 3, and 4 focused on deviants, individuals whose behavior makes them subject to the sanctions of social control agents. In chapters 5 through 9, the focus will shift to deviance, the forbidden behavior. Just as deviants organize in various ways, *deviant transactions* display different patterns of organization. A teenager's suicide, a group of tramps sharing a bottle of wine on skid row, an addict buying heroin from a dealer, a mugger robbing a victim, and a burglar opening a safe are all examples of deviant transactions. A transaction is deviant if at least one participant's actions are likely to being defined as deviant and subject to social control agents' sanctions. The social organization of deviance refers to the structure of the deviant transaction, the pattern of relations between its roles.

A transaction occurs whenever one or more persons orient their activity toward a particular goal. Transactions vary in many ways: they can last from a few seconds to many months; they can involve one or more persons; and the participants can be face-to-face or physically separated. The defining feature of a transaction is whether the activity is purposeful, whether the actors intend to produce some result. All transactions, whether deviant or respectable, have three properties (cf. Shibutani, 1961:32-35). First, the participants orient themselves toward a common end, the achievement of which brings gratifications of some sort to some or all of the participants. There may be considerable variation in the degree to which the participants understand the objective, the types and magnitudes of gratifications they expect to receive, and their assessment of the objective's propriety. Second, transactions have a division of labor, an allocation of tasks among those involved. Achieving a common end requires that participants perform their roles in coordination with one another. In some cases, a transaction may involve nothing more than one person performing alone; other transactions require two or more actors, each providing a different contribution. Third, transactions involve flexible coordination, "that high degree of adaptability which makes it possible to meet the peculiarities and changes that occur in each situation" (Shibutani, 1961:35). Participants need flexibility to adjust their responses to unexpected events, so that the transaction can continue in spite of disruptions.

Deviant transactions vary along a dimension of organizational complexity. Complexity refers to the minimum number of actors required for the transaction and the relationship between the roles they must perform. Some deviant transactions can be accomplished by a single person, but others require two actors. These are minimum requirements; there is no upper limit on the number of people who might be present during a transaction. In transactions featuring several persons, participants may share a common role; but transactions requiring at least two actors involve two distinct roles. The relationship between these roles can range from cooperation to conflict. The more people required for a transaction, and the more their roles conflict, the more complex the transaction's organization.

Three major forms of deviant transactions can be arrayed along the dimension of complexity: individual deviance, deviant exchange, and deviant exploitation (see Table II-1). Individual deviance requires only one person to accomplish the deviant

Table II-1 FORMS OF DEVIANT TRANSACTIONS

FORM OF TRANSACTION	MINIMUM ORGANIZATIONAL REQUIREMENTS
Individual Deviance	One Actor Performing a Deviant Role
Deviant Exchange	Two Actors Performing Cooperative Deviant Roles
Deviant Exploitation	Two Actors in Conflict: One Performing a Deviant Role (Offender); One Performing a Respectable Role (Target)

operation. Deviant exchange demands two or more actors performing cooperative deviant roles. Finally, deviant exploitation requires two actors in conflict, one performing a deviant role (the offender) and one performing a respectable or quasi-respectable role (the target). Each of these basic organizational forms has identifiable subtypes.

Classifying deviant transactions according to their complexity of organization offers two analytic advantages. First, the scheme of classification identifies underlying similarities in seemingly dissimilar forms of deviance. This perspective reveals that suicide has much in common with skid row drinking, homosexuality with drug dealing, and murder with business fraud. An examination of the different forms of deviant transactions shows that each constrains the activities of deviants and social control agents. Second, where deviants' lives involve several kinds of deviant transactions, those transactions—which may have different properties—can be distinguished using these classifications. Thus, when addicts use drugs, they engage in individual deviance, but their drug purchases and the thefts to support their habits are instances of deviant exchange and deviant exploitation, respectively. The type of transaction has important consequences for deviants; for instance, addicts must take very different matters into account then they use drugs, buy drugs, and steal.

While this classification is useful, it should be used with care. The descriptions of the forms of deviant transactions and their subtypes which follow are idealized. In practice, deviant transactions are not always easy to classify. Sometimes two or more transactions occur at the same time, as when drug use takes place during a drug sale. On other occasions, a transaction's participants have different understandings about what is occurring. For example, a drug buyer may believe that the transaction is a deviant exchange, while the seller plans to exploit the buyer by selling adulterated drugs. The analysis of transactions' organization inevitably describes ideal types, ignoring some of the complexities of social life. Further, these chapters rely heavily on studies of deviance in contemporary America. This classification of deviant transactions may not fit deviance in other societies or in other periods. There may be other forms of deviant transactions or some of the forms identified here may have different features in other cultures. These possibilities deserve further study.

The five chapters which follow describe the three forms of deviant transactions and their subtypes and examine some consequences of organizational complexity. Chapter 5 treats individual deviance and chapter 6 examines deviant exchange. Chapters 7 and 8 discuss varieties of deviant exploitation. Finally, chapter 9 examines the consequences of the social organization of deviance for deviants and social control agents.

CHAPTER FIVE
INDIVIDUAL DEVIANCE

Individual deviance is a transaction that can be accomplished by a single person. There are two principal types of individual deviance. First individual deviance can involve the provision of illicit services to oneself. In suicide, the actor kills himself or herself; in self-induced abortion, the actor rids herself of an unwanted fetus. Other examples include the excessive use of alcohol and the use of illicit drugs. Second, individual deviance can involve the subscription to a prohibited version of reality. In some forms of mental illness, such as schizophrenia, the actor withdraws from the conventional reality embraced by others, constructs an imaginary world, and acts on the basis of what he or she imagines. Religious heresy and the adoption of a forbidden political philosophy also exemplify this form of individual deviance. (Some sociologists would identify a third type of individual deviance—spoiled social identities [F. Davis, 1961; Goffman, 1963b; Truzzi, 1968]. While dwarves, people with visible handicaps, and the obese sometimes receive treatment similar to the responses to deviance, they will not be considered here. The definition of deviance developed in chapter 1 specified that deviance involves forbidden behavior. In cases of spoiled social identities, it is the actor's condition, rather than behavior, which is at issue.)

The person who engages in individual deviance can act alone or in the company of others. The individual deviant may perform in isolation, as in most instances of suicide or self-induced abortion. Or the deviant may perform in the presence of others. They can be bystanders who are not directly involved in deviance but witness the actor's performance. For example, bystanders may spot a group of skid row tramps sharing a bottle or see someone hallucinating in public. The individual deviant also can perform in the presence of deviant associates. Here, two or more actors engage in individual deviance together. This can add to the transaction's complexity, requiring a division of labor among the participants and adherence to a set of norms governing their activities. Recreational drug users, for instance, may get together in a private place and share illicit drugs. One person may supply the drugs and another may prepare the drugs for consumption, and all of the participants are expected to share the drugs equally. Thus, individual deviance does not mean that the deviant must operate alone. The issue is not whether other persons, respectable or deviant, are present, but whether the individual's action, taken alone, would merit a deviant label.

Individual deviance often is viewed as nonsocial behavior. When someone uses illicit drugs, drinks to excess, commits suicide, or subscribes to a prohibited version of reality, some biological or personality disorder generally is believed to account for the deviance. This mode of explanation seems to fit individual deviance because, if only one actor needs to be involved in the transaction, the cause of deviance appears to lie within that person. However, biological and psychiatric explanations ignore an important fact: most individual deviance is socially organized behavior. It is organized in the sense that the performance is shaped by the actor's social relations. Social relations affect individual deviance in two ways: the actor's socialization shapes the deviant performance; and the actual or anticipated actions of others affect the transaction.

Socialization shapes the deviant performance. Through interaction with others, every person learns the perspective of the group to which he or she belongs (Shibutani, 1961:115-22). Specifically, the actor learns the shared understandings about the many objects comprising the world—their central attributes, the basic distinctions between them, the appropriate ways in which to relate to them under various circumstances, and the correct ways in which to refer to them. Once the actor acquires this perspective, he or she can respond to situations in ways that are consistent with his or her group's practices. The actor's perspective may encourage him or her to define a specific situation as appropriate for undertaking a form of individual deviance. For example, to obtain pleasure during leisure time, some groups encourage persons to have a cocktail, while other groups encourage persons to use illicit drugs. Further, the actor's perspective may direct the manner in which he or she undertakes and experiences the deviant performance. Thus, an experienced drug user teaches a novice how to prepare and smoke marijuana (Becker, 1963:41-58). Instruction includes techniques for smoking so as to maximize pleasure and minimize discomfort. The novice also may be taught how to interpret the physiological effects of marijuana—dizziness should be recognized as a pleasurable effect, for instance. Once the actor learns these lessons, he or she will be able to enjoy smoking marijuana, even when he or she is alone.

The actual or anticipated actions of others also influence individual deviance. When a deviant performs among deviant associates, his or her actions are affected by them. Associates may decide that an occasion is appropriate for deviance, and they may supply the necessary equipment for carrying it out. In addition, associates may expect the deviant's actions to conform with their norms. Thus, smoking marijuana in the company of peers is an activity guided by a set of rituals and expectations. The joint or pipe must be passed around to everybody present; each member is expected to share in sociable talk or activity; and, within the limits of the marijuana available, each member can smoke as much as he or she wants (Zimmerman and Wieder, 1977:200-202). Failure to fulfill associates' expectations can lead to ostracism.

Even when the actor is alone, his or her behavior may be shaped by others' actions. Others may contribute to the actor's decision to engage in individual deviance. For example, feeling that friends and family members are unsupportive, an actor may decide that suicide is the only way out of a personal dilemma. The anticipated actions of others also may influence the actor's performance. Believing that friends and family members will blame themselves for his or her suicide, the deviant writes a note explaining that no one else is to blame (Jacobs, 1967). Thus, even when performed in isolation, individual deviance is socially organized behavior.

The fact that the actor's deviance makes him or her eligible for official sanctions affects the nature of the transaction. If the deviant is capable of self-control, he or she usually takes precautions to avoid identification and processing by social control agents. Precautions typically center on self-discretion, the control of discrediting information about one's deviant involvement (Goffman, 1963b). Information control may be accomplished in any of several ways. The actor may restrict the deviant performance to protected or isolated settings which outsiders do not normally enter. The deviant may restrict conversations about his or her involvement in deviance; some actors tell no one about their involvement, while others confide in a few deviant associates or sympathetic nondeviants. Discrediting information also may be controlled by cloaking symbols of deviant involvement, as when a drug addict covers needle tracks with clothing. When the deviant is not discreet, he or she is vulnerable to social control efforts. Because they lack the resources to drink in private, skid row tramps usually share a bottle in public places, making them susceptible to police intervention (Wiseman, 1970).

This chapter focuses on the social organization of three cases of individual deviance. It begins with two deviant self-services—suicide, typically a solitary act, and excessive drinking by groups of skid row tramps. Then it considers mental illness, a case of subscribing to a prohibited version of reality.

DEVIANT SELF-SERVICES

In everyday life, people do many things for themselves, such as eating and dressing. In performing these self-services, individuals serve as both the agent and object of action; they do things to themselves. Some self-services occur in isolation—people typically clean and dress themselves in privacy. Other self-services take place in public, as when people sit down to a family dinner or run in a marathon. One need not be alone to perform a self-service.

Some self-services are deviant—a type of individual deviance. The actor tries to satisfy a personal need or cope with a personal problem by performing a deviant self-service. Two subtypes of deviant self-services can be identified. First, the actor can consume an intoxicating substance in an illicit fashion. The use of illicit drugs (Blumer, 1967; Carey, 1968; Stoddart, 1974) and the excessive consumption of alcohol (Cahalan and Room, 1974; Spradley, 1970) illustrate this subtype. Second, one can remove an unwanted personal feature in an illicit manner. This includes self-induced abortion, removing an unwanted fetus (N. Lee, 1969), and suicide, ridding oneself of life (Douglas, 1967; Jacobs, 1967).

Deviant self-services vary along several dimensions. Like respectable self-services, they may be performed in private or in public. Those who remove an unwanted feature usually act in private, while deviants who consume an illicit substance often perform with others. Second, the transaction may be episodic or systematic. Self-induced abortion typically is an isolated episode—the woman performs this service only once in her life. However, the consumption of illicit drugs may become systematic—an addict uses heroin daily. Third, persons who engage in deviant self-services organize in different ways. Suicides typically are loners, while recreational drug users often organize as peers, associating with one another to obtain, prepare, and use drugs.

People generally use psychiatric explanations to account for deviant self-services. For example, the public typically defines alcoholism and drug addiction as diseases, requiring treatment (Linsky, 1970; Pattison et al., 1968). However, deviant self-services can be viewed as socially organized transactions, shaped by the actor's social relations. Other people, deviant or respectable, influence the actor's performance. First, others may contribute to the actor's personal need or problem or constrain the actor's options for managing it. For example, self-induced abortion may become a plausible means for dealing with a pregnancy when the father does not want the child, one's physician refuses to abort the fetus, and friends cannot help to find an abortionist (N. Lee, 1969:79-81). Second, others may provide the knowledge and skill for performing the self-service. Experienced drug users may transmit an ideology justifying drug use, and women may pass along techniques for self-induced abortion. Third, others may supply the equipment needed to perform the self-service. Respectable shopkeepers sell catheters which can be used for abortion, and deviant peers supply one another with illicit drugs. Fourth, others may schedule the transaction. For instance, the time and place for using recreational drugs may be determined by mutual agreement among peers. In these ways, others help to organize the individual's deviant self-service.

This section examines two instances of deviant self-services. It begins with suicide, a transaction in which a person, usually operating as a loner, uses death to resolve a personal dilemma. It then considers bottle gang drinking, a more complex transaction where skid row tramps, operating as peers, share a bottle of wine for pleasure.

Suicide

Suicide is the ultimate act of self-destruction. In his classic study of the subject, Durkheim (1951: 44) defined suicide as "death resulting directly or indirectly from a positive or negative act of the victim himself, which he knows will produce this result." This definition emphasizes two important points. First, suicide is a conscious, intentional act; the actor realizes what he or she is doing and intends to die. Durkheim excluded all life-threatening activities in which "the victim is either not the author of his own end or else only its unconscious author" (Durkheim, 1951:44). Second, suicide varies in method. The actor may commit a self-destructive act, such as shooting oneself, or make a self-destructive omission, such as refusing to eat or drink. The actor may inflict his or her own death, or use another person as the instrument of death, such as jumping before a moving car.

Suicide constitutes one of the simplest forms of individual deviance. Most cases involve only one person, although there are situations where a couple carries out a suicide pact, and even cases where an entire group commits suicide in the face of a serious threat (as in the 1978 Jonestown incident). In most cases, however, suicide is a solitary transaction (cf. Stengel, 1964). The actor chooses a method for committing suicide, acquires the necessary equipment, and commits suicide in an isolated or protected setting.

Although suicide is a solitary transaction, it does not lack social organization. Suicide is a learned behavior pattern (Akers, 1973:245-252). Through socialization, individuals learn about situations in which suicide is common and possibly appropriate, such as when confronting a painful, terminal illness or the loss of one's business. Individuals also learn common techniques for committing suicide, such as shooting and poisoning. Thus, everyone acquires social meanings about suicide through socialization.

Suicide is social in another sense. Most research suggests that suicide is not a product of irrational impulse, but a conscious and deliberate action, shaped by the actor's social relations. Essentially, the actor faces an insurmountable personal problem, examines the possible alternatives for dealing with it, selects suicide as the best alternative, and attempts suicide (Breed, 1972; Douglas, 1967; Jacobs, 1967; 1971). The nature of the personal problem, the alternatives examined, and the selection of suicide as the best alternative are affected by the actor's primary relationships. Jacobs' (1971) research provides a useful framework for understanding the step-by-step process through which individuals reach the point of attempting and possibly completing suicide.

Using data derived from suicide notes and interviews with youngsters who attempted suicide, Jacobs (1971) sought to explain adolescent suicide. Generally, he found that suicide occurs when the actor experiences progressive isolation from meaningful, primary relationships. Jacobs identified five stages in this social process. (In an earlier investigation, Jacobs [1967] developed a comparable model of suicide for adults.)

Stage 1. A long history of childhood problems. Jacobs compared a group of fifty adolescent suicide attempters with a control group of thirty-one adolescents who had never attempted suicide. The two groups were matched in age, race, sex, and level of mother's education. Examining the adolescents' life histories, Jacobs found that the suicide attempters experience more debilitating events than members of the control group. Debilitating events include the death of a family member, a home broken by divorce or separation, an alcoholic parent, residential moves, and school changes. In short, the suicide attempters have relatively disorienting and unhappy lives.

Stage 2. An escalation of problems during adolescence. Although members of the control group experience personally troublesome events in their early lives, the number and severity of these problems decline as they move into adolescence. For instance, the heavy drinking by parents ceases as the youngsters reach adolescence. In contrast, the suicide attempters' problems escalate as they reach adolescence. Not only are earlier problems still unresolved, but they now face additional problems. For example, an unwanted stepparent enters the previously broken home.

Stage 3. Progressive isolation from meaningful social relationships. The escalation of problems leads to progressive isolation from significant others. For instance, a change in residence and school can lead to isolation from friends, or a home broken by divorce or the death of a parent can bring isolation from family members. This isolation makes the adolescent unhappy. The adolescent uses adaptive techniques to manage this unhappiness and restore relationships with significant others. Adaptive techniques range from rebellion (disobedience, sassiness, and defiance) to withdrawal into oneself (gloominess and refusal to talk) or physical withdrawal (running away from home). These techniques are attempts to make others, particularly one's parents, aware that the adolescent has important problems requiring their attention. Rebellion, for example, should alert parents that the adolescent requires their understanding and help. If rebellion fails to elicit the understanding and assistance of parents, the adolescent might escalate the adaptive process by withdrawing into himself or herself; if this fails, the adolescent might try running away from home. When members of the control group express their unhappiness through these adaptive techniques, their parents respond by "talking it over" with their youngsters, often at the early, rebellious stage. However, the parents of suicide attempters are more likely to define these activities as "behavioral problems" requiring some kind of punishment. These parents respond to their youngsters' adaptive techniques by withholding privileges, nagging, yelling, or physical punishment. The adolescent defines such reactions as unfair, as evidence of parental rejection. Consequently, these adolescents experience further isolation from their parents.

Other research confirms Jacobs' claim that isolation from meaningful social relations is associated with attempting suicide. The more individuals are integrated into primary social groups, such as the family and work group, the lower their rate of suicide (Henry and Short, 1954; Maris, 1969). In a study of suicides among school children, it was found that "in every case of suicide, the child was described as having no close friends with whom he might share confidences or from whom he received psychological support"(Jan-Tausch, cited in Jacobs, 1971:16). In his analysis of adult suicides, Breed (1972) identified three events occurring shortly before the self-destructive act: (1) a failure in an important social sphere, such as being fired or demoted at work; (2) a sense of "shame" engendered by the negative reactions of significant others to the failure; and (3) isolation from others because of this shame. Another detailed investigation of five adults, four successful suicides and one suicide attempter, found that suicide is affected more by how others react to the actor's pleas for understanding and assistance than by the nature of the actor's personal problems (Kobler and Stotland, 1964). A threat to commit suicide is a technique for coping with isolation:

> Our conception views suicidal attempts and verbal or other communications of suicidal intent as efforts, however misdirected, to solve problems of living, as frantic pleas for help and hope from other people: help in solving the problems, and hope that they can be solved. (Kobler and Stotland, 1964:1).

Whether or not the individual attempts suicide depends, in large part, on the manner in which others respond to these signals. If others respond with understanding and assistance, suicide is unlikely. But if others react negatively, reaffirming the actor's sense of isolation and hopelessness, a suicide attempt is likely.

Stage 4. Reaching the end of hope.   Immediately before the suicide attempt, the adolescent experiences further isolation from his or her remaining primary relationships. For example, a broken romance, serious illness, suspension from school, or confinement in a juvenile detention center serves to isolate the youngster from friends and relatives. These events occur abruptly and unexpectedly. Further, the adolescent defines them as intolerable; they cannot be resolved through such adaptive techniques as rebellion or withdrawal, for these techniques have already proven ineffective, and significant others cannot provide understanding and assistance, for the actor already feels isolated from these others. By themselves, the new problems might not appear to be serious enough to cause a suicide. But, as Jacobs emphasizes, these events must be seen within the larger context of the adolescent's life history. From the adolescent's standpoint, the isolating events break the limits of endurance. The progressive isolation from significant others coupled with a constriction of techniques for managing isolation and a need to resolve the new problems lead to the serious consideration of suicide.

Other research confirms that a sense of hopelessness is common among those who commit suicide. One study found that hopelessness develops when individuals experience extremely threatening events and feel incapable of responding effectively. In turn, this sense of hopelessness leads to seriously considering suicide as a means of coping with the threat (Farber, 1968). Similarly, Neuringer (1964) discovered that individuals who commit suicide have a heightened sense of impotency; they believe that they are weak and ineffectual in shaping their life course. Also consistent with Jacobs' claims, Ringel (1977) found that suicide is preceded by a sense that problems are all-encompassing, a constriction of problem-solving alternatives, and a decision that there is no way out of the predicament except by suicide.

Stage 5. Justifying suicide to oneself.   Considering suicide as a means of solving one's predicament does not mean that the adolescent will necessarily make a suicide attempt. American society condemns suicide; life is seen as a sacred trust, something which people must protect. Adolescents considering suicide must align their conceptions of themselves as trusted persons—persons who should safeguard life—with suicide—behavior which violates that trust. Before an actor can attempt suicide, he or she must overcome these moral and social constraints. The neutralization of constraints involves a mental process through which one consciously comes to see oneself as blameless. The adolescent defines the situation so that his or her predicament can be understood to be: 1) not of his or her own making; (2) unresolved in spite of his or her efforts to deal with it; and

(3) not resolvable except through death (Jacobs, 1971:87). By defining the situation in this manner, the actor recognizes that death is the only hope and that, since there is no choice in the matter, suicide is less sinful or immoral. Jacobs derived this final stage from an examination of suicide notes left by 112 persons (both adolescents and adults) who successfully committed suicide. While he found some variation in the reasoning given in the notes, most notes indicated that the actor neutralized the moral constraints against suicide before carrying out the act (Jacobs, 1967).

Once the actor decides that suicide is a justified means of dealing with his or her life situation, he or she mobilizes the resources required for suicide. In some cases, the individual uses no special equipment; jumping from a high place requires nothing more than access to a tall building. More commonly, the individual uses some sort of equipment, readily available through conventional channels, to commit suicide. Firearms and explosives are the most common suicide equipment for both white and nonwhite men and women (Farberow, 1977:535). Given the necessary equipment, the actor ordinarily commits suicide in a private setting. Suicide attempts often occur in settings which either contain others or are near others, making intervention possible or probable (Stengel, 1964). However, individuals who successfully kill themselves choose settings where intervention is unlikely.

Suicide is a form of individual deviance in which the actor typically acts alone. Although suicide is a solitary transaction, the choice of suicide is affected by the character of the actor's primary relationships. The actor usually encounters a series of personal problems which isolate him or her from significant others. Various techniques for solving these problems not only fail to restore primary relationships but lead to further isolation. The actor eventually reaches a point where his or her life situation becomes unendurable. The actor then considers suicide as an available alternative, and, after neutralizing moral constraints, chooses self-destruction as the way out.

Drinking on Skid Row

Drinking alcoholic beverages is a socially respectable activity which most Americans enjoy on occasion. Moderate consumption of alcohol by adults in an appropriate context, e.g., a wedding reception or cocktail party, is not considered deviant. However, under other circumstances, drinking is considered deviant and the actor is liable to social control. Drinking by minors is unlawful and can lead to juvenile court action. Drinking outside of licensed public places, such as taverns and restaurants, or private places, such as homes and hotel rooms, is also unlawful (Spradley, 1970:118). Drinking to the point of intoxication is considered deviant in some situations, e.g., while driving, and makes the individual eligible for legal processing. Alcoholism, habitually drinking to excess, is also subject to social control efforts, such as treatment in detoxification centers or alcohol abuse programs.

Like suicide, drinking involves learned patterns of behavior. It is commonly thought that drinking physiologically affects behavior by reducing the individual's inhibitions (Chafetz and Demone, 1962). Alcohol supposedly produces a toxic reaction that releases the lower brain centers from the control of the higher brain centers, permitting the individual to say and do things which ordinarily are controlled by internalized social restraints. However, social scientists argue that behavior while drinking is shaped by the individual's socialization (Straus, 1971:236-243). The individual's drinking practices, including the purpose of drinking, the times and places of consumption, the choice of beverage, and the amounts ingested, are influenced by the group to which he or she belongs (Bacon, 1962; Straus and Bacon, 1953). Importantly, the individual's behavior under the influence of alcohol is affected by the group's culture. In a cross-cultural study, MacAndrew and Edgerton (1969:165) concluded that "the way people comport themselves when they are drunk is determined not by alcohol's toxic assault upon the seat of moral judgment, conscience, and the like, but by what their society makes of and imparts to them concerning the state of drunkenness." They demonstrate that drunken comportment varies from society to society. For example, intoxicated members of Aritama (a North Colombian village) behave in a controlled, somewhat somber fashion, while members of Takashima (a Japanese village) display camaraderie, laughter, songs and dances (MacAndrew and Edgerton, 1969:24-25, 32-33). Members of the Abipone of Paraguay and the Pondo of South Africa refrain from promiscuity when drunk, while the Tarahumara of Mexico and the Lepcha of Sikkim become impassioned and promiscuous (MacAndrew and Edgerton, 1969:76-77, 80-81, 93-94). They also show that drunken comportment can vary from one social setting to another within the same community. For instance, in Taira (a rural Okinawan village), intoxicated men exhibit peaceful and controlled behavior in the presence of women, but they are boisterous and aggressive in all-male settings (MacAndrew and Edgerton, 1969:54). Thus, an individual's drunken comportment is shaped by his or her group; intoxication may lead to less inhibition, little change from sobriety, or more inhibition, depending on what the individual learns is appropriate behavior when drinking. Therefore, drunken comportment—whether it is related to deviant or respectable drinking—involves socially organized behavior patterns.

Deviant drinking is more complexly organized than suicide. While it can take place in solitude, most deviant drinking occurs with a group, often organized as peers. Juveniles, skid row tramps, and alcoholics typically drink in the company of their fellows. When people drink together, their individual deviance becomes more complexly organized. There may be some division of labor among the participants, with one person setting the time and place for their drinking and another buying the alcohol. Moreover, the presence of others may influence the individual. Deviant associates can influence the kind of alcohol used, the manner in which it is consumed, and behavior while drinking. One form of deviant drinking, skid row bottle gang drinking, illustrates these organizational features.

Tramps, homeless men and women, populate the skid rows of large American cities (Spradley, 1970). Drinking by skid row tramps is considered deviant because they often become intoxicated in public. Public intoxication makes the tramp liable to processing by social control agents. In some cities, drinking or being drunk in public is illegal; in others, public intoxication is not illegal, but intoxicated persons are subject to arrest if they are thought to present a danger to themselves or others (Spradley,1970:121; Wiseman, 1970:70-71).

Drinking is a basic activity in the lives of skid row inhabitants (Rubington,1958; 1968; Wallace, 1965:181-182; Wiseman, 1970:20). Popularly, the tramp's drinking is seen as evidence of alcoholism, an inability to refrain from habitual drinking to intoxication (Spradley, 1970:66-69). This is an oversimplification. One recent study estimated that only one third of homeless men and women are problem drinkers, another third are moderate drinkers, and the remainder drink little at all (Bahr, 1973). A relatively small proportion of skid row residents are forced into the area because of their excessive drinking (Siegel, et al., 1975). Moreover, of those tramps who do drink to excess, few consider themselves alcoholics (Spradley, 1970: 70-71; Straus and McCarthy, 1951). Tramps learn the drinking practices that are considered normal on skid row; their peers expect them to follow particular drinking practices, and reward them for doing so (Spradley, 1970:117; Wallace, 1965:182).

Tramps typically drink in groups (Wallace, 1965:184). J. Jackson and Connor (1953) distinguish between two types of group drinkers on skid row: "lushes" prefer whiskey and can afford to drink together in skid row taverns, while "winos" cannot afford to drink in taverns. Rather, winos band together and consume a cheaper drink, usually wine, but sometimes a nonbeverage alcohol, such as hair tonic, after shave lotion, or the alcohol squeezed from shoe polish or canned heat (Spradley, 1970:260). Some individuals move between the two groups, but many tramps are winos who drink in bottle gangs.

A bottle gang is a short-lived group of tramps who come together, pool their financial resources, purchase a bottle of wine, share it in some public place, and disperse once the wine is gone (Rubington, 1968; Spradley, 1970:117). A bottle gang serves two important functions: "(1) it permits individuals with very limited financial resources to purchase the maximum amount of alcohol per monetary unit; (2) the interpersonal association resulting from this transaction permits satisfaction of emotional needs for personal contact" (Rooney, 1961:449). Rubington (1968) identifies six stages in the life of a skid row bottle gang:

Stage 1. Salutation.   Salutation brings the potential bottle gang participants together. They casually spot one another in a common area and move into one another's presence. They pass the time of day and prepare to negotiate sharing a bottle of wine.

Stage 2. Negotiation.   Negotiation is the process through which potential participants agree to collectively purchase a bottle of wine for shared consumption. One tramp, the leader, initiates negotiation by saying that he or she has a certain amount of money (perhaps a dime or quarter) and is willing to invest it in a bottle. If they are interested, the others report their holdings and then turn them over to the leader. The leader adds the combined sum and, if it is less than the price of a bottle, states how much more they need and perhaps leads the gang to others who may want to invest in a bottle. "The solicitor has the obligation to inform the prospective partner of the amount of money collected and the number of men with whom he will have to share the wine" (Rooney, 1961:450). Once the group acquires sufficient funds, it is ready to make the purchase.

Stage 3. Procurement.   Procurement involves purchasing the bottle of wine. The leader picks one person to buy the bottle, to "make the run." The person who is selected must not be shabbily dressed or visibly intoxicated; he or she must be dependable, a person who can be trusted to return with the bottle. In the meantime, the others pick a safe place to drink and wait there (Spradley, 1970:119-120; Wiseman,1970:21-26). A place is considered safe when it is protected against the intrusion of police officers, predators (such as delinquents who might attack), and freeloaders (persons who wish to drink without contributing financially).

Stage 4. Consumption.   Consumption is collective drinking of the wine. After the runner returns with the bottle, the leader initiates the drinking by either taking two short drinks and passing the bottle to the left. or immediately passing it to the left and taking his or her drinks after the bottle has made the round. Each person takes two short drinks and passes the bottle to the left. Once the bottle makes the full circle, the leader puts it away. The gang members sit back and talk.

Stage 5. Affirmation.   Affirmation involves communicating support for the leader and the bottle gang. The leader serves as the "host." He or she "has the major obligation of leading the conversation, which consists of ego-building mechanisms and recapitulations of past experiences, with frequent disparagement of the local police force as grossly unjust, and condemnation of the gospel missions as 'rackets'" (Rooney, 1961:452). The others affirm the leader's comments and criticisms; they compliment the leader on his or her character and ability, and they criticize the police and freeloaders. The leader decides when the next round of drinking will take place. The bottle once again circles the group, with each person taking two short drinks.

Stage 6. Dispersal.   When the bottle is empty, the gang is ready to disband. The bottle is thrown away, the gang members announce their immediate plans, and they leave.

Drinking within a skid row bottle gang is structured. There are norms regulating members' participation in the transaction; these norms are learned and shared by tramps (Rubington, 1958:67). Participants are re-warded with drink and social acceptance for complying with the norms. When participants violate these norms they are liable to sanctioning by the group. Rubington (1968) describes several violations and their punish-ments. Procurement violations occur when the runner fails to return or returns with a bottle that has been opened and partially consumed. The runner is labeled undependable, and he or she may be excluded from immediate participation (if he or she returns with a partially consumed bottle) or from future bottle gangs (if he or she does not return). A member breaks consumption rules by drinking too fast, taking more than two short drinks, or refusing to pass the bottle to the left. These violations may be pointed out, or the bottle may be plucked from the offender's hand. Af-firmation violations include talking about subjects inconsistent with the topics chosen by the leader or criticizing the leader or other bottle gang members without immediate cause. The violater is labeled troublesome, and he or she may be excluded from future bottle gangs. Thus, bottle gang norms and sanctions affect the manner in which skid row winos drink and act while drinking.

Unlike suicide, deviant drinking usually occurs in a group context. This makes the activity more complex, for it can entail some division of labor as well as rules regulating the participants' drinking. In the skid row bottle gang, there is a division of labor, with one person serving as the leader, another as the runner, and the remainder as contributors. Norms govern their drinking and sanctions are imposed on individuals who violate these norms. Although only one person is required—each of the tramps could drink alone—the activity is structured by the tramps' contacts with their associates.

Social Constraints on Self-Services

Suicide and bottle gang drinking represent two cases of deviant self-services. These transactions have very different goals. In suicide, the deviant uses self-destruction to resolve a severe personal dilemma. In bottle gang drinking, the deviant drinks wine to reach a pleasurable state and to enjoy the company of others. These transactions also vary in complexity. Suicide is a relatively simple transaction. The actor typically operates alone and in private; he or she supplies the necessary resources and uses knowledge obtained through conventional channels to justify and carry out the act. Bottle gang drinking is more complex. The actor performs among deviant peers, and he or she relies on them for the resources and knowledge needed to undertake the operation. The transaction is bound by norms regulating the ways in which the wine is obtained and consumed. In both cases, as in self-induced abortion and illicit drug use, the deviant's actions lead to a desired personal end.

The fact that some self-services are deviant reflects the intrusion of the social world on individuals' lives. Societies which prohibit some self-services insist that people should not choose their own courses of action without guidance. Prohibitions against these actions argue that the self-services, however attractive they may seem to individuals, threaten the social order. Sometimes this rationale emphasizes the harm which comes to the deviant, so that the prohibition is said to exist for the deviant's "own good." Thus, prohibitions against the use of illicit drugs presumably protect the user from the drugs' ill effects. Less commonly, the rules against deviant self-services rest on beliefs that the activities harm others; self-induced abortion is an obvious example. In either case, social control agents assume the right to interrupt the deviant's actions.

DEVIANT REALITY
SUBSCRIPTION

Reality is what people perceive the world to be. This is not to deny that there exists an actual world, one independent of thoughts and deeds. But what people know about the world is socially constructed, a product of group participation (Berger and Luckmann, 1966; Shibutani, 1961:118). Through socialization, people acquire a cognitive perspective, a body of shared understandings about the world. Their perspective includes shared conceptions of the central objects which comprise the world, the basic features of those objects, what should and should not be done with them in various circumstances, and the like. In the course of life, people come to reaffirm some of these conceptions, question others, and revise still others. Thus, reality is a social construction.

Complex societies have coexisting, overlapping realities. Shibutani (1961:129-130) observes: "Modern mass societies are made up of a bewildering array of social worlds—the underworld, the world of high finance, the world of the theater, the world of horse racing, the world of Protestant missionaries." Social worlds or realities sometimes overlap; they share some conceptions about the actual world. Yet, they also differ; horse racers and Protestant missionaries see the world very differently, focusing on different objects, defining the same objects differently, and so on. Although many realities coexist peacefully, perhaps supplementing one another, other realities conflict. Importantly, some realities are considered acceptable or tolerable by authorities, while other realities are considered unacceptable or intolerable. In some instances, these latter realities are prohibited, and individuals who subscribe to them are considered deviant, liable to social control efforts.

Two subtypes of deviant reality subscription can be identified. First, it may be deviant to subscribe to a reality that opposes the reality embraced by the government. For example, totalitarian governments may prohibit adherence to an opposing political ideology. Subscription to communism may be prohibited in fascist nations, while subscription to fascism may be declared deviant in communist nations (Connor, 1972a; Loney, 1973). Another example is heresy, where an individual subscribes to a prohibited religious ideology (Erikson,1966). Second, subscription to a reality that departs radically from the overlapping, unquestioned truths shared by most societal members may be defined as deviant. A large part of mental illness falls within this category; the individual adopts a perspective that violates what "everyone knows to be true" (Scheff, 1966; Szasz, 1961). Thus, a man who believes that he is God's agent while all others are demons is defined as schizophrenic.

Subscription to a deviant reality varies in the degree to which that reality can be shared with others. In general, deviants do not share realities that depart from the unquestioned truths held by "normal" societal members. Schizophrenics do not share their imaginary worlds with others, not even other schizophrenics. Mental illness is individualized; the deviant operates as a loner. However, realities that challenge those in power often are shared. Deviants who share a forbidden political or religious ideology can organize in different ways. In early stages of development, deviants subscribing to a prohibited ideology may organize as peers; in later stages, they may develop a formal organization. Whatever the form of deviant organization, subscription to a deviant reality is individual deviance—an activity which can be performed by a single person.

Deviant reality subscription often is attributed to the individual's pathological mental state, ignorance, or foolishness. However, deviant reality subscription is socially organized. A prohibited reality may develop as a reaction to the reality imposed by others, as when a deviant political ideology evolves as an alternative to the reality embraced by those in power. Further, subscription to a prohibited reality may be influenced by others who share that reality. Associates may transmit the deviant reality, giving instruction in its conceptions, providing norms regulating practice, and supplying necessary equipment, such as special costumes, materials for conducting rituals, and so forth.

This section examines one instance of deviant reality subscription— mental illness. Here, the deviant, operating as a loner, subscribes to an unshared, imaginary reality. While most people argue that mental illness is nonsocial, caused by mental disorder, mental illness is socially organized, shaped by others.

Mental Illness

Mental illness is difficult to define. It usually refers to maladaptive behavior caused by a physical or personality disorder (cf. Coleman, 1964; Mechanic, 1969). The American Psychiatric Association (1968:32-46) identifies several types of mental illness. The most general distinction is between organic and functional mental illness. Organic types of mental illness result from a physiological disorder, such as brain damage or neurological disease. For instance, senile psychoses are caused by hardening of the arteries in the brain; they manifest themselves in a loss of memory, an inability to concentrate, and, in some cases, delusions. Paresis involves degeneration of the brain cells caused by syphilis and manifests itself in depression and a loss of memory. Functional types of mental illness arise from personality, rather than physical, disorders. Functional disorders have been divided into neuroses and psychoses. Neuroses "entail emotional discomfort and impairment of functioning, often in a limited realm of behavior, but entail no sharp break with reality" (Clausen, 1971b:35). For example, in obsessive-compulsive reactions, a person experiences an incessant, unwanted thought, such as the pain of death, or persistently performs an unnecessary activity, such as frequent hand-washing. Psychoses "entail a gross de-rangement of mental processes and inability to evaluate external reality correctly" (Clausen, 1971b:35). Psychoses include schizophrenia and manic-depression. Schizophrenia involves dissociation from the community's conventional reality. The individual withdraws and, in some cases, constructs an imaginary world, with its own system of ideas, concepts, and language, in which he or she lives. Manic-depression involves drastic shifts in emotion and behavior. In the manic phase, the person is elated and hyperactive; in the depression phase, he or she is despondent.

Although these mental disorders have their own characteristics, they share three features. First, mental illness becomes manifest through behavior. For instance, several patterns of behavior may be taken as evidence of schizophrenia: the individual may stand mute, without acknowledging the presence of others; or he or she may deal with others from an entirely foreign standpoint, perhaps claiming to be some historic figure or speaking to others in an alien tongue. Mentally ill behavior may be oriented toward oneself, as when a person with a phobia fears certain situations, or the behavior may be oriented toward others, as when a person suffering from paranoia (a form of schizophrenia) threatens others.

Second, the mentally ill actor adopts a personal reality which others do not ratify. The deviant violates widely shared expectations regarding the propriety of behavior in particular situations (Goffman, 1963a:3). As Scheff

(1966:32) states, mentally ill behavior "violates the assumptive world of the group, the world that is construed to be the only one that is natural, decent, and possible." Precisely which norms constitute the assumptive world, which background expectancies are shared by competent members of the community for particular situations, are difficult to specify. Scheff (1966; 1974) argues that mental illness is a label for a broad and ambiguous category of deviance which he terms "residual rule-breaking."

> The culture of the group provides a vocabulary of terms for categorizing many norm violations: crime, perversion, drunkenness, and bad manners are familiar examples. Each of these terms is derived from the type of norm broken, and ultimately, from the type of behavior involved. After exhausting these categories, however, there is always a residue of the most diverse kinds of violations, for which the culture provides no explicit label. For example, although there is great cultural variation in what is defined as decent or real, each culture tends to reify its definition of decency and reality, and so provides no way of handling violations of its expectations in these areas. The typical norm governing decency or reality, therefore, literally "goes without saying" and its violation is unthinkable for most of its members. For the convenience of the society in construing those instances of unnamable rule-breaking which are called to its attention, these violations may be lumped together into a residual category: witchcraft, spirit possession, or, in our own society, mental illness. . . . the diverse kinds of rule-breaking for which our society provides no explicit label, and which, therefore, sometimes lead to the labeling of the violator as mentally ill, will be considered to be technically *residual rule-breaking*.(Scheff, 1966:33-34, emphasis in original)

Thus, such activities as withdrawal, hallucination, and senseless fears violate residual norms, those rules "which are so taken for granted that they are not explicitly verbalized" (Scheff, 1966:38).

Finally, the individual's violation of background expectancies cannot be explained in terms of motives which are current, popular, and ratified within the community (Cressey, 1962:455). As a consequence, the behavior appears "senseless" or "irrational" to respectable community members. For instance, a claustrophobic person in an enclosed space, such as an elevator, may behave in an apprehensive or fearful manner, demanding to be near the exit or trembling uncontrollably. From the standpoint of others, this behavior seems bizarre, for there are no rational grounds for fear. When an individual violates the assumptive, taken-for-granted world, and this violation cannot be explained in terms of what others consider sensible and rational, then such behavior may be interpreted as an indication that the individual suffers from mental illness and lacks the capacity to function as a competent member of the community (Blum, 1970:38). This interpretation may begin a process in which the individual is labeled mentally ill and subjected to social control actions aimed at curing his or her affliction.

What causes residual rule-breaking? Answers to this question vary, but most modern authorities adopt the medical model of illness. According to the medical model, residual rule-breaking is only a *symptom* of a deeper disease or disturbance. The nature of the disturbance is debated; advocates of competing psychiatric theories locate the disorder's cause in different psychological processes. Nonetheless, they share the assumption that residual rule-breaking is analogous to the symptoms of a physical disease—the behavior points to the presence of a mental disorder.

Although the medical model dominates the field of mental health, it is a controversial way of viewing mental illness, for it is based on a questionable conception of human behavior. Many sociologists and some psychiatrists argue that the medical model slights the role of social relations in the production and progression of mentally ill behavior (Akers, 1973:255-65; Clausen, 1971b; Laing, 1967; Laing and Esterson, 1964; Scheff, 1966; 1967; 1974; Szasz, 1960).[1] Conventional psychiatric theory pays limited attention to the individual's social relationships. It holds that a child's relations with authority figures affect the structure and development of his or her personality. Once developed, that personality largely determines behavior for the remainder of one's life, independent of later life experiences. The medical model ignores the possibility that the social world shapes the individual's behavior, often times facilitating the actor's residual rule-breaking. It also overlooks the possibility that being labeled and treated as mentally ill contributes to the actor's development of a mentally ill role.

A sociological alternative to the medical model holds that residual rule-breaking is socially organized behavior, shaped by the individual's interpersonal relations. There is little doubt that residual rule-breaking is disturbing and sometimes disruptive, but it is not necessary to explain it in terms of a disorder located within the individual (Laing and Esterson,1964; Szasz, 1960). Rather, this type of individual deviance can be explained and understood in terms of the same processes involved in conventional behavior. This position rests on several points.

First, many behavioral psychologists and sociologists argue that the behavior patterns indicative of mental illness are learned:

> From a social-learning perspective, behaviors that may be detrimental to the individual or that depart widely from the accepted social and ethical norms are considered not as manifestations of an underlying pathology, but as ways, which persons have learned, of coping with environmental and self-imposed demands. (Bandura, 1969:62).

Residual rule-breaking may represent behavior patterns learned through reinforcement from others (Akers, 1973:275-284). For instance, an individual may develop psychosomatic complaints in order to obtain attention and sympathy from others. When others attend to and sympathize with the individual's complaint, their responses reinforce the residual rule-breaking, and this behavior pattern becomes part of the individual's behavioral repertoire. Studies show that residual rule-breaking can be reduced by manipulating the individual's schedule of reinforcement and punishment (Ullman and Krasner, 1965).

Second, residual rule-breaking resembles socially respectable forms of problem-solving. Residual rule-breaking is the individual's attempt, albeit defective in the eyes of others, to manage troublesome social situations. In his critique of the medical model, Szasz (1960) argues that psychiatry envisions a world where social relationships would be harmonious, satisfying, and secure were it not for the disrupting effects of mental illness. Szasz objects to this image, arguing instead that "The diversity of human values and the methods by means of which they may be realized is so vast, and many of them remain so unacknowledged, that they cannot fail but to lead to conflicts in human relations" (Szasz, 1960:117). Residual rule-breaking may be a strategy, unsuitable from the standpoint of others, for coping with stressful, difficult social situations, with a "world in conflict." Laing and Esterson (1964) take a more extreme position. Examining the family contexts of young women diagnosed as schizophrenic, they conclude that "the experiences and behaviour of schizophrenics is much more socially intelligible than has come to be supposed by most psychiatrists" (Laing and Esterson, 1964:27). They argue that these women were not "sick"; rather, they were attempting to manage stressful, seemingly insane situations created by their families.

Lemert's (1967:197-211) research on paranoia illustrates the use of residual rule-breaking as a strategy for managing troublesome social situations. Lemert claims that paranoid behavior develops as a strategy for dealing with the hostile, conspiratorial, and exclusionary behavior of others. The process begins with interpersonal difficulties between the individual and others, such as family members, work associates, or neighbors. These difficulties arise from bona fide problems, such as a loss of status from a demotion at work. In response, the individual begins to treat others in an unpleasant manner, exhibiting arrogance or insulting them. The others' tolerance of the individual's behavior diminishes; they come to evaluate the individual as troublesome, as someone who is "untrustworthy," "unreliable," or "to be avoided." Increasingly, they treat the individual in a manner consistent with their evaluations—they patronize, redirect conversation toward inconsequential topics, or avoid contacts. Importantly, the others develop a coalition to oppose the individual and exclude him or her from normal interaction. The individual comes to realize that he or she is being excluded and isolated, and this is disturbing:

> As channels of communication are closed to the paranoid person, he has no means of getting feedback on consequences of his behavior, which is essential for correcting his interpretations of the social relationships and organization which he must rely on to define his status and give him a sense of identity. (Lemert, 1967:207)

In an attempt to make others respond, the individual tries to provoke strong reactions from them—he or she accuses them of conspiracy or acts in a blunt or insulting manner. Such actions elicit further exclusion and isolation from others, which, in turn, intensifies the individual's efforts to generate meaningful communication. This interactive process escalates until the individual is labeled "mentally ill" and treated as such by others, including, in some cases, social control agents.

Third, labeling the individual as mentally ill facilitates the development of a mentally ill role which includes systematic residual rule-breaking. Most people violate background expectancies from time to time. However, comparatively few engage in residual rule-breaking systematically. Scheff (1966; 1974) advances a theory which explains why some individuals develop mentally ill careers. Essentially, mental illness is a role, learned through interaction with others. Most instances of residual rule-breaking are not interpreted by others as manifestations of mental illness; they are normalized, considered understandable given the situation (Mechanic, 1962; Yarrow et al.,1955). But some residual rule-breaking is interpreted as symptomatic of mental illness, and the rule violator is labeled mentally ill. Once labeled, others increasingly respond as if the individual is mentally ill, rewarding him or her for acting in a manner consistent with the mentally ill role. Psychiatrists, nurses, mental hospital attendants, family, and friends expect the individual to be "sick," and they reinforce him or her for accepting the label and acting mentally ill (Goffman, 1971). Other mental patients also may pressure the individual to accept his or her illness and act accordingly:

NEW PATIENT: "I don't belong here. I don't like all these crazy people. When can I talk to the doctor? I've been here four days and I haven't seen the doctor. I'm not crazy."
ANOTHER PATIENT: "She says she's not crazy." (Laughter from patients.)
ANOTHER PATIENT: "Honey, what I'd like to know is, if you're not crazy, how did you get your ass in this hospital?"
NEW PATIENT: "It's complicated, but I can explain. My husband and I. . . ."
FIRST PATIENT: "That's what they all say." (General laughter.) (Scheff, 1966:86).

At the same time, respectable others keep the individual from performing conventional roles; they exclude him or her from positions of trust and responsibility (Farina and Ring, 1965; Lamy, 1966; D. Miller and Dawson, 1965). This theory has been criticized for ignoring the mental patient's real problems (cf. Gove, 1970; 1975), but there is evidence that commitment to a mental hospital promotes the acquisition of a mentally ill role. The hospital strips the individual of his or her conventional identity, rewards for accepting and punishes for rejecting his or her mental illness, and isolates the individual from respectable members of the community. In response, institutionalized individuals sustain or increase their residual rule-breaking (Dunham and Weinberg, 1960; Goffman, 1961).

Residual rule-breaking is carried out by a single person. The actor may operate in solitude or in the presence of others. In either case, the actor's behavior flows from the subscription to a prohibited, nonshareable reality. While others may be incorporated into that reality, they do not subscribe to it; they may not even understand it. The actor's behavior challenges the assumptive world and appears senseless and irrational to others, but this does not mean that it is senseless. From the actor's standpoint, residual rule-breaking may be sensible, a means for acquiring attention and sympathy from others, or a strategy for managing a troublesome situation. Because it can be shaped by the actions of others, residual rule-breaking can be viewed as socially organized.

Shared Realities and Social Impact

Mental illness, heresy, and adoption of forbidden political ideologies are instances of deviant reality subscription. In each case, the individual perceives and acts toward the world from a prohibited standpoint. Each instance also can be viewed as socially organized, influenced by the activities of others, some deviant, some respectable. Cases of deviant reality subscription vary in several important ways. Adherence to forbidden religious or political ideologies usually involves subscribing to a shared reality, while mentally ill individuals rarely find anyone willing to share their realities. Those who share a deviant ideology may offer a direct challenge to the existing order; these deviants may organize to overthrow their respectable opponents. Thus, prohibited ideologies can form the basis for social movements. If the movement gains power, members may be able to demand respectable status for their beliefs. The evolution of early Christianity from a forbidden cult to a dominant church illustrates this process. Sometimes the change is more dramatic; members of the forbidden movement may revolt and overthrow the existing order, as in political revolutions. In either case, an alliance of individuals who share a prohibited reality provides the basis for coordinated action.

Not all deviant realities offer this potential. Mental illness does not involve a shared reality. The individual's reality departs from the everyday, taken-for-granted assumptions of most people in ways which others cannot recognize as reasonable. Without the ratification of one's reality by others, the individual remains a loner. As a consequence, the impact of these individualized deviant realities ordinarily is restricted to those who encounter the deviant face-to-face.

CONCLUSION

Any deviant transaction that can be performed by a single person is individual deviance. Individual deviance can be subdivided into the provision of deviant self-services and the subscription to a prohibited reality. Although a single person can accomplish individual deviance, it is not restricted to loners. Some forms of individual deviance usually involve loners; for example, suicide is normally a solitary act, and the mentally ill person's reality is generally not shared. Other forms of individual deviance typically are performed with deviant associates, often organized as peers; deviant drinking and recreational drug use usually occur in the company of associates. When persons engage in individual deviance together, their operations are likely to be more complex, with a division of labor and a set of norms and sanctions regulating conduct. Whether the act is performed alone or with others does not matter; it is an instance of individual deviance if one person's action, taken alone, merits a deviant label.

Although most explanations for individual deviance focus on physiological or personality disorders, individual deviance is socially organized. Psychiatric explanations argue that residual rule-breaking, suicide, excessive drinking, and drug use are symptoms of mental disorder. However, the actor's social relations shape individual deviance, just as they shape conventional actions. Actors learn from others the knowledge and skill needed to perform the deviant activity. As members of their culture, people learn about the situations in which suicide is common and perhaps justifiable, as well as the methods for committing suicide; tramps learn the rules for skid row drinking from the other skid row inhabitants. Moreover, the actual or anticipated actions of others can affect the actor's deviant performance. In paranoia, the actor's perception that others are progressively excluding him or her from group participation leads to residual rule-breaking. Thus, the actor's social relations shape the character of individual deviance.

Despite some similarities, individual deviance differs from comparable conventional activities in one important respect. Individual deviance makes the actor liable to social control efforts. This liability requires the actor to be discreet. The failure to be discreet increases the risks of detection and subsequent apprehension. To be sure, the capacity for discretion varies among those involved in individual deviance; some people who engage in residual rule-breaking are unable to control their conduct and keep it hidden. Further, the capacity to be discreet varies with the deviant's resources; some persons can control private settings for their deviance, while others cannot. The more public the deviance, the greater the risks of discovery and apprehension. Although individual deviants may take others into account, their deviance demands only one actor. The social organization of deviance becomes more complex in deviant exchange and deviant exploitation—transactions which require a second actor.

NOTES

[1]There are other criticisms of the medical model. Some critics argue that the medical model lends itself to circular reasoning, for there is virtually no way that a causal connection can be empirically established between an internal, mental state and behavior. As a result, mentally ill behavior is taken as evidence of the inner mental state, while the inner mental state is said to explain the behavior. The medical model also lacks a broad base of empirical support. For example, treatment efforts that are consistent with the model have not met with much success. See Akers (1973:255-265).

CHAPTER SIX
DEVIANT EXCHANGE

Deviant exchange is a transaction in which two or more individuals voluntarily exchange illicit goods or services. Any prohibited commodity — illicit goods, such as illicit drugs, pornography, or smuggled material, or illicit services, such as illegal abortions or forbidden sexual services—can be the basis for an exchange. Like individual deviance, deviant exchange is socially organized. Exchange participants share a cognitive perspective which shapes their actions. Each participant also affects the other—together, they must come to terms over the conditions for the exchange, including their division of labor and respective payoffs, and they must coordinate their actions. The participants also work together to avoid detection and apprehension by social control agents. Deviant exchange is more complex than individual deviance because it requires at least two participants who cooperate in reciprocal roles.

Exchange transactions are common in respectable as well as deviant life. When two friends trade confidences, or when a customer buys something in a store, an exchange takes place. Both deviant and respectable forms of exchange share several properties (cf. Blau, 1964:1-32, 88-114; Homans, 1974:51-69, 94-138). First, exchange requires that the participants have compatible interests. Participants mutually benefit from their interaction by providing one another with rewarding goods or services which they cannot provide for themselves. Second, exchange is cooperative. The participants voluntarily enter the exchange and work together to produce mutually beneficial results. Third, while exchange involves compatible interests, the participants nonetheless enter the exchange out of self-interest. They expect their efforts will be profitable; they expect rewards greater than the costs incurred from participation. When a transaction does not yield the expected profits, the participants may negotiate to change the rate at which the goods or services are exchanged or withdraw from the operation altogether.

There are two principal forms of deviant exchange—trades and sales. In a "trade," the simpler form of deviant exchange, the participants perform roughly comparable deviant tasks—each participant provides the other with a similar service. Examples of deviant trades include homosexual intercourse in public places and swinging (sometimes called "wifeswapping"). In a "sale," the more complex form of deviant exchange, the participants perform different deviant tasks—one party sells a good or service, while another party buys it. Examples of deviant sales include illegal abortions, prostitution, the sale of illicit drugs, fencing, and bookmaking.

Trades and sales differ along three dimensions. First, they vary in the degree of differentiation between the participants' roles. In deviant trades, the participants perform roughly comparable roles, although there may be a division of labor. The participants in homosexual intercourse, for instance, may perform different acts, but each gives and receives sexual satisfaction, making their roles comparable. In deviant sales, the participants perform very different roles—one party acts as a seller, the other as a customer. Second, trades and sales differ in the amount of knowledge and skill necessary to perform the roles. Deviant trades generally require relatively unsophisticated knowledge and skill which the participants can learn in conventional social life. For example, swingers require little special sexual training. In deviant sales, the seller, and perhaps the customer, need relatively sophisticated knowledge and skill. A bookmaker must be able to compute odds, collect bets, and lay off large bets, and a prostitute must know how to collect payments, manage troublesome customers, and the like. The special knowledge and skill necessary to perform as a bookmaker or prostitute are learned from experienced deviants. Third, trades and sales differ in their division of authority. In trades, there is minimal division of authority; the participants enter the exchange as equals and coordinate their actions through collective problem-solving and negotiation. In sales, however, the seller usually directs the interaction, setting the stage and determining the conditions of the sale, such as the price of the good or service. While the customer can negotiate these conditions and decide whether to make a purchase, the seller structures the transaction, including the customer's participation in it.

Despite these basic differences, both trades and sales require their participants to manage four problems. First, they must locate a market—

prospective partners with whom illicit goods or services can be exchanged. In respectable exchanges, locating a market is easy; advertisements and telephone directories list sellers as well as the times and places they can be contacted. But in deviant exchange, markets are concealed. The participants are vulnerable to social control efforts; by advertising publicly, they would risk detection and apprehension. Alternate channels of information are needed to locate deviant markets. An individual may locate a prospective partner using social networks or geographic knowledge. A newcomer can find a deviant market using a social network, asking others how to find it. In extreme cases, a long chain of contacts, perhaps through a friend of a friend of a friend, develops before the market can be located (N. Lee, 1969). A second method for finding a market uses geographic knowledge, going where deviants are thought to frequent. A simple strategy for finding a prostitute is to go to the "red light" district.

Second, participants must come to terms over the conditions for the exchange. In respectable exchanges, these terms often are conventionally established and nonnegotiable; a grocery store, for instance, sets the quantity, quality, and prices of items for sale and the customer pays without question. In deviant exchange, the terms are more often at issue. The participants may need to agree on a time and place for the exchange. More importantly, they need to agree on precisely what each participant will contribute to the transaction. In trades, the participants may negotiate about what specific services will be exchanged. In sales, the participants must come to terms on the price and the goods or services provided for payment. The participants also may agree that they will not exploit their relationship by providing less than promised, blackmailing or stealing from the partner, or informing outsiders of the partner's deviance.

Third, the participants must carry out the deviant exchange. As in a respectable exchange, the participants must coordinate their actions to produce mutually beneficial results. Living up to the terms of the bargain can be particularly troublesome in deviant exchange. Also, because they are involved in deviance, participants cannot turn to social control agencies if one party fails to live up to terms. Deviant exchange is based on trust— the participants will not exchange illicit goods or services unless they trust one another to operate honestly, to keep the terms of the agreement. Because there is always a possibliity that partners will violate this trust, the participants may take precautions to protect themselves from their partners' betrayal.

Fourth, the participants must protect their marketplace. They are vulnerable, both to social control agents and to predators, persons who exploit deviants through assault, theft, or blackmail. Exchanges must be arranged and performed secretly, often in protected settings which outsiders are unlikely to enter. There is a tension here—the marketplace must be accessible enough for deviants to locate it, yet it must be secure against outsiders' observation and invasion.

The remainder of this chapter focuses on the organization of four cases of deviant exchange. It begins by examining two cases of deviant trades—homosexual relations in public restrooms and swinging. It then considers two instances of deviant sales—fencing and the sale of illicit drugs.

TRADES

Trades are deviant exchanges where the actors perform comparable roles. The most obvious examples are types of deviant sexual intercourse—each partner seeks sexual satisfaction and each provides sexual services for the other's satisfaction. As in any exchange, participation is voluntary—rape is not a trade. In theory, contemporary Americans only approve of sexual relations between married partners. This excludes a wide range of sexual activities performed by consenting partners—premarital intercourse (I. Reiss, 1970), extramarital intercourse (Hunt, 1969), male homosexuality (A. Bell and Weinberg, 1978; M. Weinberg and Williams, 1974), female homosexuality (A. Bell and Weinberg, 1978; Ponse, 1976; Tanner, 1978), sadomasochism (Kamel, 1980; T. Weinberg and Falk, 1980), and swinging (Bartell, 1971). Many state penal codes prohibit all or some of these activities. In practice, however, sex outside of marriage is not always considered deviant. Most laws against sexual relations between consenting partners are rarely enforced, and there is widespread tolerance for some formerly forbidden activities, such as premarital intercourse and homosexuality.

Although some types of deviant sexual conduct are being vindicated, other sexual activities retain their deviant status. This is particularly true when individuals have intercourse in public places or when they perform unfamiliar sexual practices. Tearoom trades—homosexual intercourse in public restrooms—remain deviant to many people who tolerate homosexual behavior in private places. Similarly, swinging—deliberately exchanging marital partners for sexual relations—involves an element of calculation which sets it apart from more conventional sexual practices. These two cases provide examples for this section.

Tearoom Trades

Homosexual relations are as varied as those of heterosexuals. At one extreme, couples live together monogamously for years. At the other extreme, two individuals meet, have intercourse, and part, sometimes in the space of a few minutes. These fleeting relationships are impersonal—they are conducted anonymously, without commitment or obligation beyond sheer sexual satisfaction. They let people enjoy homosexual experiences while minimizing the chances that their involvement will become public knowledge; homosexuality is segregated to this one sector of the individual's life. While impersonal sex is not representative of all homosexuality, it highlights the essential elements of a deviant trade, precisely because the participants' relationship is limited to their brief encounter.

Sociologists have studied impersonal sex between homosexuals in a variety of settings, including gay bathhouses and highway rest areas (Corzine and Kirby, 1977; Delph, 1978; M. Weinberg and Williams, 1975). The most detailed study of impersonal sex, Laud Humphreys' *Tearoom Trade* (1970), examines homosexual contacts in public restrooms or "tearooms." Because Humphreys provides a wealth of information about the social organization of these impersonal contacts, this discussion will focus on tearoom trades.

The men who participate in impersonal sexual relations in tearooms differ from those who attend openly gay settings, such as gay bars or discos (Humphreys, 1970:11, 104-30). Tearooms attract only a minority of the gay men who are active in the larger homosexual community. Tearooms also attract men who do not define themselves as homosexual or avoid participating in the homosexual community ("closet queens"). Some 54 percent of the men observed by Humphreys in tearoom encounters were married and living with their wives, and another 24 percent were unmarried yet maintained heterosexual appearances in public life. Thus, the overwhelming proportion of tearoom participants keep their homosexual contacts secret; they do not want to be labeled as gay, or even be seen with those who are identified as homosexual.

Tearoom participants enter their exchange expecting sexual satisfaction with little cost (Humphreys, 1970:46). Because their contacts are impersonal, participants need not invest time and effort in developing or maintaining a relationship with their sex partners. Their relations are unencumbered by the many obligations characteristic of courting and love relationships. While some men define tearoom sex as only a substitute for heterosexual sex, other men look on tearoom relations as a unique and exciting experience.

Tearooms offer several advantages to men who want impersonal sex (Humphreys, 1970:3-15, 96-97). They are easily accessible, located in public places, such as bus stations, YMCAs, and public parks. Within these larger public settings, tearooms are reasonably private; they are protected against outside observation by walls, doors, and the like. Tearooms provide participants with an alibi should they be discovered there. A person who would have difficulty explaining his presence in a gay bar or bathhouse can easily account for his presence in a public restroom.

As in any exchange, tearoom participants must locate the marketplace—those restrooms where men meet to have sex. Not all public restrooms are tearooms. Several features of restrooms determine which ones become scenes for impersonal sex, and participants search for restrooms with these features (Humphreys, 1970:6-9). Tearooms are relatively isolated from the main traffic flow. For instance, in a public park, those restrooms which become tearooms are usually located furthest from the heavily used park facilities. Tearooms also have outside surroundings that can be surveyed easily by those inside. One or more of the windows may have small cracks, so that persons inside can peer through to watch for outsiders. Inside the restroom, the walls may be filled with graffiti, indicating that it is frequented by men who engage in homosexual relations. And the walls of the toilet stalls may have small holes in them, used by men inside the stalls to peer into the restroom and evaluate others.

The tearoom serves as a rallying point for prospective partners. Once he finds a tearoom, a man must locate a partner with whom to exchange sexual services. Usually, a man will wait outside the tearoom for a time to see whether the police are near, former partners are present, or desirable persons also seem to be waiting (Humphreys, 1970:60-61). If he observes a desirable man entering the restroom, he will follow immediately. Or he may enter the restroom in hope of signaling the other to follow him inside. If no one approaches or leaves the tearoom while he watches, he may enter the tearoom to determine what is happening. If the tearoom is unoccupied, promising little action, he may search for another tearoom and a sex partner.

Once two participants locate one another inside a tearoom, they must come to terms on the conditions for their exchange. Specifically, they must establish their intent to engage in impersonal sex and agree on what service each participant will provide the other. The participants in tearoom encounters perform different roles (Humphreys, 1970:49). The two principal actors exchange sexual services: the "insertor" inserts his penis into the mouth of the other, and the "insertee" is the fellator. In addition, there are three roles for onlookers. The "waiter" waits for a particular kind of partner, or an opportunity to get in on the action. The "masturbator" masturbates, either as an end in itself or in the course of waiting. Lastly, the "voyeur" simply watches the others engage in intercourse. These onlookers serve an important function—they alert the principal actors when outsiders approach the tearoom, giving the men time to halt their sexual relations before the others enter.

To engage in impersonal sex, the prospective partners must communicate their desire to participate in the deviant exchange. Typically, they do this nonverbally. After the men enter the tearoom, they quickly size up the situation and position themselves. One man may move directly to a stall and sit on the toilet seat; this usually signifies to others that he intends to serve as the insertee. Another may move to one of the urinals; this generally indicates his desire to serve as the insertor. The prospective insertor conveys his intention to participate by "signaling." Standing back from the urinal, thereby exposing his penis to others, he casually masturbates. One tearoom participant states:

> The thing he (the potential insertee) is watching for is "handling," to see
> whether or not the guy is going to play with himself. He's going to pretend

like he is masturbating, and this is the signal right there. . . . (Humphreys, 1970:63)[1]

The prospective insertor must show an erection—"the one essential and invariable means of indicating a willingness to play" (Humphreys, 1970:64). The prospective insertee, seated in the stall, watches the insertor through a small hole in the stall's wall. The insertee communicates his desire to participate either by motioning the insertor to the stall or by moving to one of the urinals.

Once the men communicate their desire to participate in an exchange, they must agree on a "contract," setting forth who will perform which roles. In general, contracts are initiated in one of two ways—the man who wishes to perform as the insertee takes hold of his prospective partner's exposed, erect penis; or the man who wishes to perform as the insertor steps into the stall where his prospective partner is seated. The contract is ratified when the prospective partner does not reject the other's move. In some cases, a gesture, such as manipulating the initiator's penis, signifies consent; in other cases, a "lack of negative response from the recipient of the action is enough to seal the contract" (Humphreys, 1970:66).

After coming to terms, the partners engage in oral intercourse with the insertee fellating the insertor (Humphreys, 1970:71-75). Their exchange may be occur in front of the urinals or inside a stall. Other participants, such as the voyeur, may approach and observe their activity, or they may simply give the partners some privacy and wait their turn. In any case, several norms govern the deviant trade. Once the act is initiated, neither partner backs down from the agreement—oral intercourse continues until either orgasm is reached or outsiders threaten to enter the tearoom. Because they operate under the threat of outside intervention, the partners finish their exchange quickly. Fellatio is usually completed in anything from ten seconds to five minutes. Lastly, the partners conduct their exchange without a word.

Once the exchange is completed, one or both participants leave the setting. In most cases, the insertor departs immediately. Sometimes the insertee also leaves, but frequently he waits in the tearoom for another partner. After leaving, some men go home or back to work. Others return to their cars, parked in a lot near the tearoom, and await the arrival of new players. Still other men venture to another tearoom in search of more action.

Tearoom participants run serious risks. First, they risk social damage (Humphreys, 1970:82-84). What tearoom participants fear most is the discovery of their activities by their family, friends, co-workers, and neighbors:

Sometimes, when I come out of a tearoom, I look up at the sky just to make sure some plane isn't flying around up there, writing "(JOHN JONES) IS A PERVERT"! (Humphreys, 1972:82)

Exposure is feared because of its irreparable harm to one's social relations—it can break up a man's marriage or jeopardize his livelihood. Second, tearoom participants risk blackmail. Anyone who discovers their secret, including police officers, acquaintances, or other tearoom participants, can demand money to remain silent. Of course, the dangers of exposure and blackmail are greatest for participants who live apparently heterosexual lives. Discovery in a tearoom poses fewer risks for men who openly acknowledge their homosexuality (Humphreys, 1970:131-34). Finally, participants risk physical attack. Defining tearoom participants as fair game because they are both despised and unlikely to complain to the police, teenagers and other "toughs" may injure or kill men found in tearooms.

Tearoom participants devise techniques to protect themselves from these dangers. To avoid exposure and blackmail by their partners, tearoom participants avoid giving away biographical information. Exchanging names and addresses renders personal what should be an impersonal encounter, adding to the risks. This norm is observed to the point that participants often maintain total silence during their encounters (Humphreys, 1970:47). To avoid identification and apprehension by the authorities, one or more men may serve as lookouts, to warn of intruders. In fact, when a tearoom contains only an insertor and insertee, the pair may move toward a cracked window so the insertor can watch for outsiders during intercourse. To avoid physical attack by predators, participants avoid any sexual interaction with juveniles, who may attack, injuring or killing the participants.

Tearoom sex is a relatively simple deviant trade. The participants find sexual gratification without the costs of undertaking a love relationship. They locate public restrooms where men pair up for brief, casual sexual contacts. They find partners within these tearooms, establish their mutual desire to participate, assign roles, and perform fellatio. This entire process occurs quickly and nonverbally. By maintaining silence, the participants can insure a measure of discretion on the part of their partners, reducing the risks of exposure and blackmail. Further, by watching the area surrounding the tearoom, the participants can avoid detection and subsequent exposure or attack.

Swinging

Swinging is a deviant trade in which married couples agree to have sexual relations with other persons in one another's presence (Wolshok, 1971: 488). Unlike extramarital affairs, which typically occur without the spouse's knowledge or consent, swinging involves mutual knowledge and approval of sexual relations with others by both the husband and wife (L. Smith and Smith, 1974). And unlike some instances of open marriage, where a husband and wife agree to have sexual relations with others in privacy, swinging occurs in the spouse's presence. There are three basic types of swinging (cf. Bartell, 1971; Thio, 1978:279-282). In *closed swinging*, two couples exchange mates and then move to separate rooms to conduct their sexual relations. In *open swinging*, two couples exchange mates and engage in sexual relations in the same room. Finally, the *swinging party* involves three or more couples who gather together, exchange mates, and swing, either in separate rooms or in the same room.

Swinging resembles tearoom trades in several respects. First, the participants exchange sexual services in order to receive personal satisfaction. Most participants expect sexual gratification from the transaction, but many swingers also anticipate additional rewards (Fang, 1976; Palson and Palson, 1972; Stephenson, 1973; Wolshok, 1971). "The comments of many committed swingers suggest that co-marital sexuality has served to solidify their marriages, to expand their circle of friends, and to contribute to a more general sense of well-being" (Wolshok, 1971:493). Many people begin swinging in the hope of enhancing their marriages as well as their everyday lives. They expect swinging to add excitement and novelty to their marital routine (Palson and Palson, 1972). One woman observed that prior to swinging, her marriage was lifeless:

> We didn't fight, because there was nothing to fight about. We just felt the inevitability of being together for the rest of our lives—something like brother and sister without the blood. (Palson and Palson, 1972:31)

Another swinger reported that he yearned for a variety of sexual experiences, something he had missed in his early life:

> I told Helen (his wife) that I missed terribly the experiences that other men had as kids. I was always too busy with school to ever have a good time dating. I only had a date once in high school, for the senior prom, and I only had one girl friend in college. I felt that whole stage of my life was totally absent. I wanted to do these things that I had missed out on—then maybe I'd feel more able to cope with our problems. Much to my surprise, Helen felt that she too had missed out. (Palson and Palson, 1972:34)

Second, like tearoom relations, swinging is an impersonal encounter with no strong emotional attachments between sex partners (Ramey, 1977:44). Swingers usually do not want to invest time and effort in the development and maintenance of love relationships with their sex partners, for this can lead to jealousy by their mates and disruption of their marriages. Some swingers prefer swinging parties because they guarantee impersonal contact—there are more participants than in open or closed swinging, and an individual can enjoy a series of brief sexual contacts. These brief contacts make it difficult for an individual to become emotionally attached to specific sex partners, reducing the liklihood of jealousy and subsequent complications. Many swingers who prefer open or closed swinging also maintain impersonal relationships with their sex partners. They swing with one couple only once or twice and then move on to another couple, without trying to develop strong, binding relationships with specific couples.

Third, like tearoom participants, swingers are discreet about their deviant involvement. While tearoom relations occur in public restrooms, swinging usually takes place in a private home where there is less risk of detection or intervention by outsiders, unless the gathering becomes loud or unruly (Bartell, 1971:183). Still, the participants want to avoid exposing their activities because swinging violates conventional norms of marriage and sexual relations and because it can bring negative sanctions from others. Swingers, like tearoom participants, must trust their partners to be discreet, to protect their identities and activities from outsiders (Stephenson, 1973:181). Some swingers prefer the anonymity of swinging parties where, except for the host and hostess, participants may know nothing more than one another's first names.

Although swinging and tearoom relations share some basic properties, swinging is a more complex transaction. The process of locating prospective sex partners is more complicated in swinging. Swingers locate one another in any of four ways (Fang, 1976:224-226). First, they can use a personal reference. Veteran couples pass along the names and telephone numbers of past partners to new couples, or they arrange for the couples to meet. Second, swingers can place or answer advertisements in swingers' magazines or newspapers. Ads are anonymous, describing only the couple's qualifications and interests:

> Attractive couple in late 30's. She 5'7", 145, 38-28-38. He 6', 180. Would like to hear from similar couples in Chicago area. Object: conversation, cocktails, and beginning of swinging interests. Photo of both a must.

> Discreet, attractive couple 21 and 25 wish to meet couples and singles 21-35 for exciting and fun-loving adult relationships. Open-minded but not way out. No prejudices. Full length photo, address, and detailed letter assures same. (Bartell, 1971:85)

Swingers may answer the ads with letters describing themselves and their interests. Letters are mailed to the publisher along with a forwarding fee. The publisher forwards the letters to the advertisers, who may respond by arranging to meet the writers (Stephenson, 1973:180; Thio, 1978:278-279). Third, swingers can meet other couples in swingers' bars or clubs. Participants learn about these establishments through advertisements in swingers' publications, such as *LaPlume, Select, National Informer, Swinger's Life*, and *Kindred Spirits*. Like those who frequent singles bars or gay bars, swingers enter the bar, look around for attractive couples, walk over and begin a conversation, and determine whether the other couple is interested in swinging with them (Thio, 1978:278). Fourth, swingers can recruit newcomers. A veteran couple casually brings up the topic of swinging to a prospective couple and assesses their reactions. If the recruits seem interested in swinging, the veterans may suggest a trade. This approach is rare, probably because the veterans must reveal their deviance to outsiders. While the new couple might decide to swing, they also might respond with shock, or even by exposing the recruiters to other nonswingers.

Like tearoom participants, swingers come to terms before engaging in sexual trades. In tearoom trades the participants establish their intent and assign roles quickly and nonverbally. In swinging, however, the process of coming to terms is more complicated. Unlike tearoom relations, where only two persons must come to terms, swinging involves two or more couples. Members of each couple must first agree to participate in the deviant trade. In some cases, both husbands and wives want to participate. In other cases, however, one spouse agrees to participate at the other's request. Often the husband brings up the topic and reveals his desire to swing; while the wife may resist, she eventually yields (cf. L. Smith and Smith, 1974; Symonds, 1971). Given agreement between spouses, the couples must then come to terms with one another. The prospective partners explicitly state their sexual interests and agree about the kinds of sexual activities they will perform, the kinds of activities they wish to avoid, and the style of swinging they will adopt. They also may negotiate about related activities; for instance, one couple may want the other to agree to abstain from drinking. Finally, they arrange a time and place to meet and agree to be discreet about their partners' identities and activities. While tearoom participants come to terms immediately before intercourse, swingers' negotiations often take place through ads, letters, and meetings in bars before the couples get together to swing (Bartell, 1971).

In swinging, the sexual exchange is part of a larger social occasion. The evening may begin with nonsexual activities, such as eating or dancing. Sometime during the course of socializing, men and women start pairing up for sexual relations. Further, their sexual contracts typically last longer than those in tearooms. Tearoom trades are fleeting because of the risks of outside intrusion, but swingers face minimal risks of outside intrusion and couples can devote an entire evening to swinging.

While swinging shares some features with tearoom trades, it is a more complex transaction. In both, the participants exchange sexual services in an impersonal trade. But swinging involves a more elaborate process for locating prospective partners, often involving special communication channels (for example, publications and letters) or intermediaries (for example, veteran swingers). Swinging also involves more people—two or more couples must come to terms, first as each couple agrees to swing and then as the different couples arrange a mutually acceptable gathering. Because more people are involved, issues must be discussed explicitly to insure that each member consents.

Equality and Immediacy

When participants in trades locate a marketplace, negotiate terms, carry out the exchange, and try to protect themselves, they are solving problems which confront participants in all deviant exchanges. However, trades have two characteristics which set them apart from the more complexly organized deviant sales—participants typically have equal status, and successful trades have few long-term consequences.

Partners in a deviant trade may perform different, yet complementary roles. In a tearoom trade, one man acts as insertor, the other as insertee. While these roles are different, the actors have roughly equal status in the transaction. Each participant can influence the terms of the exchange by refusing to participate. Neither has the authority to make the other co-operate. When one partner exerts more influence in the transaction, it often reflects that person's greater experience with deviant trades—veterans guide newcomers, teaching them the knowledge and skill needed to participate in the deviant marketplace. Differences in roles or experience usually do not negate the essential equality of the participants.

In deviant trades, participants seek immediate satisfaction with few long-term consequences. While there may be a period of negotiation in which participants come to terms, trades often have abrupt endings. Swingers may spend several hours with prospective partners before deciding to swing together; they are less likely to maintain their relationship beyond a few sexual trades. In fact, participants often withhold their names and other information about themselves so that they can avoid future contacts with their partners. Of course, deviant trades occasionally develop into enduring relationships—some sadists and masochists establish long-term relationships as regular sexual partners (Kamel, 1980). But tearoom trades, swinging encounters, and most other trades are designed to minimize long-term consequences. Participants seek to avoid the attention of social control agents, but they also want to avoid future contact with their partners as a way of protecting themselves from exposure and blackmail.

SALES

Sales are more complex exchanges than trades. The participants perform distinct roles—one as the seller of the deviant good or service, the other as the buyer. Any prohibited good or service can become the basis for a deviant sale, including sexual services (Bryan, 1965; Heyl, 1979; Pittman, 1971; Rasmussen and Kuhn, 1976), pornography (Karp, 1973; Sundholm, 1973), smuggled goods (T. Green, 1969), and bookmaking (Hindelang, 1971; Lesieur, 1977), as well as the two examples considered below, stolen goods and drugs. Typically, the buyer pays the seller in cash and the seller makes a profit on their exchange. Some deviants support themselves by selling. Because sellers usually deal with many different customers, they have more experience with the exchange transaction than their partners. In most cases, both the seller and the customer are considered deviant, but social control agents view the seller's action as more serious and they devote more effort to apprehending and sanctioning sellers.

Both the seller and the customer are vulnerable to exploitation by the other. Partners can rob each other or betray one another to social control agents. Because the seller usually has more experience and runs greater risks from social control efforts, the seller directs the exchange. Sellers pick the setting for the exchange, set the terms for the sale, and direct their customers through the transaction. To minimize their risks, customers often return to sellers who dealt fairly with them in the past, so that established business relationships develop between some buyers and sellers. These elements—distinct roles, a profit motive, differences in risk, experience, and authority, and established relationships—make exchanges more complicated than the relatively simple trades in tearooms and swinging.

The two examples considered in this section represent different sales situations. Fencing—purchasing stolen property for resale—is often a small, independent enterprise. In contrast, drug sales are usually tied to a larger distribution network. Stolen goods normally are fenced only once, but illicit drugs are sold and resold as they pass through the network.

Fencing

Fencing involves an exchange between a thief and a fence who buys and then resells the stolen property. Not all stolen goods are fenced; some thieves keep the goods they steal or sell them directly to a customer who plans to use them. But often thieves turn to a receiver, a middleman who buys stolen property from thieves and sells it to customers. There are different kinds of receivers. The receiver can be a member of a mob of thieves, who sells stolen goods on behalf of the mob, a "piece man," "who accepts merchandise from thieves and transfers it to the real buyer for a percentage or 'piece' of the value of the goods" (Klockars, 1975:172, note 15), or an "occasional receiver," who irregularly buys stolen goods for resale (Hall, 1952:156). A final type of receiver is the fence.

Fences can be arrayed along several dimensions. First, they vary in their commitment to fencing. Some persons make fencing a full-time occupation, but most limit it to a sideline, with other activities serving as their central source of income (Walsh, 1977:51; 111-113). Second, fences vary in the legitimacy of their other operations. In some cases, the fence is a "criminal entrepreneur"—fencing is a sideline to other illicit pursuits, such as loansharking or bookmaking (Walsh, 1977:107-111). But usually the fence is a "businessman-fence," a proprietor of a legitimate business who buys and sells stolen goods under the cover of the business. Businessman-fences operate various establishments, including antique stores, restaurants, taverns, salvage companies, and auto parts shops (Walsh, 1977:45-51). Third, fences vary in the kinds of stolen goods they handle. At one pole is the "generalist," a fence who will buy and sell virtually anything a thief offers, from clothing to jewelry, appliances to computer tapes (Klockars, 1975:106). At the other pole is the "specialist," who handles only certain kinds of goods, such as auto parts or televisions. Most fences are specialists (Walsh, 1977:54-60).

The fence interacts with two publics. "As a fence he provides much needed disposal services to a criminal population (thieves) and at the same time purveys wanted goods to an array of customers" (Walsh, 1977:52). The fence relates to these publics in different ways. Thieves are the fence's clients; they receive important services, including cash for stolen goods (and sometimes bail and legal services) and advice on what goods to steal and the techniques of theft (Klockars, 1975:152-55; Shover, 1972). To customers, the fence sells stolen goods at a comparatively low price. This section focuses on the exchange between the fence and thief, for it clearly exemplifies deviant sales. While customers may not be aware that goods they purchase from a fence are stolen, thieves know that they are involved in a deviant exchange.

At first glance, the fence appears to be the customer and the thief the seller. After all, the thief sells stolen goods to the fence. However, "the fence is more than a buyer of the thief's product; he is a *seller* of services as well" (Walsh, 1977:71, italics in original). The thief requires an outlet for stolen property. Stolen goods usually mean little to the thief; one can use only so many televisions, appliances, and cameras. The thief needs to transform stolen goods into a more negotiable medium—cash. The fence provides the thief with this important service (Walsh, 1977:175). The exchange will ultimately prove to be profitable for the fence. The fence purchases the thief's stolen goods at far less than their market value, making resale to customers a profitable venture (Klockars, 1975:77).

To carry out their exchange, the thief and fence must locate one another. They may use various methods to find one another. Vincent Swaggi, a professional fence interviewed by Klockars (1975), describes the gradual cultivation of a source of stolen goods:

> . . . you have to "open a guy up" so he'll do business with you. Like you can't just go up to somebody who is managing a warehouse and tell him you want him to send you hot merchandise. I started out with this Pep Boys guy buying dented stock, dead merchandise, overloads, anything I could steal [buy cheaply]. Once he got to know me he started sending me current stock at real good prices. Then after we was doin' business good for a couple of months he knew I'd take whatever he could get with no questions. (Klockars, 1975:50-51)[2]

Swaggi also observed that the thieves tell each other about a fence: "This whole business is word-of-mouth. One driver tells another, one thief tells another, one guy who owns a store tells somebody else who owns one" (Klockars, 1975:62). Or the thief and fence may share a social network, leading to mutual recognition of one another's status (as a thief or fence) (Walsh, 1977:117-138). Kinship is one such network—the thief and fence hear about each other from family members involved in theft or fencing.

For every deal, the thief and fence must come to terms on the price to be paid for the stolen property. The fence dominates pricemaking, for outcome value and outcome scarcity favor the fence (cf. Thibaut and Kelley, 1959:101-102). The commodity which the fence controls (cash) has greater rewarding value for the thief than the rewarding value for the fence of the commodity controlled by the thief (stolen goods). Indeed, during their negotiations, the fence may warn the thief that, while a fence does not need a thief to make a good living, the thief needs the fence to dispose of stolen goods and make ends meet. Moreover, a thief has more trouble finding alternate partners than the fence. The fence often knows a large number of thieves who provide a steady stream of stolen goods. In contrast, a thief may know only one or two fences, providing limited options for disposing of stolen goods. Even when the thief knows about other fences, access to them may be restricted by collusion. Although fences are theoretically in competition with one another, they may conspire against a thief who makes the rounds trying to get the highest price for goods. Here, the fence tells other fences that the thief is shopping around and asks them to quote a similar low price should the thief contact them. This collusion serves to constrict the thief's alternatives (Walsh, 1977:73-74). Thus, the fence's capacity to reward the thief is greater than the thief's capacity to reward the fence, making the fence the dominant partner in the transaction.

While the fence dominates price making, the actual price paid for stolen goods is negotiable. The thief wants to get the best price for stolen property. Customarily, the thief expects one-third the retail price—"a norm that has governed the asking price of thieves for centuries . . ." (Klockars, 1975:114). However, the fence wants to pay the lowest possible price in order to maximize resale profit. Consequently, the fence may quote a price considerably lower than one-third the retail price. The stage is set for negotiation.

The final price can be affected by several conditions (Walsh, 1977:71-76). First, the price paid for stolen goods depends on the type of thief. The better the thief—the greater the thief's skill, experience, and consistency—the better the terms offered by the fence. Knowledge about the quality and value of stolen goods and the intricacies of the fencing business affect the price obtained for stolen goods. An inexperienced thief does not completely understand the business of fencing:

> Unlike the legitimate consumer, he may have no real knowledge about the product he has in his possession. If the item is not labeled he may have no idea of its price. Even if it is labeled, he probably will not know if the price marked is competitive. Judgments about quality, market demand, and wholesale mark-up are difficult for the most sophisticated consumer; for the thief they may well be impossible. Finally, with high-cost items marketed to a social class different from his own, or items specific to a particular industry, he may have not only no notion of their price but also no idea of their purpose or use. (Klockars, 1975:115)

Given their ignorance, such thieves are easily deceived by the fence. The fence may tell them that the stolen goods are out of season, or unfinished, or of poor quality; the fence may even show them an outdated catalogue and quote them prices which have since increased (Klockars, 1975:116-120). As a consequence, inexperienced thieves may obtain only 10 percent of the goods' retail value. In contrast, experienced thieves understand fencing and know the value of their stolen goods. Consequently, they can evaluate the fence's offers better. With their knowledge, these thieves can get a better price—often 30 to 50 percent of retail value.

A second condition which affects the price is the fence's desire to guide the thief. Fluctuations in the market for stolen goods affect the fence's need for particular kinds and amounts of goods. For instance, if certain brands of watches are in demand, the fence wants a large and stable supply. In order to insure this supply, the fence sets a standard price for these watches. Thieves favor standard prices: ". . . it interjects an element of certainty into the exchange transaction which the thief rarely finds in dealings with the fence. It tells the thief not only what to steal, but also how much to steal in order to earn a specific monetary goal" (Walsh, 1977:73).

A third condition affecting price is competition among fences. Where competitors handle the same products, a fence may pay higher prices to obtain goods. Fences try to outbid their competitors under one or two conditions. First, if a fence's business drops because other fences are expanding, he or she will increase prices to regain a portion of the local business. Second, if a fence needs a large supply of particular products, he or she will outbid competitors in order to fill that need (Walsh, 1977:73). Competitive pricing is often temporary. "There is significant pressure within the industry to maintain low-level prices" (Walsh, 1977:73).

Because the sale is an illicit transaction, the participants must be cautious, using discretion to keep their dealings secret. Sometimes, caution can be built into the transaction. Fences "dress their illegal traffic in all the paraphernalia of lawful enterprise" (Hall, 1952:195). For the businessman-fence, the business provides a "front" behind which stolen goods can be bought and sold (Klockars, 1975:79-93). The legitimate front "renders the moving of merchandise, the discussion of price, the examination of cargoes, and the dealings with samples all entirely normal" (Klockars, 1975:89).

From the standpoint of outsiders, the fence and the thief are indistinguishable from a legitimate seller and customer.

Similarly, the exchange itself is conducted discreetly. While a fence may ask a thief to steal particular goods in order to fill a demand, most thieves initiate the transaction by bringing stolen goods to the fence. In such cases, the fence may insist the thief take precautions, such as moving the goods to a location where the fence cannot be linked to them should they be discovered (Klockars, 1975:86-87). Once the setting appears safe from outsiders, the fence may ask the thief to fetch all or samples of the goods for the fence's inspection. According to Swaggi:

> You see, I school my thieves and drivers. Watch sometime when one of my boosters comes in the store. First thing he does, he puts his bag down by the front door. Then he just looks around at the shelves like he's lookin' for something to buy. When I'm ready I'll give him the OK to come over and tell me what he's got. Remember I still ain't looked at his merchandise. Maybe I'll give him a little bullshit about how I ain't interested in what he's got, but then I'll have him bring it over. See, all that time if somebody's followin' him they're gonna come in. So if I didn't buy nothin' there's nothin' nobody can do. (Klockars, 1975:86)

The fence may also require the thief to remove all identifying information from the stolen goods, such as name tags from clothing and stock number slips from warehouse cartons (Klockars, 1975:87). Negotiations occur in relative privacy. Finally, once the exchange is made, the thief and fence devise an alibi. If the police catch the fence with the stolen goods, the fence needs an alibi corroborated by concrete evidence. A businessman-fence can use the false-bill-canceled-check procedure (Plate, 1975:72). Here, the fence pays the thief cash for the stolen property. He or she then writes a check drawn from bank account A for an amount representing the approximate wholesale price of the goods obtained, making the check out to a fictitious name. The thief endorses the check with the fictitious name and returns it to the fence, who then endorses the check and deposits the sum in bank account B. Should the police find the fence in possession of stolen goods, the fence has a solid alibi. The fence claims that he or she paid the customer with a check. However, because the customer needed the money right away, he or she took the check to the bank and cashed it. The double endorsement on the canceled check is used as proof of the legitimate sale.

Either the thief or the fence can exploit the other during their illicit transaction. On the one hand, the thief can cheat the fence. Typically, this involves "burning" the fence, obtaining some or all of the cash payment and failing to deliver the goods. On the other hand, the fence can exploit the thief by deceiving him or her about the quality or quantity of the stolen goods (cf. Klockars, 1975:113-129). The fence may falsely appraise the quality of the goods. Or, the thief may steal a carton with an unbroken seal, containing different items. The fence opens the carton, surreptitiously checks its contents, and finds that the assortment includes some valuable goods. The fence then announces that the carton contains the same, relatively cheap item. Similarly, the fence may undercount the stolen items, paying the thief for only some of the items delivered. Of course, thieves are not equally vulnerable to deception by the fence; a fence will not exploit thieves with whom he or she has developed a stable, long-term relationship. And fences usually will not deceive better thieves—they are knowledgeable and their trade is worth keeping because they bring valuable merchandise and little trouble if arrested (Klockars, 1975:125).

Given the potential for exploitation, the participants attempt to control each other's actions. The thief may use techniques similar to those employed by consumers in legitimate markets. Should the fence try to deceive the thief, the thief may refuse to sell and avoid that fence in the future. The thief may also "tip" the police, telling them that the fence is planning to buy or already has purchased stolen goods, or "set up" the fence, helping officials entrap the fence in an actual deal. The fence, in turn, exerts considerable control over the thief. The fence typically refuses to advance money before taking possession of the stolen goods. The fence who has a "drop," a place where stolen goods are stored, may keep its location secret, minimizing the risk of arrest on a tip. But even without these precautions, the thief will be reluctant to exploit the fence. The fence provides the thief with highly valued services. Further, the fence has a virtual monopoly over these services, for the thief is likely to know only one or two fences. The fence is a powerful figure in the thief's life—the fence can not only cut the thief off from other fences (by warning them that the thief cannot be trusted) but also inform the authorities about the thief's activities (Chappell and Walsh, 1978:189).

In summary, fencing involves an exchange between a thief and a fence; the fence provides the thief with an important service—converting stolen property into cash. The participants locate one another through various social networks, such as kinship or work. The thief brings the fence stolen goods, and they come to terms on a price. Although convention sets the price at one-third the resale value, the actual price is negotiable, depending on the thief's experience, the demand for the goods, and the fence's competition. The deviant sale is managed cautiously—the thief and fence want to avoid identification by authorities or exploitation by their business partners.

Dealing in Illicit Drugs

Drug dealing is a deviant sale which differs from fencing in some important ways. While fencing involves the sale of a service, drug sales involve an illicit good. The two also differ in their ties to a larger deviant network. Fencing typically is a small-scale, independent operation—the fence often owns a small business and buys and sells stolen property as a sideline, subject to such constraints as the thief's experience and the extent of local competition. But drug dealing often involves a large distribution network. Illicit drugs may pass through several organizational tiers, being sold and resold before reaching the ultimate user. This affects several features of the lower-level transactions, including the drug's price. This discussion examines the exchange between the drug retailer and drug user, because the largest number of drug sales occur at this level. First, however, the larger distribution network must be outlined.

The market in illicit drugs is complex, involving several basic tiers (cf. Carey, 1968:68-121; Redlinger, 1975). At the highest level are the manufacturers. They grow, harvest, and refine opium poppies or hemp or produce hallucinogens, amphetamines, or barbiturates; they sell the drugs to wholesalers. At the second level, the wholesaler purchases a large stock of illicit drugs from a manufacturer and transports them to a local market for distribution to retailers. Essential to wholesaling are establishing stable, trusting relations with manufacturers, possessing and investing a considerable amount of money in bulk purchases of illicit drugs, and establishing and maintaining a pool of retail buyers. Retailers form the third level. The retailer purchases a portion of the wholesaler's stock and sells the drugs to a clientele of users, possibly keeping some for personal consumption. Retailing requires connections with wholesalers, enough money to purchase a fairly large amount of drugs, and a location for selling to users. At the fourth tier are the ultimate users of illicit drugs, who buy from retailers. Of course, the number of tiers in the distribution network varies. In rare cases, the manufacturer sells directly to the user, as when a grower of marijuana sells to friends. In especially complex networks, drugs filter down through several additional tiers before reaching the retailer (cf. D. Goddard, 1978; Sabbag, 1976).

Although drug sales at any level involve an exchange of money for illicit drugs, as one moves from manufacturer to user, the character of drug dealing changes (Redlinger, 1975). First, the higher the level of dealing, the greater the seller's profits. While the retailer makes very little profit, owing to personal consumption of drugs, discounts to close friends, and pilferage, both the wholesaler and manufacturer turn handsome profits. Second, the higher the level of dealing, the more complex the organization of the parties to the transaction. Users often make purchases alone, on their own behalf. Retailers sometimes employ one or two assistants to distribute drugs to users. Wholesalers and manufacturers usually employ a small group of workers to prepare and transport goods, package the drugs for marketing, and distribute them to retailers. Also, lawyers and accountants may assist wholesalers and manufacturers. Third, the higher the level of dealing, the greater the parties' stability in the marketplace. Users and retailers have short careers—they may tire of the activity, find that it is not as profitable as they had assumed, or be apprehended and punished. Wholesalers and manufacturers, in contrast, enjoy high profits and relative invulnerability from social control efforts, leading to long, stable careers in drug dealing.

Like other deviant sales, the exchange between the retailer and user is an economic transaction. While the parties may socialize, they enter the exchange to buy and sell drugs. The user wants drugs, either to achieve the satisfactions of the drug experience or to ward off the effects of withdrawal from narcotics (Akers et al., 1968). Yet, the customer has no legitimate way of getting them. In turn, the retailer has a financial stake in the transaction. The retailer expects to make enough money to exceed the overhead—the costs incurred in purchasing the drugs, storing and preparing them for distribution, and transporting them to users—as well as the cost of personal consumption of drugs (Carey, 1968:71-73; Langer, 1977; Redlinger, 1975). Even hippies, whose ideology argues against profitmaking, expect to make a profit in their drug deals (Cavan, 1972:120-133).

Before the user can purchase illicit drugs, he or she must locate a retailer. Usually, this is not difficult—the user and retailer are linked by friendship. A popular stereotype is that retailers, out to make enormous profits, push drugs to the young, innocent, weak members of society. The seller is portrayed as a stranger who infiltrates young people's primary groups, provides them with free samples, and ultimately converts them to systematic drug use (cf. Clausen, 1971a:206). This stereotype is false. People introduce their friends to illicit drug use at social gatherings, such as parties and dates; rather than being naive, most people begin illicit drug use deliberately (Carey, 1968:51-60; Duster, 1970; E. Goode, 1970: 251-57; Redlinger, 1975). Moreover, most illicit drugs are distributed through a network of friends (Carey, 1968:80; E. Goode, 1970; Redlinger, 1975). The occasional user often receives illicit drugs from friends at cost or without charge; for example, a host offers hashish to guests at a party. The systematic user generally purchases small quantities from a friend who happens to be a retailer. Drug dealing is limited to friends for an important reason: a friend can be trusted. Because the customer is a friend, someone about whom much is known, the seller can assume that the customer is not an undercover police officer or a police informant and that the customer will be discreet in telling others about his or her source. Thus, many sellers refuse to deal with strangers:

> I make it a policy to never sell it to anybody I don't know . . . that's a groovy policy. Usually if someone you don't know comes in to make a buy, you can, unless it's a friend of a friend, you can make a pretty good assumption that he's the MAN so you don't talk to him. (Carey, 1968:80)[3]

Once the user locates the retailer, they must come to terms. The central issue is price. Drugs purchased through the illicit market cost substantially more than those in a legitimate market. While there is a large demand for illicit drugs, the supply is limited and often concentrated among a small number of deviant networks. Because customers have difficulty shopping for the lowest price, and because the demand for some drugs, particularly heroin, is inelastic (customers want the drug regardless of price), illicit drugs are expensive. Within any illicit drug market, prices are informally fixed. Sellers and customers know the price ranges of particular kinds and amounts of drugs, and the retailer and user generally negotiate within the commonly recognized range (Carey, 1968:70). Yet, the price range is somewhat flexible. In marijuana sales, "the price . . . will depend on the closeness of the friendship, the amount asked (joints will be given away, lids charged for), the number of times the friend asks for the favor, and one's mood at the moment" (Carey, 1968:70; cf. Cavan, 1972:120-133). A dealer's customers may request special discounts or credit arrangements on the basis of their faithfulness or friendship; thus, a heroin dealer's "good" customers can negotiate for a reduced price (Redlinger, 1975:288). Once the user and retailer agree on a price, they may consider payment. Retailers usually do not extend credit to customers; the buyer must pay on receipt of the drugs, to prevent him or her from exploiting the dealer by absconding. In some cases, however, the customer can "come up short." Here, the seller allows the customer to purchase drugs without paying the full amount. Although there is a limit to how short a customer can be, these sellers make sales on the promise of future payment. As in legitimate sales, this practice reflects the belief that extending credit will sustain the seller's clientele (Redlinger, 1975).

The user and retailer may also negotiate over the quality and quantity of drugs to be purchased. The user may wish to establish that the drugs meet certain standards before making payment. The quality and quantity of illicit drugs differ from those of legitimate drugs. The quality of a product is a measure of how good it is compared to similar products or an established standard. In legitimate drug markets, the government requires that drugs meet or exceed certain minimal standards of quality. In illicit drug markets, however, official standards of quality are absent, and the retailer and user are often uncertain about the product's quality, for it is difficult to determine to what degree the manufacturers and wholesalers "cut" the drug. Cutting drugs refers to the process of adding inexpensive substances of similar color and consistency so as to increase the apparent amount of the product; for instance, one ounce of heroin can be doubled by adding an ounce of milk-sugar, lactose, or quinine. Legitimate markets also are bound by law to employ standardized weights and measures in preparing and packaging drugs. In the illicit drug marketplace, however, standardized weights and measures are not used, because there is no means of enforcement. While retailers and users speak about such units as grains, grams, ounces, pounds, kilograms, and the like, there is considerable variability in the actual measures. For instance, while a kilogram weighs 2.2 pounds, the "kilograms" of heroin sold by dealers range from 2.0 to 2.4 pounds (Cavan, 1972:120-33; Redlinger, 1975).

The user may check quality and quantity in two ways. One common technique is simply to ask the retailer about the product. The customer expects the seller to be knowledgeable about the drugs he or she handles and to provide accurate information about them. On the basis of first-hand experience, sellers are expected to know about the amounts of active ingredients in their products and the size and weight of specific items. Users also expect sellers to know about the effects of illicit drugs; they serve users as pharmacological advisors (Carey, 1968:92; Langer, 1977:381). As one dealer observed:

> If I couldn't talk about drugs and the things that I was selling, I wouldn't be accepted as a dealer. A dealer is the person who is knowledgeable about drugs, who's experienced, who has tried most the stuff around. (Langer, 1977:381)

Another technique used is more subtle. In many cases, the participants couple their exchange with sociable drug use. Although the apparent purpose is sociable, it also serves as a test. By immediately using some portion of the drugs, the customer can test their quality before the seller leaves. The seller may encourage sociable drug use, but for a different reason— it helps to establish a stable clientele. Sociable drug use is part of salesmanship. In smoking marijuana with a customer, the seller presents an air of confidence which puts the customer at ease and encourages his or her return business (Langer, 1977:380-81).

Because participants in illicit drug dealing are liable to arrest and punishment, they must be discreet. The seller and customer attempt to carry out their exchange at a time and place which will not attract attention. The seller may discourage customers from arriving late at night, for continuous activity at odd hours may alert outsiders that the seller is engaged in illicit activities (Carey, 1968:75). The successful seller will refuse to meet customers in places where police surveillance is possible—some sellers operate in private places, such as their personal residence or a special house or apartment used only for dealing, and others deal in public places which are shielded from outsiders' observations. The sellers and customer also try to present themselves to outsiders as ordinary, legitimate members of the setting. Carey (1968:82) notes, "the best pusher, just like the best agent, is one who you would never expect to be one. Ideally, the pusher is 'uncool.' He blends in with the crowd." Conversely, "the pusher most likely to get caught is the one whose dealings are most flamboyant" (Carey, 1968:73). Similar restrictions affect customers.

In retail drug dealing, the user has little difficulty in locating the retailer, for they usually are linked by friendship. Like other kinds of deviant sales, the user and retailer may negotiate over the price, and the user may check the quality and quantity of the goods before making payment. Both parties try to avoid detection and apprehension by conducting their exchange cautiously; they operate at times and places and in ways which do not attract attention. To avoid exploitation by the user, the retailer may require payment on delivery. In turn, the user asks the retailer about the drugs and may even test them before the retailer leaves. Drug dealing is a relatively complex deviant exchange. The user and retailer are individuals, operating on their own behalf, but their transaction is constrained by outside conditions. The price, quality, and availability of illicit drugs are affected by other deviants who manufacture and distribute them to retailers. These other deviants set the boundaries within which the deviant sale occurs.

Repetition and Authority

Deviant trades are sharply bounded transactions. Participants expect to achieve gratification during the encounter and they try to avoid long-term entanglements with one another. Some deviant sales share these features—streetwalkers do not expect to serve the same customer on more than one occasion. However, many deviant sales develop into extended relationships where the seller and customer repeat their transaction on many occasions—thieves repeatedly offer their stolen goods to the same fence, and drug users return to the same dealer. In fact, some customers even seek out familiar streetwalkers (B. Cohen, 1980:140-41). An extended relationship is one way deviants cope with the uncertainties of the exchange. For customers, patronizing the same seller solves the problem of locating a deviant market; for sellers, repeat business insures a stable income. And both actors know that the risks of exploitation by one's partner are reduced by dealing with someone who was honest and discreet in previous transactions. Where deviant trades involve special risks, participants also establish extended relationships. Masochists, for example, carefully screen potential partners before letting themselves be bound and punished. Once a reliable partner is found, the pair tends to remain together (Kamel, 1980; T. Weinberg and Falk, 1980).

The seller's authority over the deviant sale adds further stability. Sellers tend to be more experienced and they usually face greater risks than their customers. As a consequence, they often direct the transaction. The seller's authority also springs from another source: he or she controls the supply of the deviant good or service that the customer wants. Although illicit markets fluctuate, customers generally have more difficulty finding sellers than sellers have finding customers. The demand for the illicit commodity, coupled with many customers' inability to locate more than one seller, forces most customers to comply with the seller's directions. Thus, deviant sales are not only more complex than deviant trades, but extended customer-seller relationships and the seller's authority also make them relatively stable transactions.

CONCLUSION

Deviant exchange is a transaction in which two or more individuals voluntarily exchange illicit goods or services. Exchange can take two general forms. In a trade, the parties perform roughly comparable deviant roles, although there may be some division of labor, as found in tearoom trades, where one man fellates another. Trades also have a minimal division of authority—participants treat one another as equals. In a sale, a customer buys an illicit good or service from a seller. The division of labor is clear and there is often a clear division of authority, with the seller directing the transaction. The fence and the drug dealer set the time and place for the sale, the price range of the goods, and the precautions their customers must take.

To accomplish their exchange, whether it is a trade or a sale, the participants must solve four problems. They must first locate a deviant market—partners with whom to exchange the illicit good or service. They may search for a specific partner or a place that is likely to house prospective partners. The participants must then come to terms on the conditions for the exchange. In trades, such conditions can include the roles participants will perform, the time and place for the exchange, and the need for discretion. In sales the participants may negotiate over additional conditions, such as the price and quality of an illicit good or service. After coming to terms, the participants must carry out their exchange, performing in the agreed upon manner. Lastly, the participants must protect their transaction—they may choose a safe, protected setting, keep a lookout, or conduct themselves in a manner that is unlikely to attract attention.

Deviant exchange has a larger social context. The transaction may be linked to other social spheres that affect the nature of the exchange. First, deviant sales may be linked to a larger exchange network which supplies the seller with illicit goods or controls the distribution of illicit services. The retail drug dealer, for instance, purchases illicit drugs from a wholesaler, and the wholesaler's price shapes the retailer's price to customers; when the wholesaler increases the price, the retailer passes along the increase to users. The sexual services provided by the prostitute often are controlled by a manager, such as a pimp, madam, or owner of a massage parlor. The manager can determine the kinds of customers the prostitute meets, the kinds of services she provides, and the prices she charges (N. Davis,

1978:215-220; Winick and Kinsie, 1971:97-120). Second, the exchange may be linked to those who teach the participants their deviant roles. For example, a prostitute may be trained by a manager or an experienced prostitute, learning how to manage difficult clients, handle money, and perform some sexual skills (Bryan, 1965; Heyl, 1979). Third, the transaction may be linked to those who provide services to the deviant.In prostitution, cab drivers may refer clients, while hotel employees supply rooms and, occasionally, assist in emergencies (Prus and Vassilakopoulos, 1979).

The social context of deviant exchange also contains risks for the participants. Predators and control agents pose dangers. Predators can exploit participants through threats of exposure or physical attacks. For example, men who wish to conceal their homosexual activities are attractive targets for blackmail or beatings because they are reluctant to complain to the authorities. Social control agents pose the obvious risks of apprehension and punishment. Less obvious is the danger that social control agents will abuse their authority. Because there is no complainant in deviant exchange, and because officers use their initiative to detect and apprehend participants, it is easy for officers to convert a possible arrest into blackmail or some other exploitative response.

Deviants adopt various tactics to minimize these risks. First, they perform exchanges in relatively protected places, safe from outsiders' observation or intrusion. Second, the participants attempt to be discreet, careful not to reveal their deviance to outsiders. Third, deviants demand discretion from their associates. In some cases, the structure of the transaction facilitates discretion. In tearoom trades and swinging parties, participants learn little about one another; therefore, they cannot inform outsiders about their partners' identities. In other cases, where the participants have greater personal knowledge of one another, they expect each other to be discreet and they may make this expectation an explicit part of their agreement. The drug dealer and fence may demand their customers' silence, threatening severe consequences for informing the police about their operations.

Partners in deviant exchange are also able to exploit one another. One partner may attack the other, knowing that the individual cannot turn to the authorities for aid. A drug user may rob the dealer, or a customer may refuse to pay the prostitute. Similarly, dealers and prostitutes can rob their customers. Partners also may expose or threaten to expose the individual's deviance to outsiders. Exposure may serve as punishment, as when a thief informs the police of a fence's illicit activities in order to punish the fence for paying poor prices, while threat of exposure may be used to extort money from the individual. One participant can also cheat the other. A fence may lie, telling the thief that the stolen goods are of little value, or a drug dealer may cut the illicit drug and misrepresent its quality.

People involved in legitimate exchanges also risk exploitation by their partners, but they can get aid. Those involved in respectable transactions can turn to social control agents for help; those involved in deviant trans-actions cannot. A prostitute who is beaten, a tearoom participant who is blackmailed, a drug dealer who is robbed, and a drug user who is cheated place little hope in officials' assistance. Therefore, deviants must devise ways to protect themselves from exploitation by their partners. They limit them-selves to exchanges with persons they can trust. In some cases, trust is based on friendship or kinship. In others, it develops through the mediation of a third party, a sponsor who introduces the participants and vouches for their reliability. In drug dealing, for instance, a customer may tell a dealer that he or she was referred to the dealer by a mutual friend. The dealer may delay the exchange until he or she can check with the sponsor. In still other cases, trust develops in the course of interaction. When the partici-pants know little or nothing about one another, they may demand proof of one another's integrity. They may insist that the other establish a stake in carrying out the exchange honestly; for example, a prostitute may require the customer to pay in advance. As an additional precaution, participants may try to minimize what their partners learn about their identity. Some exchanges involve participants linked through friendship, kinship, or a history of past deals who know a great deal about one another but others, such as tearoom trades, involve strangers who only know each other as participants in the current deviant exchange. In such cases, deviants try to remain anonymous, deliberately keeping their relations impersonal.

Deviant exchange is voluntary; the participants share consistent in-terests and cooperate in satisfying those interests. Deviant exploitation, in contrast, involves conflict between two or more participants—by means of stealth, trickery, or physical force, one party satisfies his or her interests at the other's expense. The following two chapters focus on deviant exploitation.

NOTES

[1]Excerpts copyright© 1970, 1975 by Laud Humphreys. Reprinted with permission from *Tea-room Trade* (New York: Aldine Publishing Co..

[2]Excerpts reprinted with permission of Macmillan Publishing Co., Inc. from *The Professional Fence* by Carl B. Klockars. Copyright© 1974 by The Free Press, a division of Macmillan Publishing Co., Inc.

[3]Excerpts from James T. Carey, *The College Drug Scene,* © 1968. Reprinted by permission of Prentice-Hall, Inc., Englewood Cliffs, N. J.

CHAPTER SEVEN
DEVIANT EXPLOITATION:
Coercion and Surreptitious Exploitation

Deviant exploitation is an illicit transaction in which a deviant uses stealth, trickery, or physical force to compel another person to surrender goods or services. Crimes of violence and theft are exploitative. Like deviant exchange, deviant exploitation requires a minimum of two actors performing two roles. However, deviant exploitation differs from deviant exchange in four ways. First, deviant exploitation requires only one deviant role—"offender." The other required role is "target." "Target" is a more precise term than "victim." The target is the person with whom the offender interacts, whereas the victim bears the loss. In some transactions, the target is not the victim. For example, when an offender steals from a store, the business owner is the victim, not the clerk with whom the offender interacts. While deviant exchange involves at least two actors performing deviant roles, deviant exploitation involves a deviant offender taking advantage of a usually nondeviant target.

Second, deviant exploitation is not a mutually profitable transaction (cf. Blau, 1964:22; Homans, 1974:80-91). The offender determines the payoffs, and the payoff structure favors the offender. In some cases, such as shoplifting and burglary, the target gets little or nothing in return for the loss. In other cases, the target parts with goods or services in return for something he or she had before encountering the offender. In forcible rape, for instance, the target surrenders sexual services in return for continued physical well-being. Compliance is the most attractive alternative, for resisting the rapist may lead to death or serious injury. While compliance minimizes the target's loss, the target always loses more by dealing with the offender than by not encountering the offender. At the same time, the offender gains more by dealing with the target than not.

Third, the offender and target have conflicting interests (cf. Blau, 1964: 228-32). Deviant exchange involves the voluntary cooperation of two or more deviant actors pursuing shared or compatible goals. But in deviant exploitation, the participants favor opposing outcomes based on their different interests. For example, it is in the robber's best interest to take the target's money, while it is in the target's best interest to keep that money. Although the target surrenders in the face of the offender's use of stealth, trickery, or physical force, he or she believes, or comes to believe, that the offender's interests are improper.

Fourth, deviant exploitation often generates hostility between the offender and target (cf. Blau, 1964:225; Shibutani, 1961:350-354). Because exploitation involves a conflict of interests, with the offender taking advantage of the target, the target typically feels anger and contempt for the offender. This can have important consequences for the transaction. Given these hostile feelings, the target may oppose the offender, retaliating, refusing to cooperate, or complaining to social control agents. The possibility of opposition may lead the offender to take special precautions in dealing with the target.

There are four distinct types of deviant exploitation: coercion, surreptitious exploitation, extortion, and fraud. These basic types are distinguished by the target's understanding of what is taking place. Target understanding varies along two dimensions. First, the target may or may not be aware that exploitation is occurring at the time of the transaction (cf. Glaser and Strauss, 1965). Second, understanding varies in terms of whether the target defines the transaction as an instance of exploitation or some sort of exchange (see Table 7-1).

Table 7-1   TARGET'S AWARENESS AND DEFINITION OF THE SITUATION IN DIFFERENT FORMS OF EXPLOITATION

TARGET'S AWARENESS	TARGET'S DEFINITION OF THE SITUATION	
	EXPLOITATION	EXCHANGE
Open	Coercion	Extortion
Closed	Surreptitious Exploitation	Fraud

Both coercion and extortion occur in a context of open awareness. The target recognizes exploitation for what it is, even while it is occurring, and the deviant knows that this is the target's understanding. In coercion, the target surrenders goods or services because the deviant uses actual or threatened physical force against the target. Murder, forcible rape, and robbery are examples of coercion. In extortion, the deviant threatens to injure a hostage unless the target pays a ransom. Exploitation occurs under the guise of an exchange—the target parts with the ransom in return for the hostage's safety. Thus, in blackmail, the offender agrees not to damage the target's reputation in return for payment, while in kidnapping, the deviant returns a human hostage in exchange for a ransom. Of course, coercion also involves an exchange of sorts—the target of a robbery gives in to avoid death or serious injury. The distinction between coercion and extortion lies in the degree to which the participants define the transaction as one in which a bargain is being struck. Extortion is more likely to involve overt negotiation between the deviant and the target. Whereas coercive transactions usually take a matter of minutes, the negotiations in extortion can extend over weeks or months. Extortion is less likely to involve a threat to the target's person—the target usually barters to save a reputation, a possession, or another person. Lastly, extortion is more likely to become an established relationship, as when a blackmailer or racketeer is paid off at regular intervals.

Surreptitious exploitation and fraud occur in a context of closed awareness. Although the target may come to recognize that he or she was exploited, the transaction may be over before this realization occurs. In surreptitious exploitation, the offender uses stealth to acquire or damage the target's goods without the target's knowledge. Surreptitious exploitatiion is clearly exploitative; the target would recognize it as such if he or she knew about the transaction. In some cases, surreptitious exploitation takes place outside the target's presence, as when an empty building is burglarized, an automobile is stolen, or a vacant classroom is vandalized. In others, it occurs in the target's presence, as in pickpocketing and shoplifting. In fraud, the offender uses trickery, leading the target to define the transaction as one in which they are to exchange goods or services. This exchange may appear as a legitimate sale, such as having one's roof repaired, or it may appear as a deviant sale, such as buying illicit drugs. In either case, the offender secretly intends to exploit the relationship by giving the target less than full value in the deal. Thus, the roof receives an application of a worthless substance or the illicit drugs are adulterated. In its most artful form, fraud takes place without the victim ever realizing that his or her loss was due to exploitation.

This chapter and the one following consider these four basic types of deviant exploitation. This chapter will focus on coercion and surreptitious exploitation. These are visible types of exploitation which are commonly viewed as "real crimes" deserving considerable concern. Chapter 8 will focus on extortion and fraud. These are less visible, but equally devastating offenses.

COERCION

Coercion is transaction in which an actor exacts compliance from a target by means of actual or threatened punishment. Not all instances of coercion are deviant. A parent who gets a child to eat dinner under threat of losing dessert, or a teacher who gets a student to stop talking during an exam under threat of failing the course, engages in legitimate coercion. Deviant coercion, in contrast, makes the offender eligible for sanctioning by social control agents. Deviant and legitimate coercion differ in several other respects. Deviant coercion is purely exploitative—compliance serves the offender's personal interests at the expense of the target's. Deviant coercion also involves an attack—the offender generates compliance by means of physical force, the actual or threatened infliction of bodily pain. Further, the offender monopolizes the transaction's punitive resources, such as weapons. Coercive transactions include murder (Luckenbill, 1977), assault (Athens, 1980), forcible rape (Amir, 1971), and robbery (Letkemann, 1973; Luckenbill, 1980; 1981).

Coercion usually is fleeting, lasting from a few minutes to a few hours. This is because the participants are in face-to-face contact, and compliance can be accomplished immediately. In robbery, for instance, the offender demands whatever money the target has at the time; once the money is surrendered, the offender leaves. Coercion also is unstable. At any given moment, the offender's monopoly over punitive resources can disappear, destroying the basis for the coercive transaction. The appearance of passers-by or the target's escape can end the offender's control over the transaction. Given this instability, most offenders try to complete the transaction quickly.

There are two subtypes of coercion: character coercion and instrumental coercion. Character coercion refers to transactions in which the offender tries to demonstrate strong character, and thereby establish or maintain "face," by using force against the target. Murders and assaults often result from character contests in which people respond to insults with physical force. Instrumental coercion refers to transactions in which the offender wants to obtain particular goods or services from the target. The offender uses force to either intimidate the target into surrendering the goods or services or incapacitate the target until the goods or services can be obtained. Robbery and some cases of forcible rape illustrate instrumental coercion.

Character coercion and instrumental coercion differ in several respects. First, they differ in the personal relationship between the offender and the target. In character coercion, the offender and target often are related by friendship or kinship. Because friends and relatives have greater freedom to criticize one another, and because criticism by intimates can be particularly distressing, violence sometimes develops (W. Goode, 1969). In instrumental coercion, the offender and target normally are acquaintances or strangers. Offenders avoid targets who know them because being identified can lead to apprehension (Mulvihill and Tumin, 1969:217). Second, they differ in the transaction's planning. Character coercion often is spontaneous—during the course of interaction, the offender and target escalate hostilities to the point that murder or assault occurs. Instrumental coercion commonly is scheduled, with the offender planning to exploit the target before making contact with the target. Third, they differ in the degree to which they are protected against intervention by outsiders. Spontaneous character coercion often occurs in the presence of outsiders who can intervene. In contrast, when instrumental coercion is planned ahead of time, the offender tries to choose a fairly protected setting so that outsiders will not interrupt.

This section considers two examples of coercion, representing the two basic subtypes. Murder is an example of character coercion, while robbery is an example of instrumental coercion.

Murder

Murder or criminal homicide refers to the act of intentionally and unlawfully killing a person. This definition includes several kinds of transactions—personal murder, in which the offender kills the target for personal reasons; assassination, a killing for political reasons; and murder for hire, in which a third party pays the offender to kill the target. These different forms of murder vary along several organizational dimensions, including the number of persons involved, the degree of interaction that precedes the fatal blow, and the interests served by the target's death. This discussion will focus on personal murder. Although personal murder is more mundane than assassination or murder for hire, it is the more common form of murder in American society.

Personal murder represents one of the simplest forms of coercion—most cases involve only one offender and one target, usually related by marriage, kinship, or friendship (Lundsgaarde, 1977:230-31; Mulvihill and Tumin, 1969:217; Wolfgang, 1958:88, 207). In addition, the transaction typically is unplanned—the decision to use lethal force against the target is made during interaction with the target. Personal murder is the outcome of a face-to-face interchange between the offender and target, a "character contest" in which each participant attempts to save "face" at the other's expense (Hepburn, 1973; Luckenbill, 1977; cf. Athens, 1980; Goffman, 1967:218-19, 238-57). As the contest escalates, violence becomes defined as a suitable means for settling the dispute. And once the offender decides to use violence, he or she gets whatever weapons are readily available and uses them to fell the target. Thus, personal murder typically is a situationally bounded transaction. Luckenbill (1977) identifies six stages in the development of personal murder.

Stage 1. Personal Offense.   The target opens the transaction by doing something which the offender subsequently defines as an offense to "face," a valued image of self (Goffman, 1967:5). This offensive move can take several forms. The target may say something which the offender finds personally offensive, ranging from an insult directed at a specific feature of the offender's self to a tirade disparaging the offender's overall character:

> The offender, victim, and two friends were driving toward the country where they could consume their wine. En route, the victim turned to the offender, both of whom were located in the back seat, and stated: "You know, you really got some good parents. You know, you're really a son-of-a-bitch. You're a leech. The whole time you were out of a job, you were living with them, and weren't even paying. The car you have should be your father's. He's the one who made the payments. Any time your dad goes to the store, you're the first in line to sponge off him. Why don't you grow up and stop being a leech?" (Luckenbill, 1977:179)

Or instead of insulting the offender, the target may refuse to comply with the offender's orders. The offender may come to interpret this as a challenge to his or her right or ability to command obedience. Alternatively, the target may make a nonverbal gesture which the offender finds offensive:

> When the victim finally came home, the offender told her to sit down; they had to talk. He asked her if she was "fooling around" with other men. She stated that she had, and her boyfriends pleased her more than the offender. The offender later stated that "this was like a hot iron in my gut." He ripped her clothes off and examined her body, finding scars and bruises. She said that her boyfriends liked to beat her. His anger magnified. (Luckenbill, 1977: 180)

Although the nature of the offensive move varies, it serves to disrupt the order of the occasion, beginning a process in which relative tranquility develops into an argumentative character contest.

Stage 2. Assessment.   The offender interprets the target's move as personally offensive. In many cases, the target is intentionally offensive, but sometimes the offense is committed unwittingly. In either case, the offender interprets the offense as intentional, and this assessment has important consequences for subsequent action. Often, the offender determines the meaning of the target's move through inquiries to the target and/or bystanders. They reply that the target's behavior is insulting and purposive.

> As the offender entered the back door of the house, his wife said to her lover, the victim, "There's—." The victim jumped to his feet and started dressing hurriedly. The offender, having called to his wife without avail, entered the bedroom. He found his wife nude and the victim clad in underwear. The startled offender asked the victim, "Why?" The victim replied, "Haven't you ever been in love? We love each other." The offender later stated, "If they

were drunk or something, I could see it. I mean, I've done it myself. But when he said they loved each other, well that did it." (Luckenbill, 1977:180)

In other cases, the offender imputes intent from the target's behavior in previous situations. There is an offense "routine" which the offender recognizes from past experience as a deliberate insult:

> During a family quarrel the victim had broken the stereo and several other household goods. At one point, the victim cut her husband, the offender, on the arm. He demanded that she sit down and watch television so that he could attend to his wound in peace. On returning from the bathroom, he sat down and watched television. Shortly after, the victim rose from her chair, grabbed an ashtray, and shouted, "You bastard, I'm going to kill you." As she came toward him, the offender reached into the drawer of the end table, secured a pistol, and shot her. On arrest, the offender told police officers, "You know how she gets when she's drunk? I had to stop her, or she would have killed me. She's tried it before, that's how I got all these scars," pointing to several areas on his back. (Luckenbill, 1977:181)

Such previous incidents provide the offender with an interpretive scheme for understanding the target's current behavior.

Stage 3. Retaliation.   The offender can manage the target's affront in several ways: excuse the target; leave the scene or avoid additional contact with the target; or retaliate in order to restore face and demonstrate strong character. Offenders take this latter course in transactions culminating in murder. By retaliating, the offender tries to reaffirm face by standing strong. Another alternative, such as flight, would confirm the target's challenge to face (cf. Goffman, 1967:214-39; 1969:168-69).

In retaliating, the offender expresses anger and contempt toward the target. In most cases, the offender retaliates with a verbal or physical challenge; in some cases, the offender immediately kills the target. In the latter instance, the third stage of the transaction marks the battle ending the target's life.

> The offender, victim, and group of bystanders were observing a fight between a barroom bouncer and a drunk patron on the street outside the tavern. The offender was cheering for the bouncer, and the victim was cheering for the patron, who was losing the battle. The victim, angered by the offender's disposition toward the fight, turned to the offender and said, "You'd really like to see the little guy have the shit kicked out of him, wouldn't you big man?" The offender turned toward the victim and asked, "What did you say? You want the same thing, punk?" The victim moved toward the offender and reared back. The offender responded, "OK buddy." He struck the victim with a single right cross. The victim crashed to the pavement, and died a week later. (Luckenbill, 1977:181-182)

Such cases seem one-sided, with an unwitting target taking a passive, noncontributory role. Yet, the third stage is preceded by the target's offense and the offender's assessment of it as insulting. The offender states his or her intended line of action and follows through by attacking the target.

More commonly, the third stage consists of various nonlethal moves. A common type of retaliation is a verbal challenge, often an ultimatum:

> The offender, victim, and two neighbors were sitting in the living room drinking wine. The victim started calling the offender, his wife, abusive names. The offender told him to "shut up." Nevertheless, he continued. Finally, she shouted, "I said shut up. If you don't shut up and stop it, I'm going to kill you and I mean it." (Luckenbill, 1977:182)

Alternatively, the offender may physically attack the target, but without causing death or serious injury. Or the offender may counter the target's insult with comparable gestures. In any case, the third stage is the offender's opening move to salvage face. By retaliating in nonlethal ways, the offender also reveals to the target a definition of the situation as one in which violence is suitable for settling questions of face and reputation.

Stage 4. Working Agreement.   Except for cases where the target has been killed, the offender's preceding move places the target in an awkward position—either stand up to the challenge and demonstrate strong character or place one's own face in jeopardy by apologizing or fleeing. Rather than demonstrate weakness, the target enters into a "working" agreement with the offender that the situation is suited for violence. They can strike this working agreement in different ways. The target may repeat the offensive action in spite of the offender's objections:

> The victim continued ridiculing the offender before friends. The offender finally shouted, "I said shut up. If you don't shut up and stop it, I'm going to kill you and I mean it." The victim continued his abusive line of conduct. The offender proceeded to the kitchen, secured a knife, and returned to the living room. She repeated her warning. The victim rose from his chair, swore at the offender's stupidity, and continued laughing at her. She thrust the knife deep into his chest. (Luckenbill, 1977:183)

Or the target may physically retaliate by hitting, kicking, or pushing the offender, a response short of seriously injuring the offender. The target may also issue a counterchallenge, threatening or challenging the offender.

Just as the target contributes to the escalation toward violence, so too does the audience. Bystanders generally perform one of two roles. In some cases, members of the audience actively encourage violence:

> The offender's wife moved toward the victim, and hit him in the back of the head with an empty beer bottle, stating, "That'll teach you to (molest) my boy. I ought to cut your balls off, you motherfucker." She went over to the bar to get another bottle. The victim pushed himself from the table and rose. He then reached into his pocket to secure something which some bystanders

thought was a weapon. One of the bystanders gave the offender an axe handle and suggested that he stop the victim before the victim attacked his wife. The offender moved toward the victim. (Luckenbill, 1977:184)

In other cases, onlookers are neutral, neither encouraging nor discouraging the confrontation. While neutrality may be due to fear or an attempt to ignore the escalation, the opponents can interpret it as supporting violence.

Stage 5. Battle.   By this stage, the opponents have a working agreement—the offender and, in many cases, the target appear committed to battle. They have placed their character on the line and agreed on violence as a suitable means of testing character. Because the opponents fear a display of weakness, and because the situation demands immediate resolution, they appear committed to a violent course of action. Commitment to battle is enhanced by the availability of weapons with which to support threats and challenges. At this stage, the offender finds a weapon capable of overcoming the target. In some cases, the offender already has a weapon; in others, he or she may leave temporarily to get a weapon or simply transform some existing prop, such as a beer bottle, kitchen knife, or baseball bat, into a weapon. The details of the battle vary, ranging from a single fatal blow to a lengthy struggle. The battle's conclusion comes with the target's collapse.

Stage 6. Termination.   After the target falls, the offender may flee from the setting, voluntarily wait for the police, or be held involuntarily for the police by one or more bystanders. Two conditions shape the offender's action: the relationship between the offender and target, and the response of the bystanders. When the offender and target are intimately related, the offender stays voluntarily on the scene; in fact, the offender may report the offense. But when the offender and target are acquaintances, enemies, or strangers, the offender will flee, perhaps trying to dispose of the target as well as other incriminating evidence. If the murder occurs in the presence of others, the audience adopts one of three general roles: hostile, neutral, or supportive. Hostile bystanders attempt to apprehend the offender, assist the target, and immediately notify the police. Neutral bystanders are shocked—having witnessed the killing they stand numb as the offender escapes and the target dies. Supportive bystanders, who usually encouraged the fight, assist the offender, destroy incriminating evidence, delay notifying the police, and claim ignorance when first questioned by the authorities.

    To summarize, personal murder is not a one-sided transaction with an unwitting target playing a passive, noncontributory role. Rather, murder is the outcome of a dynamic interchange between the offender, target, and bystanders. The offender and target develop lines of action, each shaped by the other's actions and focused toward saving face and demonstrating strong character. They develop a working agreement—sometimes implicit, often explicit—that violence is a suitable means for resolving questions of face and character.

Robbery

In robbery, the offender takes goods from the target, against the target's will, by means of force. The criminal law distinguishes two basic forms of robbery: "aggravated" robbery in which the offender uses a weapon, such as a firearm or knife; and "simple" or "strongarm" robbery in which the offender is unarmed. In either case, robbery involves a face-to-face confrontation between the offender and target. The offender uses punitive resources to force the target to surrender his or her goods, and the target surrenders those goods because of actual or threatened punishment. To make their demands known, generate compliance with those demands, and keep the target in line without killing anyone, offenders need skill in target manipulation (DeBaun, 1950; Letkemann, 1973:90-91).

Robbery is an example of instrumental coercion. The offender usually plans the crime, selecting the target, designing the attack, acquiring the necessary equipment, and confronting the target at a time and place that guarantees the offender's safety. Two or more offenders may cooperate, with each person performing a different task, in carrying out the robbery. Offenders may decide in advance whether they will use force, as well as what levels of force should be used to exact compliance, thwart opposition, and manage outside intervention. Whereas personal murder is a situationally bounded transaction, robbery often involves advance planning and coordination among offenders. Research identifies several stages in the development of a robbery transaction (Conklin, 1972:79-112; Einstadter, 1969; LeJuene, 1977; Letkemann, 1973:90-116; Luckenbill, 1981; Weir, 1973).

Stage 1. Planning. The offender who decides to commit a robbery, must select a target with certain characteristics. The target should possess as much money as the offender wants, and he or she should be vulnerable to attack—accessible, relatively powerless, and physically isolated from potential allies. The target should be unlikely to resist the offender, a point suggested by one street criminal:

> Say I felt like going out and robbing something, and there's a bank on one corner and there's a gas station on the other corner. Now you see the man pumping gas all day long, and he got a big old roll in his pocket. Which one would you rob? The bank, of course. Why? Less risk. The man been pumping gas all day long, he tired, he been working hard, and he's not going to give that money up as easy as a bank teller would. A bank teller in a bank behind the cage counting somebody else's money out to him or taking somebody

else's money in, they not going to get hurt for their scratch. They going to give it up. (Allen, 1977:52)[1]

The target also should be a stranger, who will have more difficulty in identifying the offender to the police.

After selecting a target, the offender prepares for the robbery. The offender may "case" the target, determining when he or she is vulnerable, where he or she can be safely approached, the best routes for entry and departure, and so on. The offender also may consider how much force should be used to manipulate the target. In sophisticated robberies, mob members may have specific tasks that must be carried out in a precise sequence. The offender may make arrangements with physicians, lawyers, and bail bondsmen prior to the robbery. Finally, the offender gets and prepares the necessary equipment.

Stage 2. Establishing copresence.   After selecting the target and preparing for the robbery, the offender establishes copresence with the target. The offender moves into striking range, a position from which he or she can attack the target. This movement must not arouse suspicion or provoke unmanageable opposition. There are two methods of establishing copresence. The offender may use speed and stealth to rush the unwitting target:

> The offender walked to the side of the gas station and saw the attendant helping several customers. He walked back to the rear of the station to wait for the customers to leave. The customers left a few minutes later. The offender donned a ski mask, pulled a handgun from his pocket, and walked to the side office window. He peered inside and saw the attendant sitting behind the desk reading. The offender crept up to the office door and pointed his handgun at the attendant. In a harsh tone of voice, the offender announced, "This is a stickup, man. Give me the money." (Luckenbill, 1981:29)

Alternatively, the offender may establish copresence by presenting a normal appearance:

> The offender entered the convenience store and moved to the cooler, getting a carton of milk. He then walked to the cashier's counter where the lone clerk was located and placed the carton on the counter. The clerk noted the price of the milk and began to ring up the sale. Before the clerk hit the last register key, the offender stuck his hand in his pocket and said, "I've got a gun. Give me all the money in the register." (Luckenbill, 1981:29-30)

Ideally, the offender confronts an unprepared target. But, in some cases, the offender alarms the target; the target spots the offender's preparation or stealthy approach or recognizes some inconsistency in the offender's normal appearance. In these cases, the robbery can break down, if the target develops a line of opposition. The offender may be reluctant or unable to carry out the robbery when the target flees the setting or prepares to defend against the robbery:

> The victim, an off-duty but uniformed police officer who was working part-time for a local business, walked up to the bank's night deposit drawer and dropped the deposit bag inside. He then heard someone running toward him from behind. He turned around and saw the hooded offender, wielding a tire iron, standing behind him. The victim, fearing impending robbery, reared back to strike the offender. The offender appeared surprised to see this particular person making the regular night deposit. The offender shouted, "Oh shit," dropped his tire iron, and tried to run past the victim. The victim managed to strike the offender with his fist. But, unhurt, the offender ran from the scene. (Luckenbill, 1981:30-31)

Stage 3. Developing coorientation.   After establishing copresence, the offender and target reorient their interaction. They transform their en-counter from a routine, tranquil frame, such as that binding a customer and a clerk, to the robbery frame (cf. Goffman, 1974). The robbery frame has two principal expectations—to avoid injury, the target should suppress op-position and surrender his or her goods to the offender; and to obtain these goods, the offender should use force to control the target's conduct and take the goods. When the opponents operate in terms of a common robbery frame, the crime usually is consummated.

The offender begins the transformation with one of two moves de-signed to provide the target with the robbery frame—the offender com-mands compliance and backs the command with a threat; or, the offender uses incapacitating force against the target. The choice of opening move depends on the strength of the offender's punitive resources and the value of the target for the transaction (Luckenbill, 1980). If the offender has "lethal" resources (a firearm or knife), then he or she commands compliance under threat of punishment. This move is based on the assumption that the target is intimidated by the offender's superior strength, a point suggested by two robbers in interviews:

> You know, if somebody came up to me and said, "Give me your money," and he had a gun or machete, I'd give him everything. I mean, it would scare the hell out of me. It would scare the hell out of anybody.

> My partner showed me a blank pistol he had. We decided it would be better with a blank gun because that way nobody would get hurt and we could scare them into cooperating with us. (Luckenbill, 1980:366-67)

The offender with "nonlethal" resources (a club or bare hands) uses in-capacitating force, on the assumption that a threat backed with nonlethal resources will not intimidate the target. The offender believes that only actual force can insure compliance:

> ... you have to put him out of commission for a few minutes. When you haven't got a gun or knife, he won't do anything. He'll tell you to go to hell or turn on you. So all you can do is knock him out. (Luckenbill, 1981:32)

The offender's opening move also depends on the target's value for the transaction. If the target has vital knowledge and skill, such as the ability to open a safe, the offender will only threaten the target; incapacitating the target would jeopardize the robbery.

Usually, the offender's opening move does not fell the target, but instead makes the target choose between accepting and rejecting the robbery frame. This choice depends, in large part, on the target's assessment of the offender's punitive capacity—whether the offender has lethal resources and is in a position to use them—and the offender's intent to use force—whether the offender intends to use force only if opposed or regardless of opposition. If the offender appears capable of inflicting death or injury and force seems to be contingent on opposition, the target accepts the robbery frame:

> I wasn't going to try anything because he had a pistol. When he's got a piece, you give him the money. That's all there is to it. If you try anything, he might shoot you. (Luckenbill, 1981:34)

However, when the offender appears incapable of inflicting death or serious injury, the target resists:

> He stuck his hand in his shirt and told me, "I'm sorry too but this is a holdup." I asked him, "Where's the gun?" I wasn't going to give him any money if he didn't have a gun. Sometimes robbers try to bluff you. They just say they have a gun, but they really don't. . . . He never showed a gun, so I never gave him money. (Luckenbill, 1981:35)

When the target believes the offender intends to use force regardless of the target's response—for example, if the offender began by using force—the target also resists; however unfeasible it may seem, opposition offers the only chance for avoiding serious harm.

If the offender and target orient themselves toward a common robbery frame, the transaction moves to the next stage. But if the target opposes the robbery frame, and the offender's subsequent efforts to overcome this opposition fail, the robbery is doomed.

Stage 4. Transferring the goods.   After accepting a common robbery frame, the offender and target must transfer the target's goods. The transfer may follow a preestablished design, when the offender seeks particular goods, or it may follow a search-and-seizure design, when the offender takes whatever valuables he or she can find. Either the offender or the target may transfer the goods. In some cases, the target stands by while the offender makes the transfer. But in many cases, the target is expected to help by getting the goods and giving them to the offender.

While the transfer is a relatively simple task, several problems can hinder it and disrupt the robbery. When the offender shifts attention from the target to the transfer, he or she may move outside striking range or drop armed surveillance over the target. Detecting an opening, the target may launch an attack or flee the setting. Or if outsiders enter and the setting becomes unsafe, the offender may decide to forfeit the robbery. Finally, the offender and target may lack the knowledge and skill needed to make the transfer.

Stage 5. Leaving.   After the goods are transferred, the offender leaves the setting, using one or more exiting strategies. The offender may plan for a speedy and stealthy departure. For instance, before the robbery, the offender parks a getaway car outside the target's view. After the transfer, the offender runs for the car. By the time the target follows, the offender is gone. Another common strategy is containing the target. The offender may verbally contain the target, warning the target not to follow, observe the getaway, or contact the authorities. Or the offender may physically contain the target, binding the target's hands and feet or using force to frighten the target against pursuit.

Robbery transactions typically involve a sequence of five stages: planning the operation; establishing copresence; transforming the transaction toward a common robbery frame; transferring the goods; and leaving the setting. The offender relies on actual or threatened force in directing the transaction. Completing all five tasks results in robbery, while failure to carry out any one of these tasks can result in disruption of the robbery and apprehension of the offender.

Force and Fear

The distinction between character coercion and instrumental coercion is not always clear. Depending on the offender's motive, the same offense can take either pattern. Some rapes, for instance, are instrumental—the rapist wants sexual satisfaction and uses force to get it. In other cases, rape is character coercion—the offender tries to establish strong character by physically dominating the target (Holmstrom and Burgess, 1979). While offenders' motives vary, coercion always involves a face-to-face confrontation in which the offender uses actual or threatened force to make the target comply.

Although other types of deviant exploitation occur more frequently, coercion is a significant public concern (Conklin, 1975). Because coercive offenses involve violent, face-to-face encounters and capture the attention of the mass media, they are especially frightening to most people. Further, because they have little experience with violence and few resources to defend themselves, most people who are attacked have little choice but surrender. Thus coercion typically is defined as "real crime," for it frightens people and reveals their inability to defend themselves from harm.

SURREPTITIOUS EXPLOITATION

In surreptitious exploitation, the offender uses stealth to take or damage the target's property without the target becoming aware of the loss while it occurs. The transaction may or may not involve face-to-face contact between the offender and target. But in either case, the target remains unaware of the exploitation until the operation is completed. The offender uses stealth to enter the target's territory, take or destroy the property kept there, and leave without the target's awareness. Examples of surreptitious exploitation include burglary (David, 1974; Shover, 1973), shoplifting (Cameron, 1964), pickpocketing (Inciardi, 1977; Maurer, 1964), and auto theft (McCaghy and Giordano, 1977), where the offender takes the target's property, and arson (Inciardi, 1970) and vandalism (Wade, 1967), where the offender damages the property.

In coercion, the offender and target engage in focused interaction—their face-to-face contact has a single, shared focus of attention (Goffman, 1963a: 24). In surreptitious exploitation, however, the offender and target engage in unfocused interaction. The operation may involve no face-to-face contact if it occurs while the target is physically absent from the setting. Or the operation may involve unfocused, face-to-face contact, where the offender and target are copresent but do not develop a shared focus of attention; in effect, the target is mentally absent from the scene. The offender depends on the target's physical or mental absence to undertake the exploitation.

Surreptitious exploitation is a fleeting transaction, lasting anywhere from a few seconds to a few hours. Like coercion, surreptitious exploitation is an unstable transaction. In coercion, instability reflects the fragile distribution of punitive resources. However, surreptitious exploitation is unstable because the target or his or her potential allies may become aware of the exploitation. The offender depends on the operation's secrecy, but this is tentative, subject to change at any moment; the residential burglar knows the target family eventually will return home. If the target becomes aware of the exploitation, he or she may interfere. Given this risk, the offender tries to complete the operation as quickly as possible.

Surreptitious exploitation may require special resources, including knowledge, skill, equipment, and teamwork. Relevant knowledge can include knowing how to select the best target, how to overcome the target's defenses, how to avoid detection, and so forth. Special skills help to insure secrecy and success. The offender must appear inconspicuous, and this requires skill at managing a normal appearance, at presenting oneself as a respectable person who belongs in the setting. The offender may need other skills to circumvent the target's defenses and carry out the operation. Special tools and equipment, such as lock picks, nitroglycerine, booster bags, and a getaway car, make it easier to enter the target's territory, carry out the operation, and depart. Finally, while one person can manage some surreptitious offenses, more complex operations often require teamwork. Deviant associates not only help take or damage the target's property, they also help maintain the operation's secrecy.

This section considers two examples of surreptitious exploitation. In burglary, the offender steals from the target's territory, usually while the target is absent. In pickpocketing, the offender steals from the target's person. The two examples differ in complexity. Burglary can be a relatively simple operation. However, pickpocketing is more complex, calling for substantial knowledge, skill, and teamwork.

Burglary

The traditional common law defined burglary as the act of breaking and entering into another's house at night with the intention of taking his or her possessions. Over the years, this definition expanded. Today, burglary is the act of breaking and entering into some structure with the intention of committing a crime. The structure may be a home, a business, or a vehicle, the crime may occur anytime, day or night; and the offender may enter with the intention of committing any crime, including kidnapping, rape, or theft. The concept of burglary, then, covers a broad swathe of deviant activity. This section focuses on a common form of burglary—entry into residences and commercial establishments for purposes of committing a theft.

In robbery, the target is directly confronted by the offender and forced to surrender goods. In burglary, however, the offender avoids direct confrontation with the target. The offender operates secretly—during the operation, the target is unaware of the exploitation (Letkemann, 1973:49). In most cases, the offender enters places when the target is phsyically absent. In the few cases when the target is present, he or she typically is asleep or otherwise indisposed. Thus, burglary features the target's physical or mental absence. If the target discovers the operation in progress, the offender faces a major problem requiring immediate management; the offender may forfeit the theft and flee or use force to control the target and continue the operation.

Burglary typically consists of four stages, each with a set of specific tasks oriented toward getting the target's goods without discovery and subsequent apprehension.

Stage 1. Planning the burglary. In most cases, the burglar selects a target location that satisfies two conditions: (1) it houses valuable goods, making the theft worthwhile; and (2) it does not pose unmanageable risks of discovery and apprehension. The value of the goods is more important than the risks of discovery and apprehension—when a place promises a large take, the offender usually selects it, even though the risks are high (Letkemann, 1973:151).

Targets are selected on the basis of tips and personal assessments (Shover, 1973:504). Sometimes an offender happens to spot a target that is both lucrative and vulnerable; on other occasions, the offender may scout for targets, canvassing an area for places that can yield a good take. (Rengert and Wasilchick, 1980). Tipsters point out still other targets. Different kinds of persons serve as tipsters, including fences, other thieves, and employees or other nondeviants who know about a particular target (Gale Miller, 1978:39-41; Shover, 1973:506). The relationship between the offender and tipster is precarious. If the tipster knows the offender is planning a burglary, the offender may be wary of the tipster, who might be working as a police agent in setting up the offender for arrest (Chambliss, 1972:26; Shover, 1972:547). Moreover, the tipster's information may be inaccurate (B. Jackson, 1972:103).

Having selected a target, the offender may case the place. Casing can range from a few observations made while walking or driving around the place to careful inspections over a period of days or weeks (Shover, 1973:504). Whatever its intensity, casing is a perceptual process in which the offender focuses on those features of the setting that might hinder or facilitate the burglary, such as the location of the place in relation to other buildings and traffic, the time when the goods are both abundant and vulnerable, and the type of alarm system used and the ways it can be circumvented (Letkemann, 1973:137-38; Gale Miller, 1978:35). There are different ways of casing. The offender may watch the place from a distance, or enter the place to observe:

> I'd go inside, see? I'd have my girl with me or something. And I'd usually hand them a hundred dollar bill for something I buy. They usually don't carry this kind of money in the till—they don't like to, anyway. And they have to go to the office. Now that's all I need to know. If I see them go in the office I know the money must be there and the safe is there. (Letkemann, 1973:144)

While casing, the offender must appear inconspicuous, so that the target will not become suspicious. To be inconspicuous, the offender attempts to appear as a person who is a legitimate part of the setting, for example, inspecting a store under the guise of a customer.

In addition to casing, the offender prepares for the burglary by tailoring equipment and contingency plans to the particular target (Shover,

1973:504). Burglars may plan the best vantage point for a lookout, the manner in which the lookout will alert associates in case of discovery, the alternate routes for fleeing if discovered, and so forth.

Stage 2. Entering the place.   Burglary involves entering a closed place which is secured and possibly equipped with alarms. There are several techniques for entering. Where there is no alarm, the offender may simply climb through an open window, kick in the door, or pry open a locked window. Places with alarms are more troublesome. In some cases, the alarm can be neutralized so that it will not go off. In other cases, the offender bypasses the alarm, entering by an unprotected route, such as a hole cut in the roof.

Entering a closed place is problematic in another sense. The offender must not arouse suspicion. In approaching the place, the offender attempts to appear as a person who belongs in the setting at that time. For instance, the apartment burglar walks past the building's doorman and residents under the pretense of having legitimate business in the building; this self-presentation is supported by dressing and acting the part, for example, wearing a suit and carrying a brief case (Plate, 1975:22). The illegal entry itself also must not arouse suspicion. When the offender operates at night or selects an isolated place, there is less risk of being observed. However, when the offender works in daytime or in a busy or heavily populated area, the management of a normal appearance may be necessary to gain entry. For example, a burglar can reduce the suspicions of neighbors by appearing as an employee of a moving company who has been sent to a residence.

Stage 3. Stealing.   Once inside the place, several tasks may be performed. The offender may locate alternate escape routes to be used if the operation is interrupted, or rig the entrances to warn of intruders or to prevent them from entering (Plate, 1975:26-27). The offender then locates the goods to be stolen. Burglars usually want either money or items which can be sold, rarely both (Letkemann, 1973:51). If the offender wants to steal money, then it may be necessary to break into a secure setting within the place, such as a cash register or safe. This may call for special skills and considerable time. In contrast, items to be sold can be taken in comparatively little time, but they must be removed from the place without observation and later converted into cash, typically by selling them to a fence.

Determining the goods' location requires skill. To be sure, some large items, such as a color television, are easy to spot, for they are openly displayed. But cash and small valuables may be more difficult to locate, for they may be hidden or kept in an unpredictable place. Consequently, the offender may have to search to find such goods.

Once the goods are located, the offender must take them. When the offender intends to steal large, accessible items, acquisition is simply a matter of taking the goods and carrying them away. However, when the offender intends to take money or small valuables from a secure location, acquisition is more difficult, requiring knowledge, skill, and equipment to gain entry. To break into a safe, for example, the offender needs knowledge, skill and special tools.

Safecracking is the most challenging method of stealing goods in a burglary. It generally is restricted to career thieves working in mobs of two to four persons. Career thieves use special techniques for cracking safes (Chambliss, 1972; B. Jackson, 1972; Letkemann, 1973:57-79). One method involves the use of explosives to blow the safe. Nitroglycerine ("grease") is poured through a funnel ("soap") into the safe, then ignited using a detonator ("knocker") and a fuse ("string"). The precise technique for blowing a safe depends on the safe's structure (round or square, one door or two) and the brand of safe. A "jam shot" involves an explosion between the safe door and its frame, so that the locking device is disengaged and the door swings open on its hinges. Too much grease will destroy the safe and its contents, while too little will result in a bulged door, which cannot be opened in most cases. If the safe door and door frame fit too tightly to make a jam shot, the safecracker will "shoot for space." Here, the thief creates a small explosion at the center of the door, trying to dent the door so that a jam shot can be attempted. When the door can withstand shooting for space, the safecracker may use a "gut shot." Here, the safe is tipped on its back, the combination dial is removed with a hammer, and grease is poured into the locking mechanism with an eyedropper. The explosion destroys the locking mechanism and permits the door to open. Blowing safes has become an undesirable method of safecracking—it is noisy, attracting the attention of outsiders, and risky, for the possession of explosives is a crime carrying stiff penalties (Inciardi, 1975:13; B. Jackson, 1972:102). As a result, non-explosive techniques have come to prevail. The safecracker may "peel" poorly constructed safes, making a hole in the safe, inserting a steel bar, and peeling away a wall panel. Using an axe or other sharp instrument, the thief then breaks through the safe's weak inner wall. Or the safecracker may "punch" the safe. The thief knocks off the combination dial, revealing a steel spindle which holds the tumblers of the locking mechanism in place. Using a hammer and long steel punch, the thief punches the spindle into the safe. The tumblers fall, and the safe door opens. Finally, the safecracker may try "drilling," a time-consuming technique in which a hole is drilled near the combination dial, and the tumblers are manipulated until the lock opens.

Stage 4. Departure.   Once the theft is completed, the offender may check the setting to insure that no incriminating evidence is left behind. The offender then checks outside for witnesses who might observe the departure. If the area is clear, the offender departs. If it is not clear, the offender may wait, use another exit, or leave in front of witnesses under a respectable guise.

After departure, the offender may take additional precautions to avoid identification. The stolen getaway car may be abandoned for a legitimate car within blocks of the crime. The offender may go directly to a fence, not only to convert the stolen property into cash but to dispose of this incriminating evidence (Shover, 1973). The offender may dispose of additional incriminating evidence, such as clothing worn during the burglary, which if it is impregnated with concrete and metal from the safe, could link the offender to the crime (Chambliss, 1972:38).

Although burglary does not involve focused interaction between the offender and target, it involves a form of social interaction. Both the offender and target adjust themselves to the actual or anticipated actions of the other. On the one hand, the target takes precautions against burglars, using monitoring systems, such as alarms or special security forces, to keep offenders from completing their operations. Further precautions, such as locks, fences, and safes, keep offenders from gaining access to the valued property. The target's goal is to make the property invulnerable to attack. On the other hand, the offender tries to penetrate the target's defenses. Using special knowledge, skill, and equipment, the burglar circumvents monitoring systems and penetrates secure locations to steal the target's property.

Pickpocketing

Pickpocketing is a form of larceny, taking money from another person against his or her will. Unlike the robber, who uses physical force against the target, or the burglar, who steals from an absent target, the pickpocket uses stealth and skill to take money from the target's person without the target's knowledge. Thus, pickpocketing is a type of sneak theft (Maurer, 1964:59).

Pickpocketing typically is practiced by career thieves. It requires so much skill and teamwork that only professionals can complete the operation safely. Consequently, comparatively unskilled, amateur thieves turn to easier forms of sneak theft. They may handle targets in a rough manner, purposely bumping or tripping targets in the course of stealing from them; often, targets are aware of the theft when it occurs. Or amateurs steal from targets who are not fully conscious—"lush workers" prowl dark halls and alleys, stealing from sleeping drunks and vagrants (Inciardi, 1975:21-22).

Professional pickpocketing typically is the work of a mob (Maurer, 1964: 56-62). Although a loner can sometimes pick pockets, the operation usually involves the coordinated actions of a team of thieves. The mob has two to four members, each responsible for specific tasks. One person is the "tool." The tool selects the target ("mark") and actually takes the money from the mark's person. The tool needs considerable skill, both to select a mark with plenty of money and to deftly take the money without the mark's knowledge. One or more other members act as "stalls." The stall may serve as the mob's "steer man." Using an encyclopedic knowledge of those settings frequented by prosperous marks, the locations being worked by other mobs, the operation of the local "fix," the best transportation routes, and the like, the steer man plans the mob's itinerary and deals with problems, such as assisting an arrested member. During the theft, the stall works near the tool and is critical to the tool's success. Once the tool selects a mark, the stall moves in to "frame" the mark, maneuvering the mark into a position where the tool can take the mark's money and holding the mark in that position until the theft is completed. While framing the mark, the stall also shields the tool's hands from the mark and potential witnesses. The stall's role requires as much skill as the tool's because framing and shielding must not arouse the attention of the mark and other persons. In some cases, the stall also takes the money from the tool once the theft is completed. This is a precautionary measure—if the tool is caught, he or she will not be holding the stolen goods. Thus, pickpocketing requires considerable skill and coordination.

The act of pickpocketing involves five stages (Inciardi, 1977:58-59; Maurer, 1964:56-82). These stages illustrate how thieves can secretly manipulate a target so that money can be stolen from his or her person without the target noticing.

Stage 1. Selecting the mark.   After finding a setting with a number of potentially prosperous people, such as a racetrack or an airport, the tool searches for a mark. The tool selects a person who appears to be carrying a considerable amount of money. The tool studies the dress, build, and behavior of people and picks out those who, on the basis of his or her past experience, are likely to be carrying a large sum. In addition, the tool may try to distinguish local residents from travelers, selecting a mark from among travelers, for they often carry larger amounts of money. The tool also looks for and tries to avoid undercover and uniformed police officers.

Stage 2. "Fanning."   Having selected the mark, the tool moves in and manually explores the mark's person to find where the money is located. This is called "fanning." In fanning, the tool skillfully runs his or her sensitive fingertips over the outside of the mark's clothes, detecting impressions of objects located in pockets and trying to determine which pockets hold the wallet, a roll of bills, and so forth. Although the tool makes physical contact, the mark remains unaware of the tool's exploration. The tool acts on the information drawn from fanning. Some tools are generalists—they can take money from almost any location on the mark's person. Others are specialists, whose skills restrict them to taking money from certain locations. For example, some specialists can steal from front and rear pants pockets, but they cannot go under overcoats. If the money is accessible, the tool moves into position vis-a-vis the mark, reaching an angle from which the theft is possible. Of course, if the mark's money is in an inaccessible location, the tool begins to search for another mark.

Stage 3. "Framing."   After the tool fans the mark and gets in position, the stall moves inconspicuously toward the mark and maneuvers the mark into a position where the tool can operate effectively. Depending on the position from which the tool wishes to make the theft, the stall may move in front, behind, or to the side of the mark. In doing so, the mark may be turned, led forward, or stopped. Once the mark is in an appropriate position, the stall "frames" the mark, blocking any further movement by the mark and keeping the mark's hands away from his or her pockets. The stall gives the mark the impression that this is just part of the normal contact one experiences in crowded places. Unaware that he or she is being framed, the mark is held in position for several seconds while the tool takes the money.

Stage 4. Stealing.   Once the mark is framed, the tool steals the money. The theft calls for great skill. To take cash from a pocket without being defected, the tool cannot place his or her entire hand into the mark's pocket; rather, the tool hooks the index finger within the crack of the pocket, taking up the pleats of the pocket lining and folding the lining between his or her fingers. This serves to shorten the pocket lining, so that the pocket's contents move upward and eventually emerge. To take a wallet from a pocket, the tool uses the index and middle fingers to fork the wallet and lift it from the pocket. While the tool takes the money, the stall not only holds the mark in position but also "shades" the tool, shielding the theft from observation by the mark and other people in the setting.

Stage 5. Departure.   After the theft, the tool moves away and the stall releases the mark from the frame. The stall may then "split" the mark, moving between the mark and the tool as the tool leaves. This reduces the possibility of the mark spotting the tool if he or she becomes aware of the theft. In some cases, the stall also takes the money from the tool immediately after the theft. This is to insure that the tool will not have the stolen goods on his or her person if apprehended by the mark or someone else. After the theft is completed, the mob resumes operations, with the tool selecting another mark.

Pickpocketing is a relatively safe operation. The deft touch of the tool and the skillful maneuvers of the stall, carefully coordinated, combine to facilitate theft and preclude detection. In some cases, however, the mark or another person observes or suspects the theft. When the tool is aware of the detection, he or she typically returns the money to the mark's pocket.

The tool immediately turns and moves away so that the mark cannot get a good look and later identify him or her for social control agents.

Like some other forms of surreptitious exploitation, the practice of picking pockets is hundreds of years old (Inciardi, 1975:20-21). Except for "slight modifications in technique made necessary by changing clothing fashions, the pickpocket of centuries ago differs little from his contemporary counterpart" (Inciardi, 1975:20). However, there is some evidence that pickpocketing is declining—there are fewer active professional pickpockets. Maurer (1964:171-172) estimates that there were approximately five to six thousand professional pickpockets working in the United States in 1945. By 1955, the number dropped to approximately one thousand. And by 1965, the number decreased still further (Inciardi, 1975:21). One professional pickpocket argues:

> Most of the ones left are old timers, and I say that there are probably no more than six or seven hundred in the whole country—if that much. There are plenty of amateurs, young ones, old ones, prostitutes, addicts, but they were never associated with the old time mobs. The kids are just not interested in it as a profession. Probably 'cause there's no money in it. And they're right. (Inciardi, 1975:21)

Inciardi (1977:61-62) estimates that, by the mid 1970s, the total number of active professional pickpockets fell to somewhere between three hundred and six hundred, far from the thousands who were involved in the activity only three decades earlier.

The decline of the professional pickpocket reflects the reduced ability of pickpockets to neutralize social control efforts (Inciardi, 1977). At the turn of the twentieth century, pickpockets worked with relative immunity, and this served an important stabilizing function:

> This immunity perpetuated contact among members of the profession, permitting the development of a subculture aimed at maintaining a low level of social visibility. An intricate network of relationships and linguistic constructions developed for the purpose of keeping out "outsiders"—amateur criminals—and a code of ethics was constructed for internal social control. A dissemination of information regarding case fixing and untrustworthy members of the profession developed to maintain a defense system against the infiltration of any representative of the wider social world. (Inciardi, 1977:62)

After the turn of the century, however, this immunity began to diminish. The professionalization of social control agencies made "fixing" more difficult, and new laws against habitual offenders and interstate flight from crime made pickpocketing riskier. With improved technology, communication between social control agencies made identification of criminals easier. These changes in the social control apparatus reduced pickpockets' security—the authorities identified, apprehended, and incarcerated more pickpockets. As a consequence, the crime is not as profitable as it once was; pickpockets cannot expect a good income at minimal risks, and fewer people seek to become professional pickpockets.

Picking pockets is more complex than other types of surreptitious exploitation. It is more difficult to steal from the target's person without being discovered. The target can easily become aware of the operation, complain, and help apprehend the offender. Successful pickpocketing requires considerable skill and teamwork. The stall must frame the target and shield the tool, and the tool must locate and steal the money. The entire operation must be completed in a few seconds, without the target becoming suspicious. Given this complexity, pickpocketing usually is restricted to mobs of experienced career thieves.

Secrecy and Awareness

The distinctive feature of surreptitious exploitation is secrecy. The offender takes or damages the target's property without the target's immediate awareness. In some cases, the offender exploits the target's property when the target is present; in others, the offender operates when the target is absent. In either event, the offender uses various resources, including special knowledge, skill, equipment, and teamwork, to keep the exploitative operation secret.

The targets of surreptitious exploitation present offenders with two problems. First, targets often anticipate surreptitious attacks against their property and prepare obstacles for offenders. Burglars face deadbolt locks and safes, shoplifters encounter one-way mirrors and specially tagged items, and pickpockets discover that some marks hide their cash in money belts. These obstacles are designed to make surreptitious exploitation more difficult. Sometimes they are effective—rather than try to overcome the target's defenses, the offender abandons the operation and searches for another target. On other occasions, particularly when the potential profits are great, the offender devises methods of overcoming the defenses. The history of safecracking illustrates this pattern—when targets installed increasingly sophisticated safes, safecrackers devised increasingly sophisticated methods of opening them (Cressey, 1972:94-95); Letkemann, 1973:86-89).

The second problem posed by targets is discovery. Surreptitious exploitation requires closed awareness—during the transaction, the target does not know what is taking place. The offender counts on closed awareness. If the target understands that exploitation is occurring, he or she may disrupt the operation by calling upon the authorities. Targets can move from closed awareness to suspicion awareness, becoming aware that exploitation might be occurring (Glaser and Strauss, 1965:47-63). In such cases, the suspicious target may check to see if anything is amiss. Faced with a suspicious target, the offender must decide whether to abandon the operation, try to allay the target's suspicions while continuing the undertaking, or transform the transaction into deviant coercion by forcibly controlling the target and continuing the operation. While the choice depends on the offender's resources, some decision must be made; secrecy is essential to surreptitious exploitation.

CONCLUSION

This chapter examined two basic types of deviant exploitation. In coercion, the offender uses physical force to exact compliance from the target. In surreptitious exploitation, the offender works secretly; ideally, the target discovers the loss only after the transaction is completed. While coercion and surreptitious exploitation are different kinds of transactions, they share a common feature—once aware, the target recognizes the transaction as exploitation. The next chapter examines two additional types of exploitation in which the target defines the transaction as an exchange of some sort.

NOTES

[1]From *Assualt with a Deadly Weapon: The Autobiography of a Street Criminal* by John Allen, edited by Dianne Hall Kelly and Philip Heymann. Copyright© 1977 by John Allen, Philip Heymann and Dianne Hall Kelly. Reprinted by permission of Pantheon Books, a division of Random House, Inc.

CHAPTER EIGHT
DEVIANT EXPLOITATION:
Extortion and Fraud

When people think about deviant exploitation, instances of coercion or surreptitious exploitation usually come to mind. All of the serious crimes catalogued in the FBI's *Uniform Crime Reports* —murder, rape, aggravated assault, robbery, larceny, burglary, and vehicle theft—involve either coercion or surreptitious exploitation. The emphasis on these familiar forms of exploitation overlooks two other, highly interesting forms: extortion and fraud. Chapter 7 examined the social organization of coercion and surreptitious exploitation. This chapter offers a parallel treatment of these less familiar forms of exploitation.

Whereas coercion relies on the actual or threatened use of physical force and surreptitious exploitation demands stealth, extortion and fraud require cooperation from the target. Without the target's cooperation, the offender cannot complete the transaction successfully. The targets of extortion and fraud perceive the deviant transaction as an exchange—they cooperate because they expect the offender to provide something in return. In the case of extortion, cooperation is exacted through a threat; the target cooperates in hopes of avoiding injury which the deviant is capable of inflicting upon a hostage. In fraud, the target cooperates because he or she has been tricked; the target's understanding of the transaction is faulty because the deviant intentionally uses deception. Thus, extortion and fraud differ from the more familiar forms of exploitation—they are organized to elicit the target's cooperation.

Naturally, targets are reluctant to cooperate in their own exploitation. Exploitation always involves a loss for the target, and deviants must arrange extortionate or fraudulent transactions so as to convince targets that cooperation, with its attendant loss, is sensible. In extortion, this is done by explicitly presenting the target with a set of choices, each carrying penalties, and then persuading the target that cooperation is the most attractive option. In fraud, targets are misled to believe that cooperation promises benefits; the discovery of their loss occurs later, if at all. In both cases, the deviant must arrange for the target's cooperation, presenting the transaction as an exchange in which cooperation will lead to the best outcome for the target.

There are several justifications for analyzing extortion and fraud. Some serious offenses fall into these categories. Kidnapping is a very serious crime—punishments are severe and major cases commonly receive heavy publicity. The losses absorbed by targets of extortion and fraud are also impressive—kidnapping ransoms have topped the $1 million mark and one extraordinary fraud cost its targets *$2 billion*. Moreover, extortion and fraud are common. Racketeering, a type of extortion, affects many businesses and labor unions, and business fraud affects all consumers. If these are not the types of exploitation which first come to mind, they are arguably among the most important types in terms of their impact.

This chapter begins by examining extortion. Two examples of extortion—kidnapping and racketeering—are considered in detail. The discussion of fraud follows, with special emphasis on confidence games and business fraud. This chapter concludes by systematically comparing extortion and fraud with the more familiar forms of exploitation—coercion and surreptitious exploitation.

EXTORTION

Extortionate transactions involve an extortionist who threatens to harm a hostage unless the target pays a ransom. These elements—extortionist, target, hostage, ransom, and threat—always appear in extortion, although they take various forms. The *extortionist* can be a lone individual, a group, or even a formal organization, and *targets* also range from individuals (in blackmail) to formal organizations (as when governments are asked to ransom kidnapped diplomats). The *hostage* may be a person (kidnapping), property (racketeering), or a reputation (blackmail). Typically, the *ransom* is a cash payment, but it can take other forms, such as the release of political prisoners, distribution of food to the poor, or publication of the deviant's message in the mass media. The *threat* depends on the type of hostage; the offender may threaten to kill a person (kidnapping), publicize damaging information (blackmail), or destroy valued property (racketeering).

Extortion is a forced exchange. Participants willingly enter a deviant exchange—they want it to occur (see chapter 6). In extortion, however, the target's participation is coerced by the offender's threats. The actors in an extortionate transaction share two basic assumptions: (1) the target values the hostage more than the ransom and is willing to part with the latter to regain or preserve the former; and (2) the extortionist values the ransom more than the hostage, and is therefore willing to return the hostage in exchange for the ransom. If both assumptions are correct, the target and the extortionist can make a deal; if either or both are wrong, the exchange is unlikely to occur.

The target must cooperate for the exchange to take place. At a minimum, cooperation involves coming to terms with the extortionist and assembling and delivering the ransom. While the target also cooperates in coercion, as when targets surrender their money to armed robbers, the target's cooperation in extortion demands more calculation. Threatened with immediate bodily harm, the robbery target often has little choice but to submit and little time in which to make the decision. The target of extortion rarely risks bodily injury; in fact, the target may never have face-to-face contact with the extortionist. The extortionist may communicate by letter or telephone in order to protect his or her identity. Usually, some time is allotted for the target to assemble the ransom. The target can choose among several options—cooperating with the extortionist's instructions, bargaining for better terms, calling upon social control agents for aid, and so forth. Because the target has these options, and because the extortionist needs the target's cooperation to gain the ransom, extortion can develop into lengthy negotiations where the extortionist and the target exchange assurances, incentives, and threats. In some cases, negotiations extend over months or even years before reaching a final settlement.

These negotiations are difficult because the participants are in conflict, with opposing goals in the transaction. Most extortionists' central goals are avoiding capture while collecting the ransom. For most targets, goals include recovering the hostage, avoiding or minimizing loss of the ransom, and bringing about the extortionist's capture. In spite of these opposing goals, the actors seek consensus in exchange. The terms of the extortionate bargain are vital. Each actor may try to manipulate the exchange so as to achieve his or her goals or block the other's efforts. They may argue over the size of the ransom, proof of the hostage's well-being, the method of delivering the ransom, or whatever else might offer an advantage to one party or the other. In extortion, tactical maneuvering is commonplace.

This section will examine two cases of extortion. Kidnapping for ransom usually involves a single episode—once the ransom is paid and the hostage returned, the transaction is over. In contrast, racketeering is systematic extortion—the target pays a ransom on several occasions. Episodic and systematic extortion pose different problems for deviants, targets, and social control agents.

Kidnapping for Ransom

Kidnapping involves the abduction or theft of a person. The term refers, both in ordinary language and in the criminal law, to a wide range of circumstances in which a person is unwillingly or illegally moved from one place to another (Alix, 1978:166-67). For example, kidnapping includes: kidnapping for ransom, where a criminal abducts a hostage in order to extort a ransom from a target; physically moving a target from one place to another in the course of another felony; and child stealing, where children are taken with the intent of keeping them. Some types of kidnapping are not extortionate; this discussion will be limited to kidnapping for ransom, emphasizing the importance of tactical maneuvering, which kidnapping shares with other types of extortion.

A typical ransom kidnapping involves five identifiable stages. First, the kidnapper must *select a target and hostage,* locating both a target, who must be able and willing to pay the desired ransom to gain the hostage's release, and a hostage who is vulnerable to capture. After making the necessary plans, the kidnapper *captures the hostage.* This involves seizing the hostage and taking him or her to a hiding place. The kidnapper can then open *negotiations.* During this stage, the kidnapper announces that he or she has the hostage, threatens to harm the hostage unless the ransom is paid, and arranges to collect the ransom. Other events, such as the target's notifying social control agents, can occur during this stage. Negotiations can become prolonged and complicated, and the tactical maneuvering during this stage provides the focus for much of this section's analysis. Once the kidnapper and target come to terms, the *delivery and collection of the ransom* occurs. Typically, cash is delivered to a specified location, where it is picked up by the kidnapper. Finally, *resolution* can take several forms: the hostage may be released; the kidnapper may withhold the hostage and demand a second ransom, reopening negotiations; or the hostage may be found dead. The kidnapper's fate must also be resolved—while some offenders avoid capture, social control agents apprehend many others.

An analysis of kidnapping must distinguish between the perspectives of the two major actors. From the kidnapper's point of view, kidnapping involves a set of practical problems: the hostage must be abducted; the target must be contacted and convinced to pay the ransom; the ransom must be collected; and so forth. The kidnapper also must avoid apprehension. At a minimum, kidnappers must conceal their location; ideally, they also can conceal their identities. But concealment is difficult because kidnappers must expose themselves at several points. During the abduction, negotiations, and ransom collection, kidnappers run the risk of revealing information which might lead to their capture. The target also has some practical concerns. Most targets want assurances that the kidnapper will keep the bargain, that is, if the ransom is paid, the hostage will be returned unharmed. Some targets also bargain to reduce the ransom. Targets who turn to social control agents for help may try to locate or identify the kidnappers so that they can be apprehended.

Because the completion of their exchange requires agreement by two parties with very different interests, negotiations over the terms of the agreement may be prolonged. In some cases, kidnapping negotiations extend over months, involving dozens of contacts between the kidnapper and the target before they complete the deal (Waller, 1961; Zierold, 1967). The themes of secrecy, character, and trust mark these negotiations and account for their length.

In kidnapping, information is an important commodity. Most kidnappers prefer to keep the crime secret from persons other than the target. If social control agents never learn about the kidnapping, the risk of apprehension is minimal. In order to discourage the target from reporting the crime, kidnappers sometimes couple their ransom demands with a threat to kill the hostage if officials are notified. Similarly, rival gangs sometimes kidnap underworld figures, assuming that the hostage's associates will be reluctant to report the crime. It is impossible to know what proportion of kidnappings go unreported. Even when the crime is reported, secrecy remains a central concern for kidnappers. Because the kidnapper usually must make more than one contact with the target, and because the target and social control agents know that the kidnapper probably will make contact in the future—if only to pick up the ransom—kidnappers must avoid revealing information about their identities and locations. They shun face-to-face contact, communicating through notes, telephone calls, or other channels which allow them to avoid direct observation. Their messages may be designed to give away as little as possible—handwriting is disguised; calls are kept short and made from public phones; the location of the ransom delivery is withheld until just before it is to take place; and so forth (Waller, 1961).

In addition to the risks posed by frequent contacts with the target, other features of the crime make secrecy important to the kidnapper. First, the hostage can gather information about the kidnapper. Once they are released, hostages may give social control agents valuable information. One recent manual advises hostages to keep this possibility in mind:

> The victim should, from the moment of his capture, make a determined effort to recover his calm and alertness so that he can start making mental notes of any details likely to help the police. . . . He should do his utmost to fix in his mind their faces, voices, dress and characteristics; how many they were; and the particulars of any vehicles that were involved. . . . He should fix in his

mind any clues he can get about his route: time, speed, distance, sharp turns, gradients, traffic lights, etc; and any sights or sound he is able to detect, such as crossing a railway or passing close to the airport; also the direction of the sun. If he has an idea whether he went north or south, he may possibly find a way of communicating this during negotiations, or in written or taped messages he is ordered to send out; even if he cannot do that, the information may help in arresting the gang later. . . . At least one hostage contributed to the eventual capture of his kidnappers because he could hear aircraft taking off from a small and recognizable airfield; and another by remembering details of the wallpaper. (Clutterbuck, 1978:104-105)

Second, the kidnapper is especially exposed while collecting the ransom. Ransom collection is obviously important to the kidnapper, but it is also an occasion when the target knows where the kidnapper will be, and the target or social control agents may arrange an ambush. Kidnappers must, then, devise a method of delivering and collecting the ransom which minimizes the information given away.

Kidnappers hope to keep their identities secret, but they want their targets to form impressions about their character. In kidnapping, as in any bargain, each party to the agreement assesses the other, trying to predict what he or she will do (Goffman, 1969). Knowing this, the shrewd bargainer attempts to foster an impression on the part of the other, deliberately displaying those qualities he or she wants the other to attribute to him or her, in order to convince the other that he or she is a certain "kind of person." Moreover, the bargainer will watch the other's actions, trying to read them for clues about the other's character. Each wants to convince the other that he or she is game—willing to carry out a plan of action and capable of doing so.

Kidnappers must establish a character which combines rationality with dangerousness. On the one hand, the target must believe that the kidnapper is rational, capable of constructing and carrying through the bargain. If the target believes that the offender is so irrational that the hostage inevitably will be killed, the ransom may be withheld. In order to foster an impression of rationality, kidnappers' messages may assure the target that they are humane, only interested in getting the ransom, aware they risk greater punishments if they harm the hostage, and so forth. However, this portrayal of rationality must not be overdone; the target also must be convinced that the kidnapper is dangerous—capable of carrying through the threat to the hostage. One political scientist calls this the paradox of face: "The nastier one's reputation, the less nasty one has to be" (Muir, 1977:41). To make the target believe the threat is real, kidnappers may lace their ransom notes with indicators of their seriousness, reminding the target that they are desperate, have nothing to lose, or are capable of carrying out their threats in the face of opposition:

I am scared stiff, and will kill the baby, at your first wrong move. (Tully, 1965:32)

> Barbara is presently alive inside a small capsule buried in a remote piece of soil. . . . Should you catch all of us, we will never admit anything as to do so would be suicide *and* again—she will die. (Gene Miller, 1971:56, italics in original)

> We are interested to send him back in gut health. . . . But we will note do so until the Police is out of the cace and the pappers are quite. The kidnaping we prepared in years so we are prepared for everyting. (Waller, 1961:26)[1]

Targets read the kidnapper's presentation for clues about the criminal's character. In letters to her relatives, written in the first days after her son's kidnapping, Anne Morrow Lindbergh's image of the kidnappers shifted:

> Their knowledge of the baby's room, the lack of fingerprints, the well-fitted ladder, all point to *professionals*, which is rather good, as it means they want only the money and will not maliciously hurt the baby.

> They think now that they are not *real* professionals, that real professionals would not walk into such a hornets' nest, that the phrasing of the letter is not hard-boiled enough for professionals. Also, the amazing knowledge of the country around here, the house, situation, etc., points more to a local gang. They think that the terrific pressure may force them to give in very soon, i.e., work for negotiations, or else it may frighten them so they don't dare negotiate.

> We seem to have pretty tangible word that the baby is safe, and *well cared for*. (Lindbergh, 1973:225-26, 229, italics in original; cf. Ross, 1876)

Where each party has reason to doubt the good will of the other, such character analysis serves as the foundation for decisions about courses of action.

The target seems to have less choice than the offender in adopting a character. Most often, two central concerns emerge. First, the target may try to appear cooperative, since a frightened or frustrated kidnapper is more likely to harm the hostage. Second, some targets work to convince the kidnapper that, while they want to cooperate, they are incapable of paying the high ransom demanded. The size of the ransom may be negotiable—kidnappers sometimes agree to lower the price.

Because the kidnapper and target are rarely face-to-face, they must trust each other to carry out their parts of the bargain. The need for trust implies the possibility of betrayal. Either party can violate the other's trust. Rather than returning the hostage upon payment of the ransom, the kidnapper can demand a second, additional ransom. Worse, the kidnapper can kill the hostage after, or even before, the ransom is paid. (In addition to betrayal by the kidnapper, the target may face interference by pseudo-kidnappers—people who learn about the crime and, claiming to be the kidnappers, open negotiations with the target, hoping to make off with the ransom before the actual kidnappers communicate with the target (Waller, 1961).) Targets also can deceive the kidnapper, usually by cooperating with the authorities to help capture the criminal. Social control agents may encourage targets to stall during the negotiations, playing for time during which the officials can locate or identify the kidnapper. They may make the ransom identifiable, for example, by marking the bills or recording their serial numbers. And, since kidnappers are most vulnerable when they collect the ransom, targets may help to arrange an ambush.

To avoid being deceived by the kidnapper, targets often insist on authenticating evidence, asking the kidnapper to prove that he or she has possession of the hostage and that the hostage is well:

> . . . frequent proof questions are needed. This will normally comprise questions to which only the victim can know the answer; or they may require a tape of his voice reading an extract from the current issue of a morning paper; or a photograph of him (sent throught the post) holding a copy of that paper; or a letter in his handwriting which, from its content (e.g. mention of a current news item) could only have been written on that day. An experienced kidnapper will appreciate that such a proof call will be required immediately negotiation begins, and at periodic intervals, and certainly at the very end, a few hours before any ransom is paid. (Clutterbuck, 1978:116)

The kidnapper must deal with the possibility of deceit in less direct ways. Threats may successfully intimidate the target into compliance. But the target may cooperate with the authorities in spite of threats, and the criminal's safest assumption is that the target is helping the officials. To avoid capture, the kidnapper must make demands which anticipate the authorities' efforts. For example, criminals often insist that the ransom conform to their specifications—that it be unmarked, in used bills, of small denominations, and with serial numbers which are not in sequence or otherwise recorded (Gene Miller, 1971; Waller, 1961). Similarly, the kidnapper must carefully arrange to collect the ransom. The target should not know the time or place for the ransom delivery until just before it is to occur. Often, the target is sent on a "treasure hunt"—ordered to go to a location where the offender can observe whether officials are following the target, then given a message to proceed to another location, and so forth, until the kidnapper is assured that no ambush is planned (Clutterbuck, 1978). While these measures offer a degree of safety, the kidnapper's ultimate protection against the target's deceit lies in delaying the hostage's release until the ransom has been collected. Cautious kidnappers may insist on further delays until the ransom has been disposed of, perhaps by selling it at a discount to other criminals.

Even using elaborate precautions, kidnappers are highly vulnerable to social control agents. In kidnapping, control agents have important advantages, particularly if they are notified while the crime is in progress. Targets may not notify the authorities if they suspect that the officials will place capturing the kidnapper ahead of recovering the hostage. Overly aggressive action on the part of social control agents can frighten a kidnapper and cost the hostage's life. In order to gain the cooperation of targets, many social control agencies adopt a policy of supporting the target's efforts. This includes counseling the target on methods of deceiving the kidnapper, such as delaying negotiations and preparing a marked ransom, advising the target to demand proof of the hostage's well-being, and investigating leads to identify or locate the kidnapper. In the meantime, each contact between the kidnapper and the target offers agents opportunities to gather additional information. Because kidnapping is defined as a serious crime, worthy of large-scale investigation, officials are willing to use considerable manpower and a wide range of scientific techniques of detection, such as the analysis of handwriting, typewriting, fingerprints, tire tracks, soil, and so forth (Collins, 1962; Tully, 1965).

Social control policies against kidnapping are effective. Beginning in the late 1920s, kidnappings rose dramatically—one survey showed 279 known cases in 1931, compared to only a handful of cases five years earlier (Alix, 1978). The Lindbergh case and other kidnappings with prominent hostages led to considerable publicity—the *New York Times* began publishing a daily box score, giving the current status of major cases. Observers attributed the wave of kidnappings to the consolidation of criminal formal organizations in major American cities, which placed many criminals, formerly employed in rival organizations, out of work, and to the Depression, which made the rich attractive targets (Renaud, 1932; Sullivan, 1932). In response, new social control methods for handling kidnappings emerged. Kidnapping laws were revised to carry stiffer penalties, and federal legislation gave the FBI jurisdiction in many kidnapping cases. By committing large teams of agents and sophisticated investigative techniques to kidnapping cases, the FBI demonstrated the kidnappers' vulnerability. During the thirty-five years after the first federal anti-kidnapping legislation, the FBI reported that all but five of over seven hundred kidnappings had been solved (*New York Times*, 1967). The difficulty of completing the crime successfully makes kidnapping unattractive to career criminals; typical kidnappers are loners or people operating on the margin of the criminal world.

Recently, another type of offender became involved in ransom kidnapping. Political terrorists concentrate on abducting diplomats, other government agents, and business executives, extorting ransoms from the hostages' employers (Baumann, 1973; Clutterbuck, 1978; Hamilton, 1976; Schreiber, 1978). Here, the aim is twofold—to extort a ransom and to demonstrate the weaknesses of the government opposed by the the terrorists. The ransoms in political kidnappings may be cash, but they often serve political ends—freedom for prisoners, distribution of food to the poor, or publicity for the kidnappers' ideology. Political kidnappings are symbolic; they demonstrate that the government has opponents and, when the kidnapping is successful, that the regime can be opposed. In political kidnappings, governments find themselves in the unaccustomed role of target. Government involvement in criminal kidnappings is limited to providing social control services, but the target governments in political kidnappings must reconsider their policies toward the crime, especially since they are vulnerable to repeated kidnappings. Some governments simply refuse to negotiate with kidnappers; others try to keep anyone from conducting such negotiations and thereby acknowledging the kidnappers' power (Baumann, 1973; Clutterbuck,1978). It is too early to evaluate the success of these strategies, but there is some evidence that kidnappers choose to avoid governments which refuse to negotiate, selecting their targets among governments with a record of cooperation (Jenkins et al., 1977).

Racketeering

Used broadly, the term "racketeering" refers to any criminal activity or to organized crime. More narrowly, racketeering refers to systematic extortion, deviant operations which regularly extort payments, usually from businesses or unions. This section focuses on racketeering in the narrow sense. Whereas the target of a kidnapping can foresee an end to the transaction, once the ransom is delivered and the hostage returned, the target of racketeering expects to continue making regular ransom payments. While kidnapping is episodic extortion, racketeering is systematic.

Rackets vary in their complexity (Gurfein, 1934). The protection racket is relatively simple. Here, the racketeer approaches the target (usually the proprietor of a small business) and offers to protect the business against unspecified dangers in return for regular payments. If the target refuses, the offender secretly attacks the establishment, escalating the damage in successive attacks until the target agrees to pay. This has all of the elements of an extortionate transaction—extortionist, target, threat (of attacks), hostage (the business), and ransom. In the protection racket, the ransom is a straightforward *tribute* to ward off the racketeer's attacks. In more complex rackets, the offenders gain control over a labor market or the supply of some good or service (such as a construction union or a city's commercial laundries) and charge their customers an exorbitant price. Customers who attempt to buy from other sources are threatened, and if they persist in buying elsewhere, they suffer attacks on their businesses or themselves. In these rackets, a gloss of apparent legitimacy helps protect the racketeer from social control efforts—without knowing about the underlying threat of violence, the transactions between racketeer and target appear to be ordinary business deals. These targets make a purchase, actually receiving some good or service, but paying more than the free market price—the *premium* being the cost of the extortion, the ransom. For example, the physical facilities for handling cargo on the New York docks at the end of World War II were inadequate. There was not enough room for trucks to load their cargo efficiently (D. Bell, 1960). Racketeers controlling the long-shoremen's union stepped in to supervise the loading—for a price. Truckers unwilling to pay the premium suffered expensive delays waiting for a turn at the docks and became targets for other intimidation.

Why do targets of racketeering, who know that the extortion will continue, cooperate? Why don't they seek help from social control agents? The answers lie in three conditions which favor the development of rack-eteering: the vulnerability of the hostage; instability in the marketplace; and inadequate social control.

Racketeers threaten vulnerable hostages. While kidnappers must hold a person captive, racketeers choose hostages which are permanently vulnerable to attack. Small businesses make ideal hostages; they must be accessible if they are to attract customers, and the proprietors usually cannot afford to relocate in order to escape the threats. These firms are vulnerable to attack:

> Restaurants may be comparatively easy targets for racketeers. They are so easily harassed, because their business is really rather fragile. Noises and bad odors and startling events can spoil the clientele, and even physical damage cannot be guarded against. (Schelling, 1971:649)

So long as the cost of protecting the hostage is greater than the cost of cooperating with the racketeer—and the cost of protective measures can be very high when the hostage is vulnerable—targets have reason to cooperate.

Cooperation is particularly likely when the target's business operates in an unstable, highly competitive marketplace. John Landesco, in his pioneering study of Chicago rackets in the 1920s, attributed the development of racketeering to two factors: "cutthroat competition among small business enterprises," and "a tradition of lawlessness and violence" (Landesco, 1968:167). He argued that markets where competitors continually reduce prices to undercut one another become so unstable that competitors sometimes organize trade associations where members agree to hold to a minimum price. If some members break ranks and begin undercutting the association's standard price, racketeering may emerge as a way of enforcing the price controls. Although paying the racketeers is an added cost, targets know that their business will not be driven out of the marketplace by a rival firm offering lower prices—the racketeers will attack these rivals. In the meantime, the extra cost of the ransom is passed along to the target's customers in the form of higher prices. Racketeers stabilize uncertain markets: truckers know that they will be able to load at the docks without expensive delays; small businesses in a competitive marketplace can avoid the risks of bankruptcy; and so forth (D. Bell, 1960; Block, 1980; Landesco, 1968). Some rackets are parasitical—the protection racket offers no benefits for targets, aside from warding off the racketeer's attacks (Gurfein, 1934). But other rackets provide a service, at the price of the racketeer's premium, by stabilizing an otherwise unpredictable marketplace. So long as the racket seems fair—targets perceive that they are being charged equally—and the price of compliance is not too high, targets may enjoy the security of a stable market, making them reluctant to resist (Schelling, 1971).

Resistance is especially unlikely if targets view social control agents as ineffective in responding to racketeering. Systematic extortion exposes the offender even more than kidnapping. Racketeers must appear regularly to make their collections, making them vulnerable to social control. As a consequence, systematic extortion tends to develop only when social control is ineffective. For example, the Sicilian mafia operated as an informal government, extorting money from peasants while maintaining order. It arose in the vacuum left by the Bourbon government, which taxed its citizens but provided few control services (Blok, 1974; Hobsbawm, 1959). Similarly, in Italian immigrant neighborhoods, the Black Hand exacted tribute because residents were suspicious, convinced the police could not offer effective protection (Nelli, 1976). Racketeers may also neutralize social control through corruption, bribing officials to ignore the racket (Block, 1980; Landesco, 1968; Nelli, 1976; Pearce, 1976). Thus, racketeers minimize resistance by intimidating vulnerable targets, by stabilizing the targets' marketplace, and neutralizing social control agencies.

Although racketeers sometimes organize as mobs (Block, 1980), racketeering is particularly suited to deviant formal organizations. It offers a potentially large, stable income, with dozens of targets, each making regular payments. A racket's scope is limited only by the number of potential hostages (businesses in the particular marketplace) and the racketeer's resources for threatening targets and collecting regular ransom payments. Formal organizations have enough members to control a marketplace through threats and make collections, as well as established contacts for corrupting officials. Rackets are most successful when they expand throughout a marketplace. Profits are maximized and targets are more likely to comply with the racketeer's threats when they believe the racketeer treats all targets equally. Racketeering offers steady income with low visibility. Targets tend to remain silent, because either they are intimidated or they view the market's stability as worth the cost of the racketeer's premium; and social control agents rarely interfere when there are no complaints. The combination of high profits and low risks suits deviant formal organizations.

The relationship between systematic extortion and deviant formal organization can be documented. The pattern often appears in preindustrial societies, where peasants pay tribute to ward off attacks by well-organized predators (McIntosh, 1975). The criminal tribes of India (McIntosh, 1973) and the Sicilian mafia (Blok, 1974; Hobsbawm, 1959) exploited peasants.

In the United States, systematic extortion developed in major cities during the twentieth century. Examples include the Black Hand, which extorted money from Italian immigrants, and the various criminal syndicates, which ran rackets beginning in the 1920s (Block, 1980; Landesco, 1968; Nelli, 1976; Pearce, 1976). In 1967, the President's Commission on Law Enforcement and Administration of Justice stated:

> Today, the kinds of production and service industries and businesses that organized crime controls or has invested in range from accounting firms to yeast manufacturing. . . . In a few instances, racketeers control nationwide manufacturing and service industries with known and respected brand names. (President's Commission, 1967a:4)

Monopolistic control over a marketplace often emerges through systematic extortion (Schelling, 1967, 1971). Rackets must be monopolistic in one sense—a marketplace usually cannot support more than one racket. Racketeers may demand a set proportion, say 25 percent, of each target's income. These targets cannot afford to pay more than one ransom. In this sense, a protection racket really does offer protection—in order to preserve their own income, offenders protect their targets from other racketeers. But the racketeer's monopoly often extends to legitimate as well as criminal enterprises. If racketeers monopolize a commodity through their control over a labor union or the supply of some product, they can extort ransoms from their targets by threatening to cut off access to that commodity. Here, the monopoly over supply serves as the extortionist's lever. In other instances, extortion can create its own monopoly. Restaurant owners may be threatened with unspecified attacks unless they agree to subscribe to the racketeer's linen service. If all targets comply, the racketeer acquires monopoly control over linen supply. Of course, one of the benefits of owning a monopoly is that pricing is no longer competitive—the racketeer can charge more than the free market price for monopolized goods or services.

Systematic extortion is not confined to respectable targets. Deviant formal organizations which distribute an illicit good or service engage in systematic extortion of deviants (Block, 1980; Schelling, 1971). For example, in a formal organization operating brothel prostitution, the brothels' madams can be viewed as the organization's targets. The organization charges the madams a fee, usually a percentage of their profits, to operate within its territory. Proprietors who fail to pay the fee can expect to suffer attacks. For example, if the city's police have corrupt ties to the organization, madams who resist may be arrested. The formal organization provides some services to the madam—notably protection from the police—in return for its percentage. This situation is analogous to rackets in legitimate marketplaces—the extortionists acquire control over their targets through their threats. Deviant enterprises make especially vulnerable targets because their proprietors cannot demand protection from social control agencies.

Whether racketeers extort from legitimate or deviant enterprises, the racket is usually invisible to outsiders (Schelling, 1971). A customer in a restaurant cannot know whether the establishment must deal with a racketeer's laundry service; similarly, a brothel's customer cannot know about the madam's enforced partnership with a deviant formal organization. These relationships become apparent only when targets complain. When racketeers provide legitimate services, such as a laundry service, it is difficult to prove that extortion occurs. Payments made to these racketeers appear to be ordinary business expenses, and targets can shift the blame, for example, criticizing laundry services for failing to police their own industry and keep out racketeers. This allows the target to view his or her own compliance to the racketeer's demands as someone else's fault.

Once racketeers control a marketplace, there may be relatively little demand for social control action against them. If complaints do arise, corruption often subverts social control efforts. Once a racket is in operation, the profits are substantial enough to pay for the cooperation of key officials. In its most systematic form, racketeering's bribes provide officials with a regular income, with weekly or monthly payments. In addition to these direct payments, officials may profit in other ways. Rackets construct an interlocking network of people who control deviant formal organizations, business firms, labor unions, and government agencies, all profiting from stability in a racket-controlled marketplace (Block, 1980; Pearce, 1976). The ordinary operation of a racket is uneventful; costs are passed along to consumers. Although grounded in extortionate threats, rackets can become institutionalized, the "way things are done around here."

Cooperation through Leverage

Kidnapping and racketeering share an underlying organization with blackmail (Hepworth, 1975), skyjacking (Baldwin, 1976), some political terrorism (Schreiber, 1978), anonymous letters threatening arson or violence (E. Thompson, 1975), and other extortionate transactions. In each case, the extortionist obtains the target's cooperation by threatening to harm the hostage unless a ransom is paid. In effect, the threat supplies the leverage with which the extortionist moves the target into reluctant cooperation. Extortion is a form of conflict where the participants maneuver—the offender trying to apply effective leverage and the target trying to reduce the extortionist's pressure. The outcome of the transaction varies among extortionate offenses. In ransom kidnapping, it is extremely difficult for the kidnapper to avoid capture once social control agents learn about the crime because repeated contacts with the target, as well as prolonged exposure to the hostage, reveal too much information about the offender's identity and location. Episodic extortion, then, is unstable. In contrast, systematic extortion, such as racketeering, can be very stable. Once in operation, the transaction's criminal aspects are concealed, resistance by targets is minimized, effective efforts by social control agents are blocked, and the racket assumes a taken-for-granted quality. The target's cooperation, while extorted, continues because there is no more attractive option.

FRAUD

Fraudulent transactions also depend upon the target's cooperation, but that cooperation is given freely. On the surface, fraud involves an exchange, usually a sale, which each participant enters willingly. Beneath the surface, however, the participants have very different understandings of what is taking place. The target's involvement is naive—he or she believes that the exchange is genuine. The deviant takes a cynical view, intending to give the target less than the target anticipates receiving in their exchange. The discrepancy between the target's expectations and the offender's intentions may take various forms. The target may get nothing, receiving no return on the investment; the target's share may be adulterated, of lower quality than promised; or it may be deficient in some other respect. In every case, the target gets less than he or she bargained for.

The essence of fraud is misrepresentation—the deviant deceives the target about the nature of the transaction, leading the target to develop exaggerated expectations for the exchange. Misrepresentation requires a deliberately staged performance by the deviant. Erving Goffman's (1959) dramaturgical perspective is helpful in understanding the offender's behavior. Goffman argues that social interaction resembles the behavior of actors on a theater stage; this analogy is particularly good for the deviant engaged in fraud. Like an actor, the deviant views his or her performance as a part, saying lines which he or she does not in fact believe. Like an actor, the deviant may supplement this performance, using a specially staged setting, props, or the assistance of other actors. The offender usually distinguishes between a front region, where the target witnesses the performance, and a backstage region, where the target is absent and the actors can safely step out of their roles to relax or plan future performances. In general, the amount of staging varies with the stakes—ambitious frauds involve large casts, special settings, and elaborate props, whereas simpler operations use minimal resources.

Frauds can be arrayed along three dimensions. First, frauds can be divided into apparently legitimate and apparently illegitimate exchanges. Sometimes the target believes that the transaction is legitimate, a respectable purchase or investment. For example, a homeowner may hire someone to repair a leaking roof or an investor may purchase real estate, only to have the roof "treated" with a worthless substance or to find that the property is located beneath a swamp. Frauds based on apparently legitimate exchanges include medical quackery (Roebuck and Hunter, 1970), home and appliance repair fraud (Vaughan and Carlo, 1975), check forgery (Lemert, 1967; Klein and Montague, 1977), land fraud (Snow, 1978), and investment fraud (N. Miller, 1965; Soble and Dallos, 1975). Other frauds involve targets who believe they are engaged in a deviant exchange. For instance, a target may purchase illicit drugs which have been overly adulterated. From the offender's perspective, frauds based on deviant exchanges have an important advantage: in reporting the fraud to the authorities, the target must reveal his or her own involvement in an illicit transaction. Naturally, many targets are reluctant to expose their deviant involvements, so these frauds rarely get reported. Any deviant exchange can be converted into a fraud; examples include frauds based on prostitution (Hong et al., 1975), and gambling (Inciardi, 1975; Polsky, 1967; Prus and Sharper, 1977).

A second dimension for classifying fraudulent transactions is the length of time required for completion. Simple frauds can often be completed in a matter of minutes. Three-card monte, for example, requires little time, space, or equipment. The target encounters a dealer who bets that the target cannot pick out one of three cards dealt face down on the ground. The target discovers something the dealer has apparently overlooked—the card to be identified has a distinctively bent corner, so that it is easily recognized. Convinced that the bet cannot be lost, the target agrees to play. However, by adeptly straightening out the bent corner on the winning card, bending a corner on another card, and then using a deceptive method of dealing, the dealer almost invariably fools the target. The entire transaction takes less than a minute. On the other hand, more elaborate frauds, usually involving much larger sums, can extend over months or years. A team of deviants must lay the groundwork for convincing the target to invest a substantial sum; if the target is a cautious investor, this process requires considerable time and care. Yet the profits can be substantial—some frauds earn millions of dollars.

Third, frauds can be classified by the target's interpretation of the loss. In the most artful frauds, the target never realizes that exploitation occurred, interpreting the loss as the result of an unfortunate error, bad luck, or some other reasonable cause. Such a naive interpretation has two important advantages for the offender—a target who does not feel defrauded is unlikely to complain to the authorities and, if assured that the error which caused the loss cannot reoccur, the target can sometimes be convinced to enter into a second fradulent exchange, only to lose again. On other occasions, of course, the target may be quick to recognize fraud for what it is.

The two examples of fraud discussed in the following section span some of these dimensions. Confidence games are a form of fraud typically carried out by career thieves. A con game usually appears to be a deviant exchange. It can be carried out over varying lengths of time, and it can go undiscovered if the offender is adroit. Investment fraud, on the other hand, is committed by apparently respectable people. The target invests in a presumably legitimate exchange, and the operation can continue for a long time before anyone discovers the ongoing fraud. Whereas confidence games typically defraud one target, large-scale investment frauds exploit many targets.

Confidence Games

Confidence games illustrate the principles behind several types of fraud. Because fraud involves major differences in the ways the target and the offender interpret their transaction, and because complicated staging may be required to maintain these different interpretations, fraudulent transactions are less straightforward than other forms of exploitation. Therefore, it will be helpful to examine one confidence game in detail, then use it to understand the general properties of con games and other types of fraud.

Maurer (1974:6) describes a big con game as a sequence of ten steps (the argot phrase for each step is given in parentheses):

1. Locating and investigating a well-to-do victim. (*Putting the mark up.*)
2. Gaining the victim's confidence. (*Playing the con for him.*)
3. Steering him to meet the insideman. (*Roping the mark.*)
4. Permitting the insideman to show him how he can make a large amount of money dishonestly. (*Telling him the tale.*)
5. Allowing the victim to make a substantial profit. (*Giving him the convincer.*)
6. Determining exactly how much he will invest. (*Giving him the breakdown.*)
7. Sending him home for this amount of money. (*Putting him on the send.*)
8. Playing him against a big store and fleecing him (*Taking off the touch.*)
9. Getting him out of the way as quickly as possible. (*Blowing him off.*)
10. Forestalling action by the law (*Putting in the fix.*)[2]

How are these steps carried out in practice? The rag, a form of big con based on the stock market, provides an example (Maurer, 1974:70-89). One member of the deviant team, called the roper, searches for potential targets. When a likely prospect or "mark" is found, the roper makes the target's acquaintance and gains his or her confidence (steps 1 and 2). The roper then arranges for the mark to meet a second member of the deviant team, the insideman. In the rag game, the roper believes that the target can be defrauded through a scheme for investing in stocks, and the insideman plays the part of a major stock market speculator (step 3). Often the introduction to the insideman is arranged so that the insideman appears to owe the target a favor; for example, the roper and the target may discover the insideman's wallet (in fact, the roper staged this discovery), and they return it. Appearing to feel indebted, the insideman explains his or her trade. He or she works for a syndicate which is illicitly manipulating the stock market; the job is to make investments as instructed—investments which guarantee profits. The insideman suggests that the mark might share these profits. (step 4). The insideman offers to invest a small sum for the target and this investment returns an immediate, impressive profit. If the target remains unconvinced, a series of small investments follows, each doubling or tripling the target's money (step 5). At this point, the insideman instructs the target and roper to visit a broker's office (which looks authentic, but is actually a "big store," a setting staged by the deviants) and invest a large amount, paying with the roper's check (which is too large to be covered by the money in the roper's bank account). They do so and immediately earn a very large profit, only to discover that the broker (another deviant team member) is angry because the check was not backed by sufficient funds. The broker refuses to pay until the target and the roper can prove that their financial resources are sufficient to cover the check. The target and roper arrange to split the responsibility for getting enough cash to cover the check and each goes to get their share (steps 6 and 7). The target is motivated by the large sum apparently waiting in the broker's office. The roper and target collect the money and return to the broker's office, only to meet the insideman, who gives them a hot new tip. The roper quickly invests all of their cash, mistakenly buying stocks rather than selling, and the money is lost (step 8). At this point, various methods are used to terminate the transaction (steps 9 and 10).

The team of deviants, the big store, and the target all play vital parts in this drama. The confidence mob is a team with a specialized division of labor (Maurer, 1974:116-80). Its members need different skills. The roper must be personable enough to strike up acquaintances with different people and perceptive enough to evaluate those people as potential targets. The mark must trust the roper while being guided into the staged world of the insideman and the big store. The insideman, in turn, must be a highly skilled salesperson. The insideman must explain the money-making scheme to the target and then convince the target to invest. This is delicate work— the target must be brought gradually into the situation and convinced that this is a sure thing. Finally, the crew which populates the big store plays a vital role. The big store is a carefully staged setting, a replica of a broker's office, a bookmaking parlor, or some other establishment. It contains several people—a manager, who appears to be in charge of the staged office and actually may be in charge of the rest of the team; shills, who act as customers in the setting, betting on horse races, investing in stocks, and so on; and others, who play the parts of employees in the establishment. Because these people fill the big store, apparently conducting major financial deals and making huge profits, the target becomes convinced that the opportunities outlined by the insideman are real.

Big stores are physical establishments, filled with props and deviant actors, often operating over periods of years. It is virtually impossible to avoid the notice of officials; too many people work in the big store for the location to remain secret. Even if the deviants could disguise their presence, some targets inevitably complain to the authorities. As a consequence, big stores need the cooperation of officials. In the early twentieth century, when big stores flourished in many cities in the United States, their locations depended partly on the corruptibility of local authorities (Maurer, 1974:181-208). When targets' complaints led to arrests, the deviants normally could fix their cases, so that their activities were relatively safe. In addition to being protected from the police, big stores offer other advantages. While a given roper can only work on one target at a time, a big store, through careful scheduling and staging, can be used for more than one target during the same week. Over a year, a successful big store can manage dozens of cons (Maurer, 1974:114).

The target must take an active part in a big con (Maurer, 1974:90-115). The most obvious requirement for a target is wealth. Big cons are expensive productions, demanding several people on the payroll, the maintenance of an elaborate setting, and enough cash to entice the mark during the con's early stages. A large return is necessary to make a profit. A second requirement is less apparent but equally important—the mark must be dishonest. All confidence games involve the mark's being given an opportunity to engage in a dishonest activity, such as manipulating the stock market or betting on a fixed horse race. Discovering a "sure thing" convinces the target to invest a large sum of cash. Where an honest person might turn away from the opportunity, the target's greed overwhelms caution. The aphorism, "You can't cheat an honest man," applies to all confidence games. While wealth and greed are necessary, other qualities are highly desirable in a target. The mark should not complain to the authorities. In some cases, the target accepts the loss without realizing that fraud was involved and then demands a second chance. (Among pool hustlers, the term "fish" describes a target who loses the money on his or her person and goes to get more [Polsky, 1967].) More commonly, the target is "cooled out," convinced to accept the loss without turning to the authorities. Deviants may cool out a mark by warning that any complaint will expose the target's dishonest intentions. Targets may also refrain from complaining to officials out of fear of being thought stupid for falling for the con. In order to preserve their respectable reputations, many targets choose to take their loss in silence. Given their corrupt ties with the authorities, their ability to conceal the fraud from some targets, and the reluctance of other targets to complain, confidence mobs minimize the risk of apprehension.

The big con game is the most elaborate example of fraud committed by career deviants, but other varieties of fraud use the same principles. Short cons share the big con's structure, with two deviants playing the roles of roper and insideman, but the mark is played only for the money on his or her person (Maurer, 1974:209-33; Roebuck and Johnson, 1964). For example, the mark may believe that he or she is conspiring with the roper to cheat the insideman at matching coins. In the course of the game, the target gives his or her cash to the roper, believing that the roper will later return with the money and split what was taken from the insideman. Instead, of course, the roper disappears. Various forms of sports hustling (discussed in Chapter 2) also resemble con games—the target agrees to bet because the odds appear to be against the hustler. Circus grifting, now in decline, is another, traditional form of fraud. Some circus and carnival workers specialize in shortchanging customers and running games which cannot be won (Inciardi, 1975:34-45). Finally, a new con recently emerged in Los Angeles (Hong et al., 1975). Male customers enter what seem to be brothels disguised as massage parlors, advertising themselves with signs like "House of Oral Love." The target gives his money to a manager who promises a private session of oral love with a woman employee. Once he and the woman go to their private room, the target discovers that "oral love" means talking about love. If the target demands sexual services, the woman indignantly responds that she is unwilling to do anything illegal. While this form of fraud lacks the finesse of the big con, the transactions share the same structure.

Confidence games, whether big cons or short cons, involve offenders who identify themselves as deviant. While some criminals specialize in armed robbery or burglary, others work confidence games (Maurer, 1974; Roebuck and Johnson, 1964). Compared to other specialties in deviant exploitation, confidence games have relatively high prestige within the world of thieves (Sutherland, 1937:197-200). Several features contribute to the con game's high status. The work can be very profitable—big cons typically involve several thousand dollars, sometimes more than one hundred thousand dollars. At the same time, there is relatively low risk; the authorities can be neutralized and targets frequently fail to complain about their losses. Even if complaints do lead to apprehension and conviction, the penalties are relatively slight. Courts generally assign longer sentences to deviants convicted of other forms of exploitation, particularly coercion and surreptitious exploitation. Fraud is viewed as less serious, perhaps because the target's cooperation and dishonest intent make the loss possible. The confidence artist's working conditions are comparatively comfortable; in order to locate, become acquainted with, and persuade wealthy targets to enter a con, the offenders must appear respectable, frequenting the habitats of the wealthy and enjoying their comforts. Finally, confidence games hinge upon the deviant's wits. The ability to understand and deceive people is the con artist's chief skill, and among deviants, as in the wider society, people who work with their heads hold higher status than those who work with their hands.

The essence of the confidence game lies in the target's character. Without the target's greed, the game would fail. The target wants something for nothing. Instead, of course, the target gets nothing in exchange for something.

Investment Fraud

While the people who manage confidence games see themselves as deviant, this is not true for offenders in all fraud. In investment fraud, offenders often define themselves as respectable business executives. They know that they are deceiving their investors and that this deception is illegal, but they justify their actions with the belief that the business will become profitable, paying back the investors before the fraud is discovered. For these executives, fraud is a way of furthering the organization's goals. Although firms engaged in investment fraud may employ many people, only a few of them know about the fraud in most cases. Under their direction, other employees may unwittingly contribute to the deception. These naive employees don't intend to commit fraud, and they will not be viewed as offenders in this discussion. Like con games, investment fraud features complex interactions between the offenders and their targets. One investment fraud, the Equity Funding case, illustrates some of these complexities. Other major investment frauds reveal similar patterns, although the details vary from case to case (cf. Hutchison, 1974; Maxa, 1977, N. Miller, 1965).

The Equity Funding scandal involved fraud on an unprecedented scale—some *$2 billion* was lost through a complicated scheme (Dirks and Gross, 1974; Soble and Dallos, 1975). The basic motivation for the fraud was straightforward: company officers of Equity Funding Corporation of America (EFCA) and its subsidiary, Equity Funding Life Insurance Company (EFLIC), wanted to increase the value of EFCA stock. During the 1960s, EFCA's stock grew in value as a consequence of the firm's outstanding performance. Each successive annual report indicated that the company was doing more business, accumulating more assets, earning greater profits, and paying higher dividends. This success story attracted investors, raising the value of the company's stock. Institutional investors, including colleges and universities, bought the stock, encouraged by security advisors who saw EFCA as an especially sound investment.

There was only one problem—much of the business reported by EFCA was fraudulent. EFLIC sold life insurance policies, but the figures reporting EFLIC's volume of business were false; many of the policies listed by the company had not, in fact, been sold. Rather, company employees created new policies, making up phony applications as well as the accompanying documentation, such as reports of physical examinations. In some years, phony files accounted for half of EFLIC's reported new policies. In turn, these policies were sold to other insurance companies, a common practice, called reinsuring, used in the insurance industry to generate cash:

> A legitimate policy with a $1,000 annual premium would cost about $1,300 to service in the first year. (A life insurance company, due to the first year commissions it pays, loses money in the first year and makes it up in renewal years.) Equity Funding would sell a legitimate policy to a reinsurance company

for $1,800. The cash profit in the first year would be $500. But for a fake policy there was no $1,300 expense. Equity Funding simply forwarded a "premium" of $1,000—and received $1,800 in return. Its profit: $800. (Dirks and Gross, 1974:243)

The problem lay in maintaining these policies. In successive years, the reinsuring company had to be paid 90 percent of the annual premium ($900 in the example), but it would not refund any of this money. Thus, the fake policies were profitable in their first year, but costly in the following years. Somehow money had to be generated to pay the second year policies. EFLIC raised this money by creating more phony policies, using the profits from new policies to pay the expenses for old ones. Each year, the number of fraudulent policies grew. While the production of fake policies was the most striking feature of the Equity Funding case, there were other fraudulent practices, including falsification of assets.

In retrospect, investigators concluded that the Equity Funding fraud should have been discovered several years before it was exposed. Discovery of the fraud was delayed for several reasons. The Equity Funding scandal demonstrated deficiencies in the mechanisms for controlling the insurance industry. Organizations dealing with EFCA had to take the company's word for the authenticity of its practices; there were few other ways to check if the company's claims were correct. The stock exchange accepted EFCA's annual reports with little additional investigation, the reinsuring companies did not check to determine the authenticity of the policies they purchased, and the various accountants, auditors, and investigators from state regulatory agencies used procedures insufficient to penetrate the layers of fraudulent records. In part, these failures were due to EFCA's computerized record system. Some of its computer programs generated fraudulent policies; others were designed to be inaccessible to auditing. The standard procedures for insuring fiscal responsibility evolved for systems based on paperwork; Equity's computerized system was unfamiliar enough and complex enough to ward off penetration. Perhaps the most important factor making the fraud possible was the knowing participation of many employees. A fraud of this size demanded participation from a relatively large number of employees, ranging from top corporation officers to clerical personnel. While most of these employees did not realize the extent of the fraud, and while some people, such as clerical personnel working up the phony policies, did not know that what they were doing was criminal, many employees recognized that something was wrong. Sometimes these people reported their misgivings to supervisors, and were reassured—told that it was a one-time illicit manipulation or that supervisors knew about and approved what was happening. But in many cases, employees realized that illegal activities occurred systematically. For reasons of job security, lack of proof, or a decision to simply accept what was taking place and, perhaps, benefit from the consequences, the fraud continued for years without evidence leaking to social control agents.

Eventually, the company fired a knowledgeable employee. Disgruntled, he notified investigators of the fraudulent activities:

> He proposed that there was a substantial amount of fake insurance on the books; that the company had made up fake death certificates; that it had created fake assets, such as certificates of deposit; that the officers of the company were not only involved in the plot but were its architects; that middle management carried out the fraud knowingly; that a substantial number of people inside and outside the company knew about the fraud; and that the fraud had evolved because of a need to boost the price of the stock so that the company could make acquisitions. (Dirks and Gross, 1974:91)

Once these claims were investigated, exposure of the fraud quickly followed. A variety of social control agents representing state boards for the regulation of the insurance industry, the Securities and Exchange Commission, and the New York Stock Exchange conducted investigations. Discovery of the fraud had important consequences for the company, which filed for bankruptcy under Chapter 10 (an arrangement whereby a company is salvaged if possible), and for many of the fraud's perpetrators. Eighteen executives pleaded guilty to federal charges—the company's president received eight years imprisonment, two executive vice-presidents received five year sentences, and the remaining members got sentences ranging from three years imprisonment to suspended sentences with probation.

The Equity Funding fraud was an exceptionally ambitious operation, but its structure resembles other investment frauds. Investors frequently lack the ability to check the actual value of their investments; they rely on reports by auditing firms and other agencies which, in turn, may fail to expose the fraud. For example, population shifts often provide the foundation for land fraud (Snow, 1978). As the demand for real estate in Florida and Arizona grew, with people purchasing lots for retirement homes, investments, and even immediate residence, some development firms saw opportunities for exploitation. The most blatant misrepresentations involved the sale of lots which hardly qualified as land; some Florida investors discovered that they owned portions of swamps. Other land frauds involve false or misleading statements about utility services. A person investing in an Arizona lot may understand that water and sewer lines already are installed or that their installation is imminent, only to discover later that the nearest facilities are miles away. The failure of control agents to supervise the development firms' claims makes the fraud possible.

Although both are based on deceit, confidence games and investment fraud differ in two important ways. First, their targets are different. The con game's mark is an individual, singled out and plucked in isolation. To make the con game profitable, the amount stolen from the target must be as large as possible. In contrast, investment frauds simultaneously deceive many targets; their goal is to attract investments from many people, even though each may pay a relatively small amount. The target in the con game must be greedy, willing to take advantage of an illicit opportunity, but the targets in investment fraud make what they believe are legitimate purchases. In the confidence game, the mark's loss cannot be concealed from him or her; the mob depends on the target's failure to perceive the loss as deliberately engineered or the target's reluctance to complain. Targets in investment fraud, on the other hand, may be slow to discover their loss.

Second, investment fraud works through a legitimate formal organization. The scenes staged in the con game's big stores are completely fraudulent—the brokerage firm in the rag game cannot really buy or sell stocks. But the firms in investment fraud often are licensed to do business—EFCA was listed on the New York Stock Exchange and highly regarded on Wall Street. Investment fraud involves deviance by members of legitimate formal organizations. It can be classified as a form of "white collar crime" (Sutherland, 1949), "business crime" (Conklin, 1977), or "organizational crime" (Schrager and Short, 1978). (These broader classifications include offenses which are not fraudulent—embezzlement and price fixing involve surreptitious exploitation, for example.) The fact that legitimate, sometimes large firms can be involved in fraud affects both offenders and social control agents.

The offenders in investment fraud often view themselves as respectable, rather than deviant. Some investment frauds are illicit from the start— the deviants create a firm with the intention of defrauding its investors and customers. But other frauds begin in business problems—the firm is a legitimate business, but economic reverses cause problems, and management, rather than accepting these losses, tries to hide them through illicit manipulations. These executives may believe that, if only they have enough time to make the necessary adjustments, the firm can become profitable again without the fraud being discovered. Some participants in the Equity Funding scheme argued that, left to its own devices, the corporation would soon have become prosperous enough to stop its fraudulent practices (Soble and Dallos, 1975). (Critics of the EFCA management responded by pointing to an apparently fatal feature of the fraud: in order to conceal the fraudulent actions of earlier years, the company had to keep paying the premiums on the fake policies, and it could only manage to do this by creating an ever larger number of policies. There was no way to bring the problem under control.) Once a fraud begins, other organizational members may learn about it, as in the Equity Funding case, and help cover it up, believing their obligations are to the firm, rather than to outsiders, such as the targets or the authorities (Jack Katz, 1977; 1979). While recognizing that the fraud is illicit, offenders and those involved in the cover-up may deny that their own actions are deviant.

Investment fraud is difficult for officials to detect. Often, the discrepancies between the offenders' claims and reality can only be discovered by experts with special technical or professional competence, such as engineers or accountants. It is not always clear which social control agencies have jurisdiction over organizational violations. Even when violations are identified, the appropriate response often remains unclear. Most social control agencies use an individualistic model of deviance—offenders are individuals who are held responsible for their illicit actions and are vulnerable to sanctions if they are apprehended. Where organizations are at fault, this model must be reexamined. Is an organization as a whole responsible for its actions, or does responsibility rest with some of its members? Should the organization be sanctioned, or should the sanctions be directed toward some members? If organizations are to be sanctioned, will the punishment's effects fall upon those who are not responsible for the deviance? For example, if social control agencies impose heavy fines on a firm, the punishment injures the company's stockholders rather than those directly responsible for the fraud. These issues become important when officials confront offenses committed by corporations and other organizations (Jack Katz, 1979; Schrager and Short, 1978; Stone, 1975; Zald, 1978). Investment fraud, like other organizational deviance, is difficult to control.

Even when the offenders in investment fraud are known, the sanctions levied against them are relatively light. The technical details of the offenses can be difficult to understand: authorities sometimes have difficulty ferreting out the details of the crime, particularly if it involves manipulations with a computer; it is not always evident how the offense fits the statutes which it supposedly violates; and the presentation of the case in a courtroom may prove hard for judges and juries to follow. Judges often are reluctant to sentence executives to prison, since these offenders already have the respectable qualities that rehabilitative programs should produce (Conklin, 1977). Why imprison executives, critics ask, if prison cannot be expected to rehabilitate them? Although the prosecutor in the Equity Funding case argued for a twenty-year sentence for the firm's president, the court sentenced him to only eight years for managing a $2 billion fraud (Soble and Dallos, 1975). At that, the penalty was far more severe than those given to the other Equity Funding defendants or in most other instances of investment fraud. Short terms of imprisonment, fines, and suspended sentences are usual outcomes in these cases.

In summary, investment fraud contains the essential elements of every fraudulent transaction—the target believes that an exchange has been arranged, but the offender engineers the deal so that the target gets less than expected. Yet the trappings of investment fraud are different from those found in con games. The deviants in an investment fraud may define themselves as respectable. The potential profits from investment fraud are far higher than those found in other forms of deviant exploitation, since these frauds can cheat large numbers of targets over what are sometimes extended periods. Furthermore, the risks of apprehension and serious punishment are not correspondingly high.

Cooperation through Trickery

Fraud is an exploitative transaction—a target loses valued property to the offender. However, fraud is distinguished from other forms of exploitation by the deviant's method. In coercion and extortion, deviants rely on actual or threatened force; in surreptitious exploitation, the offender depends on stealth. In fraud, however, the offender uses trickery—by controlling information, the deviant leads the target into an apparent exchange which is in fact exploitative. The target is tricked into cooperating with the deviant.

Because the target of fraud is tricked, societal reaction to fraud is relatively mild. This reaction reflects several factors. First, exploitation involving force or stealth is seen as more serious than fraud because targets have less chance of defending against coercive or surreptitious attacks. The target of a successful fraud loses through intentional cooperation. By failing to check the deviant's claims, the target makes unfounded assumptions about the transaction—assumptions which make the fraud possible. The victim of a mugging or a burglary has little choice in the matter, but the con mob's mark cooperates fully. Second, because the target of fraud has been fooled, fraudulent transactions sometimes appear in a comic light. The fast-talking con artist who uses disguises and a gift of gab to trick the unwary mark is a stock figure in popular culture—usually in a heroic, albeit comic role. *The Sting*, one of the top-grossing movies of all time, provides one example of this theme. Popular culture casts the con artist in a heroic role by emphasizing some features of fraud as virtues: the deviant is smart (the only one who really knows what is taking place), clever (able to manipulate others), confident, and so forth. The targets become villains—rich and arrogant, yet easily fooled. This genre extends one of the classic forms of folktale—the trickster hero. With fraud celebrated and viewed as comic, it is not surprising that actual cases of fraud seem less serious than other exploitative acts. So long as the target appears able to afford the loss, people recognize the comic undertones in fraud. Finally, there is some difficulty distinguishing investment fraud from conventional business practices. Fraud may be deviant, but "sharp" business practices are admired. Manufacturers are expected to represent their products in positive terms; at what point does this become fraudulently deceptive? In a market which advises the buyer to beware, losses to fraud seem partly the target's responsibility. In short, the larger culture recognizes the exploitative quality of fraud, but does not consider it as serious as other varieties of exploitation.

There is another sense in which trickery distinguishes fraud from other types of exploitation—if the trick is successful, the fraud may never be discovered. The targets of coercion and extortion are fully aware of their exploitation, and targets of surreptitious exploitation usually recognize their losses after they occur. While many frauds are uncovered, there is always the possibility that the target will attribute the loss to some other cause, such as bad luck, never linking it to the deviant's malicious intent.

Fraud is more likely to occur under certain circumstances. Because it involves two people who must trust one another to deal in good faith, but because the target does not know the deviant well enough to recognize the fraudulent intent, fraud tends to occur in settings where people have frequent dealings with relative strangers. While fraud can occur in rural settings, opportunities for fraud are more common in cities, where business transactions between strangers are routine. A study of crime in nineteenth century Ohio, for example, found that most types of crimes were equally common in rural and urban areas, but that fraudulent offenses occurred more frequently in the cities (Monkkonen, 1975). Similarly, the possibilities for fraud increase in financial transactions based on credit, rather than cash payment, because financial records are vulnerable to manipulation. Experts are only beginning to recognize the ways computers can be used to defraud. As cash becomes an increasingly less common mode of exchange, computerized credit offers a tempting target for offenders (Parker, 1976). The Equity Funding scandal demonstrates that modern institutions are vulnerable to massive fraud.

VARIETIES OF EXPLOITATIVE DEVIANCE

Traditionally, sociological discussions of deviant exploitation divide these offenses into crimes against persons and crimes against property. The former category includes violent attacks on the target; the latter includes various forms of theft. While this distinction has some uses, it overlooks the social organization of the exploitative transaction. This analysis identified four distinctly organized types of exploitation: coercion, surreptitious exploitation, extortion, and fraud. In general, crimes against persons are coercive or extortionate transactions, while crimes against property are surreptitious or fraudulent. But the categories advanced here are not useful only because they make finer distinctions than those found in the traditional classification. The differences in social organization have profound consequences for the actors in the different transactions (see Table 8-1).

The basis for the relationship between the deviant and the target varies from one organizational form to the next. In coercion, the relationship is based on force—the offender injures or threatens to injure the target. The coercive encounter is face-to-face, typically completed in a relatively short time. In surreptitious exploitation, the offender's stealth and the target's ignorance of what is taking place form the transaction's foundation.

Table 8-1 FEATURES OF EXPLOITATIVE TRANSACTIONS

TYPE OF EXPLOITATION	BASIS	FACE-TO-FACE	DURATION	KEY INFORMATION
Coercion	Force	Yes	Short	Offender's Identity
Surreptitious Exploitation	Secrecy	Sometimes	Short to Medium	Occurrence of Offense
Extortion	Leverage	No	Long	Offender's Identity and Intentions
Fraud	Deceit	Sometimes	Short to Long	Occurrence of Offense

Surreptitious deviants hope to complete the transaction in secrecy; keeping targets unaware of the crime is a central concern, so offenders try to minimize the transaction's length. Surreptitious exploitation may occur when the target is away, or in the target's presence. In extortion, the offender-target relationship is founded on a bargain—the deviant takes the ransom in return for not harming the hostage. Extortionate transactions rarely involve face-to-face contact, and the negotiations toward striking the bargain often are prolonged. These conditions give rise to tactical maneuvering intended to give one or both actors an advantage. Finally, fraud is based on deception—the deviant misleads the target into a disadvantageous exchange. To accomplish this trickery, the deviant manipulates the target and the situation to avoid suspicion. Fraud is often face-to-face, supported by staged settings and props, and it can continue over prolonged periods.

Forms of exploitation also vary in their distribution of information. Each form is characterized by key items of information and their pattern of distribution. In coercion, the target understands that exploitation is occurring, and the deviant knows that the target is likely to call in the authorities. Because information about the deviants' identities can be used to locate and apprehend them, offenders avoid giving away such information. Targets, on the other hand, try to learn as much as possible about the deviant's identity. In surreptitious exploitation, the deviant hopes to complete the transaction before the target recognizes what is occurring. Once the target makes this discovery, social control agents ordinarily are notified. While it remains important to avoid giving away information about identity, deviants can do this with relative ease since the target usually does not witness the deviant transaction. The key bit of information is the fact that the crime is in progress; because discovery during the transaction can lead to apprehension, the deviant tries to complete the crime in secrecy. Extortion is easily recognized by the target, who may be reluctant to notify social control agents for fear of endangering the hostage. Because extortionists confront their targets on several occasions, increasing their risks with each exposure, they must take care to avoid giving away information about identity, location, or intention. Targets who acquire such information can arrange an ambush, often at the moment when the ransom is collected.

Finally, fraud usually is hard to recognize—while some targets know when they have been defrauded, others never understand that their loss was intentional. Since the contacts necessary to persuade the target to participate in the fraudulent exchange often require face-to-face contact, the deviants are likely to concentrate on prolonging the deception, viewing recognition of fraud as the key item of information.

Forms of exploitation also differ in the rates at which they are reported. Because coercion and surreptitious exploitation often lead to complaints to social control agents, rough measures of frequency are available in official records. For example, in 1978, four major coercive offenses—criminal homicide, forcible rape, robbery, and aggravated assault—were reported to the police 1,061,826 times, leading to 469,700 arrests. (Robbery and assault accounted for over 90 percent of these offenses.) Three types of surreptitious exploitation—burglary, larceny, and motor vehicle theft—were reported on 10,079,508 occasions, leading to 1,814,700 arrests (FBI, 1979:38, 186). Thus, crimes of stealth greatly outnumbered coercive crimes. Extortion and fraud are less likely to be reported. In the former, targets fear reprisals, criticism for cooperating with criminals, and, during the transaction, injury to the hostage. In fraud, embarrassment and failure to recognize criminal intent inhibit reports. Although systematic extortion and fraud seem relatively common, they often go unreported. The FBI's annual report for 1978 lists only 77,200 arrests for forgery and counterfeiting and 262,500 for fraud; it does not present any information about extortionate offenses (FBI, 1979:186). Given the large number of cases which are not reported, it is impossible to know how often these offenses occur.

In summary, each type of deviant exploitation has a characteristic organization which affects the relationship between the offender and the target, the control and distribution of information, and the likelihood of officials learning about the transaction. Some other implications of the social organization of exploitation are considered in the next chapter.

NOTES

[1]Excerpted from *Kidnap: The Story of the Lindbergh Case* by George Waller. Copyright© 1961 by George Waller. Reprinted by permission of the Dial Press.

[2]Excerpt from David W. Maurer, *The American Confidence Man*, 1974. Courtesy of Charles C Thomas, Publisher, Springfield, Illinois.

CHAPTER NINE
THE SIGNIFICANCE OF DEVIANT TRANSACTIONS

Deviant transactions can be arrayed along a dimension of organizational complexity. Complexity refers to the minimum number of actors required for the transaction and the nature of the relationship between the roles they perform. Chapters 5 through 8 presented detailed descriptions of three principal forms of deviant transactions and their major subtypes. Individual deviance, the simplest form of deviant transaction, requires only one deviant actor; its subtypes include deviant self-services and subscriptions to prohibited realities. Deviant exchange, requiring two actors performing cooperative, deviant roles, can be subdivided into trades and sales. Finally, deviant exploitation, the most complex form of deviant transaction, requires a deviant actor (the offender) in conflict with another person (the target). Exploitation has four subtypes: coercion, surreptitious exploitation, extortion, and fraud. This chapter will compare the different forms of deviant transactions, developing six propositions about consequences of the social organization of deviance for deviants and social control agents. These propositions reflect different aspects of societal reaction to deviance. Before discussing the propositions, the nature of that reaction must be examined in some detail.

Societies differ in the ways they define and respond to deviance. Kai Erikson (1966) argues that every community's norms mark behavioral boundaries within which members are expected to limit their conduct: "A deviant is a person whose activities have moved outside the margins of the group, and when the community calls him to account for that vagrancy it is making a statement about the nature and placement of its boundaries" (Erikson, 1966:11). From this perspective, where the community draws its boundary lines is less important than the fact that those boundaries exist, separating respectable conduct from deviance. Boundaries vary over time and space—what is deviant in one society at one time may be considered respectable elsewhere or at another time. Societies expect their social control agents to patrol these boundaries and watch for deviance. When they discover deviant acts, officials try to identify, locate, and apprehend the deviants, and apply the appropriate sanctions.

Social control agencies vary from one society to another—they have different ideologies, resources, and priorities. Ideological differences are especially important for understanding social control. Every social control agency has a guiding ideology—a system of interrelated ideas which explains and justifies the agents' activities. Social control ideologies answer central questions about deviance and control: Which behaviors are deviant, and why? What causes deviance? Who commits deviance, where, when, and for what reasons? What are the appropriate responses to deviance? and, What is the social control agent's place in society? Different ideologies answer these questions differently. A brief comparison of four distinct ideologies—religious, political, legal, and medical—illustrates some of these differences.

Some societies give religious authorities the responsibility for social control (Currie, 1968; Erikson, 1966). Religious ideologies equate deviance with sin, violations of holy rules or norms. Society's members should hold orthodox religious beliefs; heresy becomes an important type of deviance. If the religion includes a belief that individuals can control spiritual forces, social control agents may search for witches. Erikson (1966) describes Puritan New England as a community where religion defined the central values and, as a consequence, religious deviance became a central concern. The church's ideology and structure set the stage for three religious "crime waves": the Antinomian heresy, the Quakers, and the Salem witchcraft hysteria. In each case, ministers accused deviants of violating religious norms, and social control agents applied sanctions to uphold the religious ideology.

In Communist countries, the central social control ideology is political (Bennett, 1977; Connor, 1972a, 1972b; Greenblatt, 1977; Loney, 1973). The Communist Party controls the apparatus for defining and controlling deviance, and social control agents focus on violations of political norms. Political deviance can range from believing in a competing political system and actively working to bring down the state (treason) to committing offenses which are not overtly political yet interfere with political programs.

For example, when the government tries to maximize industrial production through a controlled economy, loafing becomes a political offense. The boundaries marking deviance change with the political ideology. The government may mount propaganda campaigns to teach the people how to recognize newly identified forms of deviance.

Americans are most familiar with a legal ideology for social control (Black, 1976; Stone, 1975). Moral boundaries are spelled out in legal codes, and violations of these laws are considered deviant. The business of social control becomes law enforcement. Violating the criminal code is one important type of deviance for these social control agents, but the law encompasses violations other than crimes. Currently, Americans are turning to the law to control emerging social problems, such as energy, consumer safety, corporate responsibility, and ecology. In each of these cases, legislatures create new laws which define the boundaries of acceptable conduct and authorize social control agents to enforce these standards.

Finally, social control agents can use a medical ideology (Goffman, 1961). Medical ideology views deviance as illness—deviant acts are defined as symptoms of physical or mental disease. Physicians and other medical professionals act as social control agents, responsible for diagnosing and treating the deviant's illness. During the twentieth century, social control agencies based on medical ideologies expanded. Medicalization refers to the process by which medical authorities gain jurisdiction over a particular type of deviance (Conrad, 1975). For example, heavy drinking was once viewed as a crime or sin, but the offense has been medicalized and experts now speak of the disease of alcoholism (Schneider, 1978).

Different ideologies lead to different interpretations of the same deviant acts. Theft, for example, might be seen as a sin by religious agents, counterrevolutionary activity by political agents, a crime by legal agents, and a symptom of mental illness by medical agents. Agents tailor their sanctions to fit their ideological interpretation of the offense—sinners are told to repent; political deviants are reeducated; criminals get punished; and the ill receive treatment. Ideology provides the foundation for understanding patterns of social control.

Social control agencies also vary in their resources and priorities. Resources include the number of agents, their equipment and powers, and the capacity of their physical facilities for handling deviants. Agents' resources affect the scope of their activities—the greater the agents' resources, the greater their social control efforts. Because most agents' resources are insufficient for bringing all deviance under control, agencies must set priorities, placing greater emphasis on responding to certain offenses. In general, the higher an agency's priority for a particular type of deviance, the more the agents affect the deviants' lives. Social control ideologies influence agents' priorities—religious agents view some sins as more serious than others, and so forth.

Societies vary widely in their social control arrangements, this chapter cannot explore the whole range of societal reactions to deviance. The descriptions of deviant transactions in chapters 5 through 8 drew heavily on sociological studies of deviants in the United States during the late twentieth century. Deviance in other societies, such as Sicily, or at earlier points in time, such as the turn of the century, received relatively little attention. Similarly, this chapter's analysis of societal reaction to deviant transactions reflects social control in modern America. Currently, most American social control agents subscribe to either a legal ideology, as in the case of the criminal justice system, or a medical ideology, as in the case of the mental health system. This chapter presents six propositions describing consequences of the social organization of deviance. Each proposition concerns the relationship between deviance and societal reaction. Because the propositions draw on evidence from the earlier chapters, they actually describe consequences of the social organization of deviance in a society where social control agents use legal and medical ideologies. A broader analysis of the forms of deviant transactions, comparing modern America to other contemporary and historical societies, might lead to more general propositions.

The propositions should be qualified in two other ways. First, they reflect social control agents' definitions of deviance. Social control ideologies justify norms against particular behaviors, explain why deviance occurs, and specify the seriousness of violations. Adopting officials' perspectives on deviance ignores alternative interpretations. For example, officials may view marijuana smoking as a serious offense, but other people, including marijuana smokers, may see the activity as harmless, something which should not even be deviant. This chapter focuses on the societal reaction to deviance, trying to identify the impact of the social organization of deviance on that reaction. When the propositions describe societal reaction to deviance, they reflect social control agents' views; in doing so, they necessarily ignore the perspectives of others, including deviants. Second, the propositions focus on the effects of organizational complexity. This does not mean that complexity is the only, or even the most important, influence on the behavior of deviants and social control agents. However, complexity has effects, and this chapter attempts to outline some of these consequences.

Proposition 1: Persons involved in deviant exchange and deviant exploitation are more likely to be considered responsible for their deviance than those involved in individual deviance.   In everyday life, people must explain their own actions and the actions of others (Lyman and Scott, 1970:111-43). Some explanations involve a common-sense interpretation of motive, such as: "He married her because he loved her." But others are technical, expert assessments, as when a psychiatrist attributes a patient's behavior to an unresolved Oedipal complex. Explanations for behavior can be divided into those which hold the individual responsible for his or her actions and those which do not. A person held responsible for behavior is thought to deserve the credit or blame for the action. Usually, responsible actions are intentional—the person does them deliberately. But sometimes people are held responsible for unexpected consequences of their actions; one can be considered responsible for unintended harm to others if it is a consequence of one's negligence, for instance. In contrast, other explanations deny the individual's responsibility: an event may be an accident; a person may be in an altered state of consciousness, such as sleepwalking or under the influence of drugs; or, in some societies, people are thought to be possessed by demons or evil spirits. In these cases, a cause other than the individual's intent is assigned to the behavior, and responsibility is denied.

Because deviant acts are relatively rare and unexpected, people are particularly eager to explain them. Explanations for deviance also range from those which emphasize the deviant's responsibility to those which deny it (Aubert and Messinger, 1958; Stoll, 1968). The criminal law assumes responsibility on the part of the deviant—for example, it assumes that those who assault others know that their actions violate the law, yet they intentionally commit the crime. In contrast, medical explanations for deviance deny responsibility. In this view, deviance may be caused by mental disease outside the individual's control. For example, when parents beat their young children, psychiatrists argue that this child abuse is a symptom of mental disturbance. Whether they emphasize or deny responsibility, explanations are social constructions. In the case of explanations for deviance, the social control agents' ideologies determine whether deviants are held responsible for their behavior.

Explanations for a particular type of deviance can change when social control ideologies change. During the first half of the nineteenth century, Americans considered drinking alcohol a sin and drinkers responsible for their behavior; reformers concentrated on getting drinkers to repent and voluntarily stop drinking (Gusfield, 1967). By the end of the nineteenth century, reformers redefined the unrepentant drinker as an enemy, rather than a potential convert. The drinker was still seen as responsible for drinking, but reformers adopted a legal ideology to replace their religious perspective. They now saw drinking as a crime, and reform efforts focused on passing laws to prohibit drinking. After Prohibition failed, the authorities adopted a medical ideology and redefined drinkers once more; they became sick, no longer responsible for their behavior. People who were formerly called "drunkards"—a term suggesting their responsibility for moral failure—became "alcoholics"—a term for those who suffer from the disease of alcoholism. A second, more recent example involves an explanation for children's disruptive behavior (Conrad, 1975). Traditionally, children who disrupted school classrooms were seen as deliberate troublemakers who were responsible for their behavior. Advocates of a medical model now argue that these children may suffer from hyperkinesis, a physical disease caused by brain damage. Although there is no concrete proof that these behaviors have an organic foundation, medical authorities argue that these children are sick—not responsible for their actions. These examples suggest that the same offense can be viewed in different ways and that the attribution of responsibility depends more on social control agents' ideology than on the nature of the offense.

In general, deviants are more likely to be viewed as responsible for their actions if they are involved in deviant exchange or deviant exploitation. In modern America, persons involved in individual deviance are usually seen as less than fully responsible for their deviant acts. The problem drinker, the drug addict, and the mentally ill individual are thought to engage in deviance because of conditions outside their own control. Contemporary explanations for individual deviance emphasize biological and psychological causes. Even when individual deviance appears to involve a deliberate decision, such as suicide or conversion to a deviant belief system, others often attribute the deviant's action to a biological state (such as being under the influence of drugs), an abnormal mental state (such as a compulsion), or beliefs acquired through weakness, innocence, or foolishness (such as the transmission of deviant belief systems through "brainwashing").

In contrast, deviants involved in deviant exchange or deviant exploitation are usually seen as responsible for their deviance. Both forms of deviance are thought to require active, willing participation by the deviants, so that it is easy to attribute responsibility to them. This is particularly true if the deviants announce or can be presumed to have motives consistent with conventional explanations for intentional action. For example, theft is usually viewed as responsible behavior because acquiring wealth is a culturally approved goal (Cressey, 1962; Gibbons and Jones, 1975; Hartung, 1965). So long as the thief appears to have a good reason for wanting the stolen articles, stealing is deemed responsible. When psychiatrists diagnose kleptomania—a type of mental illness where the individual feels compelled to steal things—a key question is whether the theft makes sense. Thefts by a person who has more than enough money to pay for the stolen items are likely to lead to labeling the thief a kleptomaniac. By these standards, a rich person who shoplifts may be defined as ill, while a poor person committing the same offense usually is labeled a thief.

This relationship between the complexity of the deviant transaction and imputing responsibility to the deviant is not perfect. There are three principal exceptions to the pattern. First, some individual deviants are held responsible for their actions. This is particularly common when a deviant belief system challenges a central institution which controls the terms in which deviance is defined. For example, in Puritan New England, where religion was the central institution and ministers served as moral authorities, heresy was defined as deliberate, responsible behavior (Erikson, 1966). Similarly, Communist Parties, which serve as both central institutions and social control agencies in Communist states, treat subscription to alternate political ideologies as intentional behavior, as when Stalin purged people of doubtful loyalty (Connor, 1972b). In these cases, the society's leaders saw their institutions and the society itself as threatened by outside forces—the wilderness in the Puritan's case, competing political ideologies in Stalin's. In the face of these threats, the central institution demanded allegiance by the society's members; any sign of disloyalty could be interpreted as a deliberate attack on the society.

Second, those involved in deviant exchange or exploitation may be considered, or may plead to have themselves considered, less than fully responsible due to their simultaneous involvement in individual deviance. Exploitative acts committed by mentally ill individuals, drug addicts, or compulsive gamblers, for example, are viewed as related to the conditions causing the individual deviance. Where officials believe that these conditions are the direct cause of the exploitative act, the deviant is unlikely to be held responsible for his or her actions. For instance, psychiatrists argue that some murderers suffer from serious mental illness and should not be considered responsible for their crimes because they cannot control their actions. However, where the authorities view the exploitation as only indirectly related, they typically view the deviant as making a calculated choice in response to the pressure posed by the individual deviance and they hold the deviant responsible for the exploitation. For example, narcotic addiction creates a physical need for drugs, but the addict who steals to support a drug habit is viewed as making a choice to continue the habit through deviant exploitation, and the thefts are seen as responsible actions.

Finally, deviants engaged in exchange or exploitation, or those who speak for them, may lobby to redefine the deviants as not responsible. Advocates of a medical ideology sometimes argue that sexual deviance, child abuse, juvenile delinquency, and other types of deviant exchange and exploitation are caused by mental conditions outside the individual's control (cf. Pfohl, 1977). Similarly, representatives of the early homophile movement (organizations aimed at educating the public about homosexuality and extending homosexuals' rights) argued that homosexuality was involuntary, that persons were "born homosexual" (Humphreys, 1972). This argument was intended to reduce discrimination against homosexuals by suggesting that they were not deliberately deviant. (More recent spokespersons for the gay liberation movement sometimes take the opposite stance, arguing that homosexuality represents a deliberate choice of sexual preference and that homosexuals deserve the same rights and respect granted those who choose heterosexual partners.) As noted above, some of these lobbying efforts are successful. When exploitative offenses, such as child abuse, are medicalized, the deviants' responsibility is denied.

These three exceptions, appearing under specifiable circumstances, qualify the relationship between the complexity of the deviant transaction and the attribution of responsibility. It must be reemphasized that definitions of responsibility are social constructions. Although both deviants and social control agents claim to describe the way things "really are," they actually make assertions about responsibility. For example, experts disagree about the nature and causes of homosexuality and whether homosexuals are responsible for their sexual preferences. The claims and counterclaims about particular types of deviance frequently reflect the interests of those making them, as well as the nature of the deviance. As a result, changes in social control ideologies can alter dramatically the interpretations of responsibility for particular types of deviance.

Proposition 2: The more complex the deviant transaction, the more likely the deviance will be defined as serious. Societies justify their rules against deviance by claiming that it poses a threat to their members. This threat can take several forms. At the most direct level, deviance threatens specific persons. Norms against robbery, murder, rape, and other exploitative acts are justified because the deviant's target faces physical injury or the loss of property. In suicide, mental illness, and other types of individual deviance, the norms are justified by the need to protect the deviant from harm caused by his or her own actions. Or the threat may be indirect, against people who are not part of the deviant transaction—rules against the use of illicit drugs sometimes are justified by referring to the drug user's family's suffering. Finally, deviance can threaten the community's order. Rules against public drunkenness, for example, are justified as a means of keeping the streets orderly so that citizens do not witness unseemly, if otherwise non-threatening, behavior. The justification for a particular rule may refer to more than one threat. For example, justification for laws against heroin point to the ill effects on the addict's health (threat to the deviant), the suffering of the addict's family and those who the addict robs for money to supply the drug habit (indirect and direct threats to others), and the fear of addicts which keeps people from using various public facilities (threat to the community's moral order).

Some threats are judged more serious than others. In general, the threats attributed to a given type of deviance reflect the complexity of the deviant transaction; as complexity increases, the threats posed by the deviance are more likely to be defined as serious. Deviant exploitation is viewed as most serious because it inflicts direct injury on an unwilling target and because these attacks usually are unexpected and unpredictable. By harming the innocent, exploitative transactions directly challenge social control agents' ability to protect society's members from predators. Although exploitation may threaten the society in other ways, the injury to the target overrides other considerations (Conklin, 1975). Because participants enter deviant exchanges willingly, these offenses are seen as less serious than exploitation, as posing a lesser threat. Justifications for rules against deviant exchange take several forms. Some justifications mention threats to the deviants themselves—particularly when the customer in a deviant sale is a respectable community member who needs protection against his or her innocence or foolishness. For example, drug pushers supposedly corrupt naive teenagers; antidrug laws protect these innocent young people. Other justifications for norms against deviant exchange emphasize indirect threats to others (such as the deviant's family) or threats to community morality. Still others link the exchange to deviant exploitation; heroin addicts are known to steal in order to pay for their drug purchases, and those who buy pornography supposedly become violent sex offenders. Finally, individual deviance is seen as less serious than either exploitation or exchange because it directly threatens only the deviant's well-being and, insofar as the transaction is public, the community's moral order. In short, the dangers posed by deviance diminish as the deviant transaction becomes less complex.

Survey research demonstrates the relationship between the perceived seriousness of a deviant transaction and the complexity of its organization. In one study (Rossi et al., 1974), respondents rated the seriousness of 140 crimes. In general, exploitative acts ranked as more serious than deviant exchanges. As might be expected, the greater the physical harm or the monetary loss to the target, the more seriously the offense was viewed. Exchange transactions were seen as less serious, with one important exception—selling illicit drugs was viewed as very serious. Respondents ranked "selling heroin" as more serious than "forcible rape after breaking into a home" or "planned killing of a spouse," and "selling LSD" was seen as more serious than "kidnapping for ransom" or "assassination of a public official." While the survey did not ask about the buyers in drug deals, "using heroin" and "using LSD" ranked considerably below drug sales. Since the survey was limited to crimes, it did not include some types of individual deviance, such as mental illness and suicide, but those which did appear generally were ranked as less serious.

Of course, these definitions of seriousness and the justifications which support them are social constructions. They may be inaccurate or subject to change. Claims that deviants pose particular threats can be mistaken. For instance, many people believe that pornography leads to violent sex offenses (Commission on Obscenity and Pornography, 1970:27). Yet research consistently shows that this is not true. Sex offenders are no more likely to have a history of consuming pornography than other people. When Denmark eliminated its laws against pornography, the incidence of sex crimes actually dropped. While evidence suggests that there is no empirical link between pornography and violent sexual offenses, pornography's opponents continue to argue that antipornography laws prevent sexual violence. (Interestingly, this argument, traditionally associated with conservatives, recently was adopted by feminists [Lederer, 1980].) Claims about the threats posed by a particular type of deviance may reflect the ideology or political concerns of those making the claims, rather than empirical evidence about the effects of deviance.

Just as perceptions of responsibility shift over time, definitions of seriousness change. The debate over "crimes without victims" reflects this process. In an influential book, Schur (1965) argued that laws against abortion, homosexuality, and illicit drugs ignored the organizational realities of those transactions. According to Schur, the criminal justice system works best when police can count on victims to report offenses. However, crimes without victims—a term which encompasses most deviant exchanges and some individual deviance—do not lead to such reports because the participants willingly enter deviant transactions and directly threaten no one but themselves. Schur debunked claims that crimes without victims directly threaten others—drug addicts do not experience violent frenzies and homosexuals do not aggressively recruit heterosexuals. He viewed laws against crimes without victims as inappropriate and argued that these transactions should not be defined as deviant. Sociological arguments of this sort buttressed social movements to vindicate various types of individual deviance and deviant exchange. Since Schur's book appeared, restrictions against abortion, homosexuality, marijuana use, gambling, and pornography have been substantially reduced, although these activities remain the subjects of considerable political debate.

The proposition that the offense's perceived seriousness is related to the complexity of the deviant transaction must be qualified in three important ways. First, perceptions of seriousness are affected by the location of the offense. Most cities separate business centers, industrial districts, as well as residential neighborhoods for people of different social classes or ethnicity. Social control agents' activities reflect their understandings of this ecology (cf. Wilson, 1968). Agents often allocate their resources so that some districts receive more attention than others, assigning higher priorities to controlling deviance in those areas. For example, they may strictly enforce norms in some districts while being more lenient in others. Public drunkenness or streetwalking may not be tolerated in a downtown business district or an upper-middle class residential neighborhood, if only because the merchants and residents demand action from the agents. In contrast, agents may adopt an informal policy of overlooking deviance in another part of town; they argue that prostitution, public drunkenness, and some other offenses are inevitable and that it is better to keep the deviants segregated in one place than to allow them to spread. In this view, attempts to suppress deviance merely force the deviants underground. Prostitutes, for example, might set up a discreet brothel in a residential neighborhood if they cannot operate elsewhere. On the other hand, letting deviants operate in an informally designated district encourages them to congregate in that area, where the authorities "can keep an eye on them." Often, lower class neighborhoods become known for public drunkenness, streetwalking, and other visible deviance. Thus, the authorities may define the same offense as being more serious if it occurs in an upper-middle class neighborhood than in a lower class district.

The second qualification also involves social control agents applying different standards for offenders when assessing the seriousness of deviant acts. Agents may treat similar offenses differently depending upon the offender's identity. Race or social class may affect the agents' evaluation of seriousness; they may view a deviant act as more serious when the offender is black or lower class (Chambliss, 1973; LaFree, 1980; Piliavin and Briar, 1964). In part, this reflects agents' stereotypes about the threats posed by these deviants. For example, experience may teach police that lower class boys commit more delinquent acts. (If the agents allocate their resources to fit this perception, assigning more juvenile officers to lower class areas, they may uncover even more lower-class delinquency, making their prophecy self-fulfilling.) As a consequence, a police officer confronted with a lower-class delinquent may feel that the offender "shouldn't be allowed to get away with it," whereas the same offense by a middle class boy may be treated as a "mistake" or a sign that he "needs direction." In addition to stereotyping offenders, social control agents' priorities may lead them to evaluate offenses differently. The criminal justice system directs most of its attention toward what it views as "real crimes," especially interpersonal exploitation, such as murder, rape, and robbery, which are often committed by lower-class offenders. In contrast, white collar crimes, such as price fixing, embezzlement, and investment fraud, receive less attention. Offenses characteristic of the upper-middle class are seen as less serious than those of the lower class. Placing higher priorities on lower-class offenses can be an explicit social control strategy—nineteenth century police forces were created to suppress disorder in the lower or "dangerous classes" (Silver, 1967).

Finally, those who set social control policies may choose to define some offenses as less serious because they have a vested interest in the deviant operations. At one level, this involves the corruption of social control agents—in return for bribes, agents agree to overlook the deviants' activities. But the connection need not be this direct. For example, the Philippine government avoids sanctioning the fraudulent "psychic surgeons" (faith healers who perform "bloodless surgery" using sleight-of-hand techniques) because the surgeons are a major tourist attraction and source of revenue for the islands (Nolen, 1974:208). Similarly, colonial governors in the seventeenth century Caribbean permitted pirate ships to use their colonies as home bases, so long as the pirates limited their targets to the ships and towns of rival empires (Best, 1980). Watergate is a modern example; the Nixon administration overlooked bribery, burglary, and other crimes committed by its agents. In each of these cases, those in power had a vested interest in the deviants' activities and therefore defined the offenses as less serious.

The seriousness of an offense is a social construction. The complexity of the deviant transaction affects assessments of seriousness—exploitation tends to be treated very seriously, while most individual deviance is not.

However, the location of the offense, the offender's characteristics, and the interests of social control agents also affect evaluations of seriousness.

Proposition 3: The more complex the deviant transaction, the more likely the deviant will be subject to punitive sanctions.   Social control agents' reactions to deviance depend upon their ideologies and resources. When their ideologies and resources change, agents' activities also shift. The history of the last three centuries shows dramatic changes in the sanctions applied to deviants, reflecting changes in social control. In eighteenth century England and colonial America, social control agents had limited resources and a punitive ideology (Hay, 1975; Rothman, 1971). There were no professional police and few prisons. Deviants typically were executed, given corporal punishments (such as flogging), publicly humiliated (such as being held in stocks), or banished. Jails held deviants for trial, execution, or deportation, but imprisonment was an uncommon punishment. The penalty for many crimes, including minor thefts, was death. Correctional facilities had limited capacity and the social control ideology offered few programs for reforming offenders. As a consequence, the authorities sentenced many convicted criminals to death and later pardoned a large proportion of them, thereby demonstrating both the law's terrors and its mercy. Limited in their resources, control agents could do little but apply harsh sanctions and hope they deterred potential offenders.

In the nineteenth century, several new social control agencies developed, grounded in rational ideologies which claimed that deviants could be rehabilitated (Rothman, 1971; Scull, 1977). The nineteenth century saw the expansion of social control agents' resources, with the invention of the modern police, prison, and mental hospital. The agents' ideologies spelled out how they would reform deviants. For example, the prison would isolate criminals from criminogenic influences, as well as provide punishment, time to repent, and a disciplined, uniform regimen which would lead to good habits upon release. In contrast to eighteenth century responses, which could do little more than rid the community of its deviants, nineteenth century social control agents wanted to insure that deviants' future conduct would be respectable.

The nineteenth century's rationally designed control efforts evolved into contemporary agencies. Twentieth century social control ideologies emphasize the importance of individualized responses aimed at rehabilitating the deviant (Aubert and Messinger, 1958; Rothman, 1980). This theme runs through both legal and medical ideologies of control. Legal ideology argues that deviants are responsible for their crimes and that the appropriate reaction to these violations is punishment. Expanded resources for the criminal justice system, including probation, parole, and rehabilitative programs, are supposed to permit individualized responses. Modern medical ideology, grounded in psychiatry and clinical psychology, argues that deviants are not responsible for their behavior, that deviant acts are symptoms of illness, and that the correct way to respond is to treat the deviant. Again, expanded resources, such as new drugs and outpatient clinics, make it possible to tailor the authorities' reaction to the offender's case. Obviously, the use of medical rhetoric is not proof of a distinctive pattern of practice. Many treatment programs strongly resemble punitive programs in their concern for custody (Goffman, 1961). According to both legal and medical ideologies, individualized responses to deviance make rehabilitation more likely.

The two contemporary ideologies compete for command of the social control process. For example, both legal and medical authorities argue that their ideology is the best one for understanding and responding to juvenile delinquency. The relationship between perception of responsibility and the complexity of the deviant transaction was discussed above. The legal ideology's view that offenders are responsible for their actions is generally accepted for more complex transactions, while the medical ideology's claim that offenders are not responsible typically holds for less complex transactions. Therefore, offenders in more complex transactions are more likely to receive punitive sanctions.

Individual deviance usually is seen as a manifestation of illness for which the deviant should be treated. Since the principal threat of individual deviance is to the offender's well-being, treatment is justified as a way of protecting individual deviants from themselves. This response is cast in a medical vocabulary—social control facilities are called hospitals, clinics, or centers for detoxification, drug rehabilitation, or methadone treatment; and personnel bear the titles of physician, psychiatrist, nurse, counsellor, or aide. Legislative and judicial bodies acknowledge that treatment is the appropriate response—they establish and maintain the medical agents' authority to intervene. In addition, the public accepts the medical ideology. Surveys show that a large proportion of Americans not only consider mental illness, alcoholism, and drug addiction to be medical-psychiatric problems, but they also favor responding with treatment rather than punishment (Dohrenwend and Chin-Shong, 1967; Linsky, 1970; Pattison et al., 1968).

Societal reaction to participants in deviant exchange is mixed and shifting. On the one hand, individuals involved in most forms of exchange are considered responsible for their actions and, therefore, eligible for punishment. This is especially true for sellers in deviant sales—just as their offenses are defined as more serious, sellers are held more culpable than their customers. For instance, drug dealers sometimes are described as deliberately exploiting their customers, who, in turn, are seen as naive, in need of education and treatment more than punishment. On the other hand, critics of laws against crimes without victims argue that deviant exchanges are private arrangements which do little, if any, injury to others or the larger social order (Schur, 1965). In this view, social control resources should be redirected toward the more serious, exploitative offenses.

Exploitative offenders are most likely to be viewed as meriting punitive sanctions. Because exploitation directly threatens community members, these offenses are defined as "real crimes" which should be punished (President's Commission, 1967b:159-68; Conklin, 1975). Survey respondents, when asked to indicate appropriate penalties for different offenses, generally assign heavier punishment to exploitative deviants than to those involved in individual deviance or deviant exchange (Gibbons, 1969). Public condemnation includes white-collar or business crimes when those offenses have a clear exploitative element (Conklin, 1977). In spite of this public sentiment, social control agents direct relatively limited resources at business crime and the sanctions levied against such offenders are relatively lenient (M. Green et al., 1972). This restrained social control activity reflects a reluctance by officials to interfere with legitimate organizations, as well as the substantial resources which these organizations use to shield illicit practices from targets, create favorable public impressions, and neutralize enforcement efforts.

Exceptions to the relationship between the complexity of the deviant transaction and the use of punitive sanctions reflect definitions of the deviant's responsibility or the act's seriousness. For example, the medicalization of a type of deviance means that the offenders are no longer seen as responsible for their actions and, in turn, punitive sanctions become inappropriate. Child abuse might be seen as a criminal act committed by a responsible offender who deserves punishment; however, medical ideology defines the offender as ill and sanctions take the form of treatment (Pfohl, 1977). Similarly, when the seriousness of an act is questioned, sanctions become less punitive. The historical practice of punishing minor thefts with capital punishment is an example; these thefts were redefined as less serious, and more lenient sanctions replaced executions. A contemporary example of this process is the dramatic reduction in some states' penalties for possessing marijuana.

The sanctions applied by a society's social control agents reflect their ideology and resources. Developing the nineteenth century prison required an industrial society with the resources to construct and maintain large custodial facilities (Rothman, 1971). It also reflected a shift in social control ideology—a shift from viewing deviants as disruptive elements who could only be removed from the community through death or banishment to viewing them as people who were correctable through incarceration in a rationally designed penal program. Similarly, the rise of the medical ideology and the rhetoric of individualized treatment in the twentieth century reflects new resources, such as trained personnel and psychoactive drugs, and a new ideology grounded in medical science (Rothman, 1980). Currently, the legal ideology which advocates punishment and the medical ideology which recommends treatment exist side by side, with the former generally assigned responsibility for the more complex, exploitative deviant transactions and the latter given authority over most individual deviance.

Proposition 4: The more complex the deviant transaction, the greater the like-lihood the deviant will be identified and apprehended by social control agents. All deviants face the risk of social control agents' sanctions. In most cases, sanctioning is preceded by three earlier stages—the agents must learn that a deviant transaction occurred; they must learn the deviant's identity; and they must locate and apprehend the deviant. Social control depends upon gathering this information. The social organization of the deviant transaction affects this process in four ways. First, an actor's role in a deviant transaction affects the likelihood that he or she will report the offense, because actors performing different roles have different interests. Deviants usually have nothing to gain by reporting their offenses to officials, while hopes of getting revenge or restitution for their losses often motivate non-deviant targets to report offenses, and bystanders may report deviance as a civic responsibility. Second, the actor's role also affects what is reported— information from deviants is more likely to help social control agents than information from targets or bystanders, because deviants usually know more about the identities and habits of other offenders in a transaction. Third, the number of people involved in the transaction, including participants and bystanders, increases the deviant's risk. Each additional person adds a potential source from which social control agents might learn about the offense, and each person's knowledge enlarges the pool of information potentially available about the offender. Fourth, the more visible the trans-action to nondeviants, the higher the risk. Visibility involves accessibility and awareness. A transaction is accessible when it stands exposed to possible observation by nondeviants. Exploitative deviance is accessible because a target is involved. However, accessibility is not the same as awareness—re-cognizing that deviance is occurring. Some targets, particularly in fraud, never become aware of the deviance. Deviant transactions carried out in public places are highly visible. Thus, the risks of the deviant's identification and apprehension vary with the interests and the number of people involved in the transaction, and with the transaction's visibility. Because each of these features is more likely to be present in more complexly organized transac-tions, the deviant's risks increase with the organizational complexity of deviance.

By being discreet, individual deviants can minimize the risks posed by social control agents. Individual deviance requires only one actor and, if the transaction occurs where others cannot observe it, there is little risk of social control agents even learning about the offense. Individual deviants' risks increase when others are present during the transaction. Sometimes indi-vidual deviants gather together, making deviance an occasion for sociable interaction, as when several drug users get high together. So long as these deviants can rely on one another's discretion, the risks remain minimal. Individual deviants' greatest risks occur when they lack the resources or the ability to be discreet. People with limited resources cannot command private places; they must commit their deviant acts in public (Spradley, 1970; Werthman and Piliavin, 1967). For example, skid row tramps often drink in public places and delinquent gangs hang out on street corners in part because they have no private place to go. Similarly, some mentally ill individuals are unaware or unconcerned with the need for discretion and commit deviant acts in front of others. Lack of resources and an inability to be discreet combine in "space cases"—young vagrants with serious mental problems (Segal et al., 1977). Space cases' behavior contrasts with that of more successful street people who manage their poverty through panhandling, drug dealing, and the adroit use of free social services. Space cases do not have these options, their indiscreet, erratic behavior makes the other street people wary. Space cases are not trusted to deal drugs, for example. Like other individual deviants with limited resources, such as skid row tramps and older, impoverished mentally ill persons, space cases are vulnerable to social control efforts. Such deviants get apprehended repeatedly and acquire long records in misdemeanor courts and psychiatric facilities.

Because deviant exchange requires at least two actors, participants are more vulnerable to social control efforts. Each party to the exchange knows about the other's involvement in deviance and may be capable of supplying officials with enough information to bring about the other's identification and capture. However, deviant associates are unlikely to betray one another because each is implicated in the transaction and has personal reasons to be discreet. Moreover, they may have profited from the exchange and may even hope to carry out further transactions with the same partner. Deviants are most likely to inform on their associates when officials coerce them into providing the information or when they feel exploited by the exchange. For instance, pressure from police may cause an addict to inform about a drug dealer, or theft by a prostitute may lead a customer to provide an anonymous tip to vice officers. So long as associates remain discreet about their dealings, and so long as they deal fairly with each other, the risks can be minimized. As a consequence, some deviants try to limit their dealings to associates they know to be discreet and trustworthy; for example, drug dealers may refuse to sell to strangers. When exchanges take place in public, risks are much greater. Homosexual couples who have intercourse at home run few risks, but homosexuals who pick up partners in gay bars or tearooms are more vulnerable to discovery. Deals conducted in public are more often noticed and, if the illicit marketplace becomes known to the authorities, participants are vulnerable to ambushes and infiltration by social control agents.

The target makes exploitation the riskiest form of deviance. In the less complex transactions, discretion usually provides sufficient protection against social control efforts. But most targets object to being exploited, and the deviant must anticipate that, at the end of the transaction, the target will complain to the authorities and try to assist them in identifying and apprehending the offender. While individual deviance and exchange frequently occur without coming to the attention of the authorities, a much higher proportion of exploitative transactions are reported. Further, since exploitative transactions are defined as more serious, social control agents usually assign higher priority to investigating these complaints.

The degree to which exploitative deviants risk indentification and apprehension varies with the type of exploitation. In coercion, the target usually reports the violation and tries to assist in apprehending the offender, in hopes of gaining restitution or revenge. Once targets realize that surreptitious exploitation has occurred, they also usually report the offense to the authorities. However, extortion and fraud have comparatively lower rates of reporting. In extortion, the target may fear that reporting the incident will jeopardize the hostage. Targets call in officials as soon as they receive the extortionist's threat only when they believe the authorities share their concern for the hostage's safety. Otherwise, they delay complaining until the hostage's return or never complain because it would make the problem worse. For example, blackmail targets cannot complain without explaining to the social control agents why they are being blackmailed. Targets may not complain about fraud, either because they do not realize their loss was due to exploitation, as when losing gamblers fail to recognize that they were cheated, or because reporting would be personally embarrassing, as when the mark in a confidence game must reveal his or her illicit intentions.

The relationship between the complexity of the deviant transaction and the risks of identification and apprehension must be qualified in two ways. First, it is affected by the social organization of deviants. While some deviants operate as loners, most belong to a deviant social network, often cooperating with deviant associates in deviant transactions. The existence of associates poses both risks and benefits. Because they know about one's involvement in deviance, associates are capable of betraying the deviant to social control agents. This danger accounts for the establishment, particularly among deviants in more sophisticated forms of organization, of codes of conduct which emphasize secrecy and loyalty. On the other hand, deviant groups usually command greater resources than loners, resources which can be used to conceal involvement in deviance and defend members who are threatened with apprehension or sanctioning. Since these resources tend to increase as the organization of deviants becomes more sophisticated, risks diminish in the more organized groups. Thus, loners, colleagues, and peers are more vulnerable to social control efforts than members of mobs or formal organizations. The social organization of deviants affects the relationship between the complexity of the deviant transaction and risk; more sophisticated organizational forms protect their members.

Second, social control agents' priorities affect the relationship between complexity and risk. Priorities are necessary because agents' resources are insufficient to apprehend all offenders. Social control ideologies guide agents in setting priorities. Usually, priorities correspond to the perceived seriousness of the offense, so that exploitative offenses receive higher priority than less complex transactions. Exceptions to this general pattern occur during moral crusades, special campaigns which highlight the dangers of a particular type of deviance (Becker, 1963:148-155). Moral crusades can be mounted by private citizens, government leaders, or the social control agents themselves. A typical campaign uses publicity to make people aware of the threat posed by deviants, while giving social control agents more resources to react to the offense. Recent moral crusades include Anita Bryant's campaign against homosexuality and gay rights, and the movements to register handguns and outlaw abortions. Moral crusades increase the deviants' risks by making it more likely that people will report offenses and by causing social control agents to raise their priority for that type of deviance. In particular, individual deviance and deviant exchange—offenses which tend to be seen as less serious—can become high priority offenses during moral crusades.

In summary, the deviant's risks tend to increase with the deviant transaction's complexity. However, the social organization of deviants and the social control agents' priorities can alter the risks of apprehension and sanctioning.

Proposition 5: The more complex the deviant transaction, the more elaborate the tactics employed by deviants to protect themselves from social control efforts.   Deviants want to minimize their chances of being detected, identified, apprehended, and sanctioned. Because the deviant's risks increase with the transaction's complexity, deviants need more elaborate tactics to protect themselves as the organizational complexity of their deviance increases. Because each form of deviant transaction involves special risks, deviants must tailor their protective tactics to their offenses.

In individual deviance, the main defense against social control efforts is to keep the offense from coming to the agents' attention. Self-discretion is the principal tactic—the deviant tries to control information about his or her involvement in deviance. Toward this end, deviant transactions are staged in private or secluded places, where they are less likely to be observed. Deviants may conceal evidence of their deviant involvement, as when an addict wears long sleeves to cover up needle tracks, or display evidence of their commitment to respectability, as when an alcoholic tries to appear well dressed and well groomed. Again, these tactics break down when the deviants lack the resources to use them, as in the case of skid row tramps, or when they are unaware of the need for discretion or unable to be discreet, as in the case of some mentally ill persons.

In deviant exchange, as well as when individual deviants engage in deviant transactions together, there are deviant associates who can betray the offender. Self-discretion remains important, but additional tactics are required to protect against betrayal by associates. Discretion can still be fostered by staging deviant transactions in protected places and controlling evidence of one's deviance. Deviants usually count on their associates to be discreet but, as suggested above, this discretion can dissolve under certain circumstances, such as pressure from social control agents. To minimize this risk, deviants may limit their dealings to associates they know personally. However, this may be impossible. Many exchanges involve strangers—for instance, streetwalkers rarely know their customers personally and tearoom trades are anonymous. Therefore, deviants devise four supplemental tactics to protect themselves from the risks of betrayal posed by dealing with strangers. First, deviants may withhold information about their identities from their associates. Swingers, for instance, often operate on a first name basis, refusing to give one another information about their identities, occupations, or places of residence. Second, deviants may require associates to provide evidence of their trustworthiness. For example, prostitutes demand payment in advance to insure that their customers will not cheat them. Third, deviants may warn their associates that betrayal will lead to sanctions, such as ostracism or physical harm. Finally, in deviant sales, sellers may use a portion of their profits to insure their operations' safety by corrupting the authorities to overlook their violations. The latter two tactics usually involve deviants organized in relatively sophisticated forms, since they are more likely to have the resources required to enforce discipline and corrupt officials.

In deviant exploitation, deviants may use all of the protective tactics adopted by those engaged in individual deviance and deviant exchange, including self-discretion, methods of avoiding betrayal by deviant associates, and efforts to corrupt officials. In addition, exploitative deviants must develop tactics to deal with two additional problems. First, the offender must manage the target's actual or anticipated resistance. During exploitative transactions, targets must be manipulated so that they do not disrupt the operation or jeopardize the deviant's safety. In surreptitious exploitation, manipulation involves techniques for carrying out the operation without arousing the target's notice. In coercion, the deviant uses interpersonal skills to intimidate the target, convincing the target that the offender is willing to use force and that resistance would be both dangerous and futile. Armed robbers, for example, try to appear dangerous enough to make their targets comply. In extortion, the offender typically couples the leverage power of his or her control over the hostage—which should induce cooperation if the target fears for the hostage's well-being—with tactical maneuvers designed to keep the offender's identity secret, such as communicating only through notes or phone calls. In fraud, target manipulation is central to the operation, since the deviant deceives the target about the nature of their transaction. In each of these cases, the target's likely resistance to exploitation forces deviants to devise effective methods of coping.

Targets can create a second problem. The offenders must face the possibility that, after the transaction is over, the target will call upon social control agents for assistance. Unlike individual deviance and deviant exchange, where relatively few offenses come to the authorities' attention, targets of exploitation have an interest in turning to social control agents. Deviants deal with this possibility by controlling information about their identities which might link them to the offense. Methods for concealing personal identity vary with the type of exploitation. In coercion, offenders may cover up their outward appearance, for example, by wearing masks during a robbery; in surreptitious exploitation, deviants try to avoid leaving clues, for example, by wearing gloves to cover fingerprints. Extortionists usually avoid face-to-face contacts with their targets, but they remain concerned with controlling evidence of personal identity. For example, kidnappers may compose ransom notes with printed words cut from magazines, anticipating that handwriting will be analyzed. Because deviants engaged in fraud typically meet and talk to their targets, they must construct false identities for these encounters, try to keep the target from complaining by "cooling out the mark," or, ideally, keep the target from recognizing the fraud for what it is. If exploitation is reported, the offender's safety may depend on these preventative tactics. Some tactics work better than others; offenders who confront their targets—and thereby give targets considerable information about their identities—are more likely to be apprehended than offenders who work outside the targets' sight (Stinchcombe, 1963). Considering only reported offenses, surreptitious exploitation is less likely to lead to apprehension than other exploitative offenses because the target is less likely to know valuable information about the deviant's identity (Peterson and Braiker, 1980).

The social organization of deviants modifies the relationship between the deviant transaction's complexity and the deviants' range of defensive tactics. Deviants belonging to more sophisticated organizational forms can call on their associates for aid. Protective tactics require resources, such as information about social control activities, enforcers to maintain discipline among deviant associates, or funds for corrupting officials. Members of sophisticated organizational forms are more likely to command these resources. Moreover, newcomers who are socialized in more sophisticated organizational forms can learn vital lessons; experienced deviants teach novices how to recognize and evaluate the risks they face and how to devise effective tactics for coping with problems. While loners must assess the risks they face and devise protective tactics by themselves, members of mobs and deviant formal organizations can rely on their groups' established protective measures.

Deviants must tailor their protective tactics to fit the risks posed by deviant transactions. Individual deviants concentrate on being discreet and participants in deviant exchanges try to avoid betrayal, while exploitative deviants worry about managing targets and protecting their own identities. Those who belong to sophisticated organizational forms benefit from the additional protection their associates provide.

Proposition 6: Social control agents are more likely to use proactive tactics against individual deviance and deviant exchange, while they are more likely to use reactive tactics against deviant exploitation.   Several factors affect the way social control agents respond to deviance. The agents' ideology determines what they define as deviant and how they react to offenses. The relationship of social control agencies to other segments of society, including rule-making bodies, other social control agencies, the press, interest groups, and organizations which supervise or review agency activities, affects their resources and priorities. These other bodies may influence the allocation of resources, including equipment, physical facilities, and the number and quality of agents, among the society's social control agencies. By sponsoring moral crusades or pressuring social control agents to "do something" about particular types of deviance, these bodies also affect agencies' priorities. As a consequence, any given social control effort, such as the enforcement of drug laws in a particular city, reflects the political realities, the social control agency's place in the larger society (DeFleur, 1975). Finally, the nature of the deviant transaction affects agents' attempts to control deviance. This relationship between the complexity of the deviant transaction and the tactics adopted by social control agents provides the focus for this section.

Ultimately, information is the key to social control. Deviants cannot be sanctioned if they cannot be apprehended; they cannot be apprehended if they cannot be identified; and they cannot be identified by officials if their offenses do not become known to the agents (A. Reiss, 1971; Sanders, 1977). Thus, without information about their offenses, officials cannot sanction offenders. Earlier propositions pointed out that the deviant's risks and protective tactics depend upon the social organization of the deviant transaction. In turn, the tactics of social control agents also reflect organizational complexity.

Deviant transactions can be divided into those where someone informs social control agents that an offense took place and those where the agents learn about the offense through their own efforts. When someone—usually a target of exploitation, a bystander, or another social control agent—tells the appropriate agency about an offense, its agents respond by trying to identify, apprehend, and sanction the deviant. In such cases, social control agents use *reactive* tactics—they react to the report (A. Reiss, 1971). In contrast, when reports are uncommon, social control agents become responsible for discovering deviant transactions, as well as for identifying, apprehending, and sanctioning the deviants. Tactics designed to uncover deviant transactions are called *proactive* (A. Reiss, 1971). A particular offense might come to the agents' attention through either someone's report or proactive efforts. For example, police might learn about a burglary when the target discovers the loss and phones in a complaint, or when a police officer spots an open door which should be locked and decides to investigate. In most cases, deviant exploitation comes to the officials' attention through complaints, while individual deviance and deviant exchange are discovered through proactive efforts. As a consequence, officials rely more on reactive tactics in deviant exploitation and on proactive tactics in less complex transactions.

In deviant exploitation, social control agents often get cooperation from the target, who is likely to report the offense in hopes of getting revenge, restitution, or other satisfaction. As noted earlier, forms of exploitation vary in the timing and frequency of reporting. In cases of surreptitious exploitation and coercion, targets frequently report their loss. Complaints about coercion more often arrive immediately after the event, while reports of surreptitious exploitation cannot be made until the target discovers the loss—a process which may take time. Targets of extortion and fraud are less likely to inform the authorities of their losses. In extortion, targets often delay reporting because they fear for the hostage's safety while the transaction is in progress, and once it is completed, they still may be reluctant to notify the authorities out of embarrassment, either for cooperating with criminals or at having their personal secrets exposed. Of course, those targets who do report extortion while it is in progress give the authorities a better chance to apprehend the offender—for example, agents can arrange an ambush at the ransom delivery. In fraud, targets' failure to report may be due to ignorance of the exploitative nature of their loss or embarrassment at being fooled, particularly if the fraud involved an illicit exchange.

Reporting an exploitative act, whatever its form, gives social control agents valuable information. Every report notifies the officials about a probable offense and they can begin to react. The target, witnesses, the scene of the offense, and objects used in the transaction can be examined for clues about the offender's identity. Because these offenses often are reported, social control agents can rely on reactive tactics to deal with deviant exploitation. In police work, reactive methods include interviewing witnesses, analyzing physical evidence, and using informers to link the crime to a particular offender (Manning, 1977; Rubinstein, 1973; Sanders, 1977; Skolnick, 1975).

In contrast, offenders engaged in individual deviance and deviant exchange usually carry out their transactions with discretion. This means that social control agents cannot rely on others to report these offenses. The agents must discover the offenses through their own efforts. To be sure, agents do receive some complaints about these offenses from citizens, particularly when deviants with limited resources operate in public places. But such complaints are relatively uncommon—most instances of mental illness, drug sales, illicit sexual intercourse, and so on never come to the authorities' attention. If social control agencies assign a high priority to eradicating a particular type of individual deviance or deviant exchange, they must adopt proactive tactics, using their own initiative to gather information about the occurrence of deviant transactions and the offenders' identities. Proactive tactics are designed to penetrate the protected settings which ordinarily house individual deviance and deviant exchange. In police work, proactive tactics include covert observation (as when officers stake out a tearoom), undercover work (as when disguised officers make illicit drug purchases in order to get evidence against dealers), and maintaining regular informants who can tell officers "what's happening on the street" (Manning, 1977; Rubinstein, 1973; Sanders, 1977; Skolnick, 1975).

Proactive tactics carry special risks for social control agencies. When they use reactive tactics, agents respond to a complaint, a request that they deal with an offense. This means that the complainant is interested in their progress; he or she expects the agents to try to apprehend the offender. When complaints occur, an agency's effectiveness can be measured by the proportion of complaints which lead to apprehension. Of course, the police cannot hope to arrest every burglar, but the public expects them to make an effort to do so. Because citizens reported the offenses and know about them, officials' efforts are exposed to public scrutiny. In contrast, proactive tactics demand secrecy. Proactive tactics are designed to discover instances of deviance. If offenders become aware of proactive efforts, they may flee, temporarily halt their deviance, or become more discreet; lack of secrecy about proactive tactics will result in their failure. Therefore, agents must conceal their actions from respectable citizens as well as deviants. This secrecy creates special problems. Citizens expect the agents' conduct will be circumscribed by law or professional ethics. But when agents cannot be observed, they may violate these restrictions, especially if they can justify the violations in terms of some higher good, such as apprehending deviants. For example, it is virtually impossible for police to remain within the rule of the law and, at the same time, make many vice arrests (Rubinstein, 1973; Skolnick, 1975). If vice arrests have high priority, police must resort to illicit tactics, such as entrapment (tricking people into breaking the law), illegal search and seizure, false testimony about the offender's actions, planted evidence, and the deliberate support of deviant informants (such as supplying some addicts with heroin in exchange for information). Citizens are shocked when these practices are exposed because they assume that the police always work within the law. While social control agents also violate some of these rules in reactive investigations, these abuses are particularly likely to develop when agents use secretive, proactive tactics. Moreover, chances for corruption increase in proactive investigations. It is easier for agents to accept bribes when they engage in secret investigations because it will not be obvious to the public or the agents' supervisors that corruption took place. If agents agree to overlook the offenses of a few deviants who bribe them, and pay more attention to those who do not, the corruption is almost impossible to detect because the agents continue to apprehend some offenders, thereby appearing efficient.

Social control agents must adjust their tactics to the social organization of the deviant transaction. Because targets of exploitation frequently complain, reactive tactics serve as the agents' principal response. In individual deviance and deviant exchange, proactive tactics are required to uncover hidden deviant transactions. However, the secrecy of proactive investigations permits corruption and the abuse of agents' powers.

CONCLUSION

The propositions developed in this chapter reflect the relationship between deviance and social control. They argue that the complexity of the deviant transaction has important consequences for deviants and social control agents (Table 9-1). As complexity increases, deviants are more likely to be

Table 9-1   CONSEQUENCES OF THE SOCIAL ORGANIZATION OF DEVIANCE

AS THE DEVIANT TRANSACTION'S COMPLEXITY DECREASES:	AS THE DEVIANT TRANSACTION'S COMPLEXITY INCREASES:
1. The deviant is less likely to be held responsible for the deviant act.	1. The deviant is more likely to be held responsible for the deviant act.
2. The deviance is less likely to be considered serious.	2. The deviance is more likely to be considered serious.
3. The deviant is less likely to receive punitive sanctions.	3. The deviant is more likely to receive punitive sanctions.
4. The deviant is less likely to be identified and apprehended.	4. The deviant is more likely to be identified and apprehended.
5. The deviant is less likely to use elaborate protective tactics.	5. The deviant is more likely to use elaborate protective tactics.
6. Social control agents are more likely to use proactive tactics.	6. Social control agents are more likely to use reactive tactics.

held responsible for their actions, those actions are more likely to be defined as serious, the response to deviance is more likely to be punitive, the risks of the deviant's identification and apprehension become greater, the range of tactics used by deviants to avoid apprehension expands, and social control agents become more likely to emphasize reactive tactics.

These propositions were derived from reports of field research, including the studies summarized in chapters 5 through 8. While they are consistent with the bulk of that research, the propositions need further study to determine the circumstances under which they apply. This chapter qualified the propositions in two ways. First, the propositions focus on the consequences of organizational complexity and ignore the influence of other factors—factors which may have different, even opposing, effects and which may outweigh social organization in particular cases. Some instances where other factors have contrary effects were mentioned as exceptions to particular propositions. Second, the field studies which provided the foundation for these propositions generally describe deviance in the United States during the late twentieth century. Comparative research is needed to consider the impact of social organization on deviants and social control agents in different cultures and at different times.

As they stand, the propositions emphasize the links between deviance and social control. The two are opposite sides of the same coin; it is impossible to consider one without examining the other. Three ways in which deviance and social control are interrelated deserve special emphasis. First, deviance is defined through social control activities. Rulemakers specify which activities are deviant and merit sanctions, thereby establishing the domain for agents' activities. Definitions of deviance and the methods for responding to it derive from social control ideologies—the systems of ideas which justify the agents' actions. When an agency's ideology shifts, or when rival agencies with different ideologies compete for jurisdiction over some type of deviance, the definition of deviance and the methods used to control it are likely to change. Second, social control agencies' ideologies generate agendas for action. Agencies assign priorities for their efforts, based on their definitions of the seriousness of offenses and their resources. In turn, agencies' priorities affect the deviant's risks—those engaged in offenses given high priority by social control agents run greater risks than those whose offenses receive less attention. Third, deviants and social control agents affect each other through their choice of tactics. When deviants devise elaborate defensive tactics, social control agents must become more aggressive in responding to deviance. And, faced with aggressive social control tactics, deviants need more sophisticated defenses to protect themselves. Social control agents affect deviants when they define acts as deviant, set priorities for responding to deviance, and choose tactics for their responses. In turn, agents are affected by the deviants' reactions to social control. The complexity of the deviant transaction—the social organization of deviance—shapes the interactions between deviants and social control agents.

This perspective has implications beyond the study of deviance. Conventional transactions also might be located on a dimension of organizational complexity. In the course of respectable life, people frequently engage in individual operations (analogous to individual deviance), such as feeding or dressing themselves. In cooperative interaction, people engage in various forms of exchange (analogous to deviant exchange). Respectable exchanges range from formal deals, as when a customer buys something in a store, to informal exchanges, as when two people trade favors, confidences, and esteem while developing and maintaining a friendship (Blau, 1964). Whenever one party to a respectable transaction acts in his or her own interest at the expense of another, an analogy can be drawn to deviant exploitation. Examples range from the formal exercise of coercive power, as when soldiers obey orders under the threat of punishment, to mundane incidents, such as lying. This listing may not be complete—a systematic examination of conventional transactions' organization might reveal other forms which have no deviant equivalent. The propositions developed in this chapter would predict that, for conventional transactions, the more complex the transaction, the more likely the actors will be seen as responsible, their actions will be taken seriously, and so forth.

While there are analogous forms of deviant and respectable transactions, the two must be distinguished because they occupy different positions in the larger social order. Deviant transactions, unlike respectable transactions, make one or more participants subject to social control efforts. As a consequence, secrecy about deviants' operations and identities is a central theme in deviant transactions. In addition, deviant transactions are more tenuous than their respectable counterparts. Respectable transactions receive strong institutional support, backed by custom, written codes, and social control agencies of various kinds. People enter respectable transactions confident that the other participants will remain within the confines of respectability. For example, Edgerton (1979) describes behavior on an ocean beach, where perfect strangers relax in close proximity, wearing minimal clothing. Order is maintained in this setting because people understand the limits of appropriate behavior in the beach setting and because social control agents stand by, ready to sanction violations of propriety. In short, activity on the beach—and in other conventional settings—is enmeshed in a web of expectations held by the participants and protected by agencies created to ensure that those expectations are not violated. Deviant transactions do not receive comparable institutional support—deviants must rely on whatever norms govern conduct between deviant associates, as well as their own abilities to carry out operations in the face of opposition by social control agents, targets, and others. Therefore, loyalty to the group, advance planning, and precautions assume special importance for deviants. Even though its organization may resemble that found in respectable transactions, the fact that an activity is deviant turns the transaction into an occasion for secrecy and precaution.

CHAPTER TEN
SOCIAL ORGANIZATION AND THE ANALYSIS OF DEVIANCE

This chapter attempts to integrate some of the themes developed earlier in this book. Chapter 1 identified three levels of analysis for the study of deviance: social psychology, social organization, and social structure. Most sociological writing about deviance adopts either social psychological or social structural analysis; social organization receives less attention. Following the introduction, this book outlined a social organizational perspective toward deviance. Chapters 2 through 4 described the typical forms and identified several consequences of the social organization of deviants. Similarly, chapters 5 through 9 described the typical forms of the social organization of deviance and developed propositions regarding its consequences. This chapter expands the focus beyond social organization, building on the preceding analysis.

This chapter addresses three topics. First, it considers the relationship between the social organization of deviants and the social organization of deviance. Earlier, these topics were treated separately; here, they are combined. Second, it examines the relationship between social organizational analysis and the two other levels for analyzing deviance. It begins by linking the social organizational and social psychological perspectives, considering how they interrelate to affect the deviant's career. Then it links social organization to social structure, examining how social change affects the place of deviance in society. These attempts to use the social organizational perspective to enhance the two other levels of analysis form the bulk of this chapter. Finally, this chapter concludes with some directions for further research.

THE SOCIAL ORGANIZATION OF DEVIANTS AND DEVIANCE

The distinction between the social organization of deviants and the social organization of deviance is an analytic one. Obviously, every deviant transaction involves one or more deviant actors who are organized in some fashion, so that every transaction can be viewed in terms of the social organization of deviants. Similarly, all deviants carry out deviant transactions, so that deviant actors can be seen in terms of the social organization of deviance. Taken together, this means that every deviant act and every deviant actor can be examined from two distinct organizational perspectives: the social organization of deviants and the social organization of deviance. While most of this book focused on one perspective or the other, this section attempts to bring the two together.

Table 10-1 locates each of the major examples discussed in chapters 2 through 9 along both dimensions. For example, physician narcotic addicts, who were discussed as naive loners in chapter 2, engage in individual deviance, while racketeering, which was described in chapter 8, is typically carried out by a deviant formal organization.

Table 10-1   DEVIANTS, DEVIANCE, AND SOCIAL ORGANIZATION
(Numbers in parentheses refer to the chapter in which this case was described.)

DEVIANTS ORGANIZED AS	FORM OF DEVIANT TRANSACTION		
	INDIVIDUAL DEVIANCE	DEVIANT EXCHANGE	DEVIANT EXPLOITATION
Loners	Physician Addicts (2) Suicide (5) Mental Illness (5)	Tearoom Trades (6)	Embezzlers (2) Murder (7) Kidnapping (8)
Colleagues		Prostitutes (2) Fencing (6)	Pool Hustlers (2)
Peers	Recreational Drug Users (2) Bottle Gang Drinking (5)	Drug Sales (6) Swinging (6)	Delinquent Gangs (2) Burglary (7) Robbery (7)
Mobs			Road Hustlers (3) Pickpocketing (7) Confidence Games (8)
Formal Organizations		Numbers Games (3)	Large Street Gangs (3) Racketeering (8) Business Fraud (8)

Table 10-1 is useful for summarizing the cases discussed in the earlier chapters, but it is subject to inaccurate interpretation. To understand the table correctly, three qualifications should be kept in mind. First, many deviant operations can be carried out by deviants organized in different ways. For example, Table 10-1 indicates that robberies typically are committed by peers. This was true for many of the robberies described in chapter 7, where the typical offense involved a couple of friends robbing a convenience store or a filling station. But not all robberies involve peers. Loners can commit robbery—many bank robberies involve loners who approach a teller, hand over a threatening note demanding money, take the teller's cash, and leave. Mobs also carry out robberies. A bank might be the target for mob members who divide their labor, with one supplying "cover," another taking the money, and a third driving the getaway car. Thus, the claim in Table 10-1 that peers commit robberies is a simplification—robbery can be carried out by deviants in various organizational forms. A second example of this sort of simplification is tearoom trades. Table 10-1 identifies these men as loners, but tearoom participants have various relationships with other deviants. Humphreys (1970) classified some tearoom participants as "trade"—men who typically were married and used tearooms as a convenient, impersonal source of sexual satisfaction. They can be seen as loners, having no contact with other homosexuals outside the tearooms. But Humphreys classified other participants as "gay"—acknowledged homosexuals who enjoyed occasional sexual encounters in tearooms. Outside the tearooms, these men had peer relationships with other homosexuals. Thus, even in the same deviant transaction, participants may be organized differently—some tearoom participants are loners, others are peers. A particular kind of deviant operation may be carried out by deviants organized in different ways.

Second, the same deviant can engage in different forms of deviant transactions. For example, Table 10-1 distinguishes between recreational drug use (individual deviance) and illicit drug sales (deviant exchange), but heroin addicts routinely participate in both forms of transactions. In addition, many addicts steal to get money to buy drugs (deviant exploitation). Delinquents engage in a similar range of deviant transactions, from illicit drinking and drug use, to buying and selling stolen goods or drugs, to fighting and theft. As they shift from one form of transaction to another, deviants take organizational differences into account. For example, delinquents about to mug a passer-by know that they must cope with potential resistance by the target, watch out for possible witnesses, and expect the target will report the crime. These concerns are characteristic of exploitative offenses; they are far less relevant when the same delinquents discreetly use drugs together. Focusing on the deviant transaction permits the detailed analysis of a specific situation. However, a narrow focus on the transaction's roles excludes other events in the participants' lives. Consider, for example, a prostitute who is also an addict. Analyzing the social organization of deviance separates these deviant roles, focusing on either acts of prostitution or transactions linked to drug addiction. This narrow focus is useful because it permits the careful analysis of a particular transaction. At the same time, it has limitations. By classifying deviant transactions, Table 10-1 implies that the forms have no relationship. This is a simplification—a given deviant can engage in different forms of deviant transactions during his or her career.

Third, Table 10-1 does not represent all the possible combinations of deviant actors' and deviant transactions' organization. Some cells in the table are empty, others have one or two entries, and a few have three. This distribution reflects the cases chosen for inclusion in this book. They were picked to represent the range of social organization along both dimensions. To be sure, some cells are heavily represented in real life—for example, mobs typically engage in exploitative deviance, and many loners are individual deviants. While some combinations readily come to mind, it is impossible to know how many deviant actors or transactions fit a given cell, if only because deviance is a secretive activity and there is no way of learning the total numbers of deviants or deviant transactions. Nor are the four empty cells significant; some of them can be filled. Pimps are an example of colleagues who engage in individual deviance. The extravagant life style of the pimp, who lives off the earnings of prostitutes, is a form of individual deviance, and pimps share one another's company, associating as colleagues (Milner and Milner 1972). (Another facet of pimping is the relationship between pimps and their prostitutes—a relationship which can be viewed as exchange or exploitation.) The two other cells involving individual deviance—mobs/individual deviance and formal organizations/individual deviance—should indeed be empty. Members of mobs and formal organizations do engage in individual deviance; for example, many pickpockets are drug addicts (Maurer, 1964:34). However, they do not engage in individual deviance as members of these sophisticated organizational forms; typically, their individual deviance is a leisure-time activity. Mobs and formal organizations exist to amass power or make money, and individual deviance does not turn a profit. Finally, the cell for mobs/exchange is empty for the same reason—simple mobs are dedicated to profit making through theft. On the other hand, some extended mobs (discussed briefly in chapter 3) do specialize in deviant exchange. Extended mobs are small, well-coordinated teams which resemble mobs, except that their activities extend over space (as in smuggling operations) or time (as in brothels). If extended mobs are viewed as a subtype of mobs, then their operations fit the fourth empty cell.

In summary, this book developed parallel frameworks for examining the social organization of deviants and the social organization of deviance. As Table 10-1 demonstrates, any form of deviant organization or deviant transaction can be classified on both of these dimensions. But certain qualifications must be taken into account: deviant operations can be carried out by deviants organized in more than one way; a given deviant can carry out different forms of deviant transactions; and the distribution of cases in the table's cells is not a reflection of the relative numbers of deviants or deviant transactions. Table 10-1 is an attempt to integrate this book's major arguments; it is not a complete representation of everything which might be said about social organization and deviance.

Earlier chapters developed parallel arguments about the social organization of deviant actors and deviant transactions. The two combine in the social organizational perspective. As a level of analysis between the social psychological and social structural approaches, this perspective focuses on the relationships between actors involved in deviance. The next two sections consider how the social organizational perspective can be combined with each of the other two levels of analysis.

SOCIAL ORGANIZATION AND DEVIANT CAREERS

Social psychological studies of deviance frequently use the concept of career. Traditionally, career "refers to the sequence of movements from one position to another in an occupational system made by any individual who works in that system" (Becker, 1963:24). Because deviants' lives often feature dramatic changes—learning new skills and ideologies, breaking norms, acquiring new identities, getting labeled, receiving sanctions, and so on—the career concept appeals to sociologists studying deviance. The concept of a deviant career offers a way of conceptualizing these changes by suggesting that deviants follow common pathways through the deviant experience. Thus, one of the earliest studies of deviant careers argues that every novice marijuana user must first learn the technique of smoking, then learn to recognize the drug's effects, and finally learn to enjoy those effects (Becker, 1963). The career concept also draws an analogy between the lives of deviants and respectable persons. Just as respectable people pass through a series of stages in an occupational career, deviants have multiple-stage careers. In this sense, deviance resembles respectable work (Inciardi, 1975; Letkemann, 1973; Gale Miller, 1978).

Deviant careers are the subject of many social psychological analyses of deviance. Most studies narrowly focus on one or two career stages. Most commonly, sociologists examine the process of entering deviance (cf. Becker, 1963; Bryan, 1965; Dank, 1971; Goffman, 1961; Gray, 1973; Lofland, 1969; Matza, 1969; M. Weinberg, 1966). A second, less common topic is the process of leaving deviance (cf. Irwin, 1970; Livingston, 1974; Lofland, 1969; Ray, 1961; Stebbins, 1970). Social psychologists view entering and leaving deviance as key processes because they mark major changes in the individual's life, requiring a reevaluation of one's self. However, this concern with entry and exit ignores the equally interesting, intermediate stages in deviants' careers; it is as if studies of military officers' careers concentrated on recruitment and retirement while ignoring the intermediate postings, promotions, and so forth.

A few studies explore the intermediate stages in particular deviant careers, but there is no general model of these processes. This section outlines such a model, combining the social psychological and social organizational levels of analysis. It begins by comparing respectable and deviant careers. Then, using the social organizational perspective, it examines some special features of deviant careers. The result incorporates the neglected intermediate career stages, as well as the initial and final stages of the deviant career.

Respectable and Deviant Careers

Sociological analyses of respectable careers typically examine an individual's occupational movements through a formal organization (cf. Glaser, 1968). Such careers have several important features. First, the individual moves from one formally defined position to another. Movement may be horizontal—to a position of equal rank—or vertical—to a higher or lower position. Each position's relationship to others is clearly defined; typically, written codes classify positions according to their rank, responsibilities, salaries, and privileges. Ideally, an individual enters the organization and remains with it, in one position or another, throughout his or her tenure in the work force. Second, people are expected to rise through the organizational structure. Organizational mobility typically involves a prescribed sequence of positions—persons must reach one rank before moving to the next. Knowledgeable organizational members can assess one another's progress and prospects using commonly understood standards; the positions one is assigned and the length of time one holds them become predictors of future organizational progress. As members rise through the organization, they receive additional rewards, including money, fringe benefits, and status symbols. In most cases, an individual's career progress is public knowledge; movement from one position to another is visible, often marked by formal announcements or other passage rites. Third, the desirability of upward mobility is affirmed by most organizational members and the larger society. The organizational ideology values initiative, ambition, and determination to succeed. Members are expected to strive for promotion. Those who question the value of career progress risk being seen as alienated or even mentally ill.

In short, the respectable career, as described by occupational sociologists, moves upward through a well-defined structure. Becker and Strauss (1956) use the metaphor of a multistoried building to describe organizational careers. Each floor represents a position within the organization, and people ride up escalators from one floor to the next. The escalator image suggests that mobility involves short passages, along visible, established routes, from one position to the next higher one. Sociological discussions of careers sometimes imply that all careers occur within an equally orderly structure.

But deviant careers are not this orderly. Becker (1963:25-39) sketches a four-stage sequence for a deviant career: committing a deviant act; acquiring a deviant ideology; being caught and labeled; and joining a deviant group. But this model raises more issues than it answers:

> Do prostitutes, homosexuals, armed robbers, stutterers, and Communists all go through stages of a career development? Is the career the same for all these groups, or do they have in common only the fact of career? Within each such group, can common threads of development be found, which many or most individuals will follow? Or, on the other hand, are there many pathways once one has taken the first step, and in fact are there many different first steps? And do some of these paths lead "backward," away from the ultimate identity with the deviant way? (Sagarin, 1975:137-38)

These questions point to the fluidity of the deviant career. The four stages outlined by Becker resemble the orderly sequence of a respectable organizational career. But deviants' experiences can violate this sequence—one delinquent might join a gang before ever committing a deviant act; another might remain a loner, never joining a gang. Acquiring a deviant ideology often follows joining a deviant group or being labeled (and thereby thrown into the company of other deviants). Other patterns can be imagined. Deviant careers occur outside the structured confines of a respectable formal organization. There are no formal rules governing one's progress or controlling competition between rivals. Deviants are vulnerable to exploitation by other deviants and sanctions from social control agents; their careers are precarious. The model of the respectable career, with its established pathways from one well-defined position to the next, does not fit the deviant's experiences.

Career shifts, rather than orderly progress, characterize the intermediate stages of deviant careers. Career shifts can take several forms, including: (1) a deviant can shift laterally within a deviant scene, as when a professional dice "mechanic" becomes a shoot-up man; (2) a deviant can shift vertically within a deviant scene, as when a numbers runner becomes a collector; (3) a deviant can shift to a new deviant scene but perform the same deviant activity, as when a call girl later works as a streetwalker; (4) a deviant can shift to an entirely different scene, as when a safecracker turns to check forgery; and (5) a deviant can undertake additional activities within additional scenes, as when a compulsive gambler steals. With each career shift, the deviant begins a new deviant involvement. A given involvement can range from short-term to long-run, and the sequence of involvements can vary from one person to the next. For example, some prostitutes turn to drugs for recreation or refuge, while some drug addicts become prostitutes to support their drug habits. In each of these patterns, the individual remains deviant, but his or her career shifts. Career shifts lack a prescribed sequence—deviants do not move through their careers in the orderly fashion

characteristic of respectable organizational careers. The varied patterns of career shifts make it impossible to specify a standard deviant career path.

Riding escalators between floors is a poor metaphor for describing the complexities of the deviant career. A more effective image is a walk through the woods—while some people take the pathways marked by their predecessors, others strike out on their own; some walk slowly, exploring before moving further, while others run, caught up in the action. Some walkers have a destination in mind and proceed purposefully, but others view the trip as an experience, enjoying it for its own sake. Even those intent on getting somewhere may stray from the path, trying to find a shortcut, and perhaps lose sight of familiar landmarks, get lost, and find it necessary to backtrack. The analysis of deviant careers requires a framework which recognizes the relative lack of structure in the deviant experience.

By focusing on entry into and exit from deviance, most studies of deviant careers suggest an oversimplified model with three phases—becoming deviant, being deviant, and leaving deviance. However, being deviant often involves a complex series of career shifts as individuals make their way through the deviant experience. Each career shift is a process with several stages. The *preliminary stage* involves assembling the necessary equipment, knowledge, skills, contacts, and motives required for the shift to take place. For instance, an experienced marijuana user may get a sample of another illicit drug, such as LSD, as well as encouragement from other users to try it. During *commission*, the actor carries out the new line of action, sometimes in a tentative, experimental fashion. Thus, feeling sufficiently prepared, the marijuana user tries LSD for the first time. *Assessment* follows commission; the actor tries to interpret the meaning of the new experience, perhaps assessing the risks involved, the quality of the rewards, and so on. Reactions from others, including deviant associates, targets, and social control agents, can help the actor evaluate his or her performance. For example, in talking with other LSD users, the novice may compare the effects of LSD to those of marijuana. Some actors may decide not to pursue the new line of action, while others continue, entering the stage of *routine*. Here, deviants become familiar with the new activity, improving their skills with practice and constructing an integrated framework for interpreting the experience. Experienced LSD users, for example, acquire a practical pharmacology of drug lore (Stoddart, 1974). With this immersion in the now-familiar experience, the deviant may become aware of additional *options*. Such options can include opportunities for further career shifts, such as selling LSD or trying other drugs. Thus, the final stage of one career shift can mark the beginning of the preliminary stage of another shift in the deviant's career.

At each stage of a career shift, the actor can abandon the process. During the preliminary stage, for example, actors may assemble the necessary resources but then decide not to continue, perhaps calculating that the risks are too great. Similarly, actors may back out in the midst of com-

mission or, after assessing the new experience, choose not to repeat it. Persons in respectable organizational careers may find it difficult to refuse a career shift, such as a promotion, without threatening their future career prospects. But the less structured pathways taken by deviants offer a range of involvements without endangering their careers or prospects. Deviants can experiment with their careers, testing the limits of their deviant involvements. Some individuals restrict their deviance, taking only some drugs or committing only certain types of theft. The deviant who interrupts a career shift need not leave deviance altogether.

Effects of Social Organization

Given the complexities of deviant career patterns, a purely social psychological analysis of these processes is inadequate. Deviant careers occur within the context of social organization. Social organization affects deviant careers in two distinct ways. First, the social organization of deviants provides a context for the development of deviant careers. Second, the social organization of deviance constrains deviants' career development. Because deviant careers develop outside the structure of respectable formal organizations, deviants have a broad range of options, many of which become apparent only as the individual makes particular career shifts. The social organization of deviants and the social organization of deviance affect the deviant's career progress. This section identifies some of these effects, examining the differences between occupational and nonoccupational deviance, the length of the deviant career, the consequences of unregulated competition, and the impact of social control.

The first effect social organization has on the deviant career involves the purpose of deviance. Some sociologists draw an analogy between deviance and respectable work (Inciardi, 1975; Letkemann, 1973; Gale Miller, 1978). The sociology of work offers important insights for understanding some forms of deviance, but the analogy has limitations. Occupational deviance must be distinguished from nonoccupational deviance. The former includes those deviant transactions which are intended to produce income, for example, theft and drug sales. Nonoccupational deviance often involves a quest for stimulation, rather than income—illicit drug use is an example. This distinction cuts across the forms of deviant transactions. While many acts of deviant exploitation are occupational, some are not. Murder is occupational deviance for those who kill for hire, but most homicides evolve out of recreational activities, such as drinking in bars. Most theft is occupational; rape is nonoccupational. Similarly, deviant exchanges can be nonoccupational—illicit sexual relations are one example—but sellers in deviant sales profit from occupational deviance. Individual deviance usually does not produce income, but some individuals committed to deviant belief systems dedicate their lives to the cause; just as a priest has an occupation, so do political extremists. There is a tendency for more complex deviant trans-actions to involve occupational deviance, but the relationship is not perfect. The occupational-nonoccupational distinction has a stronger relationship with the social organization of deviants. Mobs and formal organizations usually pursue a profit; their members' deviance is occupational. Some lon-ers, colleagues, and peers also try to make a living through deviance, but, as noted in chapter 4, they are less likely to be successful. The greater resources of the more sophisticated forms of deviant organization make their operations more profitable.

Although it is customary to equate career with occupation, both oc-cupational and nonoccupational deviants have careers. However, their ca-reers involve different patterns. Because work is a central identity for many people, occupational careers have less flexibility than nonoccupational ca-reers—people are expected to stick with their occupational careers for pro-longed periods. (Here again, deviants can best maintain a long-term commitment to an occupational career when they are backed by the resources of a sophisticated organizational form.) Nonoccupational careers are more likely to feature short-term involvements. Respectable people typically have one long-term occupational career and several short-term nonoccupational careers, for example, in hobbies or sports. The same pattern holds for deviants. Occupational deviance is more likely to be progressive, so that, with sufficient skill, opportunity, and ambition, the deviant can gain more income, security, and other rewards. For instance, a drug dealer may hope to become more successful, moving up the ladder of distribution, trading in larger quantities, and earning more money. In contrast, nonoccupational deviance involves a smaller commitment; it usually requires less time and a smaller investment. Nonoccupational deviance usually is not progressive. A marijuana user may begin to use marijuana more frequently, use larger amounts, or experiment with other drugs, but these are options, not the next step in a well-structured, progressive career. Occupational deviants typically want to increase their profits, while the nonoccupational deviant's lower involvement makes it easier to choose widely among possible career shifts or to leave deviance altogether. In short, the social organization of deviants provides the context within which occupational and nonoccupa-tional deviance occur. Relations with deviant associates and the purpose of the deviant's operations affect the pattern of the deviant career.

A second, related link between social organization and deviant careers involves career length. The length of the individual's involvement in devi-ance varies. For some people, the deviant career has a single episode. For example, naive check forgers often lead respectable lives until they find themselves isolated and in need of funds and choose to forge a check to get the needed money (Lemert, 1967:99-108). A naive forger may limit his or her illicit activities to this one episode, returning to respectability. For others, deviance is a major phase in their lives, lasting weeks, months, or years.

Thus, delinquents often remain deviant until they enter respectable adult roles, and many prostitutes leave the life only when they age and become less competitive in their marketplace. For still others, deviance becomes a lifelong involvement. Career criminals adopt deviance as their life's work, their principal source of income. Social organization affects career length in two ways.

First, support from other deviants affects career length. The more contacts an actor has with other deviants, the longer the actor's deviant career. Other deviants supply resources necessary for deviance. Deviant transactions sometimes require special equipment, such as weapons or drugs. Because social control agents often restrict access to this equipment, many deviants get their supplies from one another. In addition to special equipment, other deviants can supply an ideology for interpreting the deviant experience. To the degree that people need equipment, instruction, or social support for continuing in deviance or making career shifts, and to the degree that they have difficulty supplying their own needs, contacts with other deviants facilitate continued involvement in deviance. These contacts expand the deviant's range of options. Through their contacts, deviants can meet still other deviants, learn about possible operations, assess opportunities for career shifts, and so forth. While loners are isolated, dependent upon themselves for career development, more sophisticated forms of deviant organization open the way to extended, diverse involvements in deviance.

Second, like respectable persons, deviants seek security in their careers. Deviants risk apprehension and sanctioning by social control agents. More sophisticated forms of deviant organization reduce this risk because the organization's resources can protect its members. Similarly, risks are lower in less complex forms of deviant transactions because the operations are easier to keep secret. As individuals commit themselves to a particular career path, they seek to reduce risks and make their career secure. In respectable careers, organizations sometimes insure members' positions through tenure or seniority systems. Deviants cannot rely on these institutional supports. Instead, those who become committed to long deviant careers may make career shifts which maximize security. For example, they may attempt to join a more sophisticated form of deviant organization. Adolescents often steal in peer groups, but those who become career criminals frequently apprentice themselves to experienced thieves and learn a specialty which allows them to join a mob. While peer group thefts involve substantial risks, mobs protect their operations through careful preparation and corruption of social control agents. Similarly, career deviants may try to move from high-risk, exploitative transactions into types of deviant exchange which bring larger profits and lower risks. For example, drug addicts who steal to support their habits may turn to drug dealing as a safer method of earning money—while thefts are likely to come to official attention, drug sales can be kept secret. By shifting toward more sophisticated forms of deviant organization or less complex forms of deviant transactions, deviants can reduce the risks of a long-term deviant career. Social organization shapes the degree of social support available to the deviant and the risks of deviance—two elements which affect the length of the deviant career.

A third link between social organization and deviant careers involves unregulated competition among deviants. Most careers involve potential conflict over scarce resources. Members of respectable formal organizations compete with each other for promotion, salary, and other rewards. Further, respectable organizations themselves often compete; businesses, for example, struggle to capture larger shares of their markets. Respectable organizations normally regulate intraorganizational and interorganizational competition with formally defined rules. Within organizations, there may be formal procedures governing promotion, seniority rules for job assignments, salary scales, and so on. Similarly, laws and regulatory agencies control interorganizational competition; state and federal agencies, such as the Interstate Commerce Commission, regulate relationships between rival organizations. Respectable careers feature competition within formally defined limits.

In contrast, competition between deviants is not formally regulated (Block, 1980). Individuals' aspirations for personal success and groups' attempts to maximize their profits exist without formal restraints. Social control agents try to disrupt deviant operations, but deviants conceal their activities and much deviance occurs outside the agents' control. As a consequence, deviants face special dangers from competition: deviants can betray their associates, informing the authorities about each other's activities; they can attack their rivals; or they can cheat one another in their dealings. When deviants exploit one another, the targets are reluctant to turn to social control agents. Asking officials for help exposes one's own activities to their inspection, and social control agents are unlikely to sympathize with complaints that illicit operations were disrupted. Informants, gang wars, and drug burns occur, in part, because deviants' competition is not regulated from the outside.

Unregulated competition threatens the stability of deviant careers. Deviants who are committed to their careers want to minimize risk and uncertainty, but they cannot rely on outside regulation to protect their operations. Therefore, the deviants' own organizations must minimize the dangers of unregulated competition. Negotiation is one method of reducing these risks. Even within deviant formal organizations, there may be considerable negotiation over important decisions. The choice of leaders, policy, targets, tactics, and the risks to be assumed in particular operations may be open to discussion (Cressey, 1969). Where members cannot accept the negotiated solutions, they may leave, perhaps to join other deviants. (Deviant formal organizations sometimes restrict this option with a code of conduct which obliges members to remain loyal to the organization.) In contrast to members of respectable organizations, deviants are more likely to have a voice in their operations.

Dividing resources according to a simple, established formula is another method of reducing conflict among deviants. Colleagues who temporarily work together, peers, and mob members commonly split their profits into equal shares. Codes of conduct for career thieves spell out the norms for dividing the profits; for example, they explain how investment capital should be treated. Where an equal split does not seem appropriate, deviants may establish another, equally clear-cut formula for allocating profits. For instance, fences typically pay one-third the value of stolen property. These rules of thumb help reduce conflict; they specify what is "fair," and thereby set an informal but well-established standard for correct conduct. Deviants know that violations of this standard are likely to meet resistance. In place of outside regulation, informal customs minimize trouble.

The supply of resources required for deviance also affects competition among deviants. Most deviant operations require scarce resources of some sort—drug users need drugs, muggers need targets, and so on. When these resources are plentiful, competition is minimized; when resources become scarce or the demand for them rises, the likelihood of conflict between deviants increases. Deviants adopt different methods of allocating scarce resources. Most obviously, they can simply pay the market price, as when drug users pay more for drugs during periods when supplies are short. Others agree on a geographical division of the spoils, as when gangs acknowledge one another's "turf" or organized crime families agree to restrict their operations to particular areas (Hoenig, 1975). A third method of controlling access to resources is through corruption, as when one mob bribes officials to let them operate without interference while their rivals remain subject to social control efforts.

Negotiation, informal rules for dividing profits, and methods for allocating resources among rivals provide ways of controlling competition among deviants. When these methods fail, rivalry may become open conflict, disrupting deviant operations and attracting the officials' attention. Deviants have an interest in regulating their competition—informal regulation reduces the risks of exploitation by other deviants, helps insure the success of deviant operations, and reduces interference by officials. When deviants avoid conflict with one another, their careers can proceed with little difficulty. When conflict breaks out, deviants may make career shifts or leave deviance altogether to avoid further problems. Deviants' social organization helps minimize conflict and insure the security needed for successful deviant careers.

Fourth, social organization affects deviant careers by mediating the impact of social control. Contacts with social control agents have a profound effect on the deviant's career. This is particularly true the first time the deviant is apprehended and labeled. Labeling has three important consequences for deviant careers. First, it affects the individual's definition of self. Labeling encourages an individual to adopt a deviant identity—the actor redefines himself or herself as a deviant, as unlike respectable people. Prior deviant acts, which may have been explained as accidents or exceptions, now become redefined as evidence of the person's deviant nature. Further, this redefinition of self can lead to secondary deviation, further involvement in deviance as an affirmation of the new deviant identity (Lemert, 1967:40-64). Adopting a deviant identity is likely to affect one's deviant career by increasing commitment to and involvement in deviance. Individuals with deviant identities are more likely to seek out other committed deviants and join sophisticated organizational forms. Individuals who develop a deviant identity also become more aware of career options and more likely to make career shifts toward greater commitment which they would have rejected when they still clung to a respectable definition of self.

Second, labeling, particularly if it is followed by incarceration, brings the deviant into contact with other deviants who can socialize the newcomer. Experienced deviants can teach deviant skills and deviant ideologies, so that newcomers learn how to carry out new deviant operations as well as how to interpret their experiences. Socialization affects the deviant career by increasing the range of options open to the individual, encouraging deeper involvement in deviance. By apprenticing themselves to more experienced deviants, newcomers can learn how to engage in more profitable, more serious offenses.

Third, by bringing newcomers into contact with experienced deviants, labeling extends the individual's contacts with the deviant social network. The newcomer and other deviants become known to one another, so that they can cooperate on future operations. When another person is needed for a particular operation, experienced deviants may turn to the newcomer. "Who you know" affects one's chances for a longer, more successful career in deviance, just as in respectable careers. By bringing newcomers into contact with experienced deviants, social control agents unwittingly shape the social organization of deviants. In turn, the deviants' organization mediates the effects of social control; sophisticated organizational forms provide socialization and support for deviant identities and offer a network of deviant contacts, fostering longer, more stable deviant careers.

Many sociologists focus on entry into deviance because labeling has such dramatic effects. However, the impact of social control continues during later stages in the deviant career. Deviant careers are disrupted whenever the offender is captured and sanctioned. The risk of disruption varies with the forms of deviant organization and deviant transaction, but all deviants must take social control efforts into account. Increased risk of apprehension, as when social control agencies assign a higher priority to a particular form of deviance, encourages deviants to make career shifts toward safer activities or forms of organization or decide to leave deviance altogether. Even deviants who never come to official attention must take precautions against discovery and capture; the risk of social control affects every deviant career.

The differences between occupational and nonoccupational deviance, career length, the effects of unregulated competition, and the impact of social control reveal social organization's impact on deviant careers. The social organization of deviants provides the context for deviant careers. Contacts with other deviants help support one's career, and links among associates, rivals, and social control agents influence career prospects. Similarly, the social organization of deviance constrains career progress. Deviant transactions differ in their risks and potential profits; these factors affect career stability. Thinking about an individual's career in strictly social psychological terms ignores the impact of social organization, of one's relationships with others.

SOCIAL ORGANIZATION AND SOCIAL STRUCTURE

Social organizational analysis also combines with the broader social structural level of analysis. Society's social structure—its overall pattern of relationships—provides the context within which deviance occurs. Several aspects of social structure affect deviance. First, every society has a system of stratification—arrangements for distributing wealth, power, and prestige among its members. Stratification usually reflects social class, ethnicity, age, or sex. Societies range from the relatively egalitarian, with minimal differences in rank, to the highly stratified. Second, societies have different economic systems, ranging from hunting and gathering to complex industrial economies. Third, societies' other institutions differ, including their political, religious, and family systems. Finally, a society's social structure is reflected in and affected by its culture. What people know and believe about their world depends upon the nature of their society. By concentrating on the contemporary United States, the preceding chapters took its social structure for granted. This section expands the focus by comparing deviance in different societies and identifying some ways social structure can affect deviance.

Comparative sociology examines differences among societies. The comparisons can be made across either time or space. Historical comparisons examine change in a society over time. For example, the social structure of the United States underwent important changes during the past two hundred years: the economic base shifted from agriculture to industry; the population moved from small towns and the rural countryside into cities and their suburbs; political participation expanded from property-holding white males to universal adult suffrage; immigration from dozens of countries contributed to a complex ethnic structure; and so forth. By comparing social patterns—such as rates of deviance—over time, it is possible to assess the effects of structural changes. Cross-national comparisons examine different societies at the same point in time. For example, today's United States might be compared to the People's Republic of China. These two countries differ in their politics, economies, and culture. Such structural differences should affect the incidence and type of deviance in these societies. Historical or cross-national comparisons offer methods of studying the effects of social structure.

Social structure affects the type and incidence of deviance in a society, as well as the ways deviants organize. Within a given society, particular types of deviance have different prospects for success or failure, and potential deviants evaluate these prospects when considering whether to commit deviant acts. The sum of these decisions determines the society's incidence of deviance; rates of deviance vary from society to society. The forms of deviant organization devised by a society's offenders also depend, in part, on the social structure. This section explores four links between the social structural and social organizational levels of analysis: structural strain, structural opportunities, structural supports, and social control.

First, structural strain is related to social organization. Some sociologists view society as a smoothly operating system in which each element has a function. This vision is too simple. Most social systems contain members with conflicting interests, and the need to coordinate these opposing factions produces strain within the social structure (Smelser, 1963). Structural strain is not an aberration or a breakdown in the system; rather, it results from conflicts of interest which are inherent in any complex social system. This discussion will examine stratification and alienation—two sources of conflict which produce structural strain. The analysis will show how a society's ordinary operations create strain which, in turn, fosters deviance, and how social organization affects this process.

Systems of stratification are an important source of structural strain. Every society has a system of stratification for distributing rewards among its members. In many societies, this system is based, in part, on the members' ascribed characteristics—those features over which they have no control, such as sex, ethnicity, or parents' social class. If an individual's chances of acquiring wealth, power, or prestige depend upon ascribed characteristics, then his or her life chances are constrained at birth. In modern America, for example, the sons of white, middle-class parents face fewer obstacles than females, blacks, or lower-class persons. The former are expected and encouraged to do well, and the social system fosters their achievements; others find their paths blocked. This system of stratification, combined with a culture which values achievement, becomes an important source of structural strain (Cloward and Ohlin, 1960; A. Cohen, 1955; Merton, 1957). For example, lower-class children watching television are bombarded with images of successful middle-class people, and they learn to want the material rewards enjoyed by the middle class. Yet they find it difficult to achieve these rewards. Blocked from achievement via the conventional avenues of mobility, they search for alternate routes. Some enter careers where talent is more important than one's ascribed characteristics—the arts and sports are examples. Others turn to deviance—another avenue usually open to people from all backgrounds. Deviance offers an arena within which the individual can become successful. Held in low regard by the larger society, some deviants receive the esteem of their associates. Others enter deviance to achieve financial success; they commit deviant acts for profit, such as the operations of mobs and deviant formal organizations. The history of career crime and organized crime in the United States parallels the history of American immigration, illustrating the choice of highly profitable forms of deviance by those who found conventional mobility routes blocked (D. Bell, 1960). In the mid-nineteenth century, when Irish immigrants faced discrimination, many professional thieves were Irish. Later, as new immigrant groups arrived and met discrimination, their members entered crime—Jews around the turn of the century, Italians somewhat later. More recently, blacks and Hispanics began to enter organized crime (Ianni, 1974; Lewis, 1980). Thus, by frustrating individuals' aspirations, systems of stratification create structural strain and lead people into deviance.

Alienation is another product of structural strain which leads to deviance. Alienated people feel isolated, cut off from the larger social world. Social norms lack their binding power when persons question the meaning of their own existence. Structural strain can produce alienation; immigrants in a city filled with foreign faces, the poor and the aged cut off from work and sufficient funds, and other members of society may find themselves isolated. In such circumstances, some individuals retreat into deviance (Merton, 1957). Individual deviance often has its roots in alienation. Feeling isolated from society and questioning the validity of norms against deviance, some turn to drugs, alcohol, mental illness, or suicide as ways of escaping the doubts and frustrations they associate with respectable life. Alienation also can lead to deviant exploitation (A. Cohen, 1955). For example, alienated from what they see as the irrelevance of formal education, some adolescents rebel, committing vandalism and other delinquent acts. Typically, they have peers who share their position in the social system. Where a social structure causes people to doubt the validity of their respectable lives, alienation and deviance are common outcomes.

Society must weigh the interests of its different factions. In modern societies, individuals' interests may vary according to their age, sex, ethnicity, education, source of income, family ties, social class, political affiliation, occupation, and so on. Most societies have limited resources, so that some members must receive fewer rewards than they want. Competition for these rewards produces conflict between factions and some parties to this conflict are likely to become disenchanted with the society's rules for allocating rewards. In turn, the disenchanted sometimes turn to deviance, reducing the strain through rule breaking. Sources of structural strain become sources of deviance. Deviance may resolve the strain by providing an alternate pathway to success or offering a method of retreating from alienation. In the process, structural strain affects the organization of both deviants and deviance.

Structural opportunities provide a second link between social organization, social structure, and deviance. Deviance requires resources and a society's social structure affects their supply. A type of deviance may be widespread in one society and nonexistent in another, simply because necessary resources are plentiful in the former and absent in the latter. By supplying the necessary human and material resources, social structure creates opportunities for deviance. Structural opportunities include technology and the availability of targets and customers.

A society's technology helps determine which material resources are available for deviance. The availability of particular tools facilitates some deviant acts. For example, most contemporary American homicides involve firearms (Morris and Hawkins, 1970). Of course, it is possible to kill another person without using a gun, but the availability of firearms makes it easier. Death is relatively unlikely to result from blows struck with fists, more common when a knife is used, and far more likely with guns. Inexpensive yet lethal firearms foster a high incidence of homicide. But technology does not always increase deviance. Crime rates dropped when cities began using street lights to reduce the dangers of traveling at night (Tobias, 1967). In some cases, a technological change may encourage one type of deviance and simultaneously disrupt another. For instance, the invention of electroplating (a process making it possible to coat base metals with silver or gold) made counterfeiting easier (because criminals could mint plated coins that looked real) but made burglary less profitable (because householders bought silverplated objects rather than the more valuable, solid silver pieces) (Tobias, 1967). A society's technology provides the context within which deviant operations occur; it makes some offenses simpler to commit and others more difficult.

Another structural opportunity involves the availability of targets. Deviant exploitation requires a target; other things being equal, exploitation will flourish when targets are plentiful and diminish when targets are rare. When a new class of targets emerges, exploitative acts increase. For example, Spanish shipments of gold and silver from their New World colonies to Spain during the late sixteenth and early seventeenth centuries provided incredibly rich targets, and pirates began patrolling the sea lanes in hopes of capturing treasure (Best, 1980). More recently, computerized financial transactions offer a target for programmers and others with knowledge about and access to computers. Specialists in computer crime are only beginning to identify the ways computerized records can be exploited (Parker, 1976). Some experts predict a cash-free economy, where all economic transactions involve electronic transfers of credit. This might reduce exploitative acts in which cash is taken from the target, while encouraging new forms of electronic theft. In deviant exploitation, opportunities reflect the availability of targets.

Illicit demand provides a parallel opportunity for deviant exchange. Typically, demand emerges when an existing good or service is forbidden and the authorities halt respectable trade in the commodity. For example, opiates were legal in the United States until the passage of the Harrison Act in 1914 (Musto, 1973). Addicts who formerly bought narcotics at pharmacies now needed new sources for drugs. Eventually, criminals who manufactured, imported, and distributed drugs to addicts met this demand (O'Donnell, 1967). A similar process occurred during Prohibition. Declaring alcohol illegal did not eliminate the huge demand; criminals took over supplying liquor. Usually, suppliers do not create the demand for an illicit good or service; demand precedes supply. The greater the demand for illicit goods or services, the greater the opportunities for deviant exchange.

Deviants organize to take advantage of the opportunities which become available to them. Expanding opportunities often lead to more sophisticated forms of deviant organization. More sophisticated organizational forms, such as mobs and formal organizations, usually are designed to produce high profits. Such profits are more certain when deviant operations can occur regularly. Deviants involved in exploitation need an ample supply of targets, while deviants involved in exchange require a steady demand for illicit goods or services. When opportunities are less certain, deviant operations become episodic, dependent on the availability of targets or customers. Limited opportunities for deviance cannot support sophisticated organizational forms, while ample opportunities encourage deviants to organize in more sophisticated forms and maximize their profits through efficient operations. The choice of an organizational form also occurs within the context of the society's technology. Deviants are limited by the materials available to them, and technological shifts may open new opportunities for successful deviant operations and more sophisticated organization. Structural opportunities affect the social organization of both deviants and deviance.

Social organization is linked to social structure in a third way—structural supports for deviance. Sociologists sometimes describe deviants as "outsiders" who stray across the society's moral boundaries; deviants may get help from deviant associates, but there is a strict division between deviants and respectable people. This picture is too simple; deviants are not totally cut off from respectable society. The two can be linked in various ways. One important link is structural supports, where deviants and respectable people make arrangements which serve to protect deviant operations from social control efforts. Structural supports include geographic control, service roles, and sponsorship.

Respectable people can support deviant activities by giving deviants effective control over a geographic region where they are safe from social control agents. The agents may stay away from the deviant area because it is outside their jurisdiction, too dangerous to enter, too far away, or unknown to them. The most familiar examples are urban: the nineteenth century English rookery—a neighborhood of thieves, prostitutes, and other deviants rarely entered by the police (Tobias, 1967); the red-light section informally set aside by the police as a vice district (Rose, 1974); or the safe city, where local authorities agree to leave fugitive criminals alone so long as they commit their crimes elsewhere. Other examples involve rural areas, such as forest or mountain camps where bandits and other outlaws hide (Hobsbawm, 1969). These examples suggest that deviants obtain geographic control by default, when the respectable society cannot enforce its norms throughout its domain. Geographic control often reflects the limited resources of social control agents. When agencies gain sufficient resources, they usually try to extend their control over these regions and suppress deviance.

Service roles involve more deliberate cooperation between respectable people and deviants. Here, persons supply deviants with services, making the deviant operations easier or safer. In some cases, the service role itself is deviant, for example, the fence or the proprietor of an after-hours club where thieves gather. In other cases, the service role is marginally respectable—hotel desk clerks who cooperate with prostitutes and the publishers of "dream books" (which translate dreams into numbers which can be bet in the numbers racket) engage in legitimate work which is intimately tied to deviance (Prus and Vassilakopoulos, 1979; McCall, 1963). Service roles involve a symbiotic relationship with deviants—service personnel make deviants' operations safer and easier, while they profit from the deviants' trade. One important service role is the corrupted official who lets deviants operate without interference. Service roles tend to emerge when deviants organize in relatively sophisticated forms. A profitable service usually requires the presence of many deviants, who typically organize as peers, mobs, or formal organzations. Moreover, deviants engaged in profitable operations—frequently carried out by sophisticated organizational forms—more often can afford services. Where deviants control a geographic region, many of the area's businesses perform service roles. For example, proprietors of skid row bars, hotels, and restaurants depend on tramps for their trade because respectable people avoid the district. Their businesses specialize in services the tramps need, such as supplying inexpensive food and lodging, extending credit, and cashing Social Security checks (Wallace, 1965). Service roles simplify the practical problems posed by deviance.

A third type of structural support is even more direct. When respectable persons find their interests coincide with those of deviants, they may sponsor the deviants' operations. Sponsorship can range from refusing to report the deviants' whereabouts to hiring them to carry out specific operations. One important form of sponsorship occurs when exploitative deviants limit their targets to individuals outside the sponsoring group. For example, bandits gain the support of peasants who believe that the bandits "rob from the rich and give to the poor" (Hobsbawm, 1959; 1969; O'Malley, 1979). Peasants support the bandits because they feel exploited by the rich. Their support includes refusing to cooperate with the authorities' antibandit efforts, hiding the bandits from officials, and giving them food and other supplies. On other occasions, powerful elements in a society may sponsor deviants' attacks on their enemies. For instance, seventeenth century colonial governors let Caribbean pirates use their colonies as bases, so long as the pirates attacked the shipping and towns of rival empires (Best, 1980). Thus, the English sponsored buccaneers' attacks on Spanish and French colonies. Similarly, government agencies and private industry sometimes hire members of organized crime families to carry out operations against their opponents (Pearce, 1976). Deviant exchange also has its sponsors. Profits from deviant sales attract respectable persons as investors. Protitution is supported by investors who own the brothels and hotels used by prostitutes and receive substantial returns from their properties (Rose, 1974; Sheehy, 1973). Sponsorship emerges where the deviants' interests coincide with those of some respectable persons.

Structural supports tend to develop when deviants organize in sophisticated forms. There are three reasons for this relationship. First, deviant operations conducted by sophisticated organizational forms tend to be more profitable, encouraging support because there is more money for purchases and a potentially higher return on supporters' investments. Second, more sophisticated forms often involve large numbers of deviants and this larger population's potential as a source of income attracts supporters. Third, the presence of supporting services makes deviance a safer enterprise; deviants can anticipate longer careers and more people enter deviance. As their numbers grow, their organization is likely to become more sophisticated as a means of coordinating operations. Structural supports, including geographic control, service roles, and sponsorship, foster deviance, even as social control agents try to eradicate it.

Finally, social structure, social organization, and deviance are linked through social control. Chapter 9 explored some effects of social control agents' ideologies, resources, and priorities and identified ways in which the definition of deviance affected the deviants' prospects. But social control can also be examined from the structural level of analysis. A society's social control apparatus reflects its social structure. Social structure influences the creation of social control agencies, the conditions under which they operate, their efficiency, and their goals.

The creation of social control agencies and the assignment of their resources and priorities reflects the perceived need for social control. When powerful groups within a society believe that additional social control is in their interest, they may create new agencies or bolster the resources of existing agents. For example, the French Revolution profoundly affected nineteenth century English perceptions of the need for social control (Silver, 1967). The English elite became increasingly concerned with the "dangerous classes"—the potentially revolutionary poor. In response, England created new social control agencies, including the first modern police force, rationally designed prisons and mental hospitals, and schools for poor children (Tobias, 1967). The presence of social control agents in a society reflects powerful members' perceptions of the threat of deviance.

The terms under which a social control agency operates locate it within the larger social structure; agents vary in their accountability and the restraints they face. In most cases, social control agents are accountable to the society's institutions, such as law, religion, or medicine, which restrain the agents' behavior to various degrees. At one extreme, agents have free rein—they are encouraged to apprehend deviants using any necessary means and their actions are rarely challenged. Such agents label large numbers of deviants but, lacking restraints, they also tend to label innocent persons (Currie, 1968). At the other extreme, social control agents are tightly supervised, required to observe elaborate rules of procedure. The society may refuse to ratify labels against persons apprehended in ways which violate those rules, and there may be special officials charged with supervising the activities of ordinary agents. Fewer deviants get labeled under these conditions, but more innocent persons avoid labeling.

Control agents' activities also vary in their efficiency. Efficiency depends upon social structure, as well as the deviants' tactics and resources, the social organization of the deviant transaction, and the agents' own resources. An increase in social control efforts usually raises the deviants' risks and eventually reduces the incidence of deviance. This involves two distinct processes. First, some control activities prevent deviance. For example, police patrols, the installation of burglar alarms, and public relations campaigns instructing people to lock their homes make it more difficult to commit a burglary, so that potential burglars choose other crimes or remain respectable. Second, social control may deter deviants. The spectacle of a deviant being apprehended, labeled, and sanctioned may (1) lead to that individual's reform (specific deterrence) and (2) discourage others from committing deviant acts (general deterrence). But, while increased social control efforts can raise the deviants' risks, it is difficult, perhaps impossible, to eliminate deviance. Some people remain willing to assume the risks; the more committed the deviant, the less effect social control activities are likely to have on his or her actions. Moreover, the costs of social control increase faster than the benefits from reduced deviance; a few simple control practices may discourage inexperienced deviants, but only expensive, elaborate efforts can hope to deter the skilled, committed offender. The benefits of reduced deviance may be counterbalanced by costs, not only in monetary terms, but in a loss of freedom.

Giving social control agents extraordinary powers may reduce the amount of deviance, but also allows those agents to interfere in the lives of all people.

Because agents rarely have the resources necessary to eradicate deviance, they may modify their goals and compromise with the deviants. Compromise sometimes involves corruption, where deviants pay social control agents to leave them alone, but it need not involve a bribe. Other bargains can be struck. In return for noninterference, agents may demand cooperation from deviants. Agents may leave some offenders alone because they supply information about other deviants' operations. Or agents may choose to regulate some types of deviance. Rather than try to eradicate deviance—a policy which drives offenders underground where they cannot be supervised—agents may informally permit deviant operations in return for the deviants' cooperation in keeping their deviance within certain limits. Thus, police may ignore a brothel so long as it is orderly—the customers are not robbed and the prostitutes call the police if trouble develops. Some agencies set aside particular areas, such as skid rows or red-light districts, where enforcement will be less strict in order to isolate deviance. Compromises by control agents reflect their priorities. They may be willing to coexist with deviance of low priority but less willing to compromise over high-priority offenses. Individual deviance and deviant exchange often lead to compromises because they are seen as less serious, of lower priority, while deviant exploitation rarely leads to compromise.

Social structure influences the creation of social control agencies and the agents' resources and priorities. It also provides the institutional context for supervising agents' actions, thereby affecting their efficiency and goals. Social organization mediates these structural effects. In general, the efficiency of social control increases with the complexity of the deviant transaction. The difficulties of enforcing rules against individual deviance and deviant exchange make control efforts less efficient. Similarly, control agents are more likely to compromise with deviants involved in these transactions, both because they are harder to apprehend and because their offenses are of lower priority. The social organization of deviants also affects social control efforts. As the sophistication of the deviants' organizational form increases, agents' operations become less efficient because the deviants command more resources, and compromise becomes more likely because the deviants can corrupt the agents.

In summary, a society's social structure affects all transactions among its members, including deviant transactions. Social structure provides the context for social interaction. In the case of deviant transactions, several processes are at work. Structural strain leads individuals to enter deviance as a response to the frustrations of their social positions. Structural opportunities and structural supports shape deviants' operations. At the same time, social control efforts constrain deviants' activities by affecting the risks of apprehension and sanctioning. Social organization mediates these structural effects. The social organization of deviants gives deviant actors a network of associates who can mobilize their resources to help one another operate within the bounds posed by social structure. Similarly, the social organization of deviance affects the practical problems faced by deviants; different transactions pose different risks and require different tactics for success. Just as social organization provides the context for deviant careers, social structure provides the context for social organization.

UNDERSTANDING DEVIANCE AND SOCIAL ORGANIZATION

This book has attempted to analyze deviance from a neglected level of analysis—social organization. The preceding chapters developed a social organizational perspective for understanding deviance. This chapter demonstrated that social organization need not be a separate level of analysis—it can be integrated with social psychological and social structural levels. Some of the arguments advanced here are speculative, drawing upon a few existing studies of deviance. But more research is needed. Specifically, six issues merit further study.

First, more research is needed about the social organization of deviants and its consequences. Descriptions of deviants should examine their patterns of relationships. Some deviants may organize in forms other than those identified, and there may be important organizational variation within a particular form. In addition, studies directly comparing the consequences of organizational differences could test the propositions presented in chapter 4.

Second, more research about the social organization of deviance and its consequences is needed. More studies of deviant transactions should consider the patterns of relationships among the participants. The scheme of classification developed in this book may not fit all deviant acts, or there may be additional subtypes within an organizational form. Further, comparisons of different organizational forms of deviant transactions are needed to evaluate the accuracy of chapter 9's propositions.

Third, research is needed to explore the interrelationships between the social organization of deviants and the social organization of deviance. Because every deviant act involves one or more deviant actors, the social organization of deviance and the social organization of deviants operate simultaneously. Deviants' contacts with their associates influence the deviant transaction, and the character of that transaction affects the deviants' social network. The nature of these interrelationships needs additional study.

Fourth, research about social organization's impact on deviants' social psychology is needed. This chapter pointed to the combined influence of social organization and social psychology on the deviant career. Additional studies of deviant careers are needed, as well as research about other topics where social organization and social psychology intersect. The deviant experience must be understood within the context of the deviant's relationships with other people.

Fifth, research is needed about the links between social structure, social organization, and deviance. This chapter identified four topics—structural strain, structural opportunities, structural supports, and social control—where these interrelationships become important. Each deserves detailed attention, and additional structural topics, such as the development and evolution of organizational forms, also merit study. When focusing on deviance and social organization, it is important to remember that social structure provides the context for all social action, including deviance.

These five research topics suggest that the social organizational analysis of deviance should not stand apart from other research in the field. Rather, social organizational analysis supplements social psychological and social structural views. The sixth issue which deserves more research extends the social organizational framework to the analysis of respectability. Deviants are distinguished from respectable people because they break rules, but in most other respects, deviants and respectable people resemble each other. Chapter 4 drew an analogy between the forms of organization of deviants and respectable people, and chapter 9 drew a parallel analogy between deviant and respectable transactions. Deviance is worth studying in its own right, but the analysis of deviance and social organization also offers insights about the social life of all people.

REFERENCES

ABRAHAMSEN, DAVID. 1960. *The Psychology of Crime*. New York: Columbia University Press.

ACHILLES, NANCY. 1967. "The Development of the Homosexual Bar as an Institution." Pp. 228-44 in John H. Gagnon and William Simon (eds.), *Sexual Deviance*. New York: Harper & Row, Pub.

AGAR, MICHAEL. 1973. *Ripping and Running*. New York: Seminar Press.

AKERS, RONALD L. 1973. *Deviant Behavior*. Belmont, CA: Wadsworth.

——, ROBERT L. BURGESS AND WELDON T. JOHNSON. 1968. "Opiate Use, Addiction, and Relapse." *Social Problems* 15:459-69.

ALBINI, JOSEPH L. 1971. *The American Mafia*. New York: Appleton-Century-Crofts.

ALIX, ERNEST KAHLAR. 1978. *Ransom Kidnapping in America, 1874-1974*. Carbondale, Ill.: Southern Illinois University Press.

ALLEN, JOHN. 1977. *Assault with a Deadly Weapon*. Edited by Dianne Hall Kelley and Philip Heymann. New York: Pantheon Books.

American Psychiatric Association, Committee on Nomenclature and Statistics. 1968. *Diagnostic and Statistical Manual of Mental Disorders*. 2nd ed. Washington, D.C.: American Psychiatric Association.

AMIR, MENACHEM. 1971. *Patterns in Forcible Rape*. Chicago: University of Chicago Press.

ANDENAES, JOHANNES. 1974. *Punishment and Deterrence*. Ann Arbor: University of Michigan Press.

ANDERSON, ELIJAH. 1978. *A Place on the Corner*. Chicago: University of Chicago Press.

ANDERSON, ROBERT T. 1965. "From Mafia to Cosa Nostra." *American Journal of Sociology* 71:302-10.

262

ATHENS, LONNIE H. 1980. *Violent Criminal Acts and Actors*. London: Routledge & Kegan Paul.

AUBERT, VILHELM. 1965. *The Hidden Society*. Totowa, N.J.: Bedminster.

_____ AND SHELDON MESSINGER. 1958. "The Criminal and the Sick." *Inquiry* 1:137-60.

BACON, SELDON D. 1962. "Alcohol and Complex Society." Pp. 78-93 in David J. Pittman and Charles R. Synder (eds.), *Society, Culture and Drinking Patterns*. New York: John Wiley.

BAHR, HOWARD M. 1973. *Skid Row*. New York: Oxford University Press.

BALDWIN, DAVID A. 1976. "Bargaining with Airline Hijackers." Pp. 404-29 in I. William Zartman (ed.), *The 50% Solution*. Garden City, NY: Anchor.

BANDURA, ALBERT. 1969. *Principles of Behavior Modification*. New York: Holt, Rinehart, & Winston.

BARTELL, GILBERT D. 1971. *Group Sex*. New York: Peter H. Wyden.

BAUMANN, CAROL EDLER. 1973. *The Diplomatic Kidnappings*. The Hague, Netherlands: Martinus Nijhoff.

BECKER, HOWARD S. 1963. *Outsiders*. New York: Free Press.

_____ . 1967. "History, Culture and Subjective Experience." *Journal of Health and Social Behavior* 8:163-76.

_____ AND ANSELM L. STRAUSS. 1956. "Careers, Personality, and Adult Socialization." *American Journal of Sociology* 62:253-63.

BEHN, NOEL. 1977. *Big Stick-up at Brink's*. New York: Putnam's.

BELL, ALAN P. AND MARTIN S. WEINBERG. 1978. *Homosexualities*. New York: Simon & Schuster.

BELL, DANIEL. 1960. *The End of Ideology*. New York: Free Press.

BENNETT, GORDON. 1977. "China's Mass Campaigns and Social Control." Pp. 121-39 in Amy A. Wilson, Sidney L. Greenblatt, and Richard W. Wilson (eds.), *Deviance and Social Control in Chinese Society*. New York: Praeger.

BERGER, PETER L. AND THOMAS LUCKMANN. 1966. *The Social Construction of Reality*. Garden City, NY: Anchor.

BEST, JOEL. 1979. "Economic Interests and the Vindication of Deviance." *Sociological Quarterly* 20:171-82.

_____ . 1980. "Licensed to Steal." Pp. 96-109 in Robert W. Love, Jr. (ed.), *Changing Interpretations and New Sources in Naval History*. New York: Garland.

_____ . 1982. "Crime as Strategic Interaction." *Urban Life* 11: in press.

BITTNER, EGON. 1970. *The Functions of the Police in Modern Society*. Rockville, MD: National Institute of Mental Health.

BLACK, DONALD J. 1976. *The Behavior of Law*. New York: Academic Press.

_____ AND ALBERT J. REISS, JR. 1970. "Police Control of Juveniles." *American Sociological Review* 35:63-77.

BLAU, PETER M. 1964. *Exchange and Power in Social Life*. New York: John Wiley.

_____ . 1974. *On the Nature of Organizations*. New York: John Wiley.

_____ AND W. RICHARD SCOTT. 1962. *Formal Organizations*. San Francisco: Chandler.

BLOCK, ALAN. 1980. *East Side-West Side*. Cardiff, Wales: University College Cardiff Press.

BLOK, ANTON. 1974. *The Mafia of a Sicilian Village, 1860-1960*. New York: Harper & Row, Pub.

BLUM, ALAN F. 1970. "The Sociology of Mental Illness." Pp. 31-60 in Jack D. Douglas (ed.), *Deviance and Respectability*. New York: Basic Books.

BLUMER, HERBERT. 1962. "Society as Symbolic Interaction." Pp. 179-92 in Arnold M. Rose (ed.), *Human Behavior and Social Processes*. Boston: Houghton Mifflin.

_____ . 1967. *The World of Youthful Drug Use*. Berkeley: University of California.

BOHANNON, PAUL. 1960. *African Homicide and Suicide*. Princeton, N.J.: Princeton University Press.

BRECHER, EDWARD M. 1972. *Licit and Illicit Drugs*. Mt. Vernon, NY: Consumers Union.

BREED, WARREN. 1972. "Five Components of a Basic Suicide Syndrome." *Life-Threatening Behavior* 2:3-25.

BRETON, RAYMOND. 1964. "Institutional Completeness of Ethnic Communities and the Personal Relations of Immigrants." *American Journal of Sociology* 70:193-205.

BRIGGS, JEAN A. 1979. "For Whom Does the Bell Toll?" *Forbes* 123 (June 25):33-36.

BRYAN, JAMES H. 1965. "Apprenticeships in Prostitution." *Social Problems* 12:287-97.

———. 1966. "Occupational Ideologies and Individual Attitudes of Call Girls." *Social Problems* 13:441-50.

BUCKNER, H. TAYLOR. 1970. "The Transvestic Career Path." *Psychiatry* 33:381-89.

CAHALAN, DON AND ROBIN ROOM. 1974. *Problem Drinking Among American Men*. New Brunswick, N.J.: Rutgers Center of Alcohol Studies.

CAMERON, MARY OWEN. 1964. *The Booster and the Snitch*. New York: Free Press.

CAPLOW, THEODORE. 1964. *Principles of Organization*. New York: Harcourt Brace Jovanovich, Inc.

CAREY, JAMES T. 1968. *The College Drug Scene*. Englewood Cliffs, NJ: Prentice-Hall.

CAVAN, SHERRI. 1972. *Hippies of the Haight*. St. Louis: New Critics.

CHAFETZ, MORRIS E. AND HAROLD W. DEMONE, JR. 1962. *Alcoholism and Society*. New York: Oxford University Press.

CHAMBLISS, WILLIAM J. 1972. *Box Man*. New York: Harper & Row, Pub.

———. 1973. "The Saints and the Roughnecks." *Society* 11:24-31.

———. 1976. "Functional and Conflict Theories of Crime." Pp. 1-28 in William J. Chambliss and Milton Mankoff (eds.), *Whose Law, What Order*. New York: John Wiley.

CHAPPELL, DUNCAN AND MARILYN WALSH. 1978. "No Questions Asked." Pp. 184-90 in Peter Wickman and Phillip Whitten (eds.), *Readings in Criminology*. Lexington, MA: Heath.

CLAUSEN, JOHN A. 1971a. "Drug Use." Pp. 185-227 in Robert K. Merton and Robert Nisbet (eds.), *Contemporary Social Problems*. 3rd ed. New York: Harcourt Brace Jovanovich, Inc.

———. 1971b. "Mental Disorders." Pp. 29-87 in Robert K. Merton and Robert Nisbet (eds.), *Contemporary Social Problems*. 3rd ed. New York: Harcourt Brace Jovanovich, Inc.

CLINARD, MARSHALL B. AND ROBERT F. MEIER. 1979. *Sociology of Deviant Behavior*. 5th ed. New York: Holt, Rinehart & Winston.

——— AND RICHARD QUINNEY. 1973. *Criminal Behavior Systems*. 2nd ed. New York: Holt, Rinehart Winston.

CLOWARD, RICHARD A. AND LLOYD E. OHLIN. 1960. *Delinquency and Opportunity*. New York: Free Press.

CLUTTERBUCK, RICHARD. 1978. *Kidnap and Ransom*. London: Faber and Faber.

COHEN, ALBERT K. 1955. *Delinquent Boys*. New York: Free Press.

———. 1965. "The Sociology of the Deviant Act." *American Sociological Review* 30:5-14.

———. 1966. *Deviance and Control*. Englewood Cliffs, NJ: Prentice-Hall.

———. 1967. "Middle-Class Delinquency and the Social Structure." Pp. 203-7 in Edmund W. Vaz (ed.), *Middle-Class Juvenile Delinquency*. New York: Harper & Row, Pub.

COHEN, BERNARD. 1980. *Deviant Street Networks*. Lexington, MA: Lexington.

COHEN, STANLEY. 1972. *Folk Devils and Moral Panics*. St. Albans, Herts.: Paladin.

COLEMAN, JAMES C. 1964. *Abnormal Psychology and Modern Life*. 3rd ed. Glencoe, IL: Scott, Foresman.

COLLINS, FREDERICK L. 1962. *The FBI in Peace and War*. New York: Putnam's.

Commission on Obscenity and Pornography. 1970. *Report*. Washington: U.S. Government Printing Office.

CONKLIN, JOHN E. 1972. *Robbery and the Criminal Justice System*. Philadelphia: Lippincott.

_____. 1975. *The Impact of Crime*. New York: Macmillan.

_____. 1977. *"Illegal but Not Criminal"*. Englewood Cliffs, NJ: Prentice-Hall.

CONNELL, K. H. 1968. *Irish Peasant Society*. Oxford: Clarendon Press.

CONNOR, WALTER D. 1972a. *Deviance in Soviet Society*. New York: Columbia University Press.

_____. 1972b. "The Manufacture of Deviance." *American Sociological Review* 37:403-13.

CONRAD, PETER. 1975. "The Discovery of Hyperkinesis." *Social Problems* 23:12-21.

CORZINE, JAY AND RICHARD KIRBY. 1977. "Cruising the Truckers." *Urban Life* 6:171-92.

COSER, LEWIS A. 1962. "Some Functions of Deviant Behavior and Normative Flexibility." *American Journal of Sociology* 68:172-81.

CRESSEY, DONALD R. 1953. *Other People's Money*. Glencoe, IL: Free Press.

_____. 1955. "Changing Criminals." *American Journal of Sociology* 61:116-20.

_____. 1962. "Role Theory, Differential Association, and Compulsive Crimes." Pp. 443-67 in Arnold M. Rose (ed.), *Human Behavior and Social Processes*. Boston: Houghton Mifflin.

_____. 1969. *Theft of the Nation*. New York: Harper & Row, Pub.

_____. 1972. *Criminal Organization*. New York: Harper & Row, Pub.

CURRIE, ELLIOTT P. 1968. "Crimes Without Criminals." *Law and Society Review* 3:7-32.

DANK, BARRY M. 1971. "Coming Out in the Gay World." *Psychiatry* 34:180-97.

DAUDISTEL, HOWARD C., WILLIAM B. SANDERS AND DAVID F. LUCKENBILL. 1979. *Criminal Justice*. New York: Holt, Rinehart & Winston.

DAVID, PEDRO R. 1974. *The World of the Burglar*. Albuquerque: University of New Mexico Press.

DAVIS, FRED. 1961. "Deviance Disavowal." *Social Problems* 9:120-32.

DAVIS, NANETTE J. 1974. "The Abortion Consumer." *Urban Life and Culture* 2:432-59.

_____. 1978. "Prostitution." Pp. 195-222 in James M. Henslin and Edward Sagarin (eds.), *The Sociology of Sex*. rev. ed. New York: Schocken.

DAWLEY, DAVID. 1973. *A Nation of Lords*. Garden City, NY: Anchor.

DEBAUN, EVERETT. 1950. "The Heist." *Harpers* 200 (February):69-77.

DECKER, JOHN F. 1979. *Prostitution*. Littleton, CO: Rothman.

DEFLEUR, LOIS, 1975. "Biasing Influences on Drug Arrest Records." *American Sociological Review* 40:88-103.

DELAMATER, JOHN. 1968. "On the Nature of Deviance." *Social Forces* 46:445-55.

DELPH, EDWARD WILLIAM. 1978. *The Silent Community*. Beverly Hills, CA.: Sage.

DENZIN, NORMAN K. 1970. "Rules of Conduct in the Study of Deviant Behavior." Pp. 62-94 in George J. McCall et al. (eds.), *Social Relationships*. Chicago: Aldine.

DIRKS, RAYMOND L. AND LEONARD GROSS. 1974. *The Great Wall Street Scandal*. New York: McGraw-Hill.

DOHRENWEND, BRUCE P. AND EDWIN CHIN-SHONG. 1967. "Social Status and Attitudes toward Psychological Disorder." *American Sociological Review* 32:417-33.

DOUGLAS, JACK D. 1967. *The Social Meanings of Suicide*. Princeton, N.J.: Princeton University Press.

DUNHAM, H. WARREN AND S. KIRSON WEINBERG. 1960. *The Culture of the State Mental Hospital.* Detroit: Wayne State University Press.

DURKHEIM, EMILE. 1938. *The Rules of the Sociological Method.* 8th ed. Chicago: University of Chicago Press.

———. 1951. *Suicide.* New York: Free Press.

DUSTER, TROY. 1970. *The Legislation of Morality.* New York: Free Press.

EDGERTON, ROBERT B. 1979. *Alone Together.* Berkeley, CA.: University of California Press.

EINSTADTER, WERNER J. 1969. "The Social Organization of Armed Robbery." *Social Problems* 17:64-83.

ELLIS, AYTOUN. 1956. *The Penny Universities.* London: Secker and Warburg.

ERICKSON, MAYNARD. 1971. "The Group Context of Delinquent Behavior." *Social Problems* 19:114-29.

ERIKSON, KAI T. 1966. *Wayward Puritans.* New York: John Wiley.

ETZIONI, AMITAI. 1964. *Modern Organizations.* Englewood Cliffs, NJ: Prentice-Hall.

FANG, BETTY. 1976. "Swinging." *Journal of Sex Research* 12:220-37.

FARBER, MAURICE L. 1968. *Theory of Suicide.* New York: Funk and Wagnalls.

FARBEROW, NORMAN L. 1977. "Suicide." Pp. 503-70 in Edward Sagarin and Fred Montanino (eds.), *Deviants.* Morristown, NJ: General Learning.

FARINA, AMERIGO AND KENNETH RING. 1965. "The Influence of Perceived Mental Illness on Interpersonal Relations." *Journal of Abnormal Psychology* 70:47-51.

Federal Bureau of Investigation. 1979. *Uniform Crime Reports for United States—1978.* Washington: U.S. Government Printing Office.

FEIDEN, DOUG. 1980. *The $10,000,000 Getaway.* New York: Jove.

FELDMAN, HARVEY W. 1968. "Ideological Supports to Becoming and Remaining a Heroin Addict." *Journal of Health and Social Behavior* 9:131-39.

FOOTE, CALEB. 1956. "Vagrancy-Type Law and Its Administration." *University of Pennsylvania Law Review* 104:603-50.

GARDINER, JOHN A. 1970. *The Politics of Corruption.* New York: Russell Sage.

GEIS, GILBERT. 1967. "White Collar Crime." Pp. 139-50 in Marshall B. Clinard and Richard Quinney (eds.), *Criminal Behavior Systems.* New York: Holt, Rinehart & Winston.

GIBBONS, DON C. 1969. "Crime and Punishment." *Social Forces* 47:391-97.

———. 1977. *Society, Crime, and Criminal Careers.* 3rd ed. Englewood Cliffs, NJ: Prentice-Hall.

———. 1979. *The Criminological Enterprise.* Englewood Cliffs, N.J.: Prentice-Hall.

——— AND JOSEPH F. JONES. 1975. *The Study of Deviance.* Englewood Cliffs, N.J.: Prentice-Hall.

GIBBS, JACK P. 1975. *Crime, Punishment and Deterrence.* New York: Elsevier North-Holland.

GINSBURG, KENNETH N. 1967. "The 'Meat-Rack.' " *American Journal of Psychotherapy* 2:170-85.

GLASER, BARNEY G. (ED.). 1968. *Organizational Careers.* Chicago: Aldine.

——— AND ANSELM L. STRAUSS. 1965. *Awareness of Dying.* Chicago: Aldine.

———. 1967. *The Discovery of Grounded Theory.* Chicago: Aldine.

GODDARD, DONALD. 1978. *Easy Money.* New York: Popular Library.

GODDARD, HENRY H. 1914. *Feeblemindedness.* New York: Macmillan.

GOFFMAN, ERVING. 1959. *The Presentation of Self in Everyday Life.* Garden City, NY: Anchor.

———. 1961. *Asylums.* Garden City, NY: Anchor.

———. 1963a. *Behavior in Public Places.* New York: Free Press.

———. 1963b. *Stigma.* Englewood Cliffs, NJ: Prentice-Hall.

———. 1967. *Interaction Ritual.* Garden City, NY: Anchor.

_____. 1969. *Strategic Interaction*. Philadelphia: University of Pennylvania Press.

_____. 1971. *Relations in Public*. New York: Harper & Row, Pub.

_____. 1974. *Frame Analysis,* New York: Harper & Row, Pub.

GOLDSTEIN, PAUL J. 1979. *Prostitution and Drugs*. Lexington, MA: Lexington.

GOODE, ERICH. 1970. *The Marijuana Smokers*. New York: Basic Books.

GOODE, WILLIAM J. 1969. "Violence Among Intimates." Pp. 941-77 in Donald J. Mulvihill and Melvin M. Tumin (eds.), *Crimes of Violence*. Washington: U.S. Government Printing Office.

GOVE, WALTER R. 1970. "Societal Reaction as an Explanation of Mental Illness." *American Sociological Review* 35:873-84.

_____. 1975. "Labelling and Mental Illness." Pp. 35-81 in Walter R. Gove (ed.), *The Labelling of Deviance*. New York: John Wiley.

GRAY, DIANA. 1973. "Turning Out." *Urban Life and Culture* 1:401-25.

GREEN, MARK J., BEVERLY C. MOORE, JR. AND BRUCE WASSERSTEIN. 1972. *The Closed Enterprise System*. New York: Grossman.

GREEN, TIMOTHY. 1969. *The Smugglers*. New York: Walker.

GREENBLATT, SIDNEY LEONARD. 1977. "Campaigns and the Manufacture of Deviance in Chinese Society." Pp. 82-120 in Amy A. Wilson, Sidney L. Greenblatt, and Richard W. Wilson (eds.), *Deviance and Social Control in Chinese Society*. New York: Praeger.

GREENWALD, HAROLD. 1970. *The Elegant Prostitute*. New York: Walker.

GURFEIN, MURRAY I. 1934. "Racketeering." Pp. 45-49 in *Encyclopedia of the Social Sciences*, Volume 13. New York: Macmillan.

GUSFIELD, JOSEPH R. 1967. "Moral Passage." *Social Problems* 15:175-88.

HALL, JEROME. 1952. *Theft, Law and Society*. 2nd ed. Indianapolis: Bobbs-Merrill.

HAMILTON, LAWRENCE C. 1976. "Political Kidnapping." Unpublished manuscript.

HARRIS, MERVYN. 1974. *The Dilly Boys*. Rockville, MD: New Perspectives.

HARRY, JOSEPH AND WILLIAM B. DEVALL. 1978. *The Social Organization of Gay Males*. New York: Praeger.

HARTUNG, FRANK E. 1965. *Crime, Law and Society*. Detroit: Wayne State University Press.

HAY, DOUGLAS. 1975. "Property, Authority and the Criminal Law." Pp. 17-63 in Douglas Hay, et al., *Albion's Fatal Tree*. New York: Pantheon.

HENRY, ANDREW F. AND JAMES F. SHORT, JR. 1954. *Suicide and Homicide*. Glencoe, IL: Free Press.

HENSLIN, JAMES M. 1967. "Craps and Magic." *American Journal of Sociology* 73:316-30.

HEPBURN, JOHN R. 1973. "Violent Behavior in Interpersonal Relationships." *Sociological Quarterly* 14:419-29.

HEPWORTH, MIKE. 1975. *Blackmail*. London: Routledge & Kegan Paul.

HESSLER, RICHARD M. 1974. "Junkies in White." Pp. 146-53 in Clifton D. Bryant (ed.), *Deviant Behavior*. Chicago: Rand McNally.

HEYL, BARBARA SHERMAN. 1979. *The Madam as Entrepreneur*. New Brunswick, NJ: Transaction.

HILLERY, GEORGE A., JR. 1968. *Communal Organizations*. Chicago: University of Chicago Press.

HINDELANG, MICHAEL J. 1971. "Bookies and Bookmaking." *Crime and Delinquency* 17:245-55.

HOBSBAWM, E. J. 1959. *Primitive Rebels*. New York: W. W. Norton & Co., Inc.

_____. 1969. *Bandits*. New York: Delacorte.

HOENIG, GARY. 1975. *Reaper*. Indianapolis: Bobbs-Merrill.

HOLMSTROM, LYNDA LYTLE AND ANN WOLBERT BURGESS. 1979. "Rapists' Talk." *Deviant Behavior* 1:101-25.

HOMANS, GEORGE C. 1974. *Social Behavior.* rev. ed. New York: Harcourt Brace Jovanovich, Inc.

HONG, LAWRENCE, K., WILLIAM DARROUGH AND ROBERT DUFF. 1975. "The Sensuous Rip-Off." *Urban Life and Culture.* 3:364-70.

HOOKER, EVELYN. 1967. "The Homosexual Community." Pp. 167-84 in John H. Gagnon and William Simon (eds.), *Sexual Deviance.* New York: Harper & Row, Pub.

HOROWITZ, RUTH AND GARY SCHWARTZ. 1974. "Honor, Normative Ambiguity and Gang Violence." *American Sociological Review* 39:238-51.

HUMPHREYS, LAUD. 1970. *Tearoom Trade.* Chicago: Aldine.

———. 1972. *Out of the Closets.* Englewood Cliffs, NJ: Prentice-Hall.

HUNT, MORTON. 1969. *The Affair.* New York: World Pub. Co.

HUTCHISON, ROBERT A. 1974. *Vesco.* New York: Praeger.

IANNI, FRANCIS A. J. 1972. *A Family Business.* New York: Russell Sage.

———. 1974. *Black Mafia.* New York: Simon & Schuster.

INCIARDI, JAMES A. 1970. "The Adult Firesetter." *Criminology* 8:145-55.

———. 1975. *Careers in Crime.* Chicago: Rand McNally.

———. 1977. "In Search of the Class Cannon." Pp. 55-77 in Robert S. Weppner (ed.), *Street Ethnography.* Beverly Hills, CA.: Sage.

IRWIN, JOHN. 1970. *The Felon.* Englewood Cliffs, NJ: Prentice-Hall.

———. 1977. *Scenes.* Beverly Hills, Ca.: Sage.

JACKSON, BRUCE. 1972. *Outside the Law.* New Brunswick, N.J.: Transaction.

JACKSON, JOAN K. AND RALPH CONNOR. 1953. "The Skid Row Alcoholic." *Quarterly Journal of Studies on Alcohol* 14:468-86.

JACOBS, JERRY. 1967. "A Phenomenological Study of Suicide Notes." *Social Problems* 15:60-72.

———. 1971. *Adolescent Suicide.* New York: John Wiley.

JANSYN, LEON R., JR. 1966. "Solidarity and Delinquency in a Street Corner Group." *American Sociological Review* 31:600-614.

JENKINS, BRIAN, JANERA JOHNSON AND DAVID RONFELDT. 1977. "Numbered Lives." Rand Corporation, P-5905.

JOHNSON, ROBBIE DAVIS. 1973. "Folklore and Women." *Journal of American Folklore* 86:211-24.

KAMEL, G. W. LEVI. 1980. "Leathersex." *Deviant Behavior* 1:171-91.

KARP, DAVID A. 1973. "Hiding in Pornographic Bookstores." *Urban Life and Culture* 1:427-51.

KATZ, JACK. 1977. "Cover-up and Collective Integrity." *Social Problems* 25:3-17.

———. 1979. "Concerted Ignorance." *Urban Life* 8:195-316.

KATZ, JONATHAN (ED.). 1976. *Gay American History.* New York: Thomas Y. Crowell.

KEISER, R. LINCOLN. 1969. *The Vice Lords.* New York: Holt, Rinehart & Winston.

KITSUSE, JOHN I. 1962. "Societal Reaction to Deviant Behavior." *Social Problems* 9:247-56.

KLEIN, JOHN F. AND ARTHUR MONTAGUE. 1977. *Check Forgers.* Lexington, MA: Lexington.

KLOCKARS, CARL B. 1975. *The Professional Fence.* New York: Free Press.

KOBLER, ARTHUR L. AND EZRA STOTLAND. 1964. *The End of Hope.* Glencoe, IL: Free Press

KORN, RICHARD R. AND LLOYD W. MCCORKLE. 1959. *Criminology and Penology.* New York: Holt, Rinehart & Winston.

LAFREE, GARY D. 1980. "The Effect of Sexual Stratification by Race on Official Reactions to Rape." *American Sociological Review* 45:842-54.

LAING, R. D. 1967. *The Politics of Experience.* New York: Ballantine.

_____. AND A. ESTERSON. 1964. *Sanity, Madness and the Family.* London: Tavistock.

LAMY, RICHARD E. 1966. "Social Consequences of Mental Illness." *Journal of Consulting Psychology* 30:450-55.

LANDESCO, JOHN. 1968. *Organized Crime in Chicago.* Chicago: University of Chicago Press.

LANGER, JOHN. 1977. "Drug Entrepreneurs and Dealing Culture." *Social Problems* 24:377-86.

LEDERER, LAURA (ED.). 1980. *Take Back the Night.* New York: Morrow.

LEE, JOHN ALAN. 1979. "The Gay Connection." *Urban Life* 8:175-98.

LEE, NANCY HOWELL. 1969. *The Search for an Abortionist.* Chicago: University of Chicago Press.

LEJEUNE, ROBERT. 1977. "The Management of a Mugging." *Urban Life* 6:123-48.

LEMASTERS, E. E. 1975. *Blue-Collar Aristocrats.* Madison: University of Wisconsin Press.

LEMERT, EDWIN M. 1967. *Human Deviance, Social Problems, and Social Control.* Englewood Cliffs, NJ: Prentice-Hall.

LERMAN, PAUL. 1967. "Gangs, Networks, and Subcultural Delinquency." *American Journal of Sociology* 73:63-72.

LESIEUR, HENRY R. 1977. *The Chase.* Garden City, NY: Anchor.

LETKEMANN, PETER. 1973. *Crime as Work.* Englewood Cliffs, NJ: Prentice-Hall.

LEWIS, GEORGE H. 1980. "Social Groupings in Organized Crime." *Deviant Behavior* 1:129-43.

LEZNOFF, MAURICE AND WILLIAM A. WESTLEY. 1956. "The Homosexual Community." *Social Problems* 3:257-63.

LIAZOS, ALEXANDER. 1972. "The Poverty of the Sociology of Deviance." *Social Problems* 20:103-20.

LINDBERGH, ANNE MORROW. 1973. *Hour of Gold, Hour of Lead.* New York: Harcourt Brace Jovanovich, Inc.

LINSKY, ARNOLD S. 1970. "The Changing Public Views of Alcoholism" *Quarterly Journal of Studies on Alcohol* 32:692-704.

LIVINGSTON, JAY. 1974. *Compulsive Gamblers.* New York: Harper & Row, Pub.

LLOYD, ROBIN. 1976. *For Money or Love.* New York: Vanguard.

LOFLAND, JOHN. 1969. *Deviance and Identity.* Englewood Cliffs, NJ: Prentice-Hall.

LOMBROSO, CESARE. 1918. *Crime.* Boston: Little, Brown.

LONEY, MARTIN. 1973. "Social Control in Cuba." Pp. 42-60 in Ian Taylor and Laurie Taylor (eds.), *Politics and Deviance.* New York: Penguin.

LUCKENBILL, DAVID F. 1977. "Criminal Homicide as a Situated Transaction." *Social Problems* 25:176-86.

_____. 1980. "Patterns of Force in Robbery." *Deviant Behavior* 1:361-78.

_____. 1981. "Generating Compliance." *Urban Life* 10:25-46.

LUNDSGAARDE, HENRY P. 1977. *Murder in Space City.* New York: Oxford University Press.

LYMAN, STANFORD M. AND MARVIN B. SCOTT. 1970. *A Sociology of the Absurd.* New York: Appleton-Century-Crofts.

MACANDREW, CRAIG AND ROBERT B. EDGERTON. 1969. *Drunken Comportment.* Chicago: Aldine.

MCCAGHY, CHARLES H. 1976. *Deviant Behavior* New York: Macmillan.

_____ AND PEGGY C. GIORDANO. 1977. "Auto Theft." *Criminology* 15:367-85.

MCCALL, GEORGE J. 1963. "Symbiosis." *Social Problems* 10:361-71.

MCINTOSH, MARY. 1971. "Changes in the Organization of Thieving." Pp. 98-135 in Stanley Cohen (ed.), *Images of Deviance.* New York: Penguin.

_____. 1973. "The Growth of Racketeering." *Economy and Society* 2:35-60.

———. 1975. *The Organisation of Crime*. London: Macmillan.

MCPHERSON, JAMES ALAN. 1969. "Chicago's Blackstone Rangers." *Atlantic* 223: Part 1 (May):74-84: Part 2 (June):92-100.

MANNING, PETER K. 1977. *Police Work*. Cambridge, MA.: MIT Press.

MARIS, RONALD. 1969. *Social Forces in Urban Suicide*. Homewood, IL: Dorsey.

MARTINDALE, DON. 1966. *Institutions, Organizations, and Mass Society*. Boston: Houghton Mifflin.

MATZA, DAVID. 1964. *Delinquency and Drift*. New York: John Wiley.

———. 1969. *Becoming Deviant*. Englewood Cliffs, NJ: Prentice-Hall.

MAURER, DAVID W. 1939. "Prostitutes and Criminal Argots." *American Journal of Sociology* 44:346-50.

———. 1964. *Whiz Mob*. New Haven, CT.: College and University Press.

———. 1974. *The American Confidence Man*. Springfield, IL: Charles C Thomas.

MAXA, RUDY. 1977. *Dare to Be Great*. New York: Morrow.

MEAD, GEORGE H. 1969. "The Psychology of Punitive Justice." Pp. 578-84 in Lewis A. Coser and Bernard Rosenberg (eds.), *Sociological Theory*. 3rd ed. New York: Macmillan.

MECHANIC, DAVID. 1962. "Some Factors in Identifying and Defining Mental Illness." *Mental Hygiene* 46:66-74.

———. 1969. *Mental Health and Social Policy*. Englewood Cliffs, NJ: Prentice-Hall.

MEDNICK, SARNOFF AND KARL O. CHRISTIANSEN (EDS.). 1977. *Biosocial Bases of Criminal Behavior*. New York: Gardner.

MENNINGER, KARL. 1968. *The Crime of Punishment*. New York: Penguin.

MERTON, ROBERT K. 1957. *Social Theory and Social Structure*. rev. ed. Glencoe, IL: Free Press.

MILESKI, MAUREEN AND DONALD J. BLACK. 1972. "The Social Organization of Homosexuality." *Urban Life and Culture* 1:131-66.

MILLER, DOROTHY AND WILLIAM H. DAWSON. 1965. "Effects of Stigma on Re-employment of Ex-Mental Patients." *Mental Hygiene* 49:281-87.

MILLER, GALE. 1978. *Odd Jobs*. Englewood Cliffs, NJ: Prentice-Hall.

MILLER, GENE. 1971. *83 Hours Till Dawn*. New York: Bantam.

MILLER, NORMAN C. 1965. *The Great Salad Oil Swindle*. New York: Coward, McCann & Geoghegan.

MILLER, WALTER B. 1958. "Lower Class Culture as a Generating Milieu of Gang Delinquency." *Journal of Social Issues* 14:5-19.

MILNER, CHRISTINA AND RICHARD MILNER. 1972. *Black Players*. Boston: Little, Brown.

MONKKONEN, ERIC H. 1975. *The Dangerous Class*. Cambridge, MA.: Harvard University Press.

MORRIS, NORVAL AND GORDON HAWKINS. 1970. *The Honest Politician's Guide to Crime Control*. Chicago: University of Chicago Press.

MOTT, PAUL E. 1965. *The Organization of Society*. Englewood Cliffs, NJ: Prentice-Hall.

MUIR, WILLIAM KER, JR. 1977. *Police*. Chicago: University of Chicago Press.

MULVIHILL, DONALD J. AND MELVIN M. TUMIN (EDS.). 1969. *Crimes of Violence*. Washington: U.S. Government Printing Office.

MUSTO, DAVID F. 1973. *The American Disease*. New Haven, CT.: Yale University Press.

MYERHOFF, HOWARD L. AND BARABRA G. MYERHOFF. 1964. "Field Observations of Middle Class 'Gangs.' " *Social Forces* 42:328-36.

NELLI, HUMBERT. 1976. *The Business of Crime*. New York: Oxford University Press.

NETTLER, GWYNN. 1974. "Embezzlement Without Problems." *British Journal of Criminology* 14:70-77.

NEURINGER, CHARLES. 1974. "Attitudes toward Self in Suicidal Individuals." *Life-Threatening Behavior* 4:96-106.

New York Times. 1967. "FBI Allows Parents to Decide on Ransom." April 7:49.

NOLEN, WILLIAM A. 1974. *Healing.* Greenwich, CT.: Fawcett, Books Group-CBS Publications.

O'DONNELL, JOHN A. 1967. "The Rise and Decline of a Subculture." *Social Problems* 15:73-84.

O'MALLEY, PAT. 1979. "Class Conflict, Land and Social Banditry." *Social Problems* 26:271-83.

PALSON, CHARLES AND REBECCA PALSON. 1972. "Swinging in Wedlock." *Society* 9:28-37.

PARKER, DONN B. 1976. *Crime by Computer.* New York: Scribner's.

PATTISON, E. MANSELL, LYALL A. BISHOP, AND ARNOLD S. LINSKY. 1968. "Changes in Public Attitudes on Narcotic Addiction." *American Journal of Psychiatry* 125:160-67

PEARCE, FRANK. 1976. *Crimes of the Powerful.* New York: Pluto.

PETACQUE, ART. 1980. "Gangs Taking Mob's Rackets." *Chicago Sun-Times* (October 5):5, 46.

PETERSILIA, JOAN, PETER GREENWOOD AND MARVIN LAVIN. 1977. *Criminal Careers of Habitual Felons.* Rand Corporation, R-2144.

PETERSON, MARK A. AND HARRIET B. BRAIKER. 1980. *Doing Crime.* Rand Corporation, R-2200.

PFOHL, STEPHEN J. 1977. "The 'Discovery' of Child Abuse." *Social Problems* 24:310-23.

PILIAVIN, IRVING AND SCOTT BRIAR. 1964. "Police Encounters with Juveniles." *American Journal of Sociology* 70:206-14.

PINCOFFS, EDMUND L. 1966. *The Rationale of Legal Punishment.* New York: Humanities Press.

PITTMAN, DAVID J. 1971. "The Male House of Prostitution." *Transaction* 8:21-27.

PLATE, THOMAS. 1975. *Crime Pays!* New York: Simon & Schuster.

POLSKY, NED. 1967. *Hustlers, Beats, and Others.* Chicago: Aldine.

PONSE, BARBARA. 1976. "Secrecy in the Lesbian World." *Urban Life* 5:313:38.

POUND, ROSCOE. 1942. *Social Control Through Law.* New Haven, CT.: Yale University Press.

President's Commission on Law Enforcement and Administration of Justice. 1967a. *Organized Crime.* Washington: U.S. Government Printing Office.

———. 1967b. *The Challenge of Crime in a Free Society.* Washington: U.S. Government Printing Office.

PRUS, ROBERT C. AND C. R. D. SHARPER. 1977. *Road Hustler.* Lexington, MA: Lexington.

——— AND STEVE VASSILAKOPOULOS. 1979. "Desk Clerks and Hookers." *Urban Life* 8:52-71.

PUTNAM, PETER L. AND EVERETT H. ELLINWOOD. 1966. "Narcotic Addiction among Physicians." *American Journal of Psychiatry* 122:145-48.

QUINNEY, RICHARD. 1974. *Critique of the Legal Order.* Boston: Little, Brown.

RAMEY, JAMES W. 1977. "Alternative Life Styles." *Society* 14:43-47.

RASMUSSEN, PAUL K. AND LAUREN L. KUHN. 1976. "The New Masseuse." *Urban Life* 5:271-92.

RAY, MARSH. 1961. "The Cycle of Abstinence and Relapse Among Heroin Addicts." *Social Problems* 9:132-40.

REDIKER, MARCUS. 1981. " 'Under the Banner of King Death.' " *William and Mary Quarterly* 38:203-27.

REDLINGER, LAWRENCE J. 1975. "Marketing and Distributing Heroin." *Journal of Psychedelic Drugs* 7:331-53.

REISS, ALBERT J., JR. 1971. *The Police and the Public.* Cambridge, MA.: MIT Press.

REISS, IRA L. 1970. "Premarital Sex as Deviant Behavior." *American Sociological Review* 35:78-88.

RENAUD, RALPH E. 1932. "The Kidnapping Profession." *Forum* 87:341-44.

RENGERT, GEORGE F. AND JOHN WASILCHICK, 1980. "Residential Burglary." Paper presented before the American Society of Criminology.

REYNOLDS, FRANK. 1967. *Freewheelin Frank.* New York: Grove.

RICH, VERNON. 1975. *Law and the Administration of Justice.* New York: John Wiley.

RINGEL, ERWIN. 1977. "The Presuicidal Syndrome." *Suicide and Life-Threatening Behavior* 6:131-49.

ROBINSON, JAMES AND GERALD SMITH. 1971. "The Effectiveness of Correctional Programs." *Crime and Delinquency* 17:67-80.

ROEBUCK, JULIAN B. AND WOLFGANG FRESE. 1976. "The After-Hours Club." *Urban Life* 5:131-64.

―――― AND ROBERT BRUCE HUNTER. 1970. "Medical Quackery as Deviant Behavior." *Criminology* 8:46-62.

―――― AND RONALD C. JOHNSON. 1964. "The 'Short Con' Man." *Crime and Delinquency* 10:235-48.

ROONEY, JAMES F. 1961. "Group Processes Among Skid Row Winos." *Quarterly Journal of Studies on Alcohol* 22:444-60.

ROSE, AL. 1974. *Storyville, New Orleans.* University: University of Alabama Press.

ROSENBERG, BERNARD AND HARRY SILVERSTEIN. 1969. *The Varieties of Delinquent Experience.* Waltham, MA: Blaisdell.

ROSS, CHRISTIAN K. 1876. *The Father's Story of Charley Ross, the Kidnapped Child.* Philadelphia: Potter.

ROSSI, PETER H., EMILY WAITE, CHRISTINE E. BOSE, AND RICHARD E. BERK. 1974. "The Seriousness of Crimes." *American Sociological Review* 39:224-37.

ROTHMAN, DAVID J. 1971. *The Discovery of the Asylum.* Boston: Little, Brown.

―――― . 1980. *Conscience and Convenience.* Boston: Little, Brown.

RUBINGTON, EARL. 1958. "The Chronic Drunkenness Offender." *Annals of the American Academy of Political and Social Science* 315:65-72.

―――― . 1968. "The Bottle Gang." *Quarterly Journal of Studies on Alcohol* 29:943-55.

―――― AND MARTIN S. WEINBERG (EDS.). 1981. *Deviance. 4th ed.* New York: Macmillan.

RUBINSTEIN, JONATHAN. 1973. *City Police.* New York: Farrar, Straus & Giroux.

SABBAG, ROBERT. 1976. *Snow Blind.* New York: Avon.

SAGARIN, EDWARD. 1975. *Deviants and Deviance.* New York: Praeger.

SALE, R. T. 1971. *The Blackstone Rangers.* New York: Popular Library.

SAMOVAR, LARRY AND FRED SANDERS. 1978. "Language Patterns of the Prostitute." *Etc.* 35:30-36.

SANDERS, WILLIAM B. 1977. *Detective Work.* New York: Free Press.

SCHEFF, THOMAS J. 1966. *Being Mentally Ill.* Chicago: Aldine.

―――― (ED.). 1967. *Mental Illness and Social Processes.* New York: Harper & Row, Pub.

―――― . 1974. "The Labeling Theory of Mental Illness." *American Sociological Review* 39:444-52.

SCHELLING, THOMAS C. 1967. "Economic Analysis of Organized Crime." Pp. 114-26 in President's Commission on Law Enforcement and Administration of Justice, *Organized Crime.* Washington: U.S. Government Printing Office.

―――― . 1971. "What Is the Business of Organized Crime?" *American Scholar* 40:643-52.

SCHNEIDER, JOSEPH W. 1978. "Deviant Drinking as Disease." *Social Problems* 25:361-72.

SCHRAGER, LAURA SHILL AND JAMES F. SHORT, JR. 1978. "Toward a Sociology of Organizational Crime." *Social Problems* 25:407-19.

SCHREIBER, JAN. 1978. *The Ultimate Weapon.* New York: Morrow.

SCHUR, EDWIN M. 1965. *Crimes Without Victims.* Englewood Cliffs, NJ: Prentice-Hall.
———. 1971. *Labeling Deviant Behavior.* New York: Harper & Row, Pub.
SCHWARTZ, GARY, PAUL TURNER AND EMIL PELUSO. 1973. "Neither Heads nor Freaks."
    Urban Life and Culture 2:288-313.
SCULL, ANDREW T. 1977. *Decarceration.* Englewood Cliffs, NJ: Prentice-Hall.
SEGAL, STEVEN P., JIM BAUMOHL AND ELISE JOHNSON. 1977. "Falling through the
    Cracks." *Social Problems* 24:387-400.
SHAW, CLIFFORD R. AND HENRY D. MCKAY. 1942. *Juvenile Delinquency in Urban Areas.*
    Chicago: University of Chicago Press.
SHEEHY, GAIL. 1973. *Hustling.* New York: Delacorte.
SHERMAN, LAWRENCE W. (ED.). 1974. *Police Corruption.* Garden City, NY: Anchor.
SHIBUTANI, TAMOTSU. 1961. *Society and Personality.* Englewood Cliffs, NJ: Prentice-
    Hall.
SHORT, JAMES F., JR. AND FRED L. STRODTBECK. 1965. *Group Process and Gang Delin-
    quency.* Chicago: University of Chicago Press.
SHOVER, NEAL. 1972. "Structures and Careers in Burglary." *Journal of Criminal Law,
    Criminology and Police Science* 63:540-49.
———. 1973. "The Social Organization of Burglary." *Social Problems* 20:499-514.
SIEGAL, HARVEY A., DAVID M. PETERSON AND CARL D. CHAMBERS. 1975. "The Emerg-
    ing Skid Row." *Journal of Drug Issues* 5:1-66.
SILVER, ALLAN. 1967. "The Demand for Order in Civil Society." Pp. 1-24 in David
    J. Bordua (ed.), *The Police.* New York: John Wiley.
SKOLNICK, JEROME H. 1975. *Justice Without Trial.* 2nd ed. New York: John Wiley.
SMELSER, NEIL J. 1963. *Theory of Collective Behavior.* New York: Free Press.
SMITH, DWIGHT C., JR. 1975. *The Mafia Mystique.* New York: Basic Books.
SMITH, LYNN G. AND JAMES R. SMITH. 1974. "Co-Marital Sex." Pp. 84-102 in Lynn
    G. Smith and James R. Smith (eds.), *Beyond Monogamy.* Baltimore: Johns Hop-
    kins University Press.
SNOW, ROBERT P. 1978. "The Golden Fleece." Pp. 133-50 in John M. Johnson and
    Jack D. Douglas (eds.), *Crime at the Top.* Philadelphia: Lippincott.
SOBLE, RONALD L. AND ROBERT E. DALLOS. 1975. *The Impossible Dream.* New York:
    Putnam's.
SPECTOR, MALCOLM AND JOHN I. KITSUSE. 1977. *Constructing Social Problems.* Menlo
    Park, CA: Cummings.
SPERGEL, IRVING. 1964. *Racketville, Slumtown, Haulburg.* Chicago: University of Chi-
    cago Press.
SPRADLEY, JAMES P. 1970. *You Owe Yourself a Drunk.* Boston: Little, Brown.
STEBBINS, ROBERT A. 1970. *Commitment to Deviance.* Westport, CT: Greenwood.
STENGEL, ERWIN. 1964. *Suicide and Attempted Suicide.* Baltimore: Pelican.
STEPHENSON, RICHARD M. 1973. "Involvement in Deviance." *Social Problems* 21:173-
    90.
STINCHCOMBE, ARTHUR. 1963. "Institutions of Privacy in the Determination of Police
    Administrative Practice." *American Journal of Sociology* 69:150-60.
STODDART, KENNETH. 1974. "The Facts of Life about Dope." *Urban Life and Culture*
    3:179-204.
STOLL, CLARICE. 1968. "Images of Man and Social Control." *Social Forces* 47:119-27.
STONE, CHRISTOPHER D. 1975. *Where the Law Ends.* New York: Harper & Row, Pub.
STRAUS, ROBERT. 1971. "Alcohol and Alcoholism." Pp. 227-69 in Robert K. Merton
    and Robert Nisbet (eds.), *Contemporary Social Problems.* 3rd ed. New York: Har-
    court Brace Jovanovich, Inc.
——— AND SHELDON BACON. 1953. *Drinking in College.* New Haven, CT.: Yale Uni-
    versity Press.
——— AND RAYMOND G. MCCARTHY. 1951. "Non-addictive Pathological Drinking
    Patterns of Homeless Men." *Quarterly Journal of Studies on Alcohol* 12:601-11.

STRAUSS, ANSELM L. 1959. *Mirrors and Masks.* Glencoe, IL: Free Press.
STYLES, JOSEPH. 1979. "Outsider/Insider." *Urban Life* 8:135-52.
SULLIVAN, EDWARD DEAN. 1932. *The Snatch Racket.* New York: Vanguard.
SUNDHOLM, CHARLES A. 1973. "The Pornographic Arcade." *Urban Life and Culture* 2:85-104.
SUTHERLAND, EDWIN H. 1937. *The Professional Thief.* Chicago: University of Chicago Press.
———. 1949. *White Collar Crime* New York: Holt, Rinehart and Winston.
——— AND DONALD R. CRESSEY. 1978. *Criminology.* 10th ed. Philadelphia: Lippincott.
SUTTLES, GERALD D. 1968. *The Social Order of the Slum.* Chicago: University of Chicago Press.
SYKES, GRESHAM M. AND DAVID MATZA. 1957. "Techniques of Neutralization." *American Sociological Review* 22:664-70.
SYMONDS, CAROLYN. 1971. "Sexual Mate-Swapping." Pp. 81-109 in James M. Henslin (ed.), *Studies in the Sociology of Sex.* New York: Appleton-Century-Crofts.
SZASZ, THOMAS S. 1960. "The Myth of Mental Illness." *American Psychologist* 15:113-118.
TALESE, GAY. 1971. *Honor Thy Father.* New York: World.
TANNER, DONNA M. 1978. *The Lesbian Couple.* Lexington, MA: Lexington.
THIBAUT, JOHN W. AND HAROLD H. KELLEY. 1959. *The Social Psychology of Groups.* New York: John Wiley.
THIO, ALEX. 1978. *Deviant Behavior.* Boston: Houghton Mifflin.
THOMPSON, E. P. 1975. "The Crime of Anonymity." Pp. 255-344 in Douglas Hay, et al., *Albion's Fatal Tree.* New York: Pantheon.
THOMPSON, HUNTER S. 1966. *Hell's Angels.* New York: Ballantine.
TOBIAS, J. J. 1967. *Crime and Industrial Society in the 19th Century.* New York: Schocken.
TRUMBACH, RANDOLPH. 1977. "London's Sodomites." *Journal of Social History* 11:1-33.
TRUZZI, MARCELLO. 1968. "Lilliputians in Gulliver's Land." Pp. 197-211 in Marcello Truzzi (ed.), *Sociology and Everday Life.* Englewood Cliffs, NJ: Prentice-Hall.
TULLY, ANDREW. 1965. *The FBI's Most Famous Cases.* New York: Morrow.
TURNER, RALPH H. 1964. "Collective Behavior." Pp. 382-425 in Robert E. L. Faris (ed.), *Handbook of Modern Sociology.* Chicago: Rand McNally.
ULLMAN, LEONARD P. AND LEONARD KRASNER (EDS.). 1965. *Case Studies in Behavior Modification.* Holt, Rinehart, & Winston.
UNRUH, DAVID R. 1979. "Characteristics and Types of Participation in Social Worlds." *Symbolic Interaction* 2:115-29.
VAUGHAN, DIANE AND GIOVANNA CARLO. 1975. "The Appliance Repairman." *Journal of Research in Crime and Delinquency* 12:153-61.
VOLD, GEORGE. 1979. *Theoretical Criminology.* Prepared by Thomas J. Bernard. 2d ed. New York: Oxford University Press.
WADE, ANDREW L. 1967. "Social Processes in the Act of Juvenile Vandalism." Pp. 94-109 in Marshall B. Clinard and Richard Quinney (eds.), *Criminal Behavior Systems.* New York: Holt, Rinehart, & Winston.
WALDORF, DAN AND CRAIG REINARMAN. 1975. "Addicts—Everything But Human Beings." *Urban Life* 4:30-53.
WALLACE, SAMUEL E. 1965. *Skid Row as a Way of Life.* Totowa, NJ: Bedminster.
WALLER, GEORGE. 1961. *Kidnap.* New York: Dial.
WALSH, MARILYN E. 1977. *The Fence.* Westport, CT: Greenwood.
WARREN, CAROL A. B. 1974. *Identity and Community in the Gay World.* New York: John Wiley.
WEBER, MAX. 1946. *From Max Weber.* Edited by Hans Gerth and C. Wright Mills. New York: Oxford University Press.

WEINBERG, MARTIN S. 1966. "Becoming a Nudist." *Psychiatry* 29:15-24.
_____ AND COLIN J. WILLIAMS. 1974. *Male Homosexuals.* New York: Oxford University Press.
_____. 1975. "Gay Baths and the Social Organization of Impersonal Sex." *Social Problems* 23:124-36.
WEINBERG, THOMAS S. AND GERHARD FALK. 1980. "The Social Organization of Sadism and Masochism." *Deviant Behavior* 1:379-93.
WEIR, ADRIANNE. 1973. "The Robbery Offender." Pp. 100-211 in Floyd Feeney and Adrianne Weir (eds.), *The Prevention and Control of Robbery.* Davis, CA: Center on Administration of Criminal Justice.
WERTHMAN, CARL AND IRVING PILIAVIN. 1967. "Gang Members and the Police." Pp. 56-98 in David J. Bordua (ed.), *The Police.* New York: John Wiley.
WILKINS, LESLIE T. 1964. *Social Deviance.* London: Tavistock.
WILSON, JAMES Q. 1968. *Varieties of Police Behavior.* Cambridge, MA.: Harvard University Press.
WINICK, CHARLES. 1961. "Physician Narcotic Addicts." *Social Problems* 9:174-86.
_____ AND PAUL M. KINSIE. 1971. *The Lively Commerce.* Chicago: Quadrangle.
WISEMAN, JACQUELINE P. 1970. *Stations of the Lost.* Englewood Cliffs, NJ: Prentice-Hall.
WOLF, DEBORAH GOLEMAN. 1979. *The Lesbian Community.* Berkeley, Ca.: University of California Press.
WOLFGANG, MARVIN E. 1958. *Patterns in Criminal Homicide.* Philadelphia: University of Pennsylvania Press.
_____ AND FRANCO FERRACUTI. 1967. *The Subculture of Violence.* London: Tavistock.
WOLSHOK, MARY LINDENSTEIN. 1971. "The Emergence of Middle-Class Deviant Subcultures." *Social Problems* 18:488-95.
YABLONSKY, LEWIS 1959. "The Delinquent Gang as a Near-Group." *Social Problems* 7:108-17.
YARROW, MARIAN, R., CHARLOTTE G. SCHWARTZ, HARRIET S. MURPHY, AND LEILA C. DEASY. 1955. "The Psychological Meaning of Mental Illness in the Family." *Journal of Social Issues* 11:12-24.
ZALD, MAYER N. 1978. "On the Social Control of Industries." *Social Forces* 57:79-102.
ZIEROLD, NORMAN. 1967. *Little Charley Ross.* Boston: Little, Brown.
ZIMMERMAN, DON H. AND D. LAWRENCE WIEDER. 1977. "You Can't Help but Get Stoned." *Social Problems* 25:198-207.
ZIMRING, FRANKLIN E. AND GORDON J. HAWKINS. 1973. *Deterrence.* Chicago: University of Chicago Press.

INDEXES

AUTHOR INDEX

SUBJECT INDEX